TOP GEAR (FLITWICK) 01525 71520
(HIGH ST)
GSF (HITCHIN) 0845 249 75
SHEFFORD AUTO PARTS 0845 3377 13
ASG 01767 310210
WEBBS SPARE PARTS 0845 408 1044
(STEVENAGE OLD TOWN)
(LETCHWORTH / HITCHIN ?)

Haynes

THE BOOK ®

Volvo S70, V70 & C70
Service and Repair Manual

RM Jex

Models covered   *(3573 - 256)*

Volvo S70, V70 and C70 models with 5-cylinder petrol engines, including special/limited editions
2.0 litre (1984 cc), 2.3 litre (2319 cc) and 2.5 litre (2435 cc)

Does not cover 4-wheel drive system, Bi-Fuel conversion, or diesel engine

© Haynes Publishing 1999

ABCDE
FGHIJ
KLMNO
PQRST

A book in the **Haynes Service and Repair Manual Series**

All rights reserved. No part of this book may be reproduced or transmitted in any form or by any means, electronic or mechanical, including photocopying, recording or by any information storage or retrieval system, without permission in writing from the copyright holder.

ISBN **1 85960 573 7**

British Library Cataloguing in Publication Data
A catalogue record for this book is available from the British Library.

Printed by **J H Haynes & Co. Ltd, Sparkford, Nr Yeovil, Somerset BA22 7JJ**

Haynes Publishing
Sparkford, Nr Yeovil, Somerset BA22 7JJ, England

Haynes North America, Inc
861 Lawrence Drive, Newbury Park, California 91320, USA

Editions Haynes S.A.
Tour Aurore - La Défense 2, 18 Place des Reflets,
92975 PARIS LA DEFENSE Cedex France

Haynes Publishing Nordiska AB
Box 1504, 751 45 UPPSALA, Sverige

Contents

LIVING WITH YOUR VOLVO S70, V70 & C70

MAINTENANCE

Routine maintenance and servicing

Contents

The Volvo S70/V70 Saloon and Estate models were introduced at the end of 1996, and are derived from the successful 850 range. Facelifted and with many detail changes beneath the skin, the new range shares the Volvo 850's transverse engine/transmission layout, front-wheel drive and state-of-the-art suspension technology.

Volvo S70 Saloon

Volvo V70 Estate

Volvo C70 Coupe

In April 1997, the AWD four-wheel-drive models were introduced, followed by the C70 sports coupe model in June 1997. The C70 represents a bold move for Volvo, serving as a flagship model, and offering further proof of Volvo's new-found commitment to driver appeal. Under the tasteful coupe exterior, the C70 shares many of its mechanical components with the Saloon and Estate models.

The engines are all fuel-injected, in-line, five-cylinder units of 1984 cc, 2319 cc or 2435 cc displacement. Both normally-aspirated and turbo-charged versions are available. The engines feature a comprehensive engine management system with extensive emission control equipment.

Transmissions are either 5-speed manual, or 4-speed automatic with computer control. The automatic transmission features mode control selection, allowing the driver to alter the transmission characteristics to suit economy, sport or winter driving requirements.

Braking is by discs all round, the handbrake acting on drums incorporated in the rear brake discs. Anti-lock braking (ABS) and power-assisted steering is standard on all models.

A wide range of standard and optional equipment is available within the range to suit virtually all tastes. As with all Volvo models, safety features are of paramount importance, and the Supplemental Restraint System and Side Impact Protection System offer an exceptional level of driver and passenger protection throughout the vehicle.

Provided that regular servicing is carried out in accordance with the manufacturer's recommendations, the Volvo S/V/C70 will provide the enviable reliability for which this marque is famous. Despite the engine's complexity, the engine compartment is relatively spacious, and most of the items requiring frequent attention are easily accessible.

Your Volvo manual

The aim of this manual is to help you get the best value from your vehicle. It can do so in several ways. It can help you decide what work must be done (even should you choose to get it done by a garage). It will also provide information on routine maintenance and servicing, and give a logical course of action and diagnosis when random faults occur. However, it is hoped that you will use the manual by tackling the work yourself. On simpler jobs it may even be quicker than booking the car into a garage and going there twice, to leave and collect it. Perhaps most important, a lot of money can be saved by avoiding the costs a garage must charge to cover its labour and overheads.

The manual has drawings and descriptions to show the function of the various components so that their layout can be understood. Tasks are described and photographed in a clear step-by-step sequence. The illustrations are numbered by the Section number and paragraph number to which they relate - if there is more than one illustration per paragraph, the sequence is denoted alphabetically.

References to the 'left' or 'right' of the vehicle are in the sense of a person in the driver's seat, facing forwards.

Acknowledgements

Thanks are due to Champion Spark Plug, who supplied the illustrations showing spark plug conditions, and to Duckhams Oils, who provided lubrication data. Certain illustrations are the copyright of Volvo Car Corporation, and are used with their permission. Thanks are also due to Draper Tools Limited, who provided some of the workshop tools, and to all those people at Sparkford who helped in the production of this manual.

We take great pride in the accuracy of information given in this manual, but vehicle manufacturers make alterations and design changes during the production run of a particular vehicle of which they do not inform us. No liability can be accepted by the authors or publishers for loss, damage or injury caused by any errors in, or omissions from the information given.

Working on your car can be dangerous. This page shows just some of the potential risks and hazards, with the aim of creating a safety-conscious attitude.

General hazards

Scalding

• Don't remove the radiator or expansion tank cap while the engine is hot.
• Engine oil, automatic transmission fluid or power steering fluid may also be dangerously hot if the engine has recently been running.

Burning

• Beware of burns from the exhaust system and from any part of the engine. Brake discs and drums can also be extremely hot immediately after use.

Crushing

• When working under or near a raised vehicle, always supplement the jack with axle stands, or use drive-on ramps. *Never venture under a car which is only supported by a jack.*
• Take care if loosening or tightening high-torque nuts when the vehicle is on stands. Initial loosening and final tightening should be done with the wheels on the ground.

Fire

• Fuel is highly flammable; fuel vapour is explosive.
• Don't let fuel spill onto a hot engine.
• Do not smoke or allow naked lights (including pilot lights) anywhere near a vehicle being worked on. Also beware of creating sparks (electrically or by use of tools).
• Fuel vapour is heavier than air, so don't work on the fuel system with the vehicle over an inspection pit.
• Another cause of fire is an electrical overload or short-circuit. Take care when repairing or modifying the vehicle wiring.
• Keep a fire extinguisher handy, of a type suitable for use on fuel and electrical fires.

Electric shock

• Ignition HT voltage can be dangerous, especially to people with heart problems or a pacemaker. Don't work on or near the ignition system with the engine running or the ignition switched on.

• Mains voltage is also dangerous. Make sure that any mains-operated equipment is correctly earthed. Mains power points should be protected by a residual current device (RCD) circuit breaker.

Fume or gas intoxication

• Exhaust fumes are poisonous; they often contain carbon monoxide, which is rapidly fatal if inhaled. Never run the engine in a confined space such as a garage with the doors shut.
• Fuel vapour is also poisonous, as are the vapours from some cleaning solvents and paint thinners.

Poisonous or irritant substances

• Avoid skin contact with battery acid and with any fuel, fluid or lubricant, especially antifreeze, brake hydraulic fluid and Diesel fuel. Don't syphon them by mouth. If such a substance is swallowed or gets into the eyes, seek medical advice.
• Prolonged contact with used engine oil can cause skin cancer. Wear gloves or use a barrier cream if necessary. Change out of oil-soaked clothes and do not keep oily rags in your pocket.
• Air conditioning refrigerant forms a poisonous gas if exposed to a naked flame (including a cigarette). It can also cause skin burns on contact.

Asbestos

• Asbestos dust can cause cancer if inhaled or swallowed. Asbestos may be found in gaskets and in brake and clutch linings. When dealing with such components it is safest to assume that they contain asbestos.

Special hazards

Hydrofluoric acid

• This extremely corrosive acid is formed when certain types of synthetic rubber, found in some O-rings, oil seals, fuel hoses etc, are exposed to temperatures above 400°C. The rubber changes into a charred or sticky substance containing the acid. *Once formed, the acid remains dangerous for years. If it gets onto the skin, it may be necessary to amputate the limb concerned.*
• When dealing with a vehicle which has suffered a fire, or with components salvaged from such a vehicle, wear protective gloves and discard them after use.

The battery

• Batteries contain sulphuric acid, which attacks clothing, eyes and skin. Take care when topping-up or carrying the battery.
• The hydrogen gas given off by the battery is highly explosive. Never cause a spark or allow a naked light nearby. Be careful when connecting and disconnecting battery chargers or jump leads.

Air bags

• Air bags can cause injury if they go off accidentally. Take care when removing the steering wheel and/or facia. Special storage instructions may apply.

Diesel injection equipment

• Diesel injection pumps supply fuel at very high pressure. Take care when working on the fuel injectors and fuel pipes.

⚠ *Warning: Never expose the hands, face or any other part of the body to injector spray; the fuel can penetrate the skin with potentially fatal results.*

Remember...

DO

• Do use eye protection when using power tools, and when working under the vehicle.

• Do wear gloves or use barrier cream to protect your hands when necessary.

• Do get someone to check periodically that all is well when working alone on the vehicle.

• Do keep loose clothing and long hair well out of the way of moving mechanical parts.

• Do remove rings, wristwatch etc, before working on the vehicle – especially the electrical system.

• Do ensure that any lifting or jacking equipment has a safe working load rating adequate for the job.

DON'T

• Don't attempt to lift a heavy component which may be beyond your capability – get assistance.

• Don't rush to finish a job, or take unverified short cuts.

• Don't use ill-fitting tools which may slip and cause injury.

• Don't leave tools or parts lying around where someone can trip over them. Mop up oil and fuel spills at once.

• Don't allow children or pets to play in or near a vehicle being worked on.

The following pages are intended to help in dealing with common roadside emergencies and breakdowns. You will find more detailed fault finding information at the back of the manual, and repair information in the main chapters.

If your car won't start and the starter motor doesn't turn

☐ If it's a model with automatic transmission, make sure the selector is in P or N.
☐ Open the bonnet and make sure that the battery terminals are clean and tight.
☐ Switch on the headlights and try to start the engine. If the headlights go very dim when you're trying to start, the battery is probably flat. Get out of trouble by jump starting (see next page) using a friend's car.

If your car won't start even though the starter motor turns as normal

☐ Is there fuel in the tank?
☐ Is there moisture on electrical components under the bonnet? Switch off the ignition, then wipe off any obvious dampness with a dry cloth. Spray a water-repellent aerosol product (WD-40 or equivalent) on ignition and fuel system electrical connectors like those shown in the photos. Pay special attention to the ignition coil wiring connector and HT leads.

A Check that the HT leads are securely connected to the distributor, and that the cap is clean and properly fitted. *Later models have no HT leads or distributor cap.*

B Check that the HT lead and wiring connections are securely connected to the ignition coil. *Later models have no HT leads, and the ignition coil is not visible.*

Check that electrical connections are secure (with the ignition switched off) and spray them with a water dispersant spray like WD-40 if you suspect a problem due to damp

C Check the mass air flow sensor or inlet air temperature sensor wiring connector for security.

D Check the security and condition of the battery terminals.

Jump starting will get you out of trouble, but you must correct whatever made the battery go flat in the first place. There are three possibilities:

1 *The battery has been drained by repeated attempts to start, or by leaving the lights on.*

2 *The charging system is not working properly (alternator drivebelt slack or broken, alternator wiring fault or alternator itself faulty).*

3 *The battery itself is at fault (electrolyte low, or battery worn out).*

When jump-starting a car using a booster battery, observe the following precautions:

✔ Before connecting the booster battery, make sure that the ignition is switched off.

✔ Ensure that all electrical equipment (lights, heater, wipers, etc) is switched off.

✔ Take note of any special precautions printed on the battery case.

Jump starting

✔ Make sure that the booster battery is the same voltage as the discharged one in the vehicle.

✔ If the battery is being jump-started from the battery in another vehicle, the two vehicles MUST NOT TOUCH each other.

✔ Make sure that the transmission is in neutral (or PARK, in the case of automatic transmission).

1 Connect one end of the red jump lead to the positive (+) terminal of the flat battery

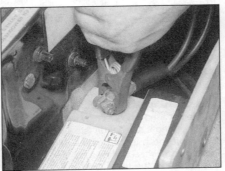

2 Connect the other end of the red lead to the positive (+) terminal of the booster battery.

3 Connect one end of the black jump lead to the negative (-) terminal of the booster battery

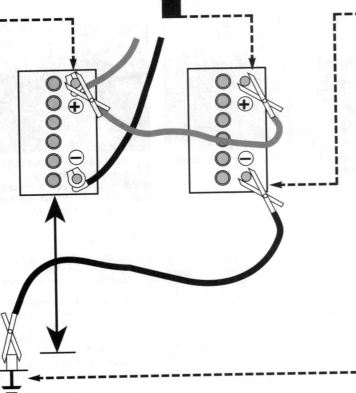

4 Connect the other end of the black jump lead to a bolt or bracket on the engine block, well away from the battery, on the vehicle to be started.

5 Make sure that the jump leads will not come into contact with the fan, drive-belts or other moving parts of the engine.

6 Start the engine using the booster battery and run it at idle speed. Switch on the lights, rear window demister and heater blower motor, then disconnect the jump leads in the reverse order of connection. Turn off the lights etc.

Wheel changing

 Warning: Do not change a wheel in a situation where you risk being hit by another vehicle. On busy roads, try to stop in a lay-by or a gateway. Be wary of passing traffic while changing the wheel - it is easy to become distracted by the job in hand.

Preparation

☐ When a puncture occurs, stop as soon as it is safe to do so.

☐ Park on firm level ground, if possible, and well out of the way of other traffic.

☐ Use hazard warning lights if necessary.

☐ If you have one, use a warning triangle to alert other drivers of your presence.

☐ Apply the handbrake and engage first or reverse gear (or Park on models with automatic transmission).

☐ Chock the wheel diagonally opposite the one being removed – a couple of large stones will do for this.

☐ If the ground is soft, use a flat piece of wood to spread the load under the jack.

Changing the wheel

1 The spare wheel and tools are stored in the luggage compartment under the carpet. Release the restraining strap, unscrew the tool and wheel clamp, and lift out the jack and wheel changing tools from the centre of the wheel.

2 Remove the wheel trim (where fitted), either by pulling it straight off (steel wheels) or by prising off the hub cap (some alloy wheels). Slacken each wheel bolt by a half turn, using the wheelbrace. If the bolts are too tight, DON'T stand on the brace to undo them - call for assistance. On models with alloy wheels, a Volvo socket may be needed to remove the security bolt - the socket should be in the glovebox.

3 Engage the jack head with the reinforced bracket located in the middle of the sill on each side of the car (don't jack the vehicle at any other point of the sill). Four-wheel-drive (AWD) models have an additional jacking point in front of the rear wheels, and this must be used in the event of a rear wheel puncture.

4 Turn the handle clockwise until the wheel is raised clear of the ground.

5 Unscrew the wheel bolts and remove the wheel.

6 Fit the spare wheel, noting that there is a special locating peg on the wheel hub, which must fit through the hole in the temporary spare wheel, or into the space inside the wheel hub on regular roadwheels.

7 Fit and screw in the bolts. Lightly tighten the bolts with the wheelbrace, then lower the vehicle to the ground. Securely tighten the wheel bolts, then refit the wheel trim or hub cap, as applicable. The wheel bolts should be slackened and retightened to the specified torque at the earliest possible opportunity.

Note: *Some models are supplied with a special lightweight 'space-saver' spare wheel, the tyre being narrower than standard, and marked TEMPORARY USE ONLY. The space-saver spare wheel is intended only for temporary use, and **must** be replaced with a standard wheel as soon as possible. Drive with particular care with this wheel fitted, especially through corners and when braking - Volvo recommend a maximum speed of 50 mph (80 km/h) when the special spare wheel is in use.*

Finally...

☐ Remove the wheel chocks.

☐ Stow the jack and tools back in the car.

☐ Check the tyre pressure on the wheel just fitted. If it is low, or if you don't have a pressure gauge with you, drive slowly to the nearest garage and inflate the tyre to the right pressure. In the case of the space-saver spare wheel, this pressure is much higher than for a normal tyre.

☐ Have the damaged tyre or wheel repaired as soon as possible.

Identifying leaks

Puddles on the garage floor or drive, or obvious wetness under the bonnet or underneath the car, suggest a leak that needs investigating. It can sometimes be difficult to decide where the leak is coming from, especially if the engine bay is very dirty already. Leaking oil or fluid can also be blown rearwards by the passage of air under the car, giving a false impression of where the problem lies.

⚠️ **Warning: Most automotive oils and fluids are poisonous. Wash them off skin, and change out of contaminated clothing, without delay.**

 HAYNES HiNT *The smell of a fluid leaking from the car may provide a clue to what's leaking. Some fluids are distinctively coloured. It may help to clean the car carefully and to park it over some clean paper overnight as an aid to locating the source of the leak.*
Remember that some leaks may only occur while the engine is running.

Sump oil

Engine oil may leak from the drain plug...

Oil from filter

...or from the base of the oil filter.

Gearbox oil

Gearbox oil can leak from the seals at the inboard ends of the driveshafts.

Antifreeze

Leaking antifreeze often leaves a crystalline deposit like this.

Brake fluid

A leak occurring at a wheel is almost certainly brake fluid.

Power steering fluid

Power steering fluid may leak from the pipe connectors on the steering rack.

Towing

When all else fails, you may find yourself having to get a tow home – or of course you may be helping somebody else. Long-distance recovery should only be done by a garage or breakdown service. For shorter distances, DIY towing using another car is easy enough, but observe the following points:
☐ Use a proper tow-rope – they are not expensive. The vehicle being towed must display an ON TOW sign in its rear window.
☐ Always turn the ignition key to the 'on' position when the vehicle is being towed, so that the steering lock is released, and that the direction indicator and brake lights will work.
☐ A towing eye is provided below each bumper. The front towing eye is hidden behind a cover panel below the right-hand end of the front bumper **(see illustration)**.

☐ Before being towed, release the handbrake and select neutral on the transmission.
☐ Note that greater-than-usual pedal pressure will be required to operate the brakes, since the vacuum servo unit is only operational with the engine running.
☐ On models with power steering, greater-than-usual steering effort will also be required.
☐ The driver of the car being towed must keep the tow-rope taut at all times to avoid snatching.
☐ Make sure that both drivers know the route before setting off.
☐ Only drive at moderate speeds and keep the distance towed to a minimum. Drive smoothly and allow plenty of time for slowing down at junctions.
☐ On models with automatic transmission or four-wheel-drive (AWD), special precautions apply. If in doubt, do not tow with the driven wheels on the ground, or transmission damage may result.

Front towing eye is located behind a cover panel in the front bumper

Introduction

There are some very simple checks which need only take a few minutes to carry out, but which could save you a lot of inconvenience and expense.

These Weekly checks require no great skill or special tools, and the small amount of time they take to perform could prove to be very well spent, for example;

☐ Keeping an eye on tyre condition and pressures, will not only help to stop them wearing out prematurely, but could also save your life.

☐ Many breakdowns are caused by electrical problems. Battery-related faults are particularly common, and a quick check on a regular basis will often prevent the majority of these.

☐ If your car develops a brake fluid leak, the first time you might know about it is when your brakes don't work properly. Checking the level regularly will give advance warning of this kind of problem.

☐ If the oil or coolant levels run low, the cost of repairing any engine damage will be far greater than fixing the leak, for example.

Underbonnet check points

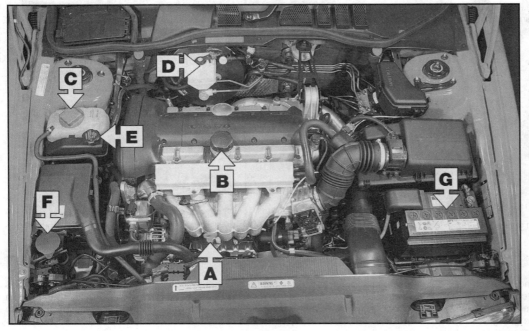

◀ **2.5 litre engine (others similar)**

A *Engine oil level dipstick*
B *Engine oil filler cap*
C *Coolant expansion tank*
D *Brake fluid reservoir*
E *Power steering fluid reservoir*
F *Screen washer fluid reservoir*
G *Battery*

Engine oil level

Before you start

✔ Make sure that your car is on level ground.
✔ Check the oil level before the car is driven, or at least 5 minutes after the engine has been switched off.

HAYNES HiNT *If the oil is checked immediately after driving the vehicle, some of the oil will remain in the upper engine components, resulting in an inaccurate reading on the dipstick!*

The correct oil

Modern engines place great demands on their oil. It is very important that the correct oil for your car is used (See Lubricants and fluids on page 0•16).

Car Care

● If you have to add oil frequently, you should check whether you have any oil leaks. Place some clean paper under the car overnight, and check for stains in the morning. If there are no leaks, the engine may be burning oil, or the oil may only be leaking when the engine is running.

● Always maintain the level between the upper and lower dipstick marks. If the level is too low severe engine damage may occur. Oil seal failure may result if the engine is significantly overfilled by adding too much oil.

1 The dipstick top is brightly coloured for easy identification (see *Underbonnet check points* on page 0•10 for exact location). Withdraw the dipstick.

2 Using a clean rag or paper towel remove all oil from the dipstick. Insert the clean dipstick into the tube as far as it will go, then withdraw it again.

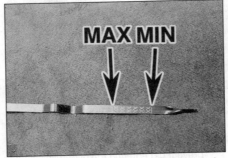

3 Note the oil level on the end of the dipstick, which should be in the hatched area between the upper (MAX) mark and lower (MIN) mark. Approximately 1.5 litres of oil will raise the level from the lower mark to the upper mark.

4 Oil is added through the filler cap. Unscrew the cap and top-up the level; a funnel may help to reduce spillage. Add the oil slowly, checking the level on the dipstick often. Don't overfill (see *Car care*).

Coolant level

⚠ **Warning: DO NOT attempt to remove the expansion tank pressure cap when the engine is hot, as there is a very great risk of scalding. Do not leave open containers of coolant about, as it is poisonous.**

Car Care

● With a sealed-type cooling system, adding coolant should not be necessary on a regular basis. If frequent topping-up is required, it is likely there is a leak. Check the radiator, all hoses and joint faces for signs of staining or wetness, and rectify as necessary.

● It is important that antifreeze is used in the cooling system all year round, not just during the winter months. Don't top-up with water alone, as the antifreeze will become too diluted.

1 The coolant reservoir is located on the right-hand inner wing. The coolant level is visible through the reservoir body. The coolant level varies with engine temperature. When cold, the coolant level should be between the MAX and MIN marks. When the engine is hot, the level may rise slightly above the MAX mark.

2 If topping up is necessary, **wait until the engine is cold**. Slowly unscrew the expansion tank cap, to release any pressure present in the cooling system, and remove it.

3 Add a mixture of water and antifreeze to the expansion tank until the coolant is at the correct level. Refit the cap and tighten it securely.

Brake and clutch fluid level

Warning:
● Brake fluid can harm your eyes and damage painted surfaces, so use extreme caution when handling and pouring it.
● Do not use fluid that has been standing open for some time, as it absorbs moisture from the air, which can cause a dangerous loss of braking effectiveness.

● Make sure that your car is on level ground.

● The fluid level in the reservoir will drop slightly as the brake pads wear down, but the fluid level must never be allowed to drop below the MIN mark.

Safety First!

● If the reservoir requires repeated topping-up this is an indication of a fluid leak somewhere in the system, which should be investigated immediately.

● If a leak is suspected, the car should not be driven until the braking system has been checked. Never take any risks where brakes are concerned.

1 The MAX and MIN marks are indicated on the reservoir. The fluid level must be kept between the marks at all times.

2 If topping-up is necessary, first wipe clean the area around the filler cap to prevent dirt entering the hydraulic system. Unscrew the reservoir cap and carefully lift it out of position, taking care not to damage the level sender float. Inspect the reservoir, if the fluid is dirty, the hydraulic system should be drained and refilled (see Chapter 1).

3 Carefully add fluid, taking care not to spill it onto the surrounding components. Use only the specified fluid; mixing different types can cause damage to the system. After topping-up to the correct level, securely refit the cap and wipe off any spilt fluid. Reconnect the fluid level wiring connector.

Power steering fluid level

Before you start

✔ Park the vehicle on level ground.
✔ Set the steering wheel straight-ahead.
✔ The engine should be turned off.

For the check to be accurate, the steering must not be turned once the engine has been stopped.

Safety First!

● The need for frequent topping-up indicates a leak, which should be investigated immediately.

1 On early models, the reservoir is mounted on the right-hand front of the engine, while later models have the reservoir on the right-hand inner wing, in front of the cooling system expansion tank. Wipe clean the area around the reservoir filler neck, and unscrew the filler cap/dipstick from the reservoir.

2 Dip the fluid with the reservoir cap/dipstick by screwing it fully back into place. When the engine is cold, the fluid level should be between the ADD mark and the COLD mark; when hot it should be between the ADD and HOT marks. Top-up when the level is at the ADD mark.

3 When topping-up, use the specified type of fluid - do not overfill the reservoir. When the level is correct, securely refit the cap.

Battery

Caution: Before carrying out any work on the vehicle battery, read the precautions given in Safety first at the start of this manual.

✔ Make sure that the battery tray is in good condition, and that the clamp is tight. Corrosion on the tray, retaining clamp and the battery itself can be removed with a solution of water and baking soda. Thoroughly rinse all cleaned areas with water. Any metal parts damaged by corrosion should be covered with a zinc-based primer, then painted.

✔ Periodically (approximately every three months), check the charge condition of the battery as described in Chapter 5A.

✔ On batteries which are not of the maintenance-free type, periodically check the electrolyte level in the battery - see Chapter 1.

✔ If the battery is flat, and you need to jump start your vehicle, see *Roadside Repairs*.

HAYNES HiNT

Battery corrosion can be kept to a minimum by applying a layer of petroleum jelly to the clamps and terminals after they are reconnected.

1 The battery is located at the front of the engine compartment on the left-hand side - where necessary, unclip and remove the cover for access. The exterior of the battery should be inspected periodically for damage such as a cracked case or cover.

2 Check the tightness of battery clamps to ensure good electrical connections. You should not be able to move them. Also check each cable for cracks and frayed conductors.

3 If corrosion (white, fluffy deposits) is evident, remove the cables from the battery terminals, clean them with a small wire brush, then refit them. Automotive stores sell a tool for cleaning the battery post . . .

4 . . . as well as the battery cable clamps

Screen washer fluid level

● On models so equipped, the screenwasher fluid is also used to clean the headlights, and on Estate models, the tailgate rear window.

● Screenwash additives not only keep the windscreen clean during foul weather, they also prevent the washer system freezing in cold weather - which is when you are likely to need it most. Don't top up using plain water as the screenwash will become too diluted, and will freeze during cold weather.

On no account use coolant antifreeze in the washer system - this could discolour or damage paintwork.

1 The washer fluid reservoir filler is located at the front right-hand side of the engine compartment, (the reservoir itself is actually located under the car).

2 Release the cap and observe the level in the reservoir by looking down the filler neck.

3 When topping-up the reservoir, a screen-wash additive should be added in the quantities recommended on the bottle.

Tyre condition and pressure

It is very important that tyres are in good condition, and at the correct pressure - having a tyre failure at any speed is highly dangerous. Tyre wear is influenced by driving style - harsh braking and acceleration, or fast cornering, will all produce more rapid tyre wear. As a general rule, the front tyres wear out faster than the rears. Interchanging the tyres from front to rear ("rotating" the tyres) may result in more even wear. However, if this is completely effective, you may have the expense of replacing all four tyres at once! Remove any nails or stones embedded in the tread before they penetrate the tyre to cause deflation. If removal of a nail does reveal that the tyre has been punctured, refit the nail so that its point of penetration is marked. Then immediately change the wheel, and have the tyre repaired by a tyre dealer.

Regularly check the tyres for damage in the form of cuts or bulges, especially in the sidewalls. Periodically remove the wheels, and clean any dirt or mud from the inside and outside surfaces. Examine the wheel rims for signs of rusting, corrosion or other damage. Light alloy wheels are easily damaged by "kerbing" whilst parking; steel wheels may also become dented or buckled. A new wheel is very often the only way to overcome severe damage.

New tyres should be balanced when they are fitted, but it may become necessary to re-balance them as they wear, or if the balance weights fitted to the wheel rim should fall off. Unbalanced tyres will wear more quickly, as will the steering and suspension components. Wheel imbalance is normally signified by vibration, particularly at a certain speed (typically around 50 mph). If this vibration is felt only through the steering, then it is likely that just the front wheels need balancing. If, however, the vibration is felt through the whole car, the rear wheels could be out of balance. Wheel balancing should be carried out by a tyre dealer or garage.

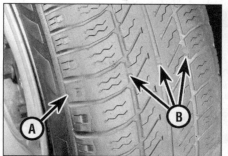

1 Tread Depth - visual check
The original tyres have tread wear safety bands (B), which will appear when the tread depth reaches approximately 1.6 mm. The band positions are indicated by a triangular mark on the tyre sidewall (A).

2 Tread Depth - manual check
Alternatively, tread wear can be monitored with a simple, inexpensive device known as a tread depth indicator gauge.

3 Tyre Pressure Check
Check the tyre pressures regularly with the tyres cold. Do not adjust the tyre pressures immediately after the vehicle has been used, or an inaccurate setting will result.

Tyre tread wear patterns

Shoulder Wear

Underinflation (wear on both sides)
Under-inflation will cause overheating of the tyre, because the tyre will flex too much, and the tread will not sit correctly on the road surface. This will cause a loss of grip and excessive wear, not to mention the danger of sudden tyre failure due to heat build-up.
Check and adjust pressures
Incorrect wheel camber (wear on one side)
Repair or renew suspension parts
Hard cornering
Reduce speed!

Centre Wear

Overinflation
Over-inflation will cause rapid wear of the centre part of the tyre tread, coupled with reduced grip, harsher ride, and the danger of shock damage occurring in the tyre casing.
Check and adjust pressures

If you sometimes have to inflate your car's tyres to the higher pressures specified for maximum load or sustained high speed, don't forget to reduce the pressures to normal afterwards.

Uneven Wear

Front tyres may wear unevenly as a result of wheel misalignment. Most tyre dealers and garages can check and adjust the wheel alignment (or "tracking") for a modest charge.
Incorrect camber or castor
Repair or renew suspension parts
Malfunctioning suspension
Repair or renew suspension parts
Unbalanced wheel
Balance tyres
Incorrect toe setting
Adjust front wheel alignment
Note: *The feathered edge of the tread which typifies toe wear is best checked by feel.*

Wiper blades

Note: *Fitting details for wiper blades vary according to model, and according to whether genuine Volvo wiper blades have been fitted. Use the procedures and illustrations shown as a guide for your car.*

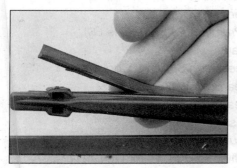

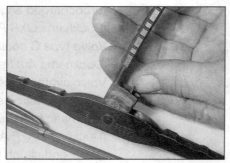

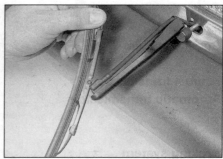

1 Check the condition of the wiper blades; if they are cracked or show any signs of deterioration, or if the glass swept area is smeared, renew them. Wiper blades should be renewed annually.

2 To remove a windscreen or tailgate wiper blade, pull the arm fully away from the glass until it locks. Swivel the blade through 90°, press the locking tab with your fingers and slide the blade out of the arm's hooked end.

3 Don't forget to check the headlight wiper blades as well. To remove the blade, lift the arm and simply pull the blade out of the arm fitting. Push the blade firmly home to refit.

Bulbs and fuses

✔ Check all external lights and the horn. Refer to the appropriate Sections of Chapter 12 for details if any of the circuits are found to be inoperative.

✔ Visually check all accessible wiring connectors, harnesses and retaining clips for security, and for signs of chafing or damage.

 HAYNES HINT *If you need to check your brake lights and indicators unaided, back up to a wall or garage door and operate the lights. The reflected light should show if they are working properly.*

1 If a single indicator light, stop-light or headlight has failed, it is likely that a bulb has blown and will need to be replaced. Refer to Chapter 12 for details. If both stop-lights have failed, it is possible that the stop-light switch is faulty (see Chapter 9).

2 If more than one indicator light or headlight has failed, it is likely that either a fuse has blown or that there is a fault in the circuit (see Chapter 12). The fuses are located in the fusebox situated in the engine compartment on the driver's side, just in front of the windscreen. Additional fuses are located in a fuse and relay box behind the left-hand suspension strut mounting, but in general, these should only be replaced by a Volvo dealer - if they have blown, a serious fault is indicated.

3 To replace a blown fuse, simply pull it out using the plastic tweezers provided. Fit a new fuse of the same rating (see Chapter 12). If the fuse blows again, it is important that you find out why - a complete checking procedure is given in Chapter 12.

Lubricants and fluids

Engine . . . . Multigrade engine oil, viscosity SAE 10W/30, 10W/40, or 15W/40, to ACEA A2 or A3 (ACEA A3 for turbocharged engines)
(Duckhams QXR Premium Petrol Engine Oil)

Cooling system . . . . Volvo type C coolant
(Duckhams Antifreeze and Summer Coolant)

Manual transmission . . . . Volvo synthetic gearbox oil 97308

Automatic transmission . . . . Volvo synthetic gearbox oil 97337 (Dexron IIE type automatic transmission fluid)
(Duckhams ATF Autotrans III)

Braking system . . . . Brake and clutch fluid to DOT 4+ (or DOT 4)
(Duckhams Universal Brake & Clutch Fluid)

Power steering . . . . Dexron type ATF
(Duckhams ATF Autotrans III)

Choosing your engine oil

Engines need oil, not only to lubricate moving parts and minimise wear, but also to maximise power output and to improve fuel economy. By introducing a simplified and improved range of engine oils, Duckhams has taken away the confusion and made it easier for you to choose the right oil for your engine.

HOW ENGINE OIL WORKS

• Beating friction

Without oil, the moving surfaces inside your engine will rub together, heat up and melt, quickly causing the engine to seize. Engine oil creates a film which separates these moving parts, preventing wear and heat build-up.

• Cooling hot-spots

Temperatures inside the engine can exceed 1000° C. The engine oil circulates and acts as a coolant, transferring heat from the hot-spots to the sump.

• Cleaning the engine internally

Good quality engine oils clean the inside of your engine, collecting and dispersing combustion deposits and controlling them until they are trapped by the oil filter or flushed out at oil change.

OIL CARE - FOLLOW THE CODE

To handle and dispose of used engine oil safely, always:

OIL CARE
FOLLOW THE CODE
OIL BANK LINE
0800 66 33 66

• **Avoid skin contact with used engine oil.** Repeated or prolonged contact can be harmful.

• **Dispose of used oil and empty packs in a responsible manner in an authorised disposal site.** Call 0800 663366 to find the one nearest to you. **Never tip oil down drains or onto the ground.**

DUCKHAMS ENGINE OILS

For the driver who demands a premium quality oil for complete reassurance, we recommend synthetic formula **Duckhams QXR Premium Engine Oils.**
For the driver who requires a straight-forward quality engine oil, we recommend **Duckhams Hypergrade Engine Oils.**

For further information and advice, call the Duckhams UK Helpline on 0800 212988.

Tyre pressures (cold)

Note: *Refer to the tyre pressure data sticker on the fuel filler flap (S70 and V70) or on the rear edge of the driver's door (C70) for the correct tyre pressures for your particular vehicle. Pressures apply only to original-equipment tyres, and may vary if other makes or type is fitted; check with the tyre manufacturer or supplier for correct pressures if necessary.*

Note: *The pressures quoted are only for use up to 100 mph (160 km/h) - for pressures suitable for continuous use at higher speeds than this, refer to the tyre pressure data sticker, or a Volvo dealer.*

S70 and V70 models

	Front	Rear
Non-turbo models, front-wheel-drive:		
S70 models:		
Up to three passengers	2.2 bar (32 psi)	2.0 bar (29 psi)
Full load	2.3 bar (33 psi)	2.5 bar (36 psi)
V70 models:		
Up to three passengers	2.2 bar (32 psi)	2.1 bar (30 psi)
Full load	2.4 bar (35 psi)	2.8 bar (41 psi)
Turbo models, front-wheel-drive:		
S70 models:		
Up to three passengers	2.3 bar (33 psi)	2.1 bar (30 psi)
Full load	2.5 bar (36 psi)	2.5 bar (36 psi)
V70 models:		
Up to three passengers	2.3 bar (33 psi)	2.2 bar (32 psi)
Full load	2.5 bar (36 psi)	2.8 bar (41 psi)
Four-wheel-drive (AWD) models:		
S70 models:		
Up to three passengers	2.2 bar (32 psi)	2.2 bar (32 psi)
Full load	2.5 bar (36 psi)	2.6 bar (38 psi)
V70 models, 15 and 16-inch wheels:		
Up to three passengers	2.2 bar (32 psi)	2.3 bar (33 psi)
Full load	2.5 bar (36 psi)	2.8 bar (41 psi)
V70 models, 17-inch wheels:		
Up to three passengers	2.5 bar (36 psi)	2.5 bar (36 psi)
Full load	2.6 bar (38 psi)	2.8 bar (41 psi)
Space saver spare	4.2 bar (61 psi)	4.2 bar (61 psi)

C70 models

	Front	Rear
16-inch wheels:		
Up to three passengers	2.3 bar (33 psi)	2.1 bar (30 psi)
Full load	2.5 bar (36 psi)	2.4 bar (35 psi)
17-inch wheels:		
Up to three passengers	2.3 bar (33 psi)	2.1 bar (30 psi)
Full load	2.5 bar (36 psi)	2.5 bar (36 psi)
18-inch wheels:		
Up to three passengers	2.4 bar (35 psi)	2.2 bar (32 psi)
Full load	2.5 bar (36 psi)	2.5 bar (36 psi)
Space saver spare	4.2 bar (61 psi)	4.2 bar (61 psi)

Notes

Chapter 1
Routine maintenance and servicing

Contents

Degrees of difficulty

 Easy, suitable for novice with little experience

 Fairly easy, suitable for beginner with some experience

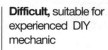 **Fairly difficult,** suitable for competent DIY mechanic

 Difficult, suitable for experienced DIY mechanic

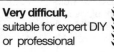 **Very difficult,** suitable for expert DIY or professional

Lubricants and fluids

Refer to end of *Weekly checks* on page 0•16

Capacities

Engine oil

Drain and refill including filter change .... 5.8 litres (plus 0.9 litres for turbo oil cooler - if drained)

Cooling system

Non-turbo engines .... 7.2 litres
Turbo engines .... 7.0 litres

Fuel tank

Front-wheel-drive models .... 68 litres
Four-wheel-drive (AWD) models .... 66 litres

Engine

Oil filter .... Champion C164

Cooling system

Specified antifreeze mixture .... 50% antifreeze/50% water
Note: *Refer to Chapter 3 for further details.*

Fuel system

Air filter .... Champion U644

Ignition system

	Type	Electrode gap
Spark plugs:		
2.0 litre engines:		
10-valve (B5202 S):		
Up to 1997	Champion RC9YCC	0.8 mm
1998-on	Champion RC89TMC	Not adjustable
20-valve non-turbo (B5204 S)	Champion RC89TMC	Not adjustable
20-valve turbo (B5204 T)	Champion RC8PYP	0.7 mm
2.3 litre engines:		
Non-turbo (B5234 S)	Champion RC89TMC	Not adjustable
Turbo (B5234 T)	Champion RC8PYP	0.7 mm
2.5 litre engines:		
Non-turbo (B5252 S and B5254 S*):		
Up to 1997	Champion RC9YCC	0.8 mm
1998-on	Champion RC89TMC	Not adjustable
Turbo (B5254 T*)	Champion RC8PYP	0.7 mm

*****Note:** *From late 1999 onwards, all 2.5 litre engine codes starting B525 have changed to B524, so B5252 S becomes B5242 S, and so on. Refer to Chapter 2A Specifications for a full list of engine codes.*

Brakes

Front brake pad minimum lining thickness .... 3.0 mm
Rear brake pad minimum lining thickness .... 2.0 mm
Handbrake lever travel:
    After adjustment .... 3 to 5 clicks
    In service .... 11 clicks maximum

Tyres

Tyre pressures .... See end of *Weekly checks* on page 0•17

Torque wrench settings

	Nm	lbf ft
Engine oil drain plug	35	26
Roadwheel bolts	110	81
Spark plugs	25	18
Transmission oil filler/level plug	35	26

The maintenance intervals in this manual are provided with the assumption that you, not the dealer, will be carrying out the work. These are the average maintenance intervals recommended by the manufacturer for vehicles driven daily under normal conditions. Obviously some variation of these intervals may be expected depending on territory of use, and conditions encountered. If you wish to keep your vehicle in peak condition at all times, you may wish to perform some of these procedures more often. We encourage frequent maintenance because it enhances the efficiency, performance and resale value of your vehicle.

If the vehicle is driven in dusty areas, used to tow a trailer, driven frequently at slow speeds (idling in traffic) or on short journeys, more frequent maintenance intervals are recommended.

Every 250 miles (400 km) or weekly
- [ ] Refer to *Weekly checks*.

Every 5000 miles (8000 km) or 6 months, whichever comes first
- [ ] Renew the engine oil and filter (Section 3).

Note: *Frequent oil and filter changes are good for the engine. We recommend changing the oil at the mileage specified here, or at least twice a year if the mileage covered is a less.*

Every 10 000 miles (16 000 km) or 12 months, whichever comes first
In addition to the items listed above, carry out the following:
- [ ] Check the condition of the brake pads (Section 4).
- [ ] Thoroughly inspect the engine for fluid leaks (Section 5).
- [ ] Check the condition and security of the steering and suspension components (Section 6).
- [ ] Check the condition of the driveshaft gaiters (Section 7).
- [ ] Inspect the clutch hydraulic components (Section 8).
- [ ] Check the manual transmission oil level (Section 9).
- [ ] Check the battery electrolyte level (Section 10).
- [ ] Inspect the underbody, brake hydraulic pipes and hoses, and fuel lines (Section 11).
- [ ] Check the condition and security of the exhaust system (Section 12).
- [ ] Check the handbrake adjustment (Section 13).
- [ ] Check the condition of the seat belts (Section 14).
- [ ] Lubricate the locks and hinges (Section 15).
- [ ] Check the headlight beam alignment (Section 16).
- [ ] Check the condition of the exterior trim and paintwork (Section 17).
- [ ] Check the automatic transmission selector cable adjustment (Section 18).
- [ ] Road test (Section 19).
- [ ] Check the automatic transmission fluid level (Section 20).
- [ ] Check the operation of the air conditioning system (Section 21).

Every 20 000 miles (32 000 km) or 2 years, whichever comes first
In addition to the items listed above, carry out the following:
- [ ] Check the condition of the auxiliary drivebelt and renew if necessary (Section 22).

Every 30 000 miles (48 000 km) or 3 years, whichever comes first
In addition to the items listed above, carry out the following:
- [ ] Inspect the distributor cap, rotor arm and HT leads (Section 23).
- [ ] Renew the spark plugs (Section 24).

Every 40 000 miles (64 000 km) or 4 years, whichever comes first
In addition to the items listed above, carry out the following:
- [ ] Renew the air cleaner element (Section 25).

Every 50 000 miles (80 000 km) or 5 years, whichever comes first
In addition to the items listed above, carry out the following:
- [ ] Renew the fuel filter (Section 26).
- [ ] Check the emission control equipment (Section 27).

Every 80 000 miles (128 000 km) or 8 years, whichever comes first
In addition to the items listed above, carry out the following:
- [ ] Renew the timing belt (Section 28) - see Note below.

Note: *It is strongly recommended that the interval is halved to 40 000 miles (64 000 km), particularly on vehicles which are subjected to intensive use, ie. mainly short journeys or a lot of stop-start driving. The actual belt renewal interval is therefore very much up to the individual owner, but bear in mind that severe engine damage will result if the belt breaks.*

Every 2 years, regardless of mileage
- [ ] Renew the coolant (Section 29).
- [ ] Renew the brake fluid (Section 30).

1

Underbonnet view of a later 2.5 litre non-turbo model

1 Cooling system expansion tank
2 Power steering reservoir
3 Main fusebox
4 Timing belt upper cover
5 Brake master cylinder reservoir
6 Spark plug cover
7 ABS modulator
8 Auxiliary fusebox
9 Suspension strut upper mounting
10 Air cleaner
11 Battery
12 Radiator fan shroud
13 Inlet manifold
14 Fuel rail
15 Oil filler cap
16 Engine oil dipstick
17 Radiator top hose
18 Power steering pump
19 Alternator
20 Washer reservoir filler

Front underside view of a later 2.5 litre model

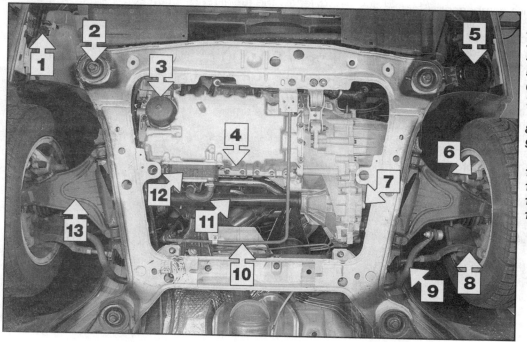

1 Windscreen washer pump
2 Subframe mounting
3 Oil filter
4 Engine oil drain plug
5 EVAP carbon canister
6 Front brake caliper
7 Manual transmission drain plug
8 Track rod end
9 Anti-roll bar connecting link
10 Power steering fluid pipes
11 Right-hand driveshaft
12 Engine oil cooler
13 Suspension control arm

Rear underside view of a 2.5 litre Estate model

1 Fuel filter
2 Exhaust centre silencer
3 Rear anti-roll bar
4 Rear suspension trailing arm
5 Handbrake cable
6 Rear shock absorber
7 Rear brake caliper
8 Exhaust rear silencer
9 Fuel tank
10 Fuel filler neck
11 Rear coil spring
12 Rear suspension transverse arm

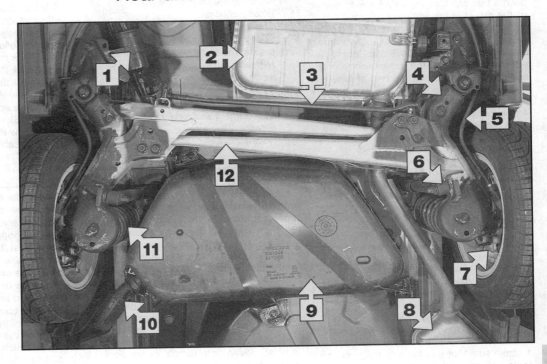

Maintenance procedures

1 Introduction

This Chapter is designed to help the home mechanic maintain his/her vehicle for safety, economy, long life and peak performance.

This Chapter contains a master maintenance schedule, followed by Sections dealing specifically with each task in the schedule. Visual checks, adjustments, component renewal and other helpful items are included. Refer to the accompanying illustrations of the engine compartment and the underside of the vehicle for the locations of the various components.

Servicing your vehicle in accordance with the mileage/time maintenance schedule and the following Sections will provide a planned maintenance programme, which should result in a long and reliable service life. This is a comprehensive plan, so maintaining some items but not others at the specified service intervals will not produce the same results.

As you service your vehicle, you will discover that many of the procedures can - and should - be grouped together, because of the particular procedure being performed, or

because of the close proximity of two otherwise-unrelated components to one another. For example, if the vehicle is raised for any reason, the exhaust should be inspected at the same time as the suspension and steering components.

The first step of this maintenance programme is to prepare yourself before the actual work begins. Read through all the Sections relevant to the work to be carried out, then make a list and gather together all the parts and tools required. If a problem is encountered, seek advice from a parts specialist or a dealer service department.

Service interval display

All models are equipped with a service interval display indicator in the instrument panel. When a predetermined mileage, time period, or number of hours of engine operation has elapsed since the display was last reset, the service light will illuminate, providing a handy reminder of when the next service is required.

The display should not necessarily be used as a definitive guide to the servicing needs of your Volvo, but it is useful as a reminder, to ensure that servicing is not accidentally overlooked. Owners of older cars, or those

covering a small annual mileage, may feel inclined to service their car more often, in which case the service interval display is perhaps less relevant.

The display should be reset whenever a service is carried out; at the time of writing, it appears that this can only be done by a Volvo dealer.

2 Regular maintenance

1 If, from the time the vehicle is new, the routine maintenance schedule is followed closely, and frequent checks are made of fluid levels and high-wear items, as suggested throughout this manual, the engine will be kept in relatively good running condition, and the need for additional work will be minimised.
2 It is possible that there will be some times when the engine is running poorly due to the lack of regular maintenance. This is even more likely if a used vehicle, which has not received regular and frequent maintenance checks, is purchased. In such cases, additional work may need to be carried out, outside of the regular maintenance intervals.

3 If engine wear is suspected, a compression test (refer to Part A of Chapter 2) will provide valuable information regarding the overall performance of the main internal components. Such a test can be used as a basis to decide on the extent of the work to be carried out. If, for example, a compression test indicates serious internal engine wear, conventional maintenance as described in this Chapter will not greatly improve the performance of the engine, and may prove a waste of time and money, unless extensive overhaul work (Chapter 2B) is carried out first.

4 The following series of operations are those often required to improve the performance of a generally poor-running engine:

Primary operations

a) *Clean, inspect and test the battery (See Weekly checks and Section 10).*
b) *Check all the engine-related fluids (See Weekly checks).*
c) *Check the condition of the auxiliary drivebelt (Section 22).*
d) *Inspect the distributor cap, rotor arm and HT leads, where applicable - up to 1999 model year (Section 23).*
e) *Renew the spark plugs (Section 24).*
f) *Check the condition of the air cleaner filter element and renew if necessary (Section 25).*
g) *Renew the fuel filter (Section 26).*
h) *Check the condition of all hoses, and check for fluid leaks (Section 5).*

Secondary operations

5 If the above operations do not prove fully effective, carry out the following operations: All the items listed under *Primary operations*, plus the following:
a) *Check the charging system (Chapter 5A).*
b) *Check the ignition system (Chapter 5B).*
c) *Check the fuel system (Chapter 4A and B).*
d) *Renew the distributor cap and rotor arm, where applicable (Section 23 and Chapter 5B).*
e) *Renew the ignition HT leads, where applicable (Section 23).*

Every 5000 miles (8 000 km) or 6 months

3 Engine oil and filter renewal

> **HAYNES HINT** *Frequent oil changes are the best preventive maintenance the home mechanic can give the engine, because ageing oil becomes diluted and contaminated, which leads to premature engine wear.*

1 Make sure that you have all the necessary tools before you begin this procedure. You should also have plenty of rags or newspapers handy, for mopping up any spills. The oil should preferably be changed when the engine is still fully warmed-up to normal operating temperature, just after a run; warm oil and sludge will flow out more easily. Take care, however, not to touch the exhaust or any other hot parts of the engine when working under the vehicle. To avoid any possibility of scalding, and to protect yourself from possible skin irritants and other harmful contaminants in used engine oils, it is advisable to wear gloves when carrying out this work.

2 Access to the underside of the vehicle is greatly improved if the vehicle can be lifted on a hoist, driven onto ramps, or supported by axle stands. (see *Jacking and vehicle support*). Whichever method is chosen, make sure that the vehicle remains level, or if it is at an angle, that the drain point is at the lowest point. On earlier vehicles it will be necessary to remove the engine undertray for access to the sump and filter.

3 Position the draining container under the drain plug, and unscrew the plug **(see illustration)**. If possible, try to keep the plug pressed into the sump while unscrewing it by hand the last couple of turns.

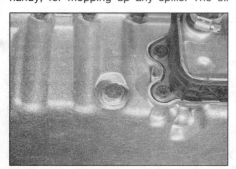

3.3 Unscrew the sump drain plug and allow the oil to drain

> **HAYNES HINT** *As the drain plug releases from the threads, move it away sharply, so the stream of oil issuing from the sump runs into the container, not up your sleeve.*

4 Allow the oil to drain into the container, and check the condition of the plug's sealing washer; renew it if worn or damaged.

5 Allow some time for the old oil to drain, noting that it may be necessary to reposition the container as the oil flow slows to a trickle; when the oil has completely drained, wipe clean the drain plug and its threads in the sump and refit the plug, tightening it to the specified torque.

6 The oil filter is located at the base of the sump on the front right-hand side.

7 Reposition the draining container under the oil filter then, using a suitable filter removal tool if necessary, slacken the filter initially, then unscrew it by hand the rest of the way; be prepared for some oil spillage **(see illustrations)**. Empty the oil in the old filter into the container.

8 Using a clean, lint-free rag, wipe clean the cylinder block around the filter mounting. Check the old filter to make sure that the rubber sealing ring hasn't stuck to the engine; if it has, carefully remove it.

9 Apply a light coating of clean engine oil to the sealing ring on the new filter **(see illustration)**. Screw the filter into position on the engine until it seats, then tighten it firmly by hand only - **do not** use any tools.

10 Remove the old oil and all tools from under the vehicle, then lower the vehicle to the ground.

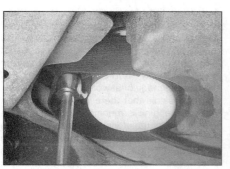

3.7a Slacken the oil filter with a suitable filter removal tool . . .

3.7b . . . then unscrew it the rest of the way by hand

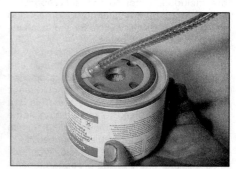

3.9 Apply a light coating of clean engine oil to the sealing ring on the new filter

11 Remove the dipstick and the oil filler cap from the engine. Fill the engine with oil, using the correct grade and type of oil (see *Specifications*). Pour in half the specified quantity of oil first, then wait a few minutes for the oil to fall to the sump **(see illustration)**. Continue adding oil a small quantity at a time, until the level is up to the lower mark on the dipstick. Adding approximately 1.5 litres will raise the level to the upper mark on the dipstick.
12 Start the engine. The oil pressure warning light will take a few seconds to go out while

the new filter fills with oil; do not race the engine while the light is on. Run the engine for a few minutes, while checking for leaks around the oil filter seal and the drain plug.
13 Switch off the engine, and wait a few minutes for the oil to settle in the sump once more. With the new oil circulated and the filter now completely full, recheck the level on the dipstick, and add more oil as necessary.
14 Dispose of the used engine oil safely and in accordance with environmental regulations (see *General repair procedures*).

3.11 Filling the engine with oil

Every 10 000 miles (16 000 km) or 12 months

4 Brake pad wear check

1 Jack up the front or rear of the vehicle in turn, and support it on axle stands (see *Jacking and vehicle support*).
2 For better access to the brake calipers, remove the roadwheels.
3 Look through the inspection window in the caliper, and check that the thickness of the friction lining material on each of the pads is not less than the recommended minimum thickness given in the *Specifications* **(see illustration)**. If any one of the brake pads has worn down to, or below, the specified limit, *all four* pads at that end of the car must be renewed as a set (ie all the front pads or all the rear pads).
4 For a comprehensive check, the brake pads should be removed and cleaned. The operation of the brake calipers can then be checked, and the brake discs can be fully examined. Refer to Chapter 9 for details.

5 Underbonnet check for fluid leaks and hose condition

Caution: Renewal of air conditioning hoses must be left to a dealer service department or air conditioning specialist who has the equipment to depressurise the system safely. Never remove air conditioning components or hoses until the system has been depressurised.

General

1 High temperatures in the engine compartment can cause the deterioration of the rubber and plastic hoses used for engine, accessory and emission systems operation. Periodic inspection should be made for cracks, loose clamps, material hardening and leaks.
2 Carefully check the large top and bottom radiator hoses **(see illustration)**, along with the other smaller-diameter cooling system hoses and metal pipes; do not forget the

heater hoses/pipes which run from the engine to the bulkhead. Inspect each hose along its entire length, replacing any that are cracked, swollen or shows signs of deterioration. Cracks may become more apparent if the hose is squeezed.
3 Make sure that all hose connections are tight. If the spring clamps that are used to secure some of the hoses appear to be slackening, they should be replaced with screw-type clips to prevent the possibility of leaks.
4 Some other hoses are secured to their fittings with screw-type clips. Where screw-type clips are used, check to be sure they haven't slackened, allowing the hose to leak. If clamps or screw-type clips aren't used, make sure the hose has not expanded and/or hardened where it slips over the fitting, allowing it to leak.
5 Check all fluid reservoirs, filler caps, drain plugs and fittings etc, looking for any signs of leakage of oil, transmission and/or brake

1

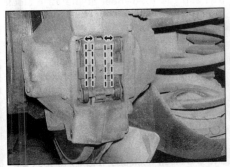

4.3 The thickness of the brake pads can be seen through the inspection window

5.2 Check all hose connections for tightness and signs of leakage

A leak in the cooling system will usually show up as white- or rust-coloured deposits on the areas adjoining the leak

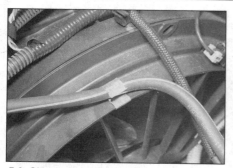

5.6 Check all vacuum hoses - ensure they are not split or crushed by their retaining clips

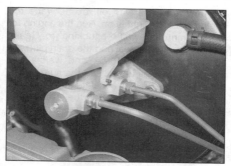

5.16 Check all metal brake lines

hydraulic fluid, coolant and power steering fluid. If the vehicle is regularly parked in the same place, close inspection of the ground underneath will soon show any leaks; ignore the puddle of water which will be left if the air conditioning system is in use. As soon as a leak is detected, its source must be traced and rectified. Where oil has been leaking for some time, it is usually necessary to use a steam cleaner, pressure washer or similar, to clean away the accumulated dirt, so that the exact source of the leak can be identified.

Vacuum hoses

6 It's quite common for vacuum hoses, especially those in the emissions system, to be numbered or colour-coded, or to be identified by coloured stripes moulded into them **(see illustration)**. Various systems require hoses with different wall thicknesses, collapse resistance and temperature resistance. When renewing hoses, be sure the new ones are made of the same material.
7 Often the only effective way to check a hose is to remove it completely from the vehicle. If more than one hose is removed, be sure to label the hoses and fittings to ensure correct installation.
8 When checking vacuum hoses, be sure to include any plastic T-fittings in the check. Inspect the fittings for cracks, and check the hose where it fits over the fitting for distortion, which could cause leakage.
9 A small piece of vacuum hose can be used as a stethoscope to detect vacuum leaks. Hold one end of the hose to your ear, and

probe around vacuum hoses and fittings, listening for the hissing sound characteristic of a vacuum leak.

⚠️ *Warning: When probing with the vacuum hose stethoscope, be very careful not to come into contact with moving engine components such as the auxiliary drivebelt, radiator electric cooling fan, etc.*

Fuel hoses

⚠️ *Warning: Before carrying out the following operation, refer to the precautions given in Safety first! at the beginning of this manual, and follow them implicitly. Petrol is a highly dangerous and volatile liquid, and the precautions necessary when handling it cannot be overstressed.*

10 Check all fuel hoses for deterioration and chafing. Check especially for cracks in areas where the hose bends, and also just before fittings, such as where a hose attaches to the fuel filter.
11 High-quality fuel line, usually identified by the word Fluoroelastomer printed on the hose, should be used for fuel line renewal. Never, under any circumstances, use unreinforced vacuum line, clear plastic tubing or water hose for fuel lines.
12 Spring-type clamps are commonly used on fuel lines. These clamps often lose their tension over a period of time, and can be 'sprung' during removal. Replace all spring-type clamps with screw clips whenever a hose is replaced.

13 If a fuel leak is suspected, remember that any leak will be more obvious with the system at full pressure, such as when the engine is running, or shortly after switching off.

Metal lines

14 Sections of metal piping are often used for fuel line between the fuel filter and the engine. Check carefully to be sure the piping has not been bent or crimped, and that cracks have not started in the line.
15 If a section of metal fuel line must be renewed, only seamless steel piping should be used, since copper and aluminium piping don't have the strength necessary to withstand normal engine vibration.
16 Check the metal brake lines where they enter the master cylinder and ABS hydraulic unit for cracks in the lines or loose fittings **(see illustration)**. Any sign of brake fluid leakage calls for an immediate and thorough inspection of the brake system.

---

6 Steering and suspension check

Front suspension and steering check

1 Apply the handbrake, then jack up the front of the vehicle and support it on axle stands (see *Jacking and vehicle support*).
2 Visually inspect the balljoint dust covers and the steering gear gaiters for splits, chafing or deterioration **(see illustration)**. Any wear of these components will cause loss of lubricant, together with dirt and water entry, resulting in rapid deterioration of the balljoints or steering gear.
3 Check the power steering fluid hoses for chafing or deterioration, and the pipe and hose unions for fluid leaks. Also check for signs of fluid leakage under pressure from the steering gear rubber gaiters, which would indicate failed fluid seals within the steering gear.
4 Check for signs of fluid leakage around the suspension strut body, or from the rubber boot around the piston rod (where fitted). Should any fluid be noticed, the shock absorber is defective internally, and renewal is necessary.
5 Grasp the roadwheel at the 12 o'clock and 6 o'clock positions, and try to rock it **(see illustration)**. Very slight free play may be felt, but if the movement is appreciable, further investigation is necessary to determine the source. Continue rocking the wheel while an assistant depresses the footbrake. If the movement is now eliminated or significantly reduced, it is likely that the wheel bearings are at fault. If the free play is still evident with the footbrake depressed, then there is wear in the suspension joints or mountings.
6 Now grasp the wheel at the 9 o'clock and 3 o'clock positions, and try to rock it as before. Any movement felt now may again be caused by wear in the wheel bearings or the

6.2 Check the balljoint dust covers for damage

6.5 Check for wear in the wheel bearing by grasping the wheel and trying to rock it

29.3a Radiator drain tap location (arrowed)

29.3b Radiator bottom hose connection

29.4 Cylinder block drain tap location (arrowed)

Every 2 years, regardless of mileage

29 Coolant renewal

⚠ *Warning: Wait until the engine is cold before starting this procedure. Do not allow antifreeze to come into contact with your skin, or with painted surfaces of the vehicle. Rinse off spills immediately with plenty of water. Never leave antifreeze lying around in an open container, or in a puddle in the driveway or on the garage floor. Children and pets are attracted by its sweet smell, but antifreeze can be fatal if ingested.*

Note: *If Volvo type C coolant, in the specified ratio, has been continuously maintained in the system, then coolant renewal will not normally be necessary. However, to be absolutely sure about the integrity of the antifreeze and anti-corrosion properties of the coolant, periodic renewal is to be recommended.*

Coolant draining

1 To drain the system, first remove the expansion tank filler cap (see *Weekly checks*).
2 If the additional working clearance is required, raise the front of the vehicle and support it securely on axle stands (see *Jacking and vehicle support*).
3 Remove the undertray under the radiator and, where fitted, the engine undertray, then place a large drain tray underneath the radiator. Open the drain tap at the bottom left-hand corner of the radiator and allow the coolant to drain into the tray. If no drain tap is fitted, carefully loosen and remove the radiator bottom hose connection **(see illustrations)**.
4 When the radiator has drained, move the tray to the rear right-hand side of the engine and unscrew the cylinder block drain tap (where fitted) **(see illustration)**.

System flushing

5 With time, the cooling system may gradually lose its efficiency, as the radiator core becomes choked with rust, scale deposits from the water, and other sediment. This is especially likely if an inferior grade of antifreeze has been used, especially if it has not been regularly renewed. To minimise this, as well as using only the specified type of antifreeze and clean soft water, the system should be flushed as follows whenever any part of it is disturbed, and/or when the coolant is renewed.
6 With the coolant drained, close the drain taps and refill the system with fresh water. Refit the expansion tank filler cap, start the engine and warm it up to normal operating temperature, then stop it and (after allowing it to cool down completely) drain the system again. Repeat as necessary until only clean water can be seen to emerge, then refill finally with the specified coolant mixture.
7 If only clean, soft water and good-quality antifreeze has been used, and the coolant has been renewed at the specified intervals, the above procedure will be sufficient to keep the system clean for a considerable length of time. If, however, the system has been neglected, a more thorough operation will be required, as follows.
8 First drain the coolant, then disconnect the radiator top and bottom hoses. Insert a garden hose into the top hose, and allow water to circulate through the radiator until it runs clean from the bottom outlet.
9 To flush the engine, remove the thermostat (see Chapter 3), insert the garden hose into the thermostat housing, and allow water to circulate until it runs clear from the bottom hose. If, after a reasonable period, the water still does not run clear, the radiator should be flushed with a good proprietary cleaning agent.
10 In severe cases of contamination, reverse-flushing of the radiator may be necessary. To do this, remove the radiator (see Chapter 3), invert it, and insert the garden hose into the bottom outlet. Continue flushing until clear water runs from the top hose outlet. A similar procedure can be used to flush the heater matrix.
11 The use of chemical cleaners should be necessary only as a last resort. Normally, regular renewal of the coolant will prevent excessive contamination of the system.

Coolant filling

12 With the cooling system drained and flushed, ensure that all disturbed components or hose unions are correctly fitted, and that the two drain taps are securely tightened. Refit the engine undertrays removed for access. If it was raised, lower the vehicle to the ground.
13 Prepare a sufficient quantity of the specified coolant mixture (see *Specifications*); allow for a surplus, so as to have a reserve supply for topping-up.
14 Slowly fill the system through the expansion tank; since the tank is the highest point in the system, all the air in the system should be displaced into the tank by the rising liquid. Slow pouring reduces the possibility of air being trapped and forming air-locks. It helps also, if the large radiator hoses are gently squeezed during the filling procedure.
15 Continue filling until the coolant level reaches the expansion tank MAX level line, then wait for a few minutes. During this time, continue to squeeze the radiator hoses. When the level stops falling, top up to the MAX level and refit the expansion tank cap.
16 Start the engine and run it at idle speed, until it has warmed-up to normal operating temperature. If the level in the expansion tank drops significantly, top-up to the MAX level line, to minimise the amount of air circulating in the system.
17 Stop the engine, allow it to cool down *completely* (overnight, if possible), then remove the expansion tank filler cap and top-up the tank to the MAX level line. Refit the filler cap, tightening it securely, and wash off any spilt coolant from the engine compartment and bodywork.
18 After refilling, always check carefully all components of the system (but especially any unions disturbed during draining and flushing) for signs of coolant leaks. Fresh antifreeze has a searching action, which will rapidly expose any weak points in the system.

1

Air-locks

19 If, after draining and refilling the system, symptoms of overheating are found which did not occur previously, then the fault is almost certainly due to trapped air at some point in the system, causing an air-lock and restricting the flow of coolant; usually, the air is trapped because the system was refilled too quickly.

20 If an air-lock is suspected, first try gently squeezing all visible coolant hoses. A coolant hose which is full of air feels quite different to one full of coolant, when squeezed. After refilling the system, most air-locks will clear once the system has cooled, and been topped up.

21 While the engine is running at operating temperature, switch on the heater and heater fan, and check for heat output. Provided there is sufficient coolant in the system, lack of heat output could be due to an air-lock in the system.

22 Air-locks can have more serious effects than simply reducing heater output - a severe air-lock could reduce coolant flow around the engine. Check that the radiator top hose is hot when the engine is at operating temperature - a top hose which stays cold could be the result of an air-lock (or a non-opening thermostat).

23 If the problem persists, stop the engine and allow it to cool down **completely**, before unscrewing the expansion tank filler cap or disconnecting hoses to bleed out the trapped air. In the worst case, the system will have to be at least partially drained (this time, the coolant can be saved for re-use) and flushed to clear the problem.

30 Brake fluid renewal

⚠ *Warning: Brake hydraulic fluid can harm your eyes and damage painted surfaces, so use extreme* caution when handling and pouring it. Do not use fluid that has been standing open for some time as it absorbs moisture from the air. Excess moisture can cause a dangerous loss of braking effectiveness.*

The procedure is similar to that for the bleeding of the hydraulic system as described in Chapter 9, except that the brake fluid reservoir should be emptied by siphoning, and allowance should be made for the old fluid to be removed from the circuit when bleeding a section of the circuit.

Since the clutch hydraulic system uses the same fluid and reservoir as the braking system, it will probably be necessary to bleed the clutch system also (see Chapter 6, Section 5).

HAYNES HiNT *Old hydraulic fluid is invariably much darker in colour than the new, making it easy to distinguish between the two.*

Chapter 2 Part A:
Engine in-car repair procedures

Contents

Degrees of difficulty

| **Easy,** suitable for novice with little experience | | **Fairly easy,** suitable for beginner with some experience | | **Fairly difficult,** suitable for competent DIY mechanic | 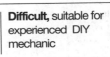 | **Difficult,** suitable for experienced DIY mechanic | | **Very difficult,** suitable for expert DIY or professional | |

Specifications

General

Engine code:
B5202 S	2.0 litre (1984 cc), 10-valve, normally-aspirated
B5204 S	2.0 litre (1984 cc), 20-valve, normally-aspirated
B5204 T	2.0 litre (1984 cc), 20-valve, turbocharged
B5234 S	2.3 litre (2319 cc), 20-valve, normally-aspirated
B5234 T	2.3 litre (2319 cc), 20-valve, turbocharged
B5252 S or B5242 S*	2.5 litre (2435 cc), 10-valve, normally-aspirated
B5254 S or B5244 S*	2.5 litre (2435 cc), 20-valve, normally-aspirated
B5254 T or B5244 T*	2.5 litre (2435 cc), 20-valve, turbocharged

*See Section 1

Bore:
2.0 and 2.3 litre engines	81.0 mm
2.5 litre engines	83.0 mm

Stroke:
2.0 litre engines	77.0 mm
All other engines	90.0 mm

Compression ratio:
B5202 S	10.0 : 1
B5204 S	10.3 : 1
B5204 T	8.4 : 1
B5234 S	10.5 : 1
B5234 T	8.5 : 1
B5252 S / B5242 S	10.0 : 1
B5254 S / B5244 S	10.3 : 1
B5254 T / B5244 T	9.0 : 1

Compression pressure:
Normally-aspirated engines	13 to 15 bar
Turbocharged engines	11 to 13 bar
Maximum difference between highest and lowest readings	2 bar
Firing order	1-2-4-5-3 (No 1 at timing belt end of engine)
Direction of crankshaft rotation	Clockwise (viewed from front of engine)

2A

Camshaft

	Inlet	Exhaust
Identification letter (stamped on end):		
10-valve engines	HEI	HEE
20-valve non-turbo engines	PGI	PGE
20-valve turbo engines	PHI	PHE
Maximum lift (inlet and exhaust):		
10-valve engines	9.60 mm	
20-valve non-turbo engines	8.45 mm	
20-valve turbo engines	7.95 mm	
Camshaft endfloat	0.05 to 0.20 mm	

Tappets (cam followers)

Diameter:	
10-valve engines	34.959 to 35.025 mm
20-valve engines	31.959 to 32.025 mm
Height	25.500 to 26.500 mm

Lubrication system

Oil pressure (warm engine @ 4000 rpm)	3.5 bars
Oil pump type	Gear, driven from crankshaft
Maximum pump gear to housing clearance	0.35 mm
Pressure relief valve spring free height:	
Non-turbo engines	82.13 mm
Turbo engines	76.22 mm

Torque wrench settings*

	Nm	lbf ft
Camshaft sprocket bolts	20	15
Crankshaft pulley-to-sprocket bolts:		
Stage 1	25	18
Stage 2	Angle-tighten a further 30°	
Crankshaft sprocket centre nut	180	133
Cylinder head lower section to block:**		
Stage 1	20	15
Stage 2	60	44
Stage 3	Angle-tighten a further 130°	
Cylinder head upper section to lower section	17	13
Engine oil drain plug	35	26
Flywheel/driveplate**		
Stage 1	45	33
Stage 2	Angle-tighten a further 65°	
Oil pump to cylinder block	10	7
Oil pressure switch	25	18
Roadwheel bolts	110	81
Spark plugs	25	18
Timing belt tensioner bolt	20	15
Timing belt idler pulley	25	18

Engine/transmission mountings (see illustration 11.7)

	Nm	lbf ft
Engine lower steady bar bracket to subframe:		
Stage 1	65	48
Stage 2	Angle-tighten a further 60°	
Engine lower steady bar bracket to transmission:**		
Stage 1	35	26
Stage 2	Angle-tighten a further 40°	
Engine lower steady bar bushes to brackets:**		
Stage 1	35	26
Stage 2	Angle-tighten a further 90°	
Engine right-hand mounting bracket to engine:		
8 mm bolt:**		
Stage 1	20	15
Stage 2	Angle-tighten a further 60°	
10 mm bolts:**		
Stage 1	35	26
Stage 2	Angle-tighten a further 60°	
Engine right-hand mounting to engine bracket:**		
Stage 1	35	26
Stage 2	Angle-tighten a further 90°	

Torque wrench settings* (continued)

	Nm	lbf ft
Engine/transmission mountings (continued) (see illustration 11.7)		
Engine right-hand mounting to subframe:**		
Stage 1	65	48
Stage 2	Angle-tighten a further 60°	
Engine upper steady bar bracket to engine:		
Lower bolts:**		
Stage 1	45	33
Stage 2	Angle-tighten a further 90°	
Upper bolt:		
Non-turbo engines	25	18
Turbo engines:		
Stage 1	35	26
Stage 2	Angle-tighten a further 60°	
Engine upper steady bar to bulkhead bracket:		
Stage 1	35	26
Stage 2	Angle-tighten a further 60°	
Engine upper steady bar to engine bracket:		
Stage 1	35	26
Stage 2	Angle-tighten a further 90°	
Transmission front mounting bracket to subframe	50	37
Transmission front mounting bracket to transmission	25	18
Transmission rear mounting nuts/bolts	50	37

*Oiled threads unless otherwise stated
New nuts/bolts must **always be used

1 General information

How to use this Chapter

This Part of Chapter 2 describes those repair procedures that can reasonably be carried out on the engine while it remains in the car. If the engine has been removed from the car and is being dismantled as described in Part B, any preliminary dismantling procedures can be ignored.

Note that, while it may be possible physically to overhaul items such as the piston/connecting rod assemblies while the engine is in the car, such tasks are not normally carried out as separate operations. Usually, several additional procedures (not to mention the cleaning of components and oilways) have to be carried out. For this reason, all such tasks are classed as major overhaul procedures, and are described in Part B of this Chapter.

Part B describes the removal of the engine/transmission from the vehicle, and the full overhaul procedures that can then be carried out.

Engine description

The five-cylinder engine is of the double overhead camshaft type, incorporating two or four valves per cylinder according to type. The cylinders are in line and the engine is mounted transversely on a subframe in the engine bay. The engine codes (which appear only where necessary) are quite logical to follow - the first digit is the number of cylinders, the second and third together give the engine capacity in litres, and the final digit is the number of valves per cylinder. A T designation after the digits denotes a turbocharged engine. Thus, the B5234 T is a five-cylinder, 2.3 litre engine, with 4 valves per cylinder (total: 20 valves) and is turbocharged.

From late 1999 onwards, it appears that all 2.5 litre engines have had their engine codes altered from B525 to B524. This is in response to an EC directive demanding that engine codes accurately reflect engine capacity, and the 2.5 litre engine being 2435 cc (and therefore nearer 2.4 litres), it was deemed that 24 rather than 25 appear in the engine code.

The entire engine is constructed of aluminium alloy, and consists of five sections. The cylinder head comprises an upper and lower section, with the cylinder block, intermediate section and sump forming the other three. The upper and lower sections of the cylinder head are mated along the centre-line of the camshafts, while the cylinder block and intermediate section are mated along the crankshaft centre-line. A conventional cylinder head gasket is used between the cylinder head and block, with liquid gaskets being used in the joints between the other main sections.

The cylinder block incorporates five cast-iron dry cylinder liners which are cast into the block and cannot be replaced. Cast-iron reinforcements are also used in the intermediate section as strengthening agents in the main bearing areas.

Drive to the camshaft is by a toothed timing belt and sprockets, incorporating an automatic tensioning mechanism. The timing belt also drives the coolant pump. All accessories are driven from the crankshaft pulley by a single multi-ribbed auxiliary drivebelt.

The cylinder head is of the crossflow type, the inlet ports being at the front of the engine and the exhaust ports at the rear. The upper section of the cylinder head functions as a combined valve cover and camshaft cover, and the camshafts run in six plain bearings integral to the two cylinder head sections. Valve actuation is by maintenance-free hydraulic tappets, acted upon directly by the camshaft lobes. The 2.0 and 2.5 litre engines are available in 10- or 20-valve configuration, while the 2.3 litre engines are all 20-valve units.

From late 1999 onwards, some 2.5 litre engines are fitted with a variable valve timing system, which acts on the inlet camshaft. Regrettably, no information was available on this system at time of writing.

The crankshaft runs in six shell type main bearings; the connecting rod big-end bearings are also of the shell type. Crankshaft endfloat is taken by thrustwashers which are an integral part of the No 5 main bearing shells.

The lubrication system is of the full-flow, pressure-feed type. Oil is drawn from the sump by a gear type pump, driven from the front of the crankshaft. Oil under pressure passes through a filter before being fed to the various shaft bearings and to the valve gear. Later non-turbo models have an external oil cooler mounted on the rear of the sump. On turbo models, an external oil cooler is fitted which is incorporated in the radiator side tank. Turbo models also have an oil feed and return for the turbocharger bearings.

2A

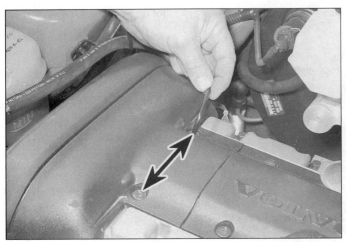

3.3a Remove the two upper cover retaining screws (arrowed) . . .   **3.3b . . . then release the clip at the front and rear of the cover . . .**

Repair operations possible with the engine in the car

The following work can be carried out with the engine in the car:
a) *Compression pressure - testing.*
b) *Timing belt - removal and refitting.*
c) *Camshaft oil seals - renewal.*
d) *Camshafts and tappets - removal and refitting.*
e) *Cylinder head - removal and refitting.*
f) *Cylinder head and pistons - decarbonising.*
g) *Crankshaft oil seals - renewal.*
h) *Oil pump - removal and refitting.*
i) *Flywheel/driveplate - removal and refitting.*
j) *Engine mountings - removal and refitting.*

2 Compression test - description and interpretation

1 When engine performance is down, or if misfiring occurs which cannot be attributed to the ignition or fuel systems, a compression test can provide diagnostic clues as to the engine's condition. If the test is performed regularly, it can give warning of trouble before any other symptoms become apparent.
2 The engine must be fully warmed-up to normal operating temperature, the battery must be fully charged, and all the spark plugs must be removed (Chapter 1). The aid of an assistant will also be required.
3 Disable the ignition system by disconnecting the RPM sensor wiring at the connector located just below and to the rear of the distributor. Also disconnect the wiring connectors to each fuel injector, to prevent fuel from damaging the catalytic converter.
4 Fit a compression tester to the No 1 cylinder spark plug hole - the type of tester which screws into the plug thread is to be preferred.
5 Have the assistant hold the throttle wide open, and crank the engine on the starter

motor; after one or two revolutions, the compression pressure should build up to a maximum figure, and then stabilise. Record the highest reading obtained.
6 Repeat the test on the remaining cylinders, recording the pressure in each.
7 All cylinders should produce very similar pressures; a difference of more than 2 bars between the highest and lowest reading indicates a fault.
8 Note that the compression should build up quickly in a healthy engine; low compression on the first stroke, followed by gradually-increasing pressure on successive strokes, indicates worn piston rings.
9 A low compression reading on the first stroke, which does not build up during successive strokes, indicates leaking valves or a blown head gasket (a cracked head could also be the cause). Deposits on the undersides of the valve heads can also cause low compression.
10 If the pressure in any cylinder is low, carry out the following test to isolate the cause. Introduce a teaspoonful of clean oil into that cylinder through its spark plug hole, and repeat the test.
11 If the addition of oil temporarily improves the compression pressure, this indicates that bore or piston wear is responsible for the pressure loss. No improvement suggests that leaking or burnt valves, or a blown head gasket, may be to blame.
12 A low reading from two adjacent cylinders is almost certainly due to the head gasket having blown between them; the presence of coolant in the engine oil will confirm this.
13 If one cylinder is about 20 percent lower than the others and the engine has a slightly rough idle, a worn camshaft lobe could be the cause.
14 If the compression reading is unusually high, the combustion chambers are probably coated with carbon deposits. If this is the case, the cylinder head should be removed and decarbonised.

15 On completion of the test, refit the spark plugs and reconnect the ignition system and fuel injectors.

3 Timing belt - removal and refitting

Note: *At the time of writing, no information was available on the variable valve timing system fitted to later 2.5 litre engines. Engines fitted with this system can be identified by having a large hub assembly bolted to the front (inlet) camshaft sprocket (refer to illustration 3.13b). Whilst it is quite likely that the timing belt renewal procedure is unaffected by this fitment, it would be wise to consult a Volvo dealer for advice before proceeding.*

Removal

1 Disconnect the battery negative lead.
2 Remove the auxiliary drivebelt as described in Chapter 1.
3 On later models without a distributor, remove the two screws and release the two spring clips securing the timing belt upper cover, and unclip the cover from the spark plug cover in the centre of the cylinder head **(see illustrations)**.

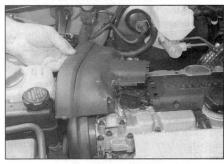

3.3c . . . and unclip it from the spark plug cover to remove

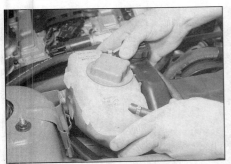

3.5 Lifting out the coolant expansion tank

3.6 Expansion tank and steering fluid reservoir can be tied clear of the working area

3.7 Removing the ECU box lid

4 Where applicable, release the turbocharger inlet ducting, then undo the six screws and remove the spark plug cover from the centre of the cylinder head.

5 Lift the cooling system expansion tank out of its mounting bracket, and place it to one side. Disconnect the wiring connector for the coolant level sensor, but there should be no need to disconnect the coolant hoses **(see illustration)**.

6 Release the power steering fluid reservoir from its mountings, and move it to one side without disconnecting the fluid hoses. Make sure the reservoir cap is secure, and that the reservoir is kept as upright as possible, to avoid fluid spillage **(see illustration)**.

7 Access may further be improved by removing the lid from the ECU box - disconnect the air supply hose, then release the two catches and remove the lid **(see illustration)**.

8 Undo the single bolt from the centre of the timing belt front cover, then pull the cover away from the engine, and lift it to release its retaining clips **(see illustrations)**.

9 Loosen the right-hand front wheel bolts, then jack up the front of the car and support it on axle stands (see *Jacking and vehicle support*). Remove the right-hand front roadwheel.

10 Release the two nuts securing the inner wheel arch liner, and fold back the liner for

access to the crankshaft pulley **(see illustrations)**.

11 Undo the bolts and remove the timing belt guard plate from behind the crankshaft pulley, where fitted **(see illustration)**.

12 On later models, temporarily refit the timing belt upper cover.

13 Using a socket on the crankshaft pulley centre nut, rotate the crankshaft clockwise (viewed from the right-hand side of the car) until the timing marks on the camshaft sprocket rims align with the notches on the timing belt rear cover (early models) or upper cover (later models) **(see illustrations overleaf)**.

14 In this position, the timing mark on the top,

3.8a Unscrew and remove the retaining bolt . . .

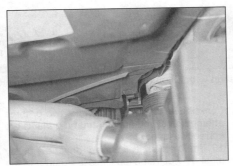

3.8b . . . then lift the cover to release the clips at the base . . .

3.8c . . . and remove the cover from the engine

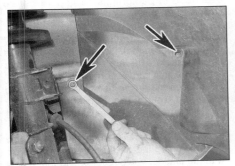

3.10a Remove the two retaining nuts (arrowed) . . .

3.10b . . . and fold back the wheel arch liner

3.11 Remove the timing belt guard plate

3.13a Timing marks on camshaft sprockets (A) aligned with the notches (B) on the belt rear cover - early models

3.13b Camshaft sprocket timing marks (A) and belt rear cover marks (B) - later models

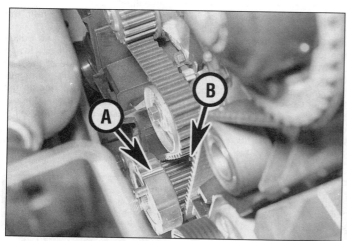

3.14 Crankshaft sprocket rib (A) should align with oil pump housing mark (B)

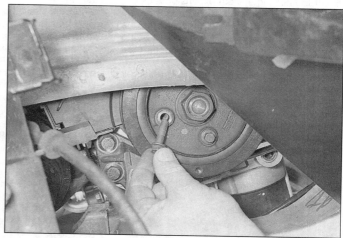

3.17a Loosen and remove two of the outer bolts . . .

outer edge of the crankshaft sprocket should also be aligned with the cast projection on the oil pump housing (see illustration).

15 The timing marks are not at all easy to see - the camshaft sprocket marks can be hardly more than faint scratches on the edges of the sprockets. Similarly, the mark on the crankshaft sprocket can only just be seen

from above. It will probably take two or three attempts until you are sure that the marks are correctly aligned.

16 The crankshaft (auxiliary drivebelt) pulley must now be removed - this is secured to the crankshaft (timing belt) sprocket by four bolts, and to the crankshaft itself by a large central nut.

17 Loosen the four outer bolts, and remove two of them. Using a home-made sprocket holding tool bolted to the pulley using the two vacated bolt holes, hold the pulley as the central nut is loosened - this is tightened to a very high torque (see illustrations).

18 Once the central nut is loose, check the alignment of the timing belt sprockets as described in paragraphs 13 and 14 before removing the pulley.

19 The crankshaft pulley locates on a roll pin, and a puller may be required to work the pulley off (see illustrations). Levering the pulley off is not advisable - the rim of the pulley itself is easily broken if care is not taken.

20 Loosen the timing belt tensioner retaining bolt, and rotate the tensioner assembly clockwise to relieve the tensioner on the belt (see illustration). If a new belt is being fitted, remove the tensioner completely, noting how the protruding lug on the tensioner engages with the engine. Volvo recommend that a new tensioner is fitted whenever a new timing belt is fitted.

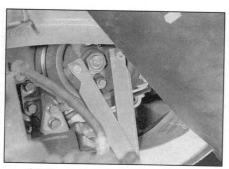

3.17b . . . then fit the home-made sprocket-holding tool . . .

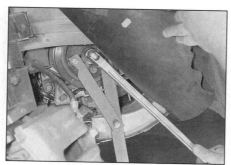

3.17c . . . and loosen the central nut

3.19a The crankshaft pulley locates on a roll pin (arrowed)

3.19b Removing the crankshaft pulley

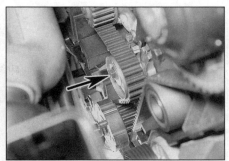

3.20 Loosen the tensioner retaining bolt (arrowed)

21 Mark the running direction of the belt if it is to be re-used, then slip it off the sprockets and idler pulleys and remove it. Clearance is very limited at the crankshaft sprocket, and a certain amount of manipulation is necessary. **Do not** rotate the crankshaft or camshafts with the belt removed.

22 Spin the idler pulley, to check for roughness or shake; renew if necessary.

23 Check the timing belt carefully for any signs of uneven wear or splitting. Pay particular attention to the roots of the teeth. Renew the belt if there is the slightest doubt about its condition.

24 If the engine is undergoing an overhaul, and has covered more than 36 000 miles (60 000 km) with the existing belt fitted, renew the belt as a matter of course, regardless of its apparent condition. The cost of a new belt is nothing when compared to the cost of repairs, should the belt break in service.

25 If signs of oil or coolant contamination are found on the old belt, trace the source of the leak, and rectify it. Wash down the engine timing belt area and all related components, to remove all traces of oil.

26 Even if the old timing belt does not show signs of coolant contamination, examine the coolant pump carefully for any indication that it may be leaking. When a coolant pump fails, it often starts leaking from the 'weep hole' in the top of the unit, just behind the pump's timing belt sprocket (see Chapter 3, Section 7). A coolant leak normally shows up as a white, crusty stain. If the engine has covered a high mileage, and is known to be using the original

pump, it would be worth considering renewing the coolant pump at the same time as the timing belt. If this is not done, and the pump subsequently starts leaking, the belt will have to be taken off again to fit a new pump.

27 Renew the tensioner assembly if there is any doubt about its condition - Volvo recommend that a new unit is fitted as a matter of course with a new belt.

Refitting and tensioning

28 Before refitting the timing belt, make sure that the sprockets are in the correct positions (paragraphs 13 and 14). It will be necessary to temporarily refit the timing belt rear cover (early models) or top cover (later models) to do this.

29 If removed, refit the belt tensioner in the same position as noted on removal. Lightly tighten the retaining bolt.

30 Slip the belt over the crankshaft sprocket. Keeping it taut, and taking care not to rotate the camshaft sprockets in particular, feed the belt over the idler pulley, front camshaft sprocket, rear camshaft sprocket, coolant pump sprocket and finally over the tensioner pulley **(see illustration)**. Observe the correct running direction if the old belt is being re-used.

31 Recheck the alignment of the sprocket marks.

32 Using a 6 mm Allen key, turn the belt tensioner anti-clockwise until its pointer reaches the stop to the right of the central notch, then turn it back to align with the central notch **(see illustrations)**. The

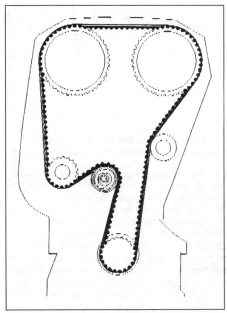

3.30 Timing belt run

tensioner must always be set in this way, so that it is being set from the right of the central position.

33 With the tensioner aligned with the central notch, hold the tensioner using the Allen key, and tighten the retaining bolt to the specified torque **(see illustration)**.

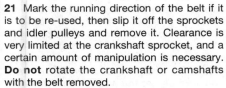

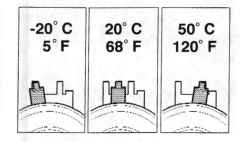

3.32a Timing belt tensioner settings at various ambient temperatures

3.32b Timing belt tensioner aligned with central notch

3.33 Hold the tensioner with an Allen key, and tighten the nut

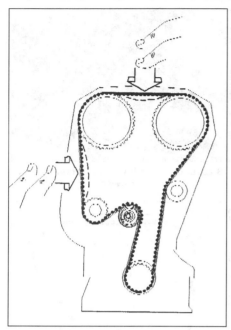

3.34 Press on the belt at each point indicated, and check the tensioner moves

34 Press on the belt at a point midway between the sprockets, and check that the tensioner pointer moves freely **(see illustration)**.

35 Turn the crankshaft clockwise through two complete revolutions, then check that all the timing marks can be realigned.

36 Also check that the tensioner pointer is aligned with the central notch. If not, loosen the tensioner retaining bolt, and reset the belt tension as described in paragraphs 31 to 35.

37 Refit the timing belt guard plate behind the crankshaft pulley, where applicable.

38 Refit the crankshaft pulley over the roll pin, then fit and tighten the central nut and the four outer bolts to the specified torques.

39 Fold back the wheel arch liner, and secure with the two nuts.

40 Refit the roadwheel and lower the car to the ground. Tighten the wheel bolts in a diagonal sequence to the specified torque.

41 Refit all the remaining components removed for access, using a reversal of the removal procedure.

4 Camshaft front oil seals - renewal

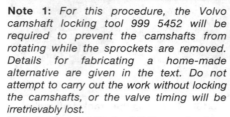

Note 1: *For this procedure, the Volvo camshaft locking tool 999 5452 will be required to prevent the camshafts from rotating while the sprockets are removed. Details for fabricating a home-made alternative are given in the text. Do not attempt to carry out the work without locking the camshafts, or the valve timing will be irretrievably lost.*

Note 2: *Models with the 2.5 litre engine from late 1999 onwards may be fitted with a variable valve timing system. Models with this system can be identified by having a large hub assembly bolted to the front (inlet) camshaft sprocket. No information on this system was available at the time of writing, and it would be wise to consult a Volvo dealer for advice before proceeding.*

1 Remove the timing belt as described in Section 3.

2 If both camshaft sprockets are to be removed, suitably mark them, inlet and exhaust for identification when refitting. The inlet sprocket is nearest the front of the car.

3 Undo the three bolts and remove the appropriate sprocket for access to the failed seal. Restrain the sprockets with a suitable tool through the holes in their faces **(see Tool Tip)**.

4 Withdraw the appropriate sprocket from the camshaft **(see illustration)**.

5 Carefully extract the seal by prising it out with a small screwdriver or hooked tool. Do not damage the shaft sealing face.

6 Clean the seal seat. Examine the shaft sealing face for wear or damage which could cause premature failure of the new seal.

7 Lubricate the new oil seal with clean engine oil. Fit the seal over the shaft, lips inwards, and tap it home with a large socket or piece of tube until its outer face is flush with the housing **(see illustration)**.

8 Before the camshaft sprocket(s) can be refitted, it is necessary to check the alignment of the camshafts (valve timing).

9 Referring to Chapter 4A, remove the air cleaner assembly and inlet ducts as

TOOL TiP

To make a camshaft sprocket holding tool, obtain two lengths of steel strip about 6 mm thick by 30 mm wide or similar, one 600 mm long, the other 200 mm long (all dimensions approximate). Bolt the two strips together to form a forked end, leaving the bolt slack so that the shorter strip can pivot freely. At the end of each 'prong' of the fork, bend the strips through 90° about 50 mm from their ends to act as the fulcrums; these will engage with the holes in the sprockets. It may be necessary to grind or cut off their sides slightly to allow them to fit the sprocket holes

necessary for clear access to the rear end of both camshafts.

10 Undo the nut and remove the bolt securing the engine upper steady bar to the bracket on the engine. Note that a new nut and bolt will be required for refitting **(see illustration)**.

11 Undo the nut securing the other end of the engine steady bar to the bulkhead bracket. Swing the steady bar to one side. Note that a new nut and bolt will be required for refitting.

12 Undo the upper nut and two lower bolts securing the steady bar bracket to the side of the engine. Note the location of the wiring connector support plates, and move them to one side. Release all the cable-ties and switch wiring connectors as necessary to allow the bracket to be removed, then prise the bracket off its locating dowels on the engine. It will be tight on the dowels, and a certain amount of levering will be necessary.

4.4 Removing the inlet camshaft sprocket

4.7 Fit the oil seal over the shaft, lips inwards

4.10 Remove the steady bar from the engine bracket

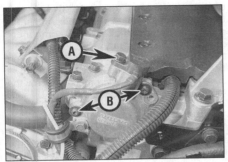

4.16 Camshaft sensor retaining bolt (A) and end cover screws (B)

13 Disconnect the camshaft position sensor wiring at the connector located at the transmission end of the engine.

14 Undo the two screws and remove the sensor housing from the cylinder head at the rear of the exhaust camshaft. Undo the bolt and remove the sensor rotor plate from the end of the exhaust camshaft.

15 On models with a distributor, undo the three screws and lift off the distributor cap and HT leads. Remove the flash shield, then undo the three screws and remove the rotor arm. Undo the bolt and remove the rotor arm mounting plate.

16 On models without a distributor, unscrew the retaining bolt and lift out the camshaft sensor from the inlet camshaft. Remove the two screws and take off the camshaft end cover **(see illustration)**.

17 Observe the position of the slots in the rear of the camshafts. Before the sprockets can be refitted, the camshafts must be positioned so that these slots are parallel to the join between the upper and lower cylinder head sections, and then locked in that position. Note also that the slots are very slightly offset from the centre-line; one slightly above and one slightly below.

18 To lock the camshafts in the correct position for refitting, obtain Volvo tool 999 5452 or fabricate a home-made alternative **(see Tool Tip)**.

19 Check that the crankshaft sprocket timing marks are still aligned, then attach the Volvo tool or the home-made alternative to the rear of the cylinder head **(see illustration)**. It may be necessary to rotate the camshafts very

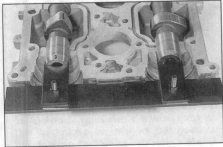

4.19 Home-made camshaft locking tool in position (cylinder head upper section shown removed for clarity)

slightly to bring their slots exactly to the horizontal position to allow the tool to fit.

20 Refit the camshaft sprocket(s), with the timing marks aligned, and secure with two of the retaining bolts for each. If only one sprocket has been removed, slacken the three bolts on the other sprocket and remove one of them. Tighten the bolts so that they just touch the sprockets, but allow the sprockets to turn within the limits of their elongated bolt holes. Position the sprockets so that the bolts are centred in their holes.

21 Carry out the operations described in Section 3, paragraphs 28 to 34 inclusive.

22 Refit the remaining bolt to each sprocket and tighten the bolts to the specified torque.

23 Remove the locking tool from the rear of the camshafts.

24 Continue with the timing belt refitting procedure as described in Section 3, paragraph 35 onwards. Do not reconnect the battery at this stage.

25 On models with a distributor, refit the mounting plate, flash shield, rotor arm, distributor cap and HT leads.

26 On models without a distributor, refit the camshaft end cover, and secure with the screws. Refit the inlet camshaft sensor, and tighten the retaining bolt securely.

27 Refit the camshaft position sensor rotor plate and housing.

28 Refit the engine steady bar bracket to the side of the engine, and secure with the nut and two bolts tightened to the specified torque. Reconnect the wiring disturbed on removal, and secure with cable-ties or the relevant clips.

29 Attach the engine steady bar to the brackets, using new nuts and bolts. Tighten the steady bar mountings to the specified torque.

30 Refit the air cleaner assembly and air ducts.

31 Check that everything has been refitted correctly, then reconnect the battery.

5 Camshaft rear oil seals - renewal

1 Disconnect the battery negative lead.

2 Refer to Chapter 4A and remove the air cleaner assembly and inlet ducts as necessary for clear access to the rear end of both camshafts.

3 Disconnect the camshaft position sensor wiring at the connector on the transmission end of the cylinder head.

4 Undo the two screws and remove the sensor housing from the cylinder head at the rear of the exhaust camshaft. Undo the bolt and remove the sensor rotor plate from the end of the exhaust camshaft.

5 On models with a distributor, undo the three screws and lift off the distributor cap and HT leads. Remove the flash shield, then undo the three screws and remove the rotor arm. Undo the bolt and remove the rotor arm mounting plate.

To make a camshaft locking tool, obtain a length of angle-iron and cut it to length so that it will fit across the rear of the cylinder head. Mark and drill two holes so that it can be bolted to a distributor cap and camshaft position sensor bolt hole. Obtain a length of steel strip of suitable thickness to fit snugly in the slots in the camshafts. Cut the strip into two lengths and drill accordingly so that both strips can be bolted to the angle iron. Using spacer washers, nuts and bolts, position and secure the strips to the angle iron so that the camshafts can be locked with their slots horizontal. Pack out the strips with spacers to cater for the offset of the slots

6 On models without a distributor, remove the two screws and take off the camshaft end cover.

7 Carefully extract the seal by prising it out with a small screwdriver or hooked tool. Do not damage the shaft sealing face.

8 Clean the seal seat. Examine the shaft sealing face for wear or damage which could cause premature failure of the new seal.

9 Lubricate the new oil seal with clean engine oil. Fit the seal over the shaft, lips inwards, and tap it home with a large socket or piece of tube until its outer face is flush with the housing **(see illustration)**.

10 Refit the components removed for access, using a reversal of removal.

11 Refit the air cleaner and ducts, then reconnect the battery.

2A

5.9 Fitting the inlet camshaft rear oil seal

6.7 One of the earth leads attached to the rear of the cylinder head

6 Camshafts and tappets - removal, inspection and refitting

Note 1: *For this procedure, Volvo tools 999 5452, 999 5453 and 999 5454 will be required to lock the camshafts in position in the cylinder head upper section during refitting, and to pull the upper section into place. Details for fabricating home-made alternatives are given in the text. Do not attempt to carry out the work without these tools. A tube of liquid gasket and a short-haired application roller (available from Volvo dealers) will also be required.*

Note 2: *Models with the 2.5 litre engine from late 1999 onwards may be fitted with a variable valve timing system. Models with this system can be identified by having a large hub assembly bolted to the front (inlet) camshaft sprocket. No information on this system was available at the time of writing, and it would be wise to consult a Volvo dealer for advice before proceeding.*

Removal

1 Disconnect the battery negative lead.

2 Drain the cooling system as described in Chapter 1.

3 Remove the timing belt as described in Section 3.

4 Suitably mark the camshaft sprockets, inlet and exhaust, for identification when refitting. The inlet sprocket is nearest the front of the car.

6.15 Remove the tappets and place them in a segmented container

5 Undo the three bolts and remove the sprockets from the camshafts. Restrain the sprockets with a suitable tool through the holes in their faces. Refer to Section 4 for details of fabricating a suitable sprocket restraining tool.

6 Carry out the operations described in Section 4, paragraphs 9 to 16 inclusive.

7 In a progressive diagonal sequence, working inwards, slacken then remove all the bolts securing the cylinder head upper section. Note the location of the earth leads on the rear bolts **(see illustration)**.

8 Using a soft-faced mallet, gently tap, or alternatively prise, the cylinder head upper section upwards off the lower section. Note that parting lugs are provided to allow the upper section to be struck or prised against without damage. Do not insert a screwdriver or similar tool into the joint between the two sections as a means of separation. In practice, the upper section will be quite tight as it is located on numerous dowels; patience is necessary.

9 Once the upper section is free, carefully lift it off. The camshafts will rise up under the pressure of the valve springs - be careful they don't tip and jam in the upper section.

10 Withdraw the sealing O-rings from the top of the spark plug recesses in the lower section. Obtain new O-rings for reassembly

11 Suitably mark the camshafts, inlet and exhaust, and lift them out complete with front and rear oil seals. Be careful of the lobes, which may have sharp edges.

12 Remove the oil seals from the camshafts, noting their fitted positions. Obtain new seals for reassembly.

13 Have ready a suitable box divided into ten or twenty segments, as applicable, or some containers and other means of storing and identifying the hydraulic tappets after removal. The box or containers must be oil-tight, and deep enough to allow the tappets to be almost totally submerged in oil.

14 Mark the segments in the box or the containers with the cylinder number for each tappet, together with identification for inlet and exhaust. On 20-valve engines, further identify each inlet and exhaust tappet as to whether it is the front or rear of the two.

15 Lift out the tappets, using a suction cup or magnet if necessary. Keep them identified for position, and place them upright in their respective positions in the box or containers **(see illustration)**. Once all the tappets have been removed, add clean engine oil to the box or container so that the oil hole in the tappet side is submerged.

Inspection

16 Inspect the cam lobes and the camshaft bearing journals for scoring or other visible evidence of wear. Once the surface hardening of the lobes has been penetrated, wear will progress rapidly.

17 No specific bearing journal diameters or

running clearances are specified by Volvo for the camshafts or journals. However, if there is a visual deterioration, then component renewal will be necessary.

18 Inspect the tappets for scuffing, cracking or other damage; measure their diameter in several places with a micrometer. Renew the tappets if they are damaged or worn.

Preparation for refitting

19 Thoroughly clean the sealer from the mating surfaces of the upper and lower cylinder head sections. Use a suitable liquid gasket dissolving agent together with a soft putty knife; do not use a metal scraper, or the faces will be damaged. As there is no conventional gasket used, the condition of the faces is of the utmost importance.

20 Clean off any oil, dirt or grease from both components and dry with a clean lint free cloth. Ensure that all the oilways are completely clean.

21 For reassembly, the camshafts are installed in the upper section, and retained in place in the correct position using special tools. This assembly is then fitted to the lower section, clamped in place against the pressure of the valve springs with more special tools, and finally bolted down. If possible, obtain the Volvo special tools mentioned in the note at the beginning of this section and use them in accordance with the instructions provided. Alternatively, fabricate a set of home-made tools as follows.

22 To position and secure the camshafts at the rear, make up the camshaft locking tool described in the Tool Tip in Section 4.

23 To secure the camshafts at the front, make up a strap as shown **(see Tool Tip below)**.

24 Finally, it will be necessary to make up a tool which will allow the upper section to be clamped down against the pressure of the valve springs **(see Tool Tip opposite)**.

To retain the camshafts in the cylinder head upper section at the front when refitting, make a retaining strap out of welding rod, bent to shape, which will locate under the camshaft projections at the front and can be secured to the upper section with two bolts

TOOL TIP

To pull the cylinder head upper section down against valve spring pressure, obtain two old spark plugs and carefully break away all the porcelain so that only the lower threaded portion remains. Drill out the centre of the spark plugs as necessary, then fit a long bolt or threaded rod to each, and secure tightly with nuts. The bolts or rods must be long enough to project up from the spark plug wells to above the level of the assembled cylinder head. Drill a hole in the centre of two 6 mm thick strips of steel which are long enough to fit across the cylinder head upper section. Fit the strips then fit a nut and locknut to each bolt or rod

Refitting

25 Commence refitting by liberally oiling the tappet bores and the camshaft bearings in the cylinder head lower section with clean engine oil.

26 Insert the tappets into their original bores (unless new tappets are being fitted). Fill new tappets with oil through the oil hole in their side before fitting.

27 Ensure that the mating faces of both cylinder head sections are clean and free of any oil or grease.

28 Check that the crankshaft timing marks are still aligned.

29 Using the short-haired roller, apply an even coating of Volvo liquid gasket solution to the mating face of the cylinder head upper section only **(see illustration)**. Ensure that the whole surface is covered, but take care to keep the solution out of the oilways; a thin coating is sufficient for a good seal.

30 Lubricate the camshaft journals in the upper section sparingly with oil, taking care not to allow the oil to spill over onto the liquid gasket.

31 Lay the camshafts in their correct locations in the upper section, remembering that the inlet camshaft must be at the front of the engine.

32 Turn the camshafts so that their slots are parallel to the upper section join, noting that the slots in each camshaft are offset with regards to the centre-line **(see illustration)**. When viewing the upper section the right way up, ie as it would be when fitted, the slot on

6.29 Apply the liquid gasket solution using a short-haired roller

the inlet camshaft is offset above the centre-line, and the exhaust camshaft slot is offset below the centre-line. Verify this by looking at the other end of the camshafts. Again, with the upper section the right way up, there should be two sprocket bolt holes above the centre-line on the inlet camshaft, and two bolt holes below the centre-line on the exhaust camshaft.

33 With the camshafts correctly positioned, lock them at the rear by fitting the rear locking and holding tool. It should not be possible to rotate the camshafts at all with the tool in place. Now secure the camshafts at the front using the holding tool or the home-made alternative.

34 Place new sealing O-rings into the recesses around each spark plug well in the lower section **(see illustration)**.

35 Lift up the assembled upper section, with camshafts, and lay it in place on the lower section.

36 Insert the pull-down tools into Nos 1 and 5 spark plug holes and tighten securely. If using the home-made tool, make sure that the bolt or threaded rod is a secure fit in the spark plug, or you will not be able to remove the tool later.

37 Lay the pull-down tool top plates, or the home-made steel strips, over the bolts or threaded rods, and secure with the nuts **(see illustration)**. Slowly and carefully tighten the nuts, a little at a time, so that the tools pull the upper section down onto the lower section. Remember there will be considerable resistance from the valve springs. Make sure that the upper section stays level, or the locating dowels will jam.

6.34 Place new sealing O-rings into the recesses around each spark plug well

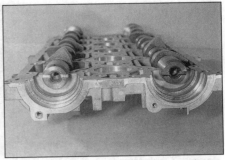

6.32 Position the camshafts so that their slots are parallel to the upper section join

38 Refit the upper section retaining bolts and tighten them in a progressive diagonal sequence, working outwards, to the specified torque. Don't forget the earth lead on the rear bolt.

39 With the upper section secure, remove the pull-down tool and the camshaft front end holding tool. Leave the rear locking tool in place.

40 Lubricate the lips of four new camshaft oil seals. Fit each seal the correct way round over the camshaft, and tap it home with a large socket or piece of tube until its outer face is flush with the housing.

41 Refit the camshaft sprockets, aligning the timing marks, and two of the retaining bolts for each. Tighten the bolts so that they just touch the sprockets, but allow the sprockets to turn within the limits of their elongated bolt holes. Position the sprockets so that the bolts are centred in their holes.

42 For the remainder of refitting, refer to Section 4 and carry out the operations from paragraph 21 onwards.

43 Refill the cooling system as described in Chapter 1 on completion.

---

7 Cylinder head - removal and refitting

Removal

1 Disconnect the battery negative lead.

2 Remove the radiator cooling fan as described in Chapter 3.

6.37 Home-made pull-down tool in position

2A

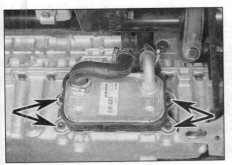

6.4 Oil cooler mounting bolts (arrowed) - later models

6.7 Undo the mounting bracket bolt and remove the oil pick-up pipe

6.8 Intermediate section bolt TIGHTENING sequence. Slacken bolts in reverse order. Slacken/tighten the bolts in matching pairs

6 Sump and intermediate section - removal

1 If not already done, drain the engine oil then remove the oil filter, referring to Chapter 1 if necessary.

2 Remove the oil pump as described in Part A of this Chapter.

3 If the pistons and connecting rods are to be removed later, position all the pistons approximately half way down their bores.

4 On models with an oil cooler mounted on the rear face of the sump, remove the four retaining bolts and take off the cooler, if possible without disconnecting the coolant pipes **(see illustration)**.

5 Undo the bolts securing the sump to the intermediate section, noting the different bolt lengths and their locations.

6 Carefully tap the sump free using a rubber or hide mallet. Recover the O-ring seals.

7 Undo the mounting bracket bolt and remove the oil pick-up pipe **(see illustration)**. Recover the O-ring seal on the end of the pipe.

8 Undo all the M7 and M8 bolts securing the intermediate section to the cylinder block in the reverse order to that shown **(see illustration)**. With all the bolts removed, undo the M10 bolts in the same order.

9 Carefully tap the intermediate section free using a rubber or hide mallet. Lift off the intermediate section complete with crankshaft lower main bearing shells. If any of the shells

have stayed on the crankshaft, transfer them to their correct locations in the intermediate section.

10 Remove the crankshaft rear oil seal.

7 Pistons and connecting rods - removal and inspection

Removal

1 Remove the cylinder head, oil pump and flywheel/driveplate as described in Part A of this Chapter. Remove the sump and intermediate section as described in Section 6.

2 Feel inside the tops of the bores for a pronounced wear ridge. Some experts recommend that such a ridge be removed (with a scraper or ridge reamer) before attempting to remove the pistons. However, a ridge big enough to damage the pistons and/or piston rings will almost certainly mean that a rebore and new pistons/rings are needed anyway.

3 Check that there are identification numbers or marks on each connecting rod and cap; paint or punch suitable marks if necessary, so that each rod can be refitted in the same position and the same way round **(see illustration)**.

4 Remove the two connecting rod bolts. Tap the cap with a soft-faced hammer to free it. Remove the cap and lower bearing shell. Note that new bolts will be needed for reassembly.

5 Push the connecting rod and piston up and out of the bore. Recover the other half bearing shell if it is loose.

6 Refit the cap to the connecting rod, the correct way round, so that they do not get mixed up.

7 Check to see if there is an arrow on the top of the piston which should be pointing toward the timing belt end of the engine. If no arrow can be seen, make a suitable direction mark yourself.

8 Without rotating the crankshaft, repeat the operations on the remaining connecting rods and pistons.

Inspection

9 Before the inspection process can be carried out, the piston/connecting rod assemblies must be cleaned, and the original piston rings removed from the pistons

10 Carefully expand the old rings and remove them from the top of the pistons. The use of two or three old feeler blades will be helpful in preventing the rings dropping into empty grooves **(see illustration)**. Be careful not to scratch the pistons with the ends of the ring. The rings are brittle and will snap if they are spread too far. They are also very sharp - protect your hands and fingers.

11 Scrape all traces of carbon from the top of the piston. A hand-held wire brush (or a piece of fine emery cloth) can be used, once the majority of the deposits have been scraped away.

12 Remove the carbon from the ring grooves in the piston, using an old ring. Break the ring in half to do this (be careful not to cut your fingers - piston rings are sharp). Be careful to remove only the carbon deposits - do not remove any metal, and do not nick or scratch the sides of the ring grooves.

13 Once the deposits have been removed, clean the piston/rod assemblies with paraffin or a suitable solvent, and dry thoroughly. Make sure the oil return holes in the ring grooves, are clear.

14 If the pistons and cylinder bores are not damaged or worn excessively, and if the cylinder block does not need to be rebored (where applicable), the original pistons can be refitted. Normal piston wear appears as even vertical wear on the piston thrust surfaces, and slight looseness of the top ring in its groove. New piston rings should always be used when the engine is reassembled.

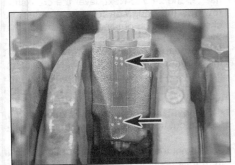

7.3 Mark the big-end caps and connecting rods with their cylinder numbers

7.10 Removing piston rings with the help of feeler blades

2B

7.23 Push the gudgeon pin out of the piston and connecting rod

7.24a Measure the piston diameters using a micrometer

7.24b Piston/cylinder grade letter stamped on the cylinder block

15 Carefully inspect each piston for cracks around the skirt, around the gudgeon pin holes, and at the ring lands (between the ring grooves).

16 Look for scoring and scuffing on the piston skirt, holes in the piston crown, and burned areas at the edge of the crown.

17 If the skirt is scored or scuffed, the engine may have been suffering from overheating and/or abnormal combustion, which caused excessively-high operating temperatures. The cooling and lubrication systems should be checked thoroughly. Scorch marks on the sides of the piston show that blow-by has occurred.

18 A hole in the piston crown or burned areas at the edge of the piston crown, indicates that abnormal combustion (pre-ignition, knocking, or detonation) has been occurring.

19 If any of the above piston problems exist, the causes must be investigated and corrected, or the damage will occur again. The causes may include inlet air leaks, incorrect fuel/air mixture or an emission control system fault.

20 Corrosion of the piston, in the form of pitting, indicates that coolant has been leaking into the combustion chamber and/or the crankcase. Again, the cause must be corrected, or the problem may persist in the rebuilt engine.

21 Examine each connecting rod carefully for signs of damage, such as cracks around the big-end and small-end bearings. Check that the rod is not bent or distorted. Damage is highly unlikely, unless the engine has been seized or badly overheated. Detailed checking

7.26 Measure the ring-to-groove clearance using a feeler blade

of the connecting rod assembly can only be carried out by an engine overhaul specialist with the necessary equipment.

22 The gudgeon pins are of the floating type, secured in position by two circlips. Where necessary, the pistons and connecting rods can be separated as follows.

23 Remove one of the circlips which secure the gudgeon pin. Push the gudgeon pin out of the piston and connecting rod **(see illustration)**.

24 Using a micrometer, measure the diameter of all five pistons at a point 10 mm from the bottom of the skirt, at right-angles to the gudgeon pin axis. Compare the measurements obtained, with those listed in the *Specifications*. Note that four standard size grades are available - the grade letter is stamped on the piston crown and on the cylinder block **(see illustrations)**. If new pistons are to be obtained, they must be of the same grade marking as the cylinder bore to which they will be fitted.

25 If the diameter of any of the pistons is out of the tolerance band listed for its particular grade, then all five pistons must be renewed. Note that if the cylinder block was re-bored during a previous overhaul, oversize pistons may have been fitted. Record the measurements and use them to check the piston-to-bore clearance when the cylinder bores are measured later in this Chapter.

26 Hold a new piston ring in the appropriate groove, and measure the ring-to-groove clearance using a feeler blade **(see illustration)**. Note that the rings are of different sizes, so use the correct ring for the groove. Compare the measurements with those listed in the *Specifications*; if the clearances are outside the tolerance range, then the pistons must be renewed.

27 Check the fit of the gudgeon pin in the connecting rod bush and in the piston. If there is perceptible play, a new bush or an oversize gudgeon pin must be fitted. Consult a Volvo dealer or engine reconditioning specialist.

28 Examine all components and obtain any new parts required. If new pistons are purchased, they will be supplied complete with gudgeon pins and circlips. Circlips can also be purchased separately.

29 Oil the gudgeon pin. Reassemble the connecting rod and piston, making sure the

rod is the right way round, and secure the gudgeon pin with the circlip. Position the circlip so that its opening is facing downward.

30 Repeat these operations for the remaining pistons.

8 Crankshaft - removal and inspection

Removal

Note: *If no work is to be done on the pistons and connecting rods, then removal of the cylinder head and pistons will not be necessary. Instead, the pistons need only be pushed far enough up the bores so that they are positioned clear of the crankpins.*

1 With reference to Part A of this Chapter, and earlier Sections of this part as applicable, carry out the following:

a) *Remove the oil pump.*
b) *Remove the sump and intermediate section.*
c) *Remove the clutch components and flywheel/driveplate.*
d) *Remove the pistons and connecting rods (refer to the Note above).*

2 Before the crankshaft is removed, it is advisable to check the endfloat. To do this, temporarily refit the intermediate section then mount a dial gauge with the stem in line with the crankshaft and just touching the crankshaft.

3 Push the crankshaft fully away from the gauge, and zero it. Next, lever the crankshaft towards the gauge as far as possible, and check the reading obtained. The distance that the crankshaft moved is its endfloat; if it is greater than specified, check the crankshaft thrust surfaces for wear. If no wear is evident, new thrustwashers (which are integral with the main bearing shells) should correct the endfloat.

4 Remove the intermediate section again, then lift out the crankshaft. Do not drop it, it is heavy.

5 Remove the upper half main bearing shells from their seats in the crankcase by pressing the end of the shell furthest from the locating tab. Keep all the shells in order.

8.11 Use a micrometer to measure the crankshaft journal diameters

Inspection

6 Clean the crankshaft using paraffin or a suitable solvent, and dry it, preferably with compressed air if available. Be sure to clean the oil holes with a pipe cleaner or similar probe to ensure that they are not obstructed.

 Warning: Wear eye protection when using compressed air!

7 Check the main and big-end bearing journals for uneven wear, scoring, pitting and cracking.

8 Big-end bearing wear is accompanied by distinct metallic knocking when the engine is running (particularly noticeable when the engine is pulling from low speed) and some loss of oil pressure.

9 Main bearing wear is accompanied by severe engine vibration and rumble - getting progressively worse as engine speed increases - and again by loss of oil pressure.

10 Check the bearing journal for roughness by running a finger lightly over the bearing surface. Any roughness (which will be accompanied by obvious bearing wear) indicates that the crankshaft requires regrinding (where possible) or renewal.

11 Using a micrometer, measure the diameter of the main and big-end journals, and compare the results with the *Specifications* **(see illustration)**. By measuring the diameter at a number of points around each journal's circumference, you will be able to determine whether or not the journal is out-of-round. Take the measurement at each end of the journal, near the webs, to determine if the journal is tapered. Compare the results obtained with those given in the *Specifications*.

12 If the crankshaft journals are outside the tolerance range specified, a new crankshaft will be needed as only graded, standard size bearing shells are available from the manufacturer. However, seek the advice of an engine overhaul specialist first, as to whether regrinding may be possible and whether graded bearing shells can be supplied to match.

13 Check the oil seal contact surfaces at each end of the crankshaft for wear and damage. If either seal has worn a deep groove in the surface of the crankshaft, consult an

engine overhaul specialist; repair may be possible, otherwise a new crankshaft will be required.

14 Refer to Section 10 for details of main and big-end bearing selection.

9 Cylinder block/crankcase - cleaning and inspection

Cleaning

1 Prior to cleaning, remove all external components and senders, and any gallery plugs or caps that may be fitted.

2 If any of the castings are extremely dirty, all should be steam-cleaned.

3 After the castings are returned from steam-cleaning, clean all oil holes and oil galleries one more time. Flush all internal passages with warm water until the water runs clear. If you have access to compressed air, use it to speed the drying process, and to blow out all the oil holes and galleries.

 Warning: Wear eye protection when using compressed air!

4 If the castings are not very dirty, you can do an adequate cleaning job with hot soapy water (as hot as you can stand!) and a stiff brush. Take plenty of time, and do a thorough job. Regardless of the cleaning method used, be sure to clean all oil holes and galleries very thoroughly, and to dry all components completely. Apply clean engine oil to the cylinder bores to prevent rusting.

5 The threaded holes in the cylinder block must be clean to ensure accurate torque readings when tightening fixings during reassembly. Carefully run the correct size tap (which can be determined from the size of the relevant bolt which fits in the hole) into each of the holes to remove rust, corrosion, thread sealant or other contamination, and to restore damaged threads. If possible, use compressed air to clear the holes of debris produced by this operation. Do not forget to clean the threads of all bolts and nuts as well.

6 Any threads which cannot be restored in this way can often be reclaimed by the use of thread inserts. If any threaded holes are damaged, consult your dealer or engine overhaul specialist and have them install any thread inserts where necessary.

7 If the engine is not going to be reassembled right away, cover it with a large plastic bag to keep it clean; protect the machined surfaces as described above, to prevent rusting.

Inspection

8 Visually check the castings for cracks and corrosion. Look for stripped threads in the threaded holes. If there has been any history of internal coolant leakage, it may be worthwhile having an engine overhaul specialist check the cylinder block/crankcase

for cracks with special equipment. If defects are found, have them repaired, if possible, or renew the assembly.

9 Check the condition of the cylinder head mating face and the intermediate section mating surfaces. Check the surfaces for any possible distortion using the straight-edge and feeler blade method described earlier for cylinder head inspection. If distortion is slight, consult an engine overhaul specialist as to the best course of action.

10 Check each cylinder bore for scuffing and scoring. Check for signs of a wear ridge at the top of the cylinder, indicating that the bore is excessively worn.

11 If the necessary measuring equipment is available, measure the diameter of each cylinder at the top (just under the ridge area), centre and bottom of the cylinder bore, parallel to the crankshaft axis using a cylinder bore gauge. Next, measure the bore diameter at the same three locations across the crankshaft axis. Note the measurements obtained. Have this work carried out by an engine overhaul specialist if you do not have access to the measuring equipment needed.

12 To obtain the piston-to-bore clearance, measure the piston diameter as described earlier in this Chapter, and subtract the piston diameter from the largest bore measurement.

13 Repeat these procedures for the remaining pistons and cylinder bores.

14 Compare the results with the *Specifications* at the beginning of this Chapter; if any measurement is beyond the dimensions specified for that grade, or any bore measurement is significantly different from the others (indicating that the bore is tapered or oval), the piston or bore is excessively-worn. Note that each cylinder is identified by a classification marking (C, D, E, or G) stamped into the rear of the cylinder block. There are four classifications (or grades) for standard diameter cylinder bores and two oversize classifications (stamped OS1 and OS2).

15 If any of the cylinder bores are badly scuffed or scored, or if they are excessively-worn, out-of-round or tapered, the usual course of action would be to have the cylinder block/crankcase rebored, and to fit new, oversized, pistons on reassembly. Consult a dealer or engine reconditioning specialist for advice.

16 If the bores are in reasonably good condition and not excessively-worn, then it may only be necessary to renew the piston rings.

17 If this is the case, the bores should be honed, to allow the new rings to bed in correctly and provide the best possible seal. Honing is an operation that will be carried out for you by an engine reconditioning specialist.

18 After all machining operations are completed, the entire block/crankcase must be washed very thoroughly with warm soapy water to remove all traces of abrasive grit produced during the machining operations.

 2B

When the cylinder block/crankcase is completely clean, rinse it thoroughly and dry it, then lightly oil all exposed machined surfaces, to prevent rusting.

19 The final step is to measure the length of the M10 bolts used to secure the intermediate section to the cylinder block. If the length of any is greater than 118 mm, they should be renewed. It is a wise precaution to renew these bolts anyway considering the significance of their location. As with all bolts that are tightened through a torque angle, they are prone to stretch, often up to the extent of their elastic limit. It is virtually impossible to judge the strain that this imposes on a particular bolt, and if any are in any way flawed, breakage when retightening, or failure in service could be the result.

10 Main and big-end bearings - inspection and selection

Inspection

1 Even though the main and big-end bearing shells should be renewed during the engine overhaul, the old shells should be retained for close examination, as they may reveal valuable information about the condition of the engine.

2 Bearing failure occurs because of lack of lubrication, the presence of dirt or other foreign particles, overloading the engine, and corrosion (see illustration). Regardless of the cause of bearing failure, the cause must be corrected (where applicable) before the engine is reassembled, to prevent it from happening again.

3 When examining the bearing shells, remove them from the cylinder block/crankcase and main bearing caps, and from the connecting rods and the big-end bearing caps, then lay them out on a clean surface in the same general position as their location in the engine. This will enable you to match any bearing problems with the corresponding crankshaft journal. *Do not* touch any of the shell's bearing surface with your fingers while checking it, or the delicate surface may be scratched.

4 Dirt or other foreign matter gets into the engine in a variety of ways. It may be left in the engine during assembly, or it may pass through filters or the crankcase ventilation system. It may get into the oil, and from there into the bearings. Metal chips from machining operations and normal engine wear are often present. Abrasives are sometimes left in engine components after reconditioning, especially when parts are not thoroughly cleaned using the proper cleaning methods.

5 Whatever the source, any foreign objects often end up embedded in the soft bearing material, and are easily recognised. Large particles will not embed in the material, and will score or gouge the shell and journal. The best prevention for this cause of bearing failure is to clean all parts thoroughly, and to keep everything spotlessly-clean during engine assembly. Frequent and regular engine oil and filter changes are also recommended.

6 Lack of lubrication (or lubrication breakdown) has a number of inter-related causes. Excessive heat (which thins the oil), overloading (which squeezes the oil from the bearing face) and oil leakage (from excessive bearing clearances, worn oil pump or high engine speeds) all contribute to lubrication breakdown. Blocked oil passages, which usually are the result of misaligned oil holes in a bearing shell, will also starve a bearing of oil, and destroy it.

7 When lack of lubrication is the cause of bearing failure, the bearing material is wiped or extruded from the shell's steel backing. Temperatures may increase to the point where the steel backing turns blue from overheating.

8 Driving habits can have a definite effect on bearing life. Full-throttle, low-speed operation (labouring the engine) puts very high loads on bearings, which tends to squeeze out the oil film. These loads cause the shells to flex, which produces fine cracks in the bearing face (fatigue failure). Eventually, the bearing material will loosen in pieces, and tear away from the steel backing.

9 Short-distance driving leads to corrosion of bearings, because insufficient engine heat is produced to drive off condensed water and corrosive gases. These products collect in the engine oil, forming acid and sludge. As the oil is carried to the engine bearings, the acid attacks and corrodes the bearing material.

10 Incorrect shell refitting during engine assembly will lead to bearing failure as well. Tight-fitting shells leave insufficient bearing running clearance, and will result in oil starvation. Dirt or foreign particles trapped behind a bearing shell result in high spots on the bearing, which lead to failure.

11 *Do not* touch any shell's bearing surface with your fingers during reassembly; there is a risk of scratching the delicate surface, or of depositing particles of dirt on it.

Selection - main and big-end bearings

12 To ensure that the main bearing running clearance will be correct, there are three different grades of bearing shell. The grades are indicated by a colour coding (red, yellow or blue) marked on each bearing shell, which denotes the shell's thickness.

13 New main bearing shells for each journal can be selected using the reference letters (A, B and C) which are stamped on the cylinder block and on the crankshaft, in accordance with the table shown (see illustration).

10.2 Typical bearing failures

	A small diameter		B medium diameter		C large diameter	
Classification markings on block	block	int. sect.	block	int. sect.	block	int. sect.
A small	yellow medium	yellow medium	yellow medium	blue thick	blue thick	blue thick
B medium	red thin	yellow medium	yellow medium	yellow medium	yellow medium	blue thick
C large	red thin	red thin	red thin	yellow medium	yellow medium	yellow medium

Crankshaft classification

10.13 Main bearing shell selection table

14 From the table, it can be seen that if the marking on the cylinder block for a particular journal was B, and the corresponding marking on the crankshaft was C, then a red bearing shell would be fitted to the cylinder block, and a yellow shell would be fitted into the intermediate section.

15 Check all the markings and select the main bearing shells necessary for all journals.

16 Big-end bearing shells are not graded and are supplied in one size only to match the dimensions of the respective journal. As the manufacturer's do not specify an actual running clearance dimension for the big-end bearings, the only safe course of action is to fit new shells whenever an overhaul is being undertaken. Assuming that the relevant crankshaft journals are all within tolerance, the running clearances will then be correct.

11 Engine overhaul - reassembly sequence

1 Before reassembly begins, ensure that all new parts have been obtained and that all necessary tools are available. Read through the entire procedure to familiarise yourself with the work involved, and to ensure that all items necessary for reassembly of the engine are at hand. In addition to all normal tools and materials, thread-locking compound will be needed in most areas during engine reassembly. A tube of Volvo liquid gasket solution together with a short-haired application roller will also be needed to assemble the main engine sections.

2 In order to save time and avoid problems, engine reassembly can be carried out in the following order:

    a) Crankshaft.
    b) Pistons/connecting rods.
    c) Sump.
    d) Oil pump.
    e) Flywheel/driveplate.
    f) Cylinder head.
    g) Camshaft and tappets.
    h) Timing belt, tensioner, sprockets and idler pulleys.
    i) Engine external components.

3 At this stage, all engine components should be absolutely clean and dry, with all faults repaired. The components should be laid out (or in individual containers) on a completely clean work surface.

12 Crankshaft - refitting

1 Crankshaft refitting is the first stage of engine reassembly following overhaul. It is assumed at this point that the cylinder block/crankcase and crankshaft have been cleaned, inspected and repaired or reconditioned as necessary. Position the cylinder block on a clean level worksurface, with the crankcase facing upwards.

2 If they're still in place, remove the old bearing shells from the block and the intermediate section.

3 Wipe clean the main bearing shell seats in the crankcase and clean the backs of the bearing shells. Insert the previously selected upper shells into their correct position in the crankcase. Press the shells home so that the tangs engage in the recesses provided.

4 Liberally lubricate the bearing shells in the crankcase with clean engine oil.

5 Wipe clean the crankshaft journals, then lower the crankshaft into position. Make sure that the shells are not displaced.

6 Inject oil into the crankshaft oilways, then wipe any traces of excess oil from the crankshaft and intermediate section mating faces.

7 Using the short-haired application roller, apply an even coating of Volvo liquid gasket solution to the cylinder block mating face of the intermediate section. Ensure that the whole surface is covered, but note that a thin coating is sufficient for a good seal.

8 Wipe clean the main bearing shell seats in the intermediate section and clean the backs of the bearing shells. Insert the previously selected lower shells into their correct position in the intermediate section. Press the shells home so that the tangs engage in the recesses provided.

9 Lightly lubricate the bearing shells in the intermediate section, but take care to keep the oil away from the liquid gasket solution.

10 Lay the intermediate section on the crankshaft and cylinder block, and insert the retaining bolts. Tighten the bolts in the five stages listed in the *Specifications*, to the specified torque and torque angle, in the sequence shown.

11 Rotate the crankshaft. Slight resistance is to be expected with new components, but there must be no tight spots or binding.

12 It is a good idea at this stage, to once again check the crankshaft endfloat as described in Section 8. If the thrust surfaces of the crankshaft have been checked and new bearing shells have been fitted, then the endfloat should be within specification.

13 Lubricate the rear oil seal location, the crankshaft, and a new oil seal. Fit the seal, lips inwards, and use a piece of tube (or the old seal, inverted) to tap it into place until flush.

13 Pistons and piston rings - assembly

1 At this stage, it is assumed that the pistons have been correctly assembled to their respective connecting rods, and that the piston ring-to-groove clearances have been checked. If not, refer to the end of Section 7.

2 Before the rings can be fitted to the pistons, the end gaps must be checked with the rings inserted into the cylinder bores.

3 Lay out the piston assemblies and the new ring sets so the components are kept together in their groups, during and after end gap checking. Position the cylinder block on the work surface, on its side, allowing access to the top and bottom of the bores.

4 Take the No 1 piston top ring and insert it into the top of the first cylinder. Push it down the bore using the top of the piston; this will ensure that the ring remains square with the cylinder walls. Position the ring near the bottom of the cylinder bore, at the lower limit of ring travel. Note that the top and second compression rings are different. The second ring is easily identified by the step on its lower surface.

5 Measure the ring gap using feeler blades.

6 Repeat the procedure with the ring at the top of the cylinder bore, at the upper limit of its travel, and compare the measurements with the figures given in the *Specifications*.

7 If new rings are being fitted, it is unlikely that the end gaps will be too small. If a measurement is found to be undersize, it must be corrected, or there is the risk that the ring ends may contact each other during engine operation, possibly resulting in engine damage. Ideally, new piston rings providing the correct end gap should be fitted; however, as a last resort the end gaps can be increased by filing the ring ends very carefully with a fine file. Mount the ring in a vice equipped with soft jaws, slip the ring over the file with the ends contacting the file face, and slowly move the ring to remove material from the ends. Take care, as piston rings are sharp and are easily broken.

8 It is equally unlikely that the end gap will be too large. If the gaps are too large, check that you have the correct rings for your engine and for the cylinder bore size.

9 Repeat the checking procedure for each ring in the first cylinder, and then for the rings in the remaining cylinders. Remember to keep rings, pistons and cylinders matched up.

10 Once the ring end gaps have been checked and if necessary corrected, the rings can be fitted to the pistons.

11 Fit the piston rings using the same technique as for removal. Fit the bottom scraper ring first, and work up. Observe the text markings on one side of the top and bottom rings; this must face upwards when the rings are fitted. The middle ring is bevelled, and the bevel must face downwards when installed **(see illustration overleaf)**. Do not expand the compression rings too far, or they will break. **Note:** *Always follow any instructions supplied with the new piston ring sets - different manufacturers may specify different procedures. Do not mix up the top and second compression rings, as they have different cross-sections.*

12 When all the rings are in position, arrange the ring gaps 120° apart.

2B

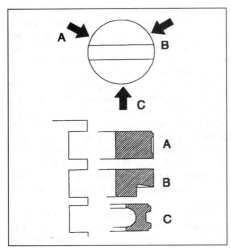

13.11 Piston ring identification and end gap positioning

Position the ring gaps (arrowed) for each ring accordingly

14 Pistons and connecting rod assemblies - refitting

1 Before refitting the piston/connecting rod assemblies, the cylinder bores must be perfectly clean, the top edge of each cylinder must be chamfered, and the crankshaft and intermediate section must be in place.
2 Remove the big-end bearing cap from No 1 cylinder connecting rod (refer to the marks noted or made on removal). Remove the original bearing shells, and wipe the bearing recesses of the connecting rod and cap with a clean, lint-free cloth. They must be kept spotlessly-clean. Ensure that new big-end bearing cap retaining bolts are available.
3 Clean the back of the new upper bearing shell, fit it to No 1 connecting rod, then fit the other shell of the bearing to the big-end bearing cap. Make sure the tab on each shell fits into the notch in the rod or cap recess.
4 Position the piston ring gaps in their correct positions around the piston, lubricate the piston and rings with clean engine oil, and attach a piston ring compressor to the piston. Leave the skirt protruding slightly, to guide the piston into the cylinder bore. The rings must be compressed until they're flush with the piston.
5 Rotate the crankshaft until No 1 big-end journal is at BDC (Bottom Dead Centre), and apply a coat of engine oil to the cylinder walls.
6 Arrange the No 1 piston/connecting rod assembly so that the arrow on the piston crown points to the timing belt end of the engine. Gently insert the assembly into the No 1 cylinder bore, and rest the bottom edge of the ring compressor on the engine block.
7 Tap the top edge of the ring compressor to make sure it's contacting the block around its entire circumference.

8 Gently tap on the top of the piston with the end of a wooden hammer handle while guiding the connecting rod big-end onto the crankpin. The piston rings may try to pop out of the ring compressor just before entering the cylinder bore, so keep some pressure on the ring compressor. Work slowly, and if any resistance is felt as the piston enters the cylinder, stop immediately. Find out what is binding, and fix it before proceeding. *Do not*, for any reason, force the piston into the cylinder - you might break a ring and/or the piston.
9 Make sure the bearing surfaces are perfectly clean, then apply a uniform layer of clean engine oil, to both of them. You may have to push the piston back up the cylinder bore slightly to expose the bearing surface of the shell in the connecting rod.
10 Slide the connecting rod back into place on the big-end journal, refit the big-end bearing cap. Lubricate the bolt threads, fit the bolts and tighten them in two stages to the specified torque.
11 Repeat the entire procedure for the remaining piston/connecting rod assemblies.
12 The important points to remember are:
a) *Keep the backs of the bearing shells and the recesses of the connecting rods and caps perfectly clean when assembling them.*
b) *Make sure you have the correct piston/rod assembly for each cylinder.*
c) *The arrow on the piston crown must face the camshaft drivebelt end of the engine.*
d) *Lubricate the cylinder bores with clean engine oil.*
e) *Lubricate the bearing surfaces before fitting the big-end bearing caps.*
13 After all the piston/connecting rod assemblies have been properly installed, rotate the crankshaft a number of times by hand, to check for any obvious binding.

15 Sump - refitting

1 Place a new O-ring on the oil pick-up pipe, and insert the pipe into its location. Secure with the bracket retaining bolt tightened to the specified torque.
2 Wipe off any oil smears from the sump and intermediate section joint faces, then locate new O-rings in the recesses in the intermediate section.
3 Using the short-haired application roller, apply an even coating of Volvo liquid gasket solution to the sump mating face. Ensure that the whole surface is covered, but note that a thin coating is sufficient for a good seal.
4 Place the sump in position, and insert four of the retaining bolts, tightened finger-tight only.
5 Using a straight edge, ensure that the rear edges of the sump and cylinder block are flush, then tighten the four bolts to just hold the sump in position.

6 Refit the remaining bolts and tighten all progressively, working towards the centre, to the specified torque.
7 On completion, where applicable, refit the oil cooler to the rear face of the sump, tightening the retaining bolts securely. Also check that the coolant hoses are undamaged, and the hose clamps secure.

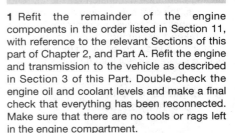

16 Engine - initial start-up after overhaul and reassembly

1 Refit the remainder of the engine components in the order listed in Section 11, with reference to the relevant Sections of this part of Chapter 2, and Part A. Refit the engine and transmission to the vehicle as described in Section 3 of this Part. Double-check the engine oil and coolant levels and make a final check that everything has been reconnected. Make sure that there are no tools or rags left in the engine compartment.
2 Remove the spark plugs and disable the ignition system by disconnecting the camshaft position sensor wiring at the connector. Disconnect the fuel injector wiring connectors to prevent fuel being injected into the cylinders.
3 Turn the engine over on the starter motor until the oil pressure warning light goes out. If the light fails to extinguish after several seconds of cranking, check the engine oil level and that the oil filter is fitted securely. Assuming these are correct, check the security of the oil pressure sensor wiring - do not progress any further until you are sure that oil is being pumped around the engine at sufficient pressure.
4 Refit the spark plugs and ignition wiring (HT leads, or ignition coils and wiring), and reconnect the camshaft position sensor and fuel injector wiring connectors.
5 Start the engine, noting that this also may take a little longer than usual, due to the fuel system components being empty.
6 While the engine is idling, check for fuel, coolant and oil leaks. Don't be alarmed if there are some odd smells and smoke from parts getting hot and burning off oil deposits. Note also that it may initially be a little noisy until the hydraulic tappets fill with oil.
7 Keep the engine idling until hot water is felt circulating through the top hose, check that it idles reasonably smoothly and at the usual speed, then switch it off.
8 After a few minutes, recheck the oil and coolant levels, and top-up as necessary (see Chapter 1).
9 If new components such as pistons, rings or crankshaft bearings have been fitted, the engine must be run-in for the first 500 miles (800 km). Do not operate the engine at full-throttle, or allow it to labour in any gear during this period. It is recommended that the oil and filter be changed at the end of this period.

Chapter 3
Cooling, heating and air conditioning systems

Contents

Degrees of difficulty

Easy, suitable for novice with little experience		Fairly easy, suitable for beginner with some experience		Fairly difficult, suitable for competent DIY mechanic		Difficult, suitable for experienced DIY mechanic		Very difficult, suitable for expert DIY or professional	

Specifications

General
System type .... Water-based coolant, pump-assisted circulation, thermostatically controlled

Thermostat
Opening commences:
  Type 1 thermostat .... 87°C
  Type 2 thermostat .... 90°C
Fully open at:
  Type 1 thermostat .... 102°C
  Type 2 thermostat .... 105°C

Torque wrench settings	Nm	lbf ft
Air conditioning compressor-to-bracket bolts	40	30
Coolant pump bolts	17	13
Radiator mounting bolts	30	22

1 General information and precautions

General information

The cooling system is of pressurised semi-sealed type with the inclusion of an expansion tank to accept coolant displaced from the system when hot and to return it when the system cools.

Water-based coolant is circulated around the cylinder block and head by the coolant pump which is driven by the engine timing belt. As the coolant circulates around the engine it absorbs heat as it flows then, when hot, it travels out into the radiator to pass across the matrix. As the coolant flows across the radiator matrix, air flow created by the forward motion of the vehicle cools it, and it returns to the cylinder block. Air flow through the radiator matrix is assisted by a two-speed electric fan, which is controlled by the engine management system ECU.

A thermostat is fitted to control coolant flow through the radiator. When the engine is cold, the thermostat valve remains closed so that the coolant flow which occurs at normal operating temperatures through the radiator matrix is interrupted.

As the coolant warms up, the thermostat valve starts to open and allows the coolant flow through the radiator to resume.

The engine temperature will always be maintained at a constant level (according to the thermostat rating) whatever the ambient air temperature.

On turbo models, bypass connections are fitted to allow cold coolant flow to cool the turbocharger.

Later non-turbo models have an oil cooler mounted on the rear of the sump - this is basically a heat exchanger with a coolant supply, to take heat away from the oil in the sump.

The vehicle interior heater operates by means of coolant from the engine cooling system. Coolant flow through the heater matrix is constant; temperature control being achieved by blending cool air from outside the vehicle with the warm air from the heater matrix, in the desired ratio.

Air entering the passenger compartment is filtered by a pleated paper filter element, sometimes known as a pollen filter, mounted in the fresh air intake duct under the bonnet. The recommended interval for replacing the filter is given on a label attached to the air intake in the engine compartment. If the pollen filter becomes blocked (or gets wet), the airflow into the cabin will be reduced, leading to poor demisting. Refer to Section 12.

The climate control (air conditioning) systems are described in detail in Section 9.

3

Precautions

 Warning: Do not attempt to remove the expansion tank filler cap, or to disturb any part of the cooling system, while it or the engine is hot, as there is a very great risk of scalding. If the expansion tank filler cap must be removed before the engine and radiator have fully cooled down (even though this is not recommended) the pressure in the cooling system must first be released. Cover the cap with a thick layer of cloth, to avoid scalding, and slowly unscrew the filler cap until a hissing sound can be heard. When the hissing has stopped, showing that pressure is released, slowly unscrew the filler cap further until it can be removed; if more hissing sounds are heard, wait until they have stopped before unscrewing the cap completely. At all times, keep well away from the filler opening.

Warning: Do not allow antifreeze to come in contact with your skin, or with the painted surfaces of the vehicle. Rinse off spills immediately with plenty of water. Never leave antifreeze lying around in an open container, or in a puddle in the driveway or on the garage floor. Children and pets are attracted by its sweet smell, but antifreeze is fatal if ingested.

Warning: Refer to Section 9 for precautions to be observed when working on vehicles equipped with air conditioning.

2 Cooling system hoses - disconnection and renewal

Note: *Refer to the warnings given in Section 1 of this Chapter before proceeding. Hoses should only be disconnected once the engine has cooled sufficiently to avoid scalding.*

1 If the checks described in Chapter 1 reveal a faulty hose, it must be renewed as follows.

2 First drain the cooling system (see Chapter 1); if the antifreeze is not due for renewal, the drained coolant may be re-used, if it is collected in a clean container.

3 To disconnect any hose, use a pair of pliers to release the spring clamps (or a screwdriver to slacken screw-type clamps), then move them along the hose clear of the union **(see illustration)**. Carefully work the hose off its stubs. The hoses can be removed with relative ease when new - on an older vehicle, they may have stuck.

4 If a hose proves to be difficult to remove, try to release it by rotating it on its unions before attempting to work it off. Gently prise the end of the hose with a blunt instrument (such as a flat-bladed screwdriver), but do not apply too much force, and take care not to damage the pipe stubs or hoses. Note in particular that the

2.3 Radiator bottom hose connection and screw-type clamp

radiator hose unions are fragile; do not use excessive force when attempting to remove the hoses.

 If all else fails, cut the hose with a sharp knife, then slit it so that it can be peeled off in two pieces. Although this may prove expensive if the hose is otherwise undamaged, it is preferable to buying a new radiator.

5 When refitting a hose, first slide the clamps onto the hose, then engage the hose with its unions. Work the hose into position, then check that the hose is settled correctly and is properly routed. Slide each clip along the hose until it is behind the union flared end, before tightening it securely.

 If the hose is stiff, use a little soapy water as a lubricant, or soften the hose by soaking it in hot water. Do not use oil or grease, which may attack the rubber.

6 Refill the system with coolant (Chapter 1).
7 Check carefully for leaks as soon as possible after disturbing any part of the cooling system.

3 Antifreeze - general information

Note: *Refer to the warnings given in Section 1 of this Chapter before proceeding.*

1 The cooling system should be filled with Volvo type C coolant (antifreeze) in a ratio of 50/50 with pure water. At this strength, the coolant will protect against freezing down to 35°C. Antifreeze also provides protection against corrosion, and increases the coolant boiling point. As the engine is of all-aluminium construction, the corrosion protection properties of the antifreeze are critical. Only Volvo antifreeze should be used in the system, and should never be mixed with different antifreeze types.
2 The cooling system should be maintained

4.2 Removing the air cleaner intake duct from the fan shroud

according to the schedule described in Chapter 1. If antifreeze is used that is not to Volvo's specification, old or contaminated coolant mixtures are likely to cause damage, and encourage the formation of corrosion and scale in the system.

3 Before adding antifreeze, check all hoses and hose connections, because antifreeze tends to leak through very small openings. Engines don't normally consume coolant, so if the level goes down, find the cause and correct it.

4 The specified mixture is 50% antifreeze and 50% clean soft water (by volume). Mix the required quantity in a clean container and then fill the system as described in Chapter 1, and *Weekly checks*. Save any surplus mixture for topping-up.

4 Radiator cooling fan - removal and refitting

Removal

1 Disconnect the battery negative lead.
2 Detach the air cleaner inlet duct and the ECU module box air duct from each side of the fan shroud **(see illustration)**.
3 On cars equipped with exhaust gas recirculation, disconnect the two hoses at the EGR controller, noting their locations.
4 Undo the two bolts each side securing the fan shroud and relay carrier to the front body panel **(see illustration)**.

4.4 Fan shroud and relay carrier left-hand retaining bolts (arrowed)

4.5 Lift up the relay carrier and disconnect the fan wiring connectors

4.7 Lift the fan shroud up and out to remove

4.9 Ensure the lower locating pegs engage with the bottom of the radiator when refitting

5 Lift up the relay carrier and disconnect the fan wiring connectors (see illustration). Lay the carrier to one side, clear of the fan shroud.
6 On turbo models, detach the intercooler air duct above the fan shroud.
7 Lift the shroud upwards to release the two lower locating pegs, and remove the shroud and fan from the car (see illustration).
8 Undo the four bolts and remove the motor and fan guard assembly from the shroud. This is the limit of dismantling as the motor, fan and guard are not available as separate components.

Refitting

9 Refitting is the reversal of removal. Ensure that the lower locating pegs engage with the bottom of the radiator as the shroud is refitted (see illustration).

5 Radiator -
removal and refitting

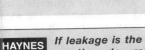
If leakage is the reason for wanting to remove the radiator, bear in mind that minor leaks can often be cured using a radiator sealant with the radiator in situ.

Removal

1 Drain the cooling system (see Chapter 1).

2 Remove the radiator cooling fan as described in Section 4.
3 Where applicable, undo the retaining bolt each side, then release the clips and remove the splash guard under the radiator (see illustrations).
4 Disconnect the top and bottom hoses, from the radiator.
5 On cars equipped with air conditioning, undo the condenser upper mounting bolt on each side. Secure the condenser to the upper body panel with string or wire to retain it in position, then undo the two lower bolts (see illustration).
6 On automatic transmission models, disconnect the fluid cooler lines from the radiator left-hand side tank. Be prepared for fluid spillage. Plug or cap the lines to keep dirt out.
7 Where fitted, disconnect the engine oil cooler pipe unions from the radiator right-hand side tank. Plug or cap the lines to keep dirt out.
8 On turbo models, detach the intercooler air ducts as necessary for radiator removal.
9 Support the radiator, then undo the lower mounting bolt on each side and lift the radiator out of the engine compartment.

Refitting

10 Refit by reversing the removal operations. With reference to Chapter 1, refill the cooling system on completion, and where applicable top-up the automatic transmission fluid and engine oil.

6 Coolant temperature sensor
- testing, removal and refitting

Testing

1 The coolant temperature sensor is located in the thermostat housing, and is used by both the engine management system and the instrument panel temperature gauge to supply an engine temperature source signal.
2 In the event of a fault in the sensor, or a loss of signal due to poor electrical connections, a fault code will be logged in the engine management system ECU, which can be read out via the diagnostic connector in the centre console (using a suitable fault code reader).
3 Should a fault code be logged, a careful check should be made of the sensor wiring and the wiring connector. Apart from testing by substitution with a new unit, further checks require the use of Volvo test equipment and should be entrusted to a dealer.

Removal

4 Partially drain the cooling system (see Chapter 1) to below the level of the sensor unit. Slacken the clip and disconnect the radiator top hose at the thermostat housing.
5 Remove the two Torx bolts, and lift off the thermostat housing.
6 Disconnect the wiring at the adjacent connector, then unscrew the sensor from its location in the thermostat housing (see illustrations).

5.3a Undo the retaining bolt each side (arrowed) . . .

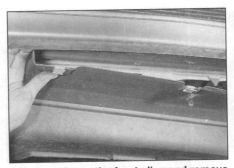

5.3b . . . release the front clips and remove the splash guard under the radiator

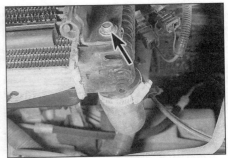

5.5 Left-hand air conditioning condenser lower mounting bolt (arrowed)

3

6.6a Disconnect the temperature sensor wiring plug above the power steering pump

Refitting

7 Screw in the new sensor unit, using a smear of sealant on the threads. Reconnect the wiring connector. Refit the thermostat housing, tightening the screws securely, and reconnect the radiator hose.
8 Top-up the coolant level as described in *Weekly checks*.

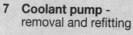
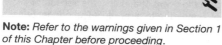

7 Coolant pump -
removal and refitting

Note: *Refer to the warnings given in Section 1 of this Chapter before proceeding.*

Removal

1 Disconnect the battery negative lead.
2 Refer to Chapter 2A and remove the timing belt. To improve access, it will also be necessary to loosen some of the timing belt rear cover fasteners.
3 Undo the seven bolts, and remove the coolant pump from its locating dowels **(see illustration)**. Access is very limited, and patience is needed. Recover the gasket after removing the pump.
4 Thoroughly clean all traces of old gasket from the pump and cylinder block mating faces.

Refitting

5 Using a new gasket, locate the pump in position.
6 Apply hydraulic sealing compound (avail-

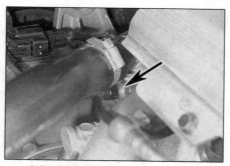

6.6b Coolant temperature sensor (arrowed)

able from Volvo dealers) to the threads of the retaining bolts, and refit the bolts. Tighten the bolts progressively and in a diagonal sequence to the specified torque.
7 Refit the timing belt as described in Chapter 2A.

8 Thermostat -
removal, testing and refitting

1 As the thermostat ages, it will become slower to react to changes in water temperature. Ultimately, the unit may stick in the open or closed position, and this causes problems. A thermostat which is stuck open will result in a very slow warm-up; a thermostat which is stuck shut will lead to rapid overheating.
2 Before assuming the thermostat is to blame for a cooling system problem, check the coolant level. If the system is draining due to a leak, or has not been properly filled, there may be an air-lock in the system (see Chapter 1, Section 29).
3 If the engine seems to be taking a long time to warm up (based on heater output or temperature gauge operation), the thermostat is probably stuck open.
4 Equally, a lengthy warm-up period might suggest that the thermostat is missing - it may have been removed or inadvertently omitted by a previous owner or mechanic. Don't drive the vehicle without a thermostat - the engine management system's ECU will then stay in

warm-up mode for longer than necessary, causing emissions and fuel economy to suffer.
5 If the engine runs hot, use your hand to check the temperature of the radiator top hose. If the hose isn't hot, but the engine is, the thermostat is probably stuck closed, preventing the coolant inside the engine from escaping to the radiator - renew the thermostat. Again, this problem may also be due to an air-lock (see Chapter 1, Section 29).
6 If the radiator top hose is hot, it means that the coolant is flowing and the thermostat is open. Consult the *Fault diagnosis* section at the end of this manual to assist in tracing possible cooling system faults.
7 To gain a rough idea of whether the thermostat is working properly when the engine is warming up, without dismantling the system, proceed as follows.
8 With the engine completely cold, start the engine and let it idle, while checking the temperature of the radiator top hose. Periodically check the temperature indicated on the coolant temperature gauge - if overheating is indicated, switch the engine off immediately.
9 The top hose should feel cold for some time as the engine warms up, and should then get warm quite quickly as the thermostat opens.
10 The above is not a precise or definitive test of thermostat operation, but if the system does not perform as described, remove and test the thermostat as described below.

Removal

Note: *Refer to the warnings given in Section 1 of this Chapter before proceeding.*
11 The engine must be completely cold before starting this procedure - the engine should have been switched off for several hours, and ideally, left to cool overnight.
12 Partially drain the cooling system (see Chapter 1) to below the level of the thermostat housing.
13 Release the radiator top hose and expansion tank hose from the thermostat housing, then undo the two housing retaining bolts **(see illustration)**.
14 Lift off the housing, and remove the thermostat and sealing ring **(see illustrations)**.

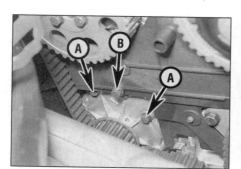

7.3 Two of the pump's mounting bolts (A) and the 'weep hole' (B)

8.13 Thermostat housing retaining bolts (arrowed)

8.14a Lift off the thermostat housing . . .

8.14b . . . and remove the thermostat

Testing

15 Check the temperature marking stamped on the thermostat, which will typically be either 87 or 90°C.

16 Using a thermometer and container of water, heat the water until the temperature corresponds with the temperature marking stamped on the thermostat.

17 Suspend the (closed) thermostat on a length of string in the water, and check that maximum opening occurs within two minutes.

18 Remove the thermostat and allow it to cool down; check that it closes fully.

19 If the thermostat does not open and close as described, or if it sticks in either position, it must be renewed. Frankly, if there is any question about the operation of the thermostat, renew it - they are not expensive.

Refitting

20 Fit a new sealing ring to the thermostat.

21 Refit the thermostat and housing and secure with the two bolts.

22 Reconnect the top hose and expansion tank hose, then refill the cooling system as described in Chapter 1 and *Weekly checks*.

---

9   Heating, ventilation and air conditioning systems - general information and precautions

---

Manual climate control system

1 On models equipped with a manual climate control system, the heater may be fitted alone, or in conjunction with a manually-controlled air conditioning unit. The same housings and heater components are used in both cases.

2 The heater is of the fresh air type. Air enters through a grille in front of the windscreen, and is filtered by a paper-element pollen filter (see Section 12). Although there is no requirement for routine renewal of the pollen filter, there will be a reduction in air flow into the car if the pollen filter becomes blocked.

3 On its way to the various vents, a variable proportion of the air passes through the heater matrix, where it is warmed by engine coolant flowing through the matrix.

4 Distribution of air to the vents, and through

or around the matrix, is controlled by flaps (dampers). These are operated by an electric motor (as is the air recirculation damper). Separate temperature controls are provided for driver and front passenger, and these are cable-operated.

5 A four-speed electric fan is fitted to boost the airflow through the heater.

6 Where manual climate control including air conditioning is fitted, the system works in conjunction with the heater to enable any reasonable air temperature to be achieved inside the car. It also reduces the humidity of the incoming air, aiding demisting even when cooling is not required.

7 The refrigeration side of the air conditioning system functions in a similar way to a domestic refrigerator. A compressor, belt-driven from the crankshaft pulley, draws refrigerant in its gaseous phase from an evaporator. The compound refrigerant passes through a condenser where it loses heat and enters its liquid phase. After dehydration the refrigerant returns to the evaporator where it absorbs heat from air passing over the evaporator fins. The refrigerant becomes a gas again and the cycle is repeated.

8 Various subsidiary controls and sensors protect the system against excessive temperature and pressures. Additionally, engine idle speed is increased when the system is in use, to compensate for the additional load imposed by the compressor.

Electronic climate control system

9 On models with electronic climate control, the temperature inside the car can be automatically maintained at the level selected by the operator, irrespective of outside temperature. The computer-controlled system operates the heater, air conditioner and fan functions as necessary to achieve this. The refrigeration side of the system is the same as for models with manual climate control; the fully automatic electronic control operates as follows.

10 An electronic control unit (ECU) receives signal inputs from sensors that detect the air duct temperatures on the driver's and passenger's side, interior temperature on the driver's and passenger's side. A solar sensor is used to detect the presence of sunlight. Signals are also received from the dampers (air flaps) on their position at any given time. Information on engine temperature, outside temperature, whether or not the engine is running, and if so, the vehicle road speed, are also sent to the ECU from the engine management system.

11 When the automatic function is engaged, the ECU can establish the optimum settings needed, based on the sensor signals, for the selected temperature and air distribution. These settings can then be maintained irrespective of driving conditions and weather.

12 Distribution of air to the various vents, and the blending of hot or cold air to achieve the

selected temperature, are controlled by dampers (flaps). These are operated by electric motors, which are in turn controlled by the ECU. A variable speed fan which can be manually or automatically controlled is used to boost airflow through the system.

13 The ECU, which is located behind the control panel, incorporates a built-in fault diagnosis facility. A fault is signalled to the driver by the flashing of the two warning lights on the control panel for approximately 20 seconds every time the engine is started.

14 Should a fault occur, the ECU stores a series of signals (or fault codes) for subsequent read-out via the diagnostic connector in the centre console.

Precautions

15 When an air conditioning system is fitted, it is necessary to observe special precautions whenever dealing with any part of the system, or its associated components. If for any reason the system must be discharged, entrust this task to your Volvo dealer or a refrigeration engineer.

⚠️ *Warning: The refrigeration circuit contains R134a liquid refrigerant, and it is therefore dangerous to disconnect any part of the system without specialised knowledge and equipment.*

16 The refrigerant is potentially dangerous, and should only be handled by qualified persons. If it is splashed onto the skin, it can cause frostbite. It is not itself poisonous, but in the presence of a naked flame (including a cigarette) it forms a poisonous gas. Uncontrolled discharging of the refrigerant is dangerous, and potentially damaging to the environment.

17 In view of the above points, removal and refitting of any air conditioning system components, except for the sensors and other peripheral items covered in this Chapter, must be left to a specialist.

---

10 Manual climate control system components - removal and refitting

---

Note: *On cars equipped with manual climate control including air conditioning, the contents of this Section are limited to those operations which can be carried out without discharging the refrigerant. Renewal of the auxiliary (compressor) drivebelt is described in Chapter 1, but all other operations except those described below must be entrusted to a Volvo dealer or air conditioning specialist. If necessary, the compressor can be unbolted and moved aside, without disconnecting the refrigerant unions, after removing the drivebelt.*

Control panel

Removal

1 Carefully pull off the rotary temperature control knobs (ie the two outer controls) from the front of the panel **(see illustration)**.

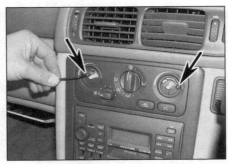

10.1 Pull off the temperature control knobs

10.2a Unscrew the panel retaining screws (arrowed) . . .

10.2b . . . then prise the panel from the facia

2 Undo the two screws now exposed behind the temperature control knobs, then carefully prise out and withdraw the control panel front plate **(see illustrations)**.

3 Disconnect the wiring plugs from the rear of the control panel, and remove **(see illustration)**.

4 If required, the three panel illumination bulbs can be removed by unscrewing the bulbholders from the rear of the panel, and pulling out the bulbs **(see illustrations)**.

5 To remove the rear section of the control panel for access to the control cables, the radio/cassette unit must be removed as described in Chapter 12.

6 With the front panel removed as described above, use a screwdriver to release the four catches (one at each corner), then carefully lower and withdraw the rear panel through the radio aperture **(see illustration)**.

7 Note the location of the control cables as an aid to refitting. Release the retaining clips securing the outer cables, and detach the inner cables from the control lever pegs **(see illustration)**.

8 Remove the control panel from the car.

Refitting

9 Refit by reversing the removal operations.

10 On completion, adjust the cables at the

heater unit as described in the following sub-section.

Control cables

Removal

11 Undo the screws and remove the trim/sound proofing panels from under the facia on the left and right-hand sides. Also unclip and detach the floor air ducts at the very front of the centre console on either side.

12 Undo the screws and remove the carpet support plates on each side of the heater unit. Bend back the carpet to allow the support plates to be withdrawn.

10.3 Disconnect the wiring plugs from the control panel

10.4a Unscrew the control panel bulbholders . . .

10.4b . . . and pull out the bulbs as required

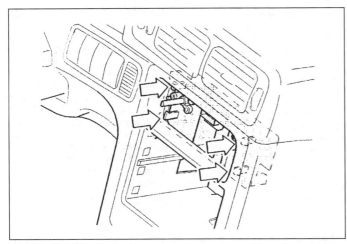

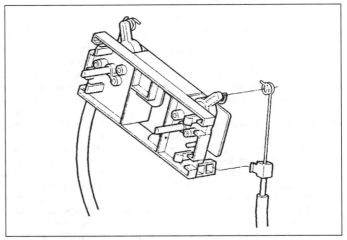

10.6 Release the four rear panel securing catches (arrowed)

10.7 Release the outer cable retaining clips, then disconnect the inner cables

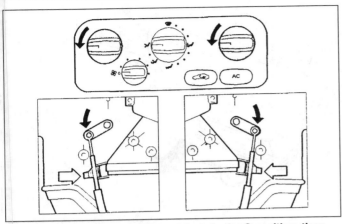

10.17 Turn the temperature controls to the O position, then reconnect the cables

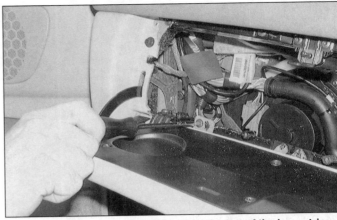

10.19a Remove the screws securing the top of the lower trim panel . . .

13 Remove the heating/ventilation control panel as described previously.

14 Note the location of the control cables at the heater unit as an aid to refitting. Release the retaining clips securing the outer cables, and detach the inner cables from the control lever pegs.

15 Remove the cables from the car.

Refitting and adjustment

16 Refit the cables to the heating/ventilation control panel, then refit the panel as described in the previous sub-section.

17 Turn the temperature control knobs on the control panel to the O position. Connect the left-hand temperature control inner cable to

the control lever peg on the heater unit. Move the control lever downwards to shut the damper, then secure the outer cable with the retaining clip (see illustration). Reconnect and adjust the right-hand cable in the same way.

18 Check the operation of the controls and cables, then refit the under-facia trim and ducting removed for access.

Heater blower motor

Removal

19 Undo the screws and remove the lower trim/sound proofing panel from under the facia on the passenger's side, disconnecting

the footwell light wiring as it becomes accessible (see illustrations).

20 Open the glovebox lid, and undo the six screws on the front face of the glovebox compartment. Pull the compartment rearwards to disengage the retaining clips, and remove from the facia.

21 Working through the glovebox aperture, disconnect the blower motor wiring connector (see illustration).

22 Detach the cable conduit from the blower motor, and move the wiring out of the way (see illustration).

23 Undo the four screws and remove the blower motor from the heater unit (see illustrations).

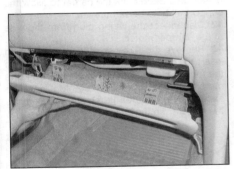

10.19b . . . then lower the panel into the footwell . . .

10.19c . . . and disconnect the footwell light wiring plug

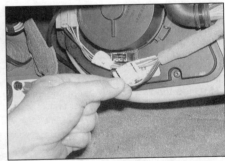

10.21 Disconnect the blower motor wiring plug

10.22 Unclip the wiring plug and cable conduit (above) from the front of the motor

10.23a Unscrew the blower motor screws (arrowed) . . .

10.23b . . . then twist the motor and remove it from the housing

3

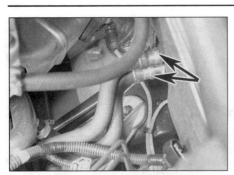

10.27 Heater matrix stubs (arrowed) at engine compartment bulkhead

Refitting

24 Refit by reversing the removal operations.

Heater matrix

Removal

Note: *Refer to the warnings given in Section 1 of this Chapter before proceeding.*

25 Disconnect the battery negative lead.
26 Depressurise the cooling system by removing the expansion tank cap. Take precautions against scalding if the coolant is hot.
27 From within the engine compartment, clamp the coolant hoses which lead to the heater matrix stubs on the bulkhead **(see illustration)**. The pipes do not have to be disconnected - the pipework is detached at a flange on the heater matrix itself, inside the car.
28 Undo the screws and remove the trim/sound proofing panels from under the facia on the left- and right-hand sides.
29 Undo the screws and remove the carpet support plates on each side of the heater unit. Bend back the carpet to allow the support plates to be withdrawn. Unclip and remove the floor duct, where necessary.
30 Unplug the drain hose from the floor in front of the unit, and fold it to one side.
31 Undo the two screws each side securing the matrix housing to the heater unit.

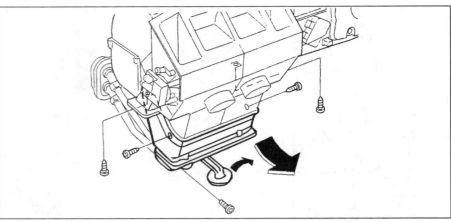

10.34 Heater matrix and housing removal details

32 Place plenty of absorbent rags and/or paper beneath the heater pipe attachment at the rear of the matrix.
33 Undo the screw securing the heater pipe flange to the rear of the matrix. Be prepared for coolant spillage.
34 Disengage the heater pipes from the flange on the heater matrix, then manoeuvre the housing rearwards and out from under the facia **(see illustration)**.
35 With the housing removed, withdraw the matrix from the housing.
36 If required, the heater supply pipes can be removed as follows. Detach the heater hoses at the bulkhead by pressing the hose connection inwards while squeezing the locking collar, then pull each hose out, noting its location. Recover the cover plate and rubber seal from around the heater matrix stubs, then move to the interior and withdraw the pipes into the passenger compartment.

Refitting

37 Refit by reversing the removal operations. Use new O-rings on the heater pipes and top-up the cooling system as described in *Weekly checks* on completion.

Air distribution damper motor

Removal

38 The air distribution damper motor is located on the left-hand side of the main heater housing (ie to the left of the central facia section).
39 On right-hand-drive models, remove the glovebox compartment as described in paragraph 20 (the glovebox lid does not have to be removed).
40 Undo the screws and remove the trim/sound proofing panels from under the left-hand side of the facia.
41 Undo the screws and remove the carpet support plate on the left-hand side of the heater unit. Bend back the carpet to allow the support plate to be withdrawn.
42 Disconnect the wiring plug from the side of the damper motor.
43 Remove the three securing screws, then insert the flat blade of a screwdriver between the motor and the damper reel, and work the motor shaft out of the reel (do not use excessive force) **(see illustrations)**. Remove the motor from the car.

10.43a Remove the three securing screws (arrowed), and disconnect the wiring plug . . .

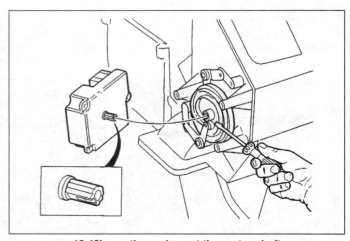

10.43b . . . then prise out the motor shaft

10.50a Disconnect the wiring plug . . .

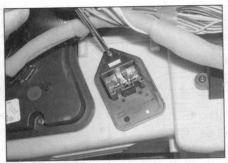

10.50b . . . remove the retaining screw . . .

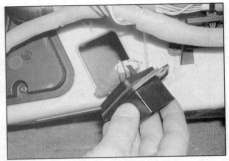

10.50c . . . and remove the blower motor resistor

Refitting

44 When refitting the motor to the damper reel, take care to engage the flat and bevelled portions of the shaft correctly with the reel, before pushing it home. Secure with the three screws, then refit the trim removed for access.

Recirculation damper motor

Removal

45 Remove the glovebox compartment as described in paragraph 20 (the glovebox lid does not have to be removed).
46 Working through the glovebox aperture, disconnect the damper motor wiring connector from the side of the heater blower housing.
47 Undo the two screws and remove the damper motor from the side of the heater blower motor housing.

Refitting

48 Refit by reversing the removal operations.

Heater blower motor resistor

Removal

49 Remove the glovebox compartment as described in paragraph 20 (the glovebox lid does not have to be removed).
50 Working through the glovebox aperture, disconnect the wiring connector, undo the screw and remove the resistor from alongside the heater blower motor housing **(see illustrations)**.

Refitting

51 Refit by reversing the removal operations.

10.52 Prising out the centre air vents - note the use of card to protect the facia

Facia panel vents

Removal

52 Carefully lever the vents out of the facia panel, using a screwdriver with a piece of card beneath it to protect the trim **(see illustration)**. To remove the side air vent(s), open the front door(s) for access (see Chapter 11, Section 29).

Refitting

53 Push the vent firmly into place to refit.

---

11 Electronic climate control system components - removal and refitting

Note: *The content of this Section is limited to those operations which can be carried out without discharging the refrigerant. Renewal of the auxiliary (compressor) drivebelt is described in Chapter 1, but all other operations except those described below must be entrusted to a Volvo dealer or air conditioning specialist. If necessary, the compressor can be unbolted and moved aside, without disconnecting the refrigerant unions, after removing the drivebelt.*

Many of the components used in the heating/ventilation side of the system are also used on cars equipped with manual climate control. Refer to Section 10 for procedures relating to the heater blower motor, heater matrix, and panel vents.

Control panel and ECU

Note: *If a new ECU is to be fitted, Volvo state that the learned values stored in the old ECU must be downloaded first, so that they can be uploaded into the new ECU on completion. If this data is lost, the new unit can still be set up, but this will take longer. In either case, dedicated Volvo test equipment must be used, so this part of the job must be entrusted to a Volvo dealer. If a new unit is fitted unprogrammed, the climate control will not work, and the green LEDs on the control panel will flash continuously.*

Removal

1 Remove the radio as described in Chapter 12.

2 Reach up through the radio aperture and depress the locking button on the underside of the unit.
3 Push out one rear corner of the unit to free it from its location, and remove it from the facia aperture.
4 Disconnect the wiring connectors and remove the unit from the car.
5 If required, the three panel illumination bulbs can be removed as follows. Remove the four screws from the rear of the unit, and separate the front panel from the rear section **(see illustration)**. Untwist the bulbholder from the rear of the panel, and pull out the bulb.

Refitting

6 Refit by reversing the removal operations. Refit the radio with reference to Chapter 12. If a new ECU has been fitted, refer to a Volvo dealer to have the unit programmed (see Note above).

Air duct temperature sensor

Removal

7 Undo the screws and remove the trim/sound proofing panel from under the facia on the passenger's side.
8 Open the glovebox lid, and undo the six screws on the front face of the glovebox compartment. Pull the compartment rearwards to disengage the retaining clips, and remove from the facia.

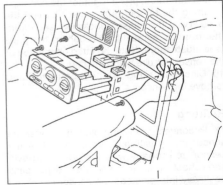

11.5 Remove the control panel and ECU, then remove four screws and separate the front panel

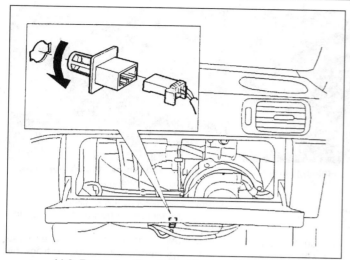

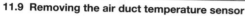

11.9 Removing the air duct temperature sensor

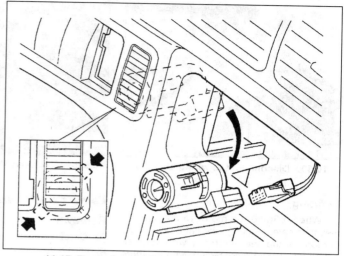

11.15 Removing the interior temperature sensor - inset shows sensor clips in fitted position

9 Twist the temperature sensor anti-clockwise and release it from the base of the blower motor housing **(see illustration)**.
10 Disconnect the wiring connector, and remove the sensor from the car.

Refitting

11 Refit by reversing the removal operations.

Interior temperature sensor

Removal

12 The temperature sensor for the car interior is located behind a small grille at the end of the switch panel next to the heater control panel.
13 Remove the control panel and ECU as described previously in this Section.
14 Reach in through the control panel aperture, and push out the switch next to the sensor grille from behind. Disconnect the wiring plug from the switch, and remove it. Look in through the switch aperture, and note the fitted position of the sensor, for use when refitting.
15 Working through the control panel and switch apertures, press together the two clips securing the temperature sensor behind the grille. Twist the sensor clockwise (seen from the front) to release it from behind the grille **(see illustration)**. Note the fitted orientation of the sensor, for use when refitting.
16 Disconnect the wiring connector and remove the sensor.

Refitting

17 Reconnect the wiring plug, then offer the sensor into position. Take care to line the sensor up properly with the holder groove, and check that the securing clips click positively into place as the sensor is twisted anti-clockwise. Check through the switch aperture that the sensor is located as noted before removal.

18 The remainder of refitting is a reversal of removal.

Air distribution and recirculation damper motors

19 Refer to the appropriate paragraphs of Section 10. On completion, switch on the ignition for approximately one minute - during this period, the ECU will self-adjust the motor positions, indicated by the green LED on the A/C switch flashing.

Temperature control damper motors

Removal

20 The driver and passenger temperature control damper motors are located on the left- and right-hand sides of the main heater housing, at the rear.
21 Undo the screws and remove the trim/sound proofing panels from the appropriate side of the facia.
22 Similarly, undo the screws and remove the carpet support plate on the side of the heater unit. Bend back the carpet to allow the support plate to be withdrawn. Also unclip and remove the floor duct, where applicable.
23 If the passenger motor is to be removed, access may be improved by removing the glovebox compartment as described in paragraph 8.
24 If removing the driver's motor on model with cruise control, remove the single screw and detach the vacuum control capsule from the heater housing - there should be no need to disconnect the vacuum hoses.
25 Remove the three securing screws, and pull the motor and shaft out of the main heater unit, noting its fitted orientation. Disconnect the wiring plug from the motor, and remove it from the car.

Refitting

26 Refit by reversing the removal operations. Take care that the motor shaft is correctly aligned with the slot in the heater housing before pushing it home and tightening the securing screws.
27 On completion, switch on the ignition for approximately one minute - during this period, the ECU will self-adjust the motor positions, indicated by the green LED on the A/C switch flashing.

Air conditioning power stage

Removal

28 Undo the screws and remove the trim/sound proofing panels from under the passenger side of the facia.
29 Open the glovebox lid, and undo the six screws on the front face of the glovebox compartment. Pull the compartment rearwards to disengage the retaining clips, and remove from the facia.
30 The relay can now be removed by pulling it up and out of the holder base.
31 Working through the glovebox aperture, disconnect the wiring connectors, then undo the screw and remove the power stage from alongside the heater blower motor housing.

Refitting

32 Refit by reversing the removal operations.

Solar sensor

Removal

33 The solar sensor is combined with the anti-theft alarm system diode, and is located on top of the facia cover.
34 Carefully prise up the sensor using a screwdriver inserted under its base at the side.
35 Disconnect the wiring connector and remove the sensor.

Refitting

36 Refit by reversing the removal operations.

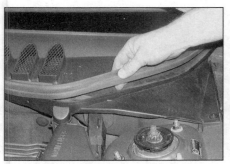

12.3 Lift off the rubber weatherseal

12.5a Release the spring clips . . .

12.5b . . . and detach the drain hoses from the cowl panel

12 Pollen filter renewal

1 The pollen filter is located beneath the windscreen cowl panels; it is located on the left side on right-hand-drive models, and the right side on left-hand drive models.
2 Remove the windscreen wiper arms as described in Chapter 12.
3 Open the bonnet, and lift up the rubber

weatherstrip from the relevant end of the top of the engine compartment bulkhead **(see illustration)**.
4 Remove the five Torx screws from the front edge of the cowl panel.
5 Using a suitable pair of pliers, release the spring clips securing the drain hoses at the front of the cowl panel, and detach the hoses from the panel **(see illustrations)**.
6 Remove the four screws securing the fusebox lid, and remove the lid **(see illustration)**.

7 Lift the cowl panel out, disengaging it from the rubber seal at the rear edge **(see illustration)**.
8 Lift the pollen filter and frame upwards and out from its location, noting which way round it is fitted **(see illustration)**.
9 Wipe clean the filter housing, then fit the new filter. Secure the filter in position and refit the cowl panel using a reversal of the removal procedure.
10 Refit the rubber seal to the engine compartment bulkhead to complete.

12.6 Remove four screws and take off the fusebox lid . . .

12.7 . . . then remove the cowl panel, unclipping it at the rear

12.8 Lifting out the pollen filter

3

Chapter 4 Part A:
Fuel systems

Contents

Degrees of difficulty

| Easy, suitable for novice with little experience | 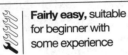 | Fairly easy, suitable for beginner with some experience | | Fairly difficult, suitable for competent DIY mechanic | | Difficult, suitable for experienced DIY mechanic | | Very difficult, suitable for expert DIY or professional | |

Specifications

System type

B5202 S and B5252 S (10-valve) engines . . . . Fenix 5.2 engine management system
B5254 S engines . . . . Bosch LH3.2-Jetronic fuel injection system, or Motronic 4.4/Denso engine management system (according to market/territory)

All other engines:
   Up to 1998 model year . . . . Bosch Motronic 4.3 or 4.4 engine management system
   1999 model year onwards . . . . Bosch ME7 engine management system

Fuel system data

Idle speed* . . . . 850 rpm
Idle mixture CO content* . . . . 0.6 ± 0.4%
Fuel pump delivery rate . . . . 1.45 to 2.41 litres/minute (at 12 volts)
Regulated fuel pressure . . . . 3.03 bars
*Non-adjustable - controlled by ECU

Recommended fuel

Octane rating:
   Recommended*:
      B5204 T2/T3 and B5234 T3/T4/T6 engines . . . . 98 RON unleaded
      All other engines . . . . 95 RON unleaded
   Minimum . . . . 91 RON unleaded
*Information correct at time of writing - consult a Volvo dealer for latest recommendations, especially if driving abroad.

Torque wrench settings

	Nm	lbf ft
Fuel gauge sender unit plastic retaining nut	30	22
Fuel pump plastic retaining nut	40	30
Fuel rail to inlet manifold:		
Stage 1	10	7
Stage 2	Angle-tighten a further 75°	
Inlet manifold bolts	20	15

1 General information and precautions

General information

The fuel system consists of a centrally-mounted fuel tank, an electric fuel pump, a fuel filter and a fully electronic fuel injection system. Further details of the fuel injection systems will be found in Section 8.

Non-turbo 20-valve engines are equipped with a variable venturi inlet system. The inlet manifold incorporates two separate inlet tracts, each of different length and diameter, for each cylinder. The shorter tracts can be opened or closed by means of vacuum-operated flap valves under the control of the ignition system ECU. At low engine speeds, both inlet tracts are opened, to allow a rapid increase in airflow when the throttle is opened. In the mid-range, the flap valves are closed, and airflow is through the longer tracts only. These are tuned for this speed range to cause the inlet air to resonate with the movement of the engine pistons and valves. These 'pulses' coincide with inlet valve opening, providing a greater inlet charge than that of a conventional system. At high engine speeds, both tracts are once again opened, to provide maximum torque in this range.

Depending on engine type, models for some market territories are also equipped with an exhaust gas recirculation (EGR) system and secondary air injection system, as part of an emissions control package. Further details of these systems will be found in Part B of this Chapter.

Depressurising the fuel system

Before working on any part of the fuel system, it is recommended that the residual fuel pressure is relieved. Even if the engine has been switched off for some time, there is a risk that, when fuel lines are disconnected, the residual fuel pressure will cause fuel to spray out uncontrollably. This is at best unpleasant (if it sprays in your face, for instance), and at worst, presents a fire risk.

Whenever a fuel line is to be disconnected, particularly if the system pressure has not been relieved, wrap plenty of absorbent rag around the connection to be disturbed. Loosen the fittings or clips slowly, and remove any pipes carefully, so that the pressure is relieved in a controlled fashion, and/or so that any fuel spillage can be contained.

To depressurise the system, using the information in Chapter 12, identify and remove the fuel pump fuse (ignition switched off). Crank the engine on the starter - the engine may fire and run, in which case let it run until it stops. After a few seconds of cranking/running, the fuel pressure should have dropped significantly, greatly reducing the dangers when disconnecting the fuel lines. Switch off the ignition and refit the fuel pump fuse on completion.

Note that a pressure relief valve is fitted in the fuel supply line to the fuel filter under the car. This valve is similar in design to a normal tyre valve, and may be used as described in Chapter 1, Section 26 to relieve system pressure.

Remember that relieving the system pressure does not remove the risk of fuel spillage - fuel will still be present in the lines, and it is wise to place absorbent rags around any connection which is to be disturbed.

Precautions

⚠️ **Warning: Petrol is extremely flammable - great care must be taken when working on any part of the fuel system. Do not smoke or allow any naked flames or uncovered light bulbs near the work area. Note that gas powered domestic appliances with pilot flames, such as heaters, boilers and tumble dryers, also present a fire hazard - bear this in mind if you are working in an area where such appliances are present. Always keep a suitable fire extinguisher close to the work area and familiarise yourself with its operation before starting work. Wear eye protection when working on fuel systems and wash off any fuel spilt on bare skin immediately with soap and water. Note that fuel vapour is just as dangerous as liquid fuel; a vessel that has just been emptied of liquid fuel will still contain vapour and can be potentially explosive. Petrol is a highly dangerous and volatile liquid, and the precautions necessary when handling it cannot be overstressed.**

Many of the operations described in this Chapter involve the disconnection of fuel lines, which may cause an amount of fuel spillage. Before commencing work, refer to the above Warning and the information in Safety first at the beginning of this manual; also see the information on depressurising the fuel system, given previously in this Section.

It is strongly advised that, wherever possible, the battery negative lead is disconnected whenever there is a danger of fuel spillage. This reduces the risk of a spark causing a fire, and also prevents the fuel pump running, which could be dangerous if the fuel lines have been disconnected.

When working with fuel system components, pay particular attention to cleanliness - dirt entering the fuel system may cause blockages which will lead to poor running.

2 Air cleaner assembly and air ducts - removal and refitting

Removal

Air cleaner assembly

1 Slacken the hose clip and detach the air inlet duct from the throttle body. Disconnect the crankcase ventilation hose at the air cleaner cover or air duct. On later models, also disconnect the secondary air inlet hose leading to the lower section of the fuel rail **(see illustrations)**.

2 Disconnect the wiring connectors from the mass airflow sensor, inlet air temperature sensor, or secondary air injection pump (as applicable) in the cover outlet **(see illustrations)**.

3 Where applicable, release the HT lead to the ignition coil from the clips at the rear of the cover.

2.1a Disconnecting the air inlet duct from the throttle body

2.1b Disconnect the crankcase ventilation hose at the base . . .

2.1c . . . and, where applicable, the secondary air hose from the top of the duct

2.2a Disconnect the wiring plug from the airflow sensor . . .

2.2b . . . and, where applicable, from the secondary air pump

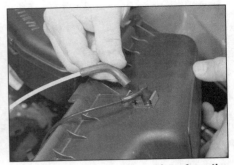

2.4 Disconnect the vacuum pipes from the temperature control valve

2.6 Pull the cold-air inlet duct rearwards to disconnect it

2.7 Detaching the warm-air inlet duct from the exhaust manifold

2.8 Removing the air cleaner housing

4 Also where applicable, disconnect the two vacuum pipes from the inlet air temperature vacuum control valve at the rear of the cover, noting their fitted positions (white pipe at the bottom) **(see illustration)**.

5 Spring back the retaining clips, lift off the cover and remove the air cleaner element.

6 Detach the cold-air inlet duct from the air inlet adjacent to the radiator **(see illustration)**.

7 Detach the warm-air inlet duct or turbocharger inlet duct, as applicable, either from the air cleaner housing, or from the exhaust manifold at the rear of the engine **(see illustration)**. On turbo models, detach the turbo control valve from the air cleaner housing (where fitted).

8 Lift the housing upwards at the engine side to release the lower retainers, then move it sideways to disengage the side locating peg. Remove the housing from the car **(see illustration)**.

Air ducts

9 All ducting is retained either by simple snap-fit connectors or by hose clips. The routing of the ducts varies between normally-aspirated and turbo models, but in all cases removal is straight forward and self-explanatory. To gain access to the lower ducts, it will be necessary to remove the air cleaner assembly as previously described.

Refitting

10 In all cases, refit by reversing the removal operations.

3 Inlet air pre-heating system - testing

1 An inlet air pre-heating system is incorporated in the air cleaner housing on non-turbo models for certain markets.

2 The system utilises a flap valve arrangement, controlled either by a wax capsule or a thermo-vacuum valve to blend cold air from the inlet adjacent to the radiator, with warm air from the exhaust manifold heat shield.

3 The capsule responds to ambient temperature to move the flap valve accordingly.

4 The thermo-vacuum valve, when warm, shuts off a vacuum supply to the flap valve diaphragm.

3.6a Remove the intake body from the air cleaner housing . . .

Removal

Wax capsule type

5 To gain access to the unit, remove the air cleaner assembly as described in Section 2.

6 Remove the inlet body from the air cleaner housing by depressing the two tabs and pulling the body free **(see illustrations)**.

7 Check the condition of the spindle bearings, capsule and spring, then test the operation of the capsule as follows.

8 Cool the unit by placing it in a refrigerator for a few minutes. Check that at a temperature of approximately 5°C or less, the flap valve has moved to shut off the cold air inlet.

9 As the unit warms in response to room temperature, check that at approximately 10°C the flap valve is in the mid-position, and that at 15°C or higher, the flap has moved to shut off the warm air inlet.

3.6b . . . for access to the pre-heating wax capsule

3.13 Air inlet temperature control valve in air cleaner housing

10 If the unit does not function as described, it should be renewed.

11 On completion, reassemble the inlet body, then refit the air cleaner assembly as described in Section 2.

Thermo-vacuum valve type

12 Remove the air cleaner top cover as described in Section 2.

13 The valve is mounted in the rear face of the top cover - before removing it, note which way round it fits **(see illustration)**.

14 With the two vacuum pipes disconnected (refer to illustration 2.4), use a small flat-bladed screwdriver to prise off the retaining plate from below the vacuum switch. The plate will probably be quite stiff, but work carefully, to avoid damaging the pipe stubs.

15 Remove the vacuum switch from the air cleaner housing, and recover the seal.

16 Refit the vacuum switch by following the removal procedure in reverse. If the seal is

4.1 Remove the cover over the accelerator cable drum and linkage

4.2a Release the outer cable retaining clip . . .

damaged or deteriorated, fit a new one when reassembling. Press the retaining plate firmly into position over the pipe stubs.

4 Accelerator cable - removal, refitting and adjustment

Note: *This Section does not apply to later models with the Motronic ME7 system, as the throttle butterfly is electronically controlled, and a cable is not fitted.*

Removal

1 Undo the screw and remove the cover over the accelerator cable drum and linkage **(see illustration)**.

2 Release the outer cable retaining clip from the cable adjuster, and unhook the inner cable from the drum **(see illustrations)**.

3 Undo the screws and remove the trim/sound proofing panel from under the facia on the driver's side. Pull the cable inner through the end of the pedal, and slide the split bush off the end of the cable.

4 On manual transmission models, release the cable grommet from the bulkhead, and pull the cable into the engine compartment. Note the routing of the cable, release it from any clips or ties, and remove it.

5 On automatic transmission models, disconnect the wiring connector from the kickdown switch attached to the cable at the bulkhead entry. Release the kickdown switch from the bulkhead by depressing the switch lugs with a screwdriver, whilst at the same time pushing the cable through. Note the routing of the cable, release it from any clips or ties, and remove it.

Refitting

6 Refit by reversing the removal operations, ensuring that on automatic transmission models the kickdown switch lugs fully engage in the bulkhead, and that the switch wiring connector is upright. Adjust the cable as follows before re-connecting it at the throttle housing end.

Adjustment

7 Check that the cable drum is seated against the idle stop on the drum bracket, and

4.2b . . . then unhook the inner cable from the drum

that the throttle lever on the throttle housing is contacting the adjusting screw. If this is not the case, slacken the link rod balljoint locknut so that the link rod will slide easily within the balljoint. Position the drum and throttle lever as just described, then tighten the locknut.

8 Reconnect the inner cable to the drum, and secure the outer cable with the retaining clip. Adjust the cable at the adjuster so that it is taut, but does not prevent the drum from closing onto the idle stop. Depress the accelerator pedal to the floor, and check that the drum reaches the full-load stop.

5 Fuel gauge sender unit - removal and refitting

Note: *Observe the precautions in Section 1 before working on any component in the fuel system.*

Removal

1 Disconnect the battery negative lead.

2 On S70 models, fold down the right-hand rear seat backrest and release the front edge of the boot carpet. Remove the support panel under the carpet. Undo the backrest catch, release the fasteners and remove the boot side trim panel

3 On V70 models, fold down the right-hand rear seat backrest, and fold back the boot carpeting. Remove the luggage cover and the side support panels. Undo the retaining screws from the luggage compartment front floor panel. Pull the panel to the rear to release the front mountings, and remove the panel.

4 On C70 models, release the boot carpet and remove the support panel underneath.

5 Undo the nuts and remove the access covers over the fuel pump and sender unit **(see illustration)**. The sender unit is beneath the cover nearest the front of the car.

6 Trace the wiring for the sender unit, which runs across the top of the fuel tank to the fuel pump, then out to the group of connectors adjacent to the shock absorber upper mounting. Disconnect the relevant connector, release any cable-ties, then feed the wiring back and through the sender unit aperture in the floor.

5.5 Remove the access cover over the sender unit

7 Unscrew the sender unit plastic retaining collar using a wide-opening pair of grips, such as a pair of water pump pliers **(see illustration)**. Certain types of oil filter removal tools are an ideal alternative.

8 Withdraw the sender unit from the fuel tank, and recover the seal. Refit the plastic collar to the tank while the sender unit is removed, to prevent the pipe stub swelling.

Refitting

9 Refitting is a reversal of removal, bearing in mind the following points:

a) *Use a new seal smeared with petroleum jelly.*

b) *Position the sender unit so that the wiring is toward the centre of the car.*

c) *Route the wiring over the top of the fuel tank and out through the fuel pump aperture. Reconnect and secure with cable-ties, where applicable.*

d) *In refitting the luggage compartment trim panels, make sure that none of the wiring gets trapped.*

6 Fuel pump -
removal and refitting

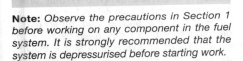

Note: *Observe the precautions in Section 1 before working on any component in the fuel system. It is strongly recommended that the system is depressurised before starting work.*

Removal

1 Carry out the operations described in Section 5, paragraphs 1 to 3.

2 Undo the nuts and remove the access cover over the fuel pump (the rearmost cover of the two).

3 Trace the wiring for the pump, which runs across to the group of connectors adjacent to the shock absorber upper mounting. Disconnect the relevant connector and release any cable-ties.

4 Identify the fuel hose connections on top of the pump as an aid to refitting. The delivery hose should be marked with a yellow band with a corresponding yellow mark on top of the pump flange **(see illustration)**. Make your own marks if none are visible.

5 Place absorbent rags around the fuel hose connections, then disconnect the quick-release couplings using a forked tool. Insert the tool under the edge of the outer sleeve of each coupling, and lever upwards without squeezing the sleeve. Be prepared for an initial release of fuel as the couplings are released.

6 Unscrew the sender unit plastic retaining nut using a wide-opening pair of grips, such as a pair of water pump pliers. Certain types of oil filter removal tools are an ideal alternative.

7 Withdraw the pump from the tank, and recover the seal. Refit the plastic nut to the tank while the pump is removed, to prevent the pipe stub swelling.

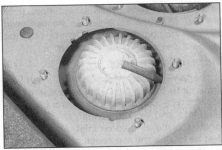

5.7 Unscrew the sender unit plastic retaining nut using a wide-opening pair of grips

Refitting

8 Lubricate a new seal sparingly with petroleum jelly and ensure it is correctly seated.

9 Refit the pump with the wiring connection towards the right-hand side of the car. Refit the plastic nut and tighten securely.

10 Lubricate the fuel hose coupling O-rings with petroleum jelly, position them squarely over the pump outlets and push down on the outer sleeves to lock. Ensure that the hoses are fitted to their correct outlets as noted during removal.

11 The remainder of refitting is a reversal of removal.

7 Fuel tank -
removal and refitting

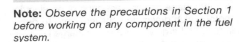

Note: *Observe the precautions in Section 1 before working on any component in the fuel system.*

Removal

1 Before the tank can be removed, it must be drained of as much fuel as possible. To avoid the dangers and complications of fuel handling and storage, it is advisable to carry out this operation with the tank almost empty. Any fuel remaining can be drained as follows.

2 Disconnect the battery negative lead.

3 Using a hand pump or syphon inserted through the filler neck, remove any remaining fuel from the bottom of the tank.

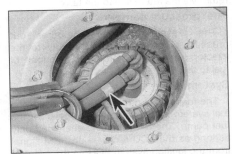

6.4 The fuel delivery hose at the pump connection should be marked with a yellow band (arrowed)

4 Alternatively, chock the front wheels then jack up the rear of the vehicle and support it on axle stands (see *Jacking and vehicle support*). Place a suitable large-capacity container under the fuel filter. Clean the fuel inlet quick-release coupling on the filter, place rags around the coupling, then disconnect it. Be prepared for an initial release of fuel as the coupling is released. Hold the disconnected fuel line over the container, and allow the fuel to drain. Store the fuel in a suitable sealed container.

5 Carry out the operations described in Section 5, paragraphs 1 to 5, and Section 6, paragraphs 3 to 5.

6 Remove the circlip securing the filler neck to the body, and release the filler neck and seals from their locations.

7 Position a trolley jack under the centre of the tank. Insert a protective wooden pad between the jack head and tank base, then raise the jack to just take the weight of the tank.

8 Undo the tank retaining straps, and carefully lower the jack and tank slightly. When sufficient clearance exists, disconnect the vent hoses leading to the front of the car. The hoses between the tank and filler tube can be left in place.

9 Lower the jack and tank, and remove the tank from under the car.

10 If the tank is contaminated with sediment or water, remove the gauge sender unit and the fuel pump as described previously, and disconnect the ventilation hoses and filler tube. Swill the tank out with clean fuel.

11 The tank is moulded from a synthetic material and if damaged, it should be renewed. However, in certain cases it may be possible to have small leaks or minor damage repaired. Seek the advice of a dealer or suitable specialist concerning tank repair.

12 If a new tank is to be fitted, transfer all the components from the old tank to the new. Always renew the filler tube seal, and the seals and plastic nuts securing the fuel pump and gauge sender unit. Once used, they may not seat and seal properly on a new tank.

Refitting

13 Refitting is a reversal of removal, bearing in mind the following points:

a) *Locate the tank in position, and tighten the rear strap mountings. Push the tank forwards, and centre the fuel gauge sender unit and fuel pump plastic nuts with respect to their access holes in the floor. Now tighten the front strap mountings.*

b) *Lubricate the filler neck seals and ensure that they are properly located. Make sure that the drain tube is on the inside of the inner seal.*

c) *On completion, refill the tank with fuel and check exhaustively for signs of leakage before driving the car on the road.*

4A

8 Fuel injection systems - general information

Bosch LH3.2-Jetronic system

The Bosch LH3.2-Jetronic system may be fitted to the non-turbo 2.5 litre 20-valve (B5254 S) engine in certain markets. Otherwise, this engine uses the Motronic 4.4 system described later in this Section.

LH3.2-Jetronic is a microprocessor-controlled fuel injection system, designed to meet stringent emission control legislation whilst still providing excellent engine performance and fuel economy. This is achieved by continuously monitoring the engine using various sensors, whose data is input to the system's electronic control unit (ECU). Based on this information, the ECU program and memory then determine the exact amount of fuel necessary, which is injected directly into the inlet manifold, for all actual and anticipated driving conditions.

The LH3.2-Jetronic ECU interacts with the EZ-129K ignition system ECU, to provide a total engine management package. In addition, it also controls various aspects of the emissions control systems described in Part B of this Chapter.

The main components of the fuel side of the system are as follows.

Electronic control unit (ECU)

The ECU is a microprocessor, which controls the entire operation of the fuel system. Contained in the unit memory is a program which controls the fuel supply to the injectors, and their opening duration. The program enters sub-routines to alter these parameters, according to inputs from the other components of the system. In addition to this, the engine idle speed is also controlled by the ECU, which uses an idle air control valve to open or close an air passage as required. The ECU also incorporates a self-diagnostic facility, in which the entire fuel system is continuously monitored for correct operation. Any detected faults are logged as fault codes which can be downloaded using a piece of equipment called a fault code reader. In the event of a fault in the system due to loss of a signal from one of the sensors, the ECU reverts to an emergency (limp-home) program. This will allow the car to be driven, although engine operation and performance will be limited.

Fuel injectors

Each fuel injector consists of a solenoid-operated needle valve, which opens under commands from the ECU. Fuel from the fuel rail is then delivered through the injector nozzle into the inlet manifold.

Coolant temperature sensor

This resistive device is screwed into the thermostat housing, where its element is in direct contact with the engine coolant. Changes in coolant temperature are detected by the ECU as a change in sensor resistance. Signals from the coolant temperature sensor are also used by the ignition system ECU and by the temperature gauge in the instrument panel.

Mass airflow sensor

The MAF sensor measures the mass of air drawn into the engine. The sensor is of the hot-film type, containing four different resistive elements and related circuitry. The unit is located in the air cleaner inlet, and uses the inlet air to alter the resistance of the elements. By comparing the changing resistance values with a calibration resistance, the ECU can establish the inlet air temperature, and from its cooling effect, the inlet air volume.

Throttle position sensor

The throttle position sensor is a potentiometer attached to the throttle shaft in the throttle housing, or to the throttle pedal on models with the Motronic ME7 system. The unit sends a linear signal to both the fuel and ignition system ECUs proportional to throttle opening.

Idle air control valve

The idle air control valve contains a small electric motor that open or shuts a bypass air passage inside the valve. The valve only operates when the throttle is closed, and in response to signals from the ECU, maintains the engine idle speed at a constant value irrespective of any additional load from the various accessories.

Fuel pump

The electric fuel pump is located in the fuel tank, and totally submerged in the fuel. The unit is a two-stage device consisting of an electric motor which drives an impeller pump to draw in fuel, and a gear pump to discharge it under pressure. The fuel is then supplied to the fuel rail on the inlet manifold via an in-line fuel filter.

Fuel pressure regulator

The regulator is a vacuum-operated mechanical device, which ensures that the pressure differential between fuel in the fuel rail and fuel in the inlet manifold is maintained at a constant value. As manifold depression increases, the regulated fuel pressure is reduced in direct proportion. When fuel pressure in the fuel rail exceeds the regulator setting, the regulator opens to allow fuel to return via the return line to the tank.

Fuel pressure damper

The pressure damper smoothes out pressure pulses in the fuel supply to the injectors, ensuring a more accurate supply of fuel to the engine.

System relay

The main system relay is energised by the fuel system ECU and provides power for the fuel pump. The relay remains energised only as long as the ECU receives an RPM signal from the ignition system ECU. In the event of that signal being lost (ie, in the event of an accident) the relay will de-energise and the fuel pump will stop.

Bosch Motronic and ME7 systems

The Motronic system components and their operation are very similar to the LH3.2-Jetronic, except that a single ECU is used to control both the fuel and ignition sides of the system. On turbo models, regulation of the turbocharger boost pressure by means of the turbo regulator valve is also controlled by the Motronic ECU.

The various generations and types of Motronic fitted to the S/V/C70 range are all but identical for all practical purposes - the only components which differ greatly are the system ECUs, and the parameters programmed into them. However, the Bosch ME7 system fitted to later models is a development of the Motronic system, having a fly-by-wire electronically-controlled throttle (with no conventional accelerator cable). The ME7 system also incorporates a MAP sensor (see below) and boasts a distributorless ignition system (see Chapter 5B).

Fenix 5.2 system

The Fenix 5.2 system is used on the 10-valve engines covered by this manual. The components and their operation are very similar to the LH3.2-Jetronic system, apart from the method of calculating the volume of air entering the engine and other minor differences which are described below. Also, as with Motronic systems, a single ECU is used to control both the fuel and ignition sides of the system.

Manifold absolute pressure (MAP) sensor

Instead of the mass airflow sensor used in the other systems, the Fenix system utilises a MAP sensor and inlet air temperature sensor to calculate the volume of air being drawn into the engine. The MAP sensor is connected to the inlet manifold via a hose, and uses a piezo-electrical crystal to convert manifold pressure to an electrical signal to be transmitted to the ECU.

Inlet air temperature sensor

This resistive device is located in the air inlet ducting, where its element is in direct contact with the air entering the engine. Changes in air temperature are detected by the ECU as a change in sensor resistance. From the signals received from the inlet air temperature sensor and pressure sensor, the ECU can calculate the volume of air inducted into the engine.

Outside air temperature sensor

This resistive device is located below the front bumper. Changes in air temperature are detected by the ECU as a change in sensor resistance. From the signals received, the ECU can more accurately determine the fuelling requirements of the engine. Information from the sensor is also displayed on the instrument panel, and is used by the electronic climate control system ECU (see Chapter 3).

9 Fuel injection system - testing and adjustment

1 If a fault appears in the fuel injection system, first ensure that all the system wiring connectors are securely connected and free of corrosion. Then ensure that the fault is not due to poor maintenance; ie, check that the air cleaner filter element is clean, the spark plugs are in good condition and correctly gapped, the cylinder compression pressures are correct, the ignition timing is correct and the engine breather hoses are clear and undamaged, referring to Chapters 1, 2A and 5B.

2 If these checks fail to reveal the cause of the problem, a diagnostic connector is located under the centre console compartment lid, into which a fault code reader can be plugged. The test equipment is capable of interrogating the engine management system electronically and accessing its internal fault log.

3 Fault codes can only be extracted from the ECU using a dedicated fault code reader. A Volvo dealer will obviously have such a reader, but they are also available from other suppliers, including Haynes. It is unlikely to be cost-effective for the private owner to purchase a fault code reader, but a well-equipped local garage or auto electrical specialist will have one.

4 Using this equipment, faults can be pinpointed quickly and simply, even if their occurrence is intermittent. Testing all the system components individually in an attempt to locate the fault by elimination is a time-consuming operation that is unlikely to be fruitful (particularly if the fault occurs dynamically), and carries high risk of damage to the ECU's internal components.

5 Experienced home mechanics equipped with an accurate tachometer and a carefully-calibrated exhaust gas analyser may be able to check the exhaust gas CO content and the engine idle speed; if these are found to be out of specification, then the vehicle must be taken to a suitably-equipped Volvo dealer for assessment. Neither the air/fuel mixture (exhaust gas CO content) nor the engine idle speed are manually adjustable; incorrect test

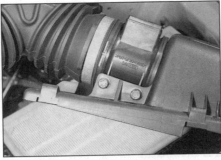

10.6 Airflow sensor mounting screws

results indicate the need for maintenance (possibly, injector cleaning) or a fault within the fuel injection system.

10 Fuel injection system components - removal and refitting

Note: Refer to the precautions in Section 1 before working on any component in the fuel system. The following procedures are applicable to all fuel injection systems unless otherwise stated.

Mass airflow sensor (all except Fenix 5.2)

Removal

1 Disconnect the battery negative lead.

2 Slacken the hose clip and detach the air inlet duct and, where applicable, the crankcase ventilation hose at the air cleaner cover.

3 Disconnect the wiring connector from the sensor.

4 Where applicable, release the HT lead to the ignition coil from the clips at the rear of the cover.

5 Spring back the retaining clips and lift off the air cleaner cover.

6 Undo the two screws and remove the sensor from the air cleaner cover **(see illustration)**.

Refitting

7 Refit by reversing the removal operations.

10.9 Prise the intake air temperature sensor out of its rubber retaining grommet (arrowed)

Inlet air temperature sensor (Fenix 5.2)

Removal

8 Carry out the operations described in paragraphs 1 to 5.

9 Carefully prise the sensor out of its rubber retaining grommet in the air cleaner cover outlet **(see illustration)**.

Refitting

10 Refit by reversing the removal operations.

Manifold absolute pressure (MAP) sensor

Fenix 5.2

11 Disconnect the battery negative lead.

12 Detach the air cleaner inlet duct and cowl from the side of the radiator fan shroud.

13 Undo the bolts each side securing the relay carrier to the front body panel above the fan shroud.

14 Lift up the relay carrier, and disconnect the vacuum hose and wiring connector from the MAP sensor **(see illustration)**.

15 Detach the pressure sensor and remove it from the centre of the relay carrier.

16 Refit by reversing the removal operations.

Motronic ME7

17 Disconnect the battery negative lead.

18 Unclip the sensor from the underside of the relay carrier above the fan shroud **(see illustrations)**.

4A

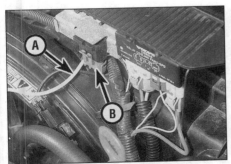

10.14 Disconnect the vacuum hose (A) and wiring connector (B) from the MAP sensor

10.18a MAP sensor location above the radiator fan shroud

10.18b Unclip the sensor from its location . . .

10.19 . . . then disconnect the wiring plug and vacuum hose from it

10.22 Disconnect the fuel feed and return pipes (arrowed) at the hose unions behind the engine

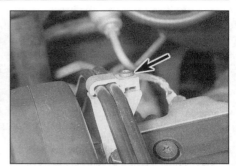

10.23 Remove the fuel pipe clamps (arrowed) from the engine

19 Disconnect the vacuum hose and wiring connector from the sensor, and remove it **(see illustration)**.
20 Refitting is a reversal of removal.

Fuel rail and injectors

Note: *If an injector problem is suspected, it might be worth trying the effect of a proprietary injector cleaner petrol treatment before removing the injectors.*

Removal - all except Motronic ME7

21 Disconnect the battery negative lead.
22 Disconnect the fuel feed and return pipes at the hose unions behind the engine **(see illustration)**. Access is difficult from above, but is slightly better from below. Place absorbent rags around the unions, and be prepared for an initial release of fuel as the unions are slackened.

23 Undo the bolts securing the two fuel pipe clamps to the engine, and remove the clamps **(see illustration)**.
24 Where applicable, release the turbocharger inlet ducting, then disconnect the wiring plug from each injector **(see illustration)**. If difficulty is experienced, pull off the fuel rail cover over the injectors for greater access.
25 Disconnect the vacuum hose from the pressure regulator on the underside of the fuel rail **(see illustration)**.
26 Undo the two bolts securing the fuel rail to the inlet manifold. Pull the rail upwards to release the injectors from the manifold, and remove the rail complete with injectors and fuel pressure regulator **(see illustrations)**.
27 Individual injectors may now be removed from the rail by simply pulling them out **(see illustration)**.

Removal - Motronic ME7

28 Disconnect the battery negative lead.
29 Disconnect the quick-release fuel line coupling in front of the fuel rail using a 17 mm spanner to push back the coupling sleeves. Be prepared for fuel spillage as the coupling is released. Plug the coupling after disconnection to prevent further loss of fuel.
30 Undo the two bolts securing the fuel rail to the inlet manifold. Pull the rail upwards to release the injectors from the manifold, and remove the rail complete with injectors and fuel pressure damper **(see illustrations)**. If required, the lower section of the fuel rail can also be pulled away and removed, after disconnecting the secondary air hose.
31 Disconnect the wiring plugs from the injectors, then remove the screws securing the injector retaining plate to the fuel rail **(see**

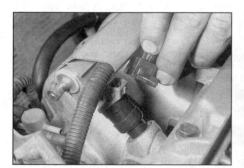

10.24 Disconnect the wiring plug from each injector

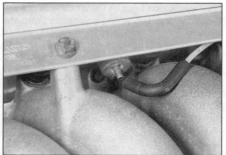

10.25 Disconnect the vacuum hose from the pressure regulator

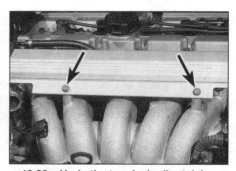

10.26a Undo the two fuel rail retaining bolts (arrowed) . . .

10.26b . . . and remove the fuel rail with injectors

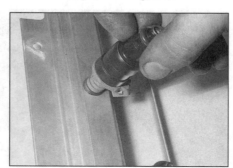

10.27 Remove the injectors by pulling them out of the fuel rail

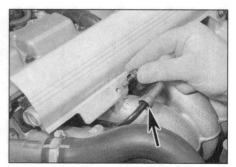

10.30a Removing one of the fuel rail bolts - note fuel line coupling (arrowed)

10.30b Withdrawing the fuel rail

10.31a Fuel injector wiring harness disconnected from all injectors

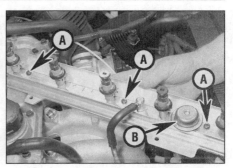

10.31b Injector retaining plate screws (A) and fuel pressure damper (B)

illustrations). The injectors can now be unclipped from the retaining plate, and removed.

Refitting - all systems

32 Refit by reversing the removal operations, and noting the following points:
  a) *Check that the injector O-rings and manifold seals are in good condition, and renew them if necessary (see illustration).*
  b) *Smear the O-rings with petroleum jelly or silicone grease as an assembly lubricant.*
  c) *Ensure that all wiring and fuel line connections are correctly and securely made.*
  d) *Tighten the fuel rail retaining bolts to the specified torque setting, first using a torque wrench, then through the specified angle using an angle-tightening gauge.*

Fuel pressure regulator (not Motronic ME7)

Removal

33 Remove the fuel rail and injectors as described previously, but leave the injectors in place in the fuel rail.
34 Undo the two bolts and remove the fuel pressure regulator from the fuel rail (see illustration).

Refitting

35 Refit the regulator to the fuel rail, then refit the fuel rail and injectors as described previously.

Fuel pressure damper (Motronic ME7)

Removal

36 Remove the fuel rail and injectors as

described previously. The fuel pressure damper can be unclipped from the fuel rail retaining plate in the same way as the injectors.

Refitting

37 Refitting is a reversal of removal.

Idle air control valve

Removal

38 Disconnect the wiring connector from the end of the valve (see illustration).
39 Release the hose clips and carefully pull the air hoses off the valve stubs.
40 Undo the mounting bracket retaining bolt and withdraw the valve from the inlet manifold.

Refitting

41 Refit by reversing the removal operations, using new hoses and clips if necessary.

Throttle housing

Removal

42 Disconnect the throttle position sensor wiring connector. On models with Motronic ME7, trace the wiring from the base of the housing, and disconnect it at the plug.
43 Disconnect the idle air control valve hose, the vacuum hoses and the air inlet duct from the housing (see illustration).
44 Where applicable, disconnect the throttle linkage balljoint from the throttle valve operating lever.
45 Remove the bolts which secure the housing and withdraw it from the manifold (see illustration). Recover the gasket.

4A

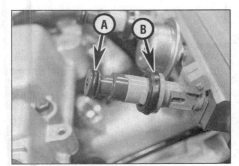

10.32 Check the condition of the injector O-rings (A) and manifold seals (B)

10.34 Undo the two bolts and remove the fuel pressure regulator

10.38 Disconnecting the idle air control valve wiring connector

10.43 Loosen the hose clip and disconnect the air inlet duct from the throttle housing

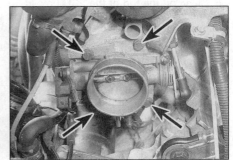

10.45 Throttle housing retaining bolts (arrowed)

10.55 Lift off the module box lid

10.56a Pull the locking lever forward . . .

10.56b . . . and withdraw the ECU

Refitting

46 Refit by reversing the removal operations, using a new gasket. Fit new hose clips if necessary.

Throttle position sensor

Removal - all except Motronic ME7

47 Disconnect the sensor wiring connector.
48 Remove the two bolts which secure the sensor and withdraw it from the throttle housing.

Removal - Motronic ME7

49 Remove the screw securing the driver's side under-facia trim panel, and pull the panel rearwards to disengage the retaining clips.
50 Disconnect the wiring plug from the sensor, which is located next to the accelerator pedal.
51 Remove the retaining screws and detach the sensor from its location.

Refitting - all systems

52 Refit by reversing the removal operations.

Coolant temperature sensor

53 Refer to Chapter 3, Section 6.

Electronic control unit

Note: *The fuel/ignition ECU and, where applicable, the automatic transmission ECU and EZ-129K ignition ECU, are all located in the ECU box, which is situated at the front right-hand side of the engine compartment in front of the cooling system expansion tank.*

Removal

54 Ensure that the ignition is switched off.
55 Clean off the top of the ECU box lid, to make sure no debris falls inside when it is removed. Release the catch on the side of the ECU module box lid. Lift off the lid and place it to one side **(see illustration)**.
56 Where applicable, pull the locking lever on top of the ECU forward, and withdraw the ECU from its location. The fuel system ECU is located in slot two, in the centre of the box **(see illustrations)**.

Refitting

57 Locate the ECU in the box, engaging it with the connector in the base.
58 Push the locking lever down to secure the ECU, and refit the box lid.

Outside temperature sensor

59 Refer to Chapter 12, Section 7.

11 Cruise control - general information

When fitted, the cruise control allows the vehicle to maintain a steady speed selected by the driver, regardless of gradients or prevailing winds.

The main components of the system are a control unit, a control switch, a vacuum servo and a vacuum pump. Brake and (when applicable) clutch pedal switches protect the engine against excessive speeds or loads should a pedal be depressed whilst the system is in use.

In operation, the driver accelerates to the desired speed, and then brings the system into use by means of the switch. The control unit then monitors vehicle speed (from the speedometer pulses) and opens or closes the throttle by means of the servo to maintain the set speed. If the switch is moved to OFF, or the brake or clutch pedal is depressed, the servo immediately closes the throttle. The set speed is stored in the control unit memory and the system can be reactivated by moving the switch to RESUME, provided that vehicle speed has not dropped below 25 mph.

The driver can override the cruise control for overtaking simply by depressing the

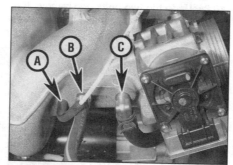

12.8 Typical inlet manifold vacuum connections

A *Inlet air temperature*   B *MAP sensor*
   control valve   C *Brake servo*

throttle pedal. When the pedal is released, the set speed will be resumed.

The cruise control cannot be engaged at speeds below 25 mph, and should not be used in slippery or congested conditions.

No specific removal, refitting or adjustment procedures were available at the time of writing. Problems should be referred to a Volvo dealer or other specialist.

12 Inlet manifold - removal and refitting

Note: *Observe the precautions in Section 1 before working on any component in the fuel system.*

Removal

1 Disconnect the battery negative lead.
2 Disconnect the air inlet duct from the throttle housing and, where applicable, release the turbocharger inlet ducting.
3 Where applicable, undo the screw and remove the cover over the accelerator cable drum and linkage. Release the outer cable retaining clip from the cable adjuster, and unhook the inner cable from the drum.
4 On early models, undo the bolts securing the two fuel pipe clamps to the engine, and remove the clamps.
5 Remove the fuel rail and injectors as described in Section 10.
6 Disconnect the wiring connector at the throttle housing.
7 Disconnect the idle air control valve hoses and the control valve wiring connector.
8 Disconnect the brake servo vacuum hose, the EGR hoses and other vacuum hoses (as applicable) from the front of the manifold **(see illustration)**.
9 Disconnect any remaining vacuum hoses which connect to services external to the manifold.
10 Release the wiring harness from the manifold cable clamps.
11 Undo the bolt securing the dipstick tube to the manifold, and the bolt securing the underside of the manifold to the steady bracket.

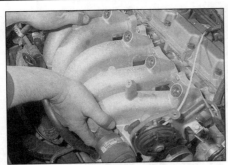

12.13 Removing the inlet manifold

12.18 Use the lower bolts to retain the gasket when refitting the manifold

12 Slacken the manifold lower retaining bolts by about two or three turns, and remove all the upper bolts.

13 Lift the manifold upwards, where applicable feed the crankcase ventilation hose through the ducts, then remove the manifold from the cylinder head **(see illustration)**. Note that the lower bolt holes are slotted, allowing the manifold to slide up and off, leaving them in position. If the manifold will not lift up, make sure that the gasket has not stuck to the manifold face; the gasket lower holes are not slotted, and it must remain on the engine to allow manifold removal.

14 With the manifold removed, take out the lower bolts and remove the gasket.

15 If required, the components remaining on the manifold can be removed with reference to earlier Sections of this Chapter.

16 On engines with a variable venturi inlet system, check the condition of the flap valves and spindles, ensuring smooth operation. If any problems are noticed in this area, entrust the necessary repair work to a Volvo dealer, as special gauges are required to install and set up the flap valve clearances.

Refitting

17 Refit by reversing the removal operations, using a new manifold gasket, and new seals and O-rings for the injectors if necessary.

18 Locate the manifold gasket on the cylinder head, and fit the lower manifold bolts a few turns, prior to placing the manifold in position **(see illustration)**. Where applicable, remember to feed the crankcase ventilation hose up between the second and third ducts. Tighten the bolts to the specified torque setting.

19 Where applicable, refit and adjust the accelerator cable as described in Section 4.

Notes

Chapter 4 Part B:
Exhaust and emission control systems

Contents

Degrees of difficulty

Easy, suitable for novice with little experience	Fairly easy, suitable for beginner with some experience	Fairly difficult, suitable for competent DIY mechanic	Difficult, suitable for experienced DIY mechanic	Very difficult, suitable for expert DIY or professional

Specifications

Torque wrench settings

	Nm	lbf ft
EGR valve bolts	50	37
Exhaust ball-and-socket clamp joint	30	22
Exhaust front pipe to manifold:		
Flexible lattice flange joint	25	18
Spring-loaded flange joint	10	7
Exhaust front pipe to turbocharger	30	22
Exhaust manifold heat shield bolts	15	11
Exhaust manifold to cylinder head	25	18
Heated oxygen sensor	45	33
Oil separator bolts	20	15
Turbocharger to manifold	25	18

1 General information

Exhaust system

The exhaust system comprises the exhaust manifold, a front section incorporating the catalytic converter and front pipe, and a rear section incorporating the intermediate pipe, silencer and tail pipe. The system is supported under the car on rubber mountings.

On turbo models, a water-cooled turbocharger is fitted to the exhaust manifold. Further information on the turbocharger is contained in Section 5.

Emission control systems

All models covered by this manual have various features built into the fuel and exhaust systems to help minimise harmful emissions. These features fall broadly into three categories; crankcase emission control, evaporative emission control, and exhaust emission control. The main features of these systems are as follows.

Crankcase emission control

To reduce the emissions of unburned hydrocarbons from the crankcase into the atmosphere, a Positive Crankcase Ventilation (PCV) system is used. The engine is sealed, and the blow-by gasses and oil vapour are drawn from inside the crankcase, through an oil separator, into the inlet tract, to be burned by the engine during normal combustion.

Under conditions of high manifold depression (idling, deceleration) the gasses will be sucked positively out of the crankcase. Under conditions of low manifold depression (acceleration, full-throttle running) the gasses are forced out of the crankcase by the (relatively) higher crankcase pressure; if the engine is worn, the raised crankcase pressure (due to increased blow-by) will cause some of the flow to return under all manifold conditions.

Evaporative emission control

The evaporative emission control (EVAP) system is used to minimise the escape of unburned hydrocarbons into the atmosphere. To do this, the fuel tank filler cap is sealed, and a carbon canister is used to collect and store petrol vapours generated in the tank. When the

engine is running, the vapours are cleared from the canister either via a vacuum operated, or by an ECU controlled electrically operated, EVAP valve, into the inlet tract, to be burned by the engine during normal combustion.

To ensure that the engine runs correctly when idling, the valve only opens when the engine is running under load; the valve then opens to allow the stored vapour to pass into the inlet tract.

As a safety measure, and to further reduce hydrocarbon emissions, a roll-over valve is incorporated into the system, which closes when the car tilts sideways by more than 45°. This prevents fuel leakage in the event of an accident.

Exhaust emission control

Oxygen sensor (or lambda sensor)

To minimise the amount of pollutants which escape into the atmosphere, all models are fitted with a catalytic converter in the exhaust system. The system is of the closed-loop type, in which a heated oxygen sensor (two sensors on later systems) in the exhaust system provides the fuel injection system ECU with constant feedback on the oxygen content of

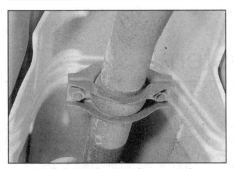

2.6 Exhaust front and rear section connecting ball-and-socket joint

the exhaust gasses. This enables the ECU to adjust the mixture by altering injector opening time, thus providing the best possible conditions for the converter to operate. The system functions in the following way.

The oxygen sensor (also known as a lambda sensor) has a built-in heating element, activated by the ECU to quickly bring the sensor's tip to an efficient operating temperature. The sensor's tip is sensitive to oxygen, and sends the control module a varying voltage depending on the amount of oxygen in the exhaust gasses; if the inlet air/fuel mixture is too rich, the exhaust gasses are low in oxygen, so the sensor sends a voltage signal proportional to the oxygen detected, the voltage altering as the mixture weakens and the amount of oxygen in the exhaust gasses rises. Peak conversion efficiency of all major pollutants occurs if the inlet air/fuel mixture is maintained at the chemically-correct ratio for complete combustion of petrol - 14.7 parts (by weight) of air to 1 part of fuel (the stoichiometric ratio). The sensor output voltage alters in a large step at this point, the ECU using the signal change as a reference point, and correcting the inlet air/fuel mixture accordingly, by altering the fuel injector opening time.

Exhaust gas recirculation (EGR) system

In addition to the catalytic converter, certain models are fitted with an exhaust gas recirculation (EGR) system. This system is designed to recirculate small quantities of exhaust gas into the inlet tract, and therefore into the combustion process. This reduces the level of oxides of nitrogen present in the final exhaust gas which is released into the atmosphere.

2.11 Exhaust silencer side mounting

The volume of exhaust gas recirculated is controlled by vacuum (supplied from the inlet manifold) via an EGR valve mounted on the inlet manifold. Before reaching the EGR valve, the vacuum from the manifold passes to an EGR controller. The purpose of which is to modify the vacuum supplied to the EGR valve according to engine operating conditions.

The EGR system is controlled by the fuel/ignition ECU, which receives information on engine operating parameters from its various sensors.

Secondary air injection system

A secondary air injection system is fitted to certain models intended for markets with stringent emission control regulations. The system is designed to inject fresh air into the exhaust passages in the cylinder head during the engine warm-up phase. This creates an afterburn effect, to reduce HC and CO emissions upstream of the catalytic converter.

The system comprises an electrically-driven air pump, solenoid, non-return valve, shut-off valve, air injection manifold and inter-connecting pipework.

Under the control of the fuel/ignition ECU, the system operates for under two minutes and starts approximately twenty seconds after the car has started to move.

2 Exhaust system - general information and component renewal

General information

1 The exhaust system consists of a front section which comprises a front pipe and catalytic converter, and a rear section comprising an intermediate pipe, silencer and tailpipe. The system is suspended from the underbody on rubber mountings, and bolted to the exhaust manifold at the front. A self-aligning ball-and-socket joint is used to connect the front and rear sections together. The front pipe-to-manifold connection is by either a spring-loaded flange joint, or a flange joint incorporating a flexible lattice type coupling.

2 The exhaust system should be examined for leaks, damage and security at regular intervals (see Chapter 1). To do this, apply the handbrake, and allow the engine to idle in a well-ventilated area. Lie down on each side of the car in turn, and check the full length of the system for leaks, while an assistant temporarily places a wad of cloth over the end of the tailpipe. If a leak is evident, stop the engine and use a proprietary repair kit to seal it. If the leak is excessive, or damage is evident, renew the section. Check the rubber mountings for deterioration, and renew them if necessary.

Removal

Front section

3 With the handbrake applied, jack up the front (and preferably the rear) of the car, and

support it on axle stands (see Jacking and vehicle support).

4 Disconnect the two heated oxygen sensor wiring connectors, and release the wiring from any cable-ties.

5 Undo the nuts securing the front pipe flange to the manifold. Recover the tension springs, where fitted. On some models, access may be improved from above after removing the heat shield over the manifold.

6 Undo the nuts and bolts at the ball-and-socket joint connecting the front and rear sections, and remove the clamps **(see illustration)**.

7 Where fitted, undo the four bolts and remove the stiffener plate from the underbody.

8 Separate the front pipe-to-manifold joint, and remove the front section from under the car.

Rear section

9 Chock the front wheels, then jack up the rear (and preferably the front) of the car, and support it on axle stands (see Jacking and vehicle support).

10 Undo the nuts and bolts at the ball-and-socket joint connecting the front and rear sections, and remove the clamps.

11 Release the tailpipe and silencer from their rubber mountings **(see illustration)**, and slide the rear section forward until the tailpipe is clear of the rear suspension. Remove the system from under the car.

Refitting

12 Refitting is a reversal of removal, bearing in mind the following points:

a) Use a new sealing ring or flange gasket, as applicable, on the front pipe-to-manifold joint.

b) When refitting the front section, loosely attach the front pipe to the manifold, and the catalytic converter to the intermediate pipe. Align the system, then tighten the front pipe-to-manifold nuts first, followed by the intermediate pipe clamp nuts.

c) Ensure that there is a minimum clearance of 20 mm between the exhaust system and underbody/suspension components.

3 Catalytic converter - general information and precautions

The catalytic converter is a reliable and simple device, which needs no maintenance in itself, but there are some facts of which an owner should be aware if the converter is to function properly for its full service life.

a) DO NOT use leaded petrol - the lead will coat the precious metals, reducing their converting efficiency, and will eventually destroy the converter.

b) Always keep the ignition and fuel systems well-maintained in accordance with the manufacturer's schedule (see Chapter 1).

c) If the engine develops a misfire, do not drive the vehicle at all (or at least as little as possible) until the fault is cured.

d) DO NOT push - or tow-start the vehicle - this will soak the catalytic converter in unburned fuel, causing it to overheat when the engine does start.

e) DO NOT switch off the ignition at high engine speeds, ie do not blip the throttle immediately before switching off.

f) DO NOT use fuel or engine oil additives - these may contain substances harmful to the catalytic converter.

g) DO NOT continue to use the vehicle if the engine burns oil to the extent of leaving a visible trail of blue smoke.

h) Remember that the catalytic converter operates at very high temperatures. DO NOT, therefore, park the vehicle in dry undergrowth, over long grass or piles of dead leaves, after a long run.

i) Remember that the catalytic converter is FRAGILE. Do not strike it with tools during servicing work.

j) In some cases, a sulphurous smell (like that of rotten eggs) may be noticed from the exhaust. This is common to many catalytic converter-equipped vehicles. Once the vehicle has covered a few thousand miles, the problem should disappear - in the meantime, try changing the brand of petrol used.

k) The catalytic converter used on a well-maintained and well-driven vehicle should last for between 50 000 and 100 000 miles. If the converter is no longer effective, it must be renewed.

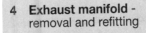

4 Exhaust manifold - removal and refitting

Removal

Left-hand drive models

1 Disconnect the battery negative lead.
2 On turbo models, remove the turbocharger as described in Section 6.
3 With the handbrake applied, jack up the front of the car and support it on axle stands (see *Jacking and vehicle support*).
4 Undo the nuts securing the exhaust front pipe flange to the manifold. Recover the tension springs, where fitted. On some models, access may be better from above after removing the heat shield over the manifold.
5 Remove the air cleaner warm-air inlet duct from the manifold heat shield.
6 Undo the nuts securing the manifold to the cylinder head.
7 Move the manifold rearwards off the cylinder head studs, then separate the front pipe flange joint. Twist the manifold through 90° to the right, and manipulate it out from the rear of the engine. On cars so equipped, take care not to

4.15 Removing the engine steady bar bracket

damage the air conditioning high pressure switch as the manifold is removed.
8 Recover the front pipe flange joint gasket or sealing ring, and the five individual manifold to cylinder head gaskets.

Right-hand drive models

9 Disconnect the battery negative lead.
10 Drain the cooling system as described in Chapter 1.
11 On turbo models, remove the turbocharger as described in Section 6.
12 Refer to Part A of this Chapter and remove the air cleaner assembly and the warm-air inlet duct from the manifold heat shield.
13 Undo the nut and remove the bolt securing the upper engine steady bar to the bracket on the engine. Note that a new nut and bolt will be required for refitting.
14 Undo the nut securing the other end of the engine steady bar to the bulkhead bracket. Swing the steady bar to one side. Note that a new nut and bolt will be required for refitting.
15 Undo the upper nut and two lower bolts securing the steady bar bracket to the side of the engine. Note the location of the wiring connector support plates, and move them to one side. Release all the cable-ties and switch wiring connectors as necessary to allow the bracket to be removed, then prise the bracket off its locating dowels on the engine **(see illustration)**. It will be tight on the dowels, and a certain amount of levering will be necessary.
16 Disconnect the two heater hoses at the pipe stubs on the side of the engine.
17 Undo the bolts securing the heat shield to the exhaust manifold, and manoeuvre the heat shield out from behind the engine. Note that clearance is **very** limited, and the shield will have to be turned and twisted until the right position is found for its removal **(see illustration)**.
18 With the handbrake applied, jack up the front of the car and support it on axle stands (see *Jacking and vehicle support*).
19 Undo the nuts securing the exhaust front pipe flange to the manifold. Recover the tension springs, where fitted.
20 Lower the car to the ground.
21 Undo the nuts securing the manifold to the cylinder head.
22 Move the manifold rearwards off the cylinder head studs, then separate the front

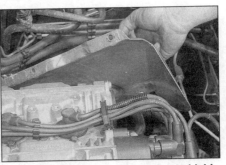

4.17 Manipulate the exhaust heat shield out from behind the engine

pipe flange joint. Twist the manifold through 90° to the right, and manipulate it out from the rear of the engine **(see illustration)**. Again, clearance is very limited, and considerable manoeuvring will be necessary. On cars so equipped, take care not to damage the air conditioning high-pressure switch as the manifold is removed.
23 Recover the front pipe flange joint gasket or sealing ring, and the five individual manifold-to-cylinder head gaskets.

Refitting

All models

24 Refitting is a reversal of removal, bearing in mind the following points:

a) Return any studs that were removed with their nuts back to the cylinder head, sealing them with suitable thread sealer. It may be advisable to renew the studs and nuts as a set, if they are badly corroded.

b) Thoroughly clean the manifold and cylinder head mating faces prior to refitting.

c) Use new manifold gaskets, and a new sealing ring or flange gasket as applicable on the front pipe-to-manifold joint.

d) Tighten all nuts and bolts to the specified torque, then further through the specified angle, where applicable. Note that angle-tightened nuts/bolts must always be renewed. Refer to Chapter 2A Specifications for the engine mounting torques.

e) On right-hand drive models, refill the cooling system as described in Chapter 1 on completion.

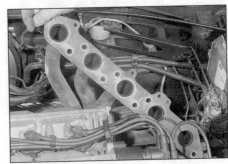

4.22 Exhaust manifold removal

4B

6.6 Turbocharger upper coolant return pipe and oil inlet pipe unions (arrowed)

5 Turbocharger - general information and precautions

General information

A water-cooled turbocharger is used on all turbo models covered by this manual. The turbocharger increases the efficiency of the engine by raising the pressure in the inlet manifold above atmospheric pressure. Instead of the air/fuel mixture being simply sucked into the cylinders, it is actively forced in.

Energy for the operation of the turbocharger comes from the exhaust gas. The gas flows through a specially-shaped housing (the turbine housing) and in so doing spins the turbine wheel. The turbine wheel is attached to a shaft, at the other end of which is another vaned wheel known as the compressor wheel. The compressor wheel spins in its own housing, and compresses the inducted air on the way to the inlet manifold.

After leaving the turbocharger, the compressed air passes through an intercooler, which is an air-to-air heat exchanger mounted with the radiator. Here the air gives up heat which it acquired when being compressed. This temperature reduction improves engine efficiency and reduces the risk of detonation.

Boost pressure (the pressure in the inlet manifold) is limited by a wastegate, which diverts the exhaust gas away from the turbine wheel in response to a pressure-sensitive actuator. The actuator is controlled by the turbocharger valve, under signals from the fuel system electronic control unit.

The turbo shaft is pressure-lubricated by means of a feed pipe from the engine's main oil gallery. The shaft floats on a cushion of oil. A drain pipe returns the oil to the sump.

Water cooling keeps the operating temperature of the turbo bearings lower than would be possible with an air-cooled unit. Water continues to circulate by convection after the engine has stopped, so cooling the turbocharger if it is hot after a long run.

Precautions

The turbocharger operates at extremely high speeds and temperatures. Certain precautions must be observed to avoid premature failure of the turbo, or injury to the operator:

a) *Do not operate the turbo with any parts exposed. Foreign objects falling onto the rotating vanes could cause extensive damage and (if ejected) personal injury.*

b) *Do not race the engine immediately after start-up, especially if it is cold. Give the oil a few seconds to circulate.*

c) *Always allow the engine to return to idle speed before switching it off - do not blip the throttle and switch off, as this will leave the turbo spinning without lubrication.*

d) *Allow the engine to idle for several minutes before switching off after a high-speed run.*

e) *Observe the recommended intervals for oil and filter changing, and use a reputable oil of the specified quality. Neglect of oil changing, or use of inferior oil, can cause carbon formation on the turbo shaft and subsequent failure.*

6 Turbocharger - removal and refitting

Removal

1 Disconnect the battery negative lead.
2 Drain the cooling system as described in Chapter 1.
3 Undo the bolts and remove the heat shield over the turbocharger.
4 Disconnect the upper air inlet pipe and rubber hose from the turbocharger inlet.
5 Disconnect the fresh air inlet hose from the side of the turbocharger and remove the second heat shield.
6 Undo the upper coolant return pipe and oil inlet pipe unions, and recover the seals **(see illustration)**.
7 Apply the handbrake, then jack up the front of the car and support it on axle stands (see *Jacking and vehicle support*).

8 Undo the bolt and remove the clamp bracket securing the oil feed and return pipes **(see illustration)**.
9 Undo the two bolts and separate the oil return pipe flange joint from the base of the turbocharger.
10 Undo the two lower nuts securing the turbocharger to the exhaust manifold, and the single lower nut securing the unit to the exhaust front pipe.
11 Undo the bolt securing the support bracket to the turbocharger, then lower the car to the ground.
12 Undo the two remaining nuts securing the front pipe to the turbocharger.
13 Undo the coolant inlet pipe union, and recover the seals.
14 Undo the turbocharger-to-manifold upper nuts, then carefully ease the unit off the manifold studs.
15 Lift the unit upwards, and disconnect the boost pressure hose (marked red), the bypass valve hose (marked white) and the pressure regulator hose (marked yellow). Note the locations of these hoses on the turbocharger, to avoid confusion when refitting **(see illustration)**.
16 Remove the turbocharger from the car, and recover the gaskets.

Refitting

17 Refitting is a reversal of removal, bearing in mind the following points:

a) *Return any studs that were removed with their nuts back to their original locations, sealing them with suitable thread sealer. If any of the studs are badly corroded, it may be advisable to renew all studs and nuts as a set.*

b) *Thoroughly clean the turbocharger and manifold mating faces prior to refitting.*

c) *Use a new manifold gasket, and use new seals on all disturbed unions..*

d) *Tighten all nuts and bolts to the specified torque.*

e) *Refill the cooling system as described in Chapter 1 on completion.*

6.8 Turbocharger pipe clamp bracket bolt, oil return pipe flange, support bracket, and manifold flange bolts (arrowed)

6.15 Disconnect the turbocharger boost pressure hose (red), the bypass valve hose (white) and the pressure regulator hose (yellow)

7 Crankcase emission control system - checking and component renewal

Checking

1 The components of this system require no attention other than to check that the hoses are clear and undamaged, and to renew the flame trap at regular intervals.

Component renewal

Flame trap (non-turbo models only)

2 Undo the securing screw, and remove the cover over the accelerator cable drum and linkage.
3 Slacken the hose clip, and detach the air outlet duct at the air cleaner cover.
4 Bend the hose forward for access to the flame trap, which is located in the duct elbow, in front of the throttle housing.
5 Turn the flame trap casing 15 mm to the left to release the bayonet fastening. Withdraw the casing, but do not disconnect the ventilation hoses **(see illustration)**.
6 Remove the flame trap from the casing, and clean the casing thoroughly. It is advisable to blow through all the hoses with compressed air, and to change the engine oil whenever the flame trap is renewed.
7 Fit the new flame trap using a reversal of the removal procedure.

Oil separator

8 The oil separator is located on the front facing side of the cylinder block, below the inlet manifold **(see illustration)**.
9 Remove the inlet manifold as described in Part A of this Chapter.
10 Remove the clips securing the connecting hoses to the cylinder block connecting sleeves. If the clips are in less than perfect condition, obtain new clips for reassembly.
11 Undo the two bolts and remove the unit from the engine.
12 Refit the oil separator using a reversal of removal. Refit the inlet manifold as described in Part A of this Chapter.

8 Evaporative emission control system - checking and component renewal

Checking

1 Poor idle, stalling and poor driveability can be caused by an inoperative canister vacuum valve, a damaged canister, split or cracked hoses, or hoses connected to the wrong fittings. Check the fuel filler cap for a damaged or deformed gasket.
2 Fuel loss or fuel odour can be caused by liquid fuel leaking from fuel lines, a cracked or damaged canister, an inoperative canister vacuum valve, and disconnected, misrouted, kinked or damaged vapour or control hoses.

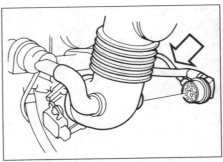

7.5 Removing the flame trap. Do not disconnect the hoses (arrowed)

3 Inspect each hose attached to the canister for kinks, leaks and cracks along its entire length. Repair or renew as necessary.
4 Inspect the canister. If it is cracked or damaged, renew it. Look for fuel leaking from the bottom of the canister. If fuel is leaking, renew the canister, and check the hoses and hose routing.

Component renewal

Carbon canister

5 The canister is located under the left-hand wheel arch at the front.
6 Note the location of the vacuum and fuel vent hose connections at the canister and carefully disconnect them.
7 Release the canister retaining strap and remove the unit from its location **(see illustration)**.
8 Refitting is a reversal of removal.

Vacuum (EVAP) valve

9 The EVAP valve is either mounted on the top of the carbon canister (vacuum-operated valve) or remotely-sited in the fuel vapour line to the canister (electronically-operated valve).
10 The vacuum-operated valve is an integral part of the carbon canister, and is renewed with that component as a unit.
11 The electronically-operated valve can be renewed by tracing back the vapour line from the canister to the valve, disconnecting the hoses and wiring connector, and removing the valve from its location.
12 Refitting is a reversal of removal.

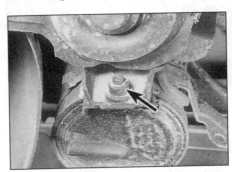

8.7 EVAP carbon canister retaining strap bolt (arrowed)

7.8 Oil separator location at the front of the engine

9 Exhaust emission control systems - checking and component renewal

Checking

1 Checking of the system as a whole entails a close visual inspection of all hoses, pipes and connections for condition and security. Apart from this, any known or suspected faults should be attended to by a Volvo dealer. At the time of writing, no specific information was available on the secondary air injection system. Detailed checks in the event of a fault in the system, or component renewal, should also be entrusted to a dealer.

Component renewal

Heated oxygen sensor (lambda sensor)

Note: *The sensor is delicate, and will not work if it is dropped or knocked, if its power supply is disrupted, or if any cleaning materials are used on it.*
2 Apply the handbrake, then jack up the front of the car and support it on axle stands (see *Jacking and vehicle support*).
3 Disconnect the two heated oxygen sensor wiring connectors, and release the wiring from any cable-ties **(see illustration)**.
4 Unscrew the sensor from the exhaust system front pipe or catalytic converter, and collect the sealing washer (where fitted) **(see illustrations)**.

9.3 Two exhaust gas sensor wiring connectors at rear of engine compartment

9.4a Exhaust gas oxygen sensor location in front pipe, just below manifold

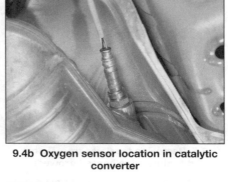

9.4b Oxygen sensor location in catalytic converter

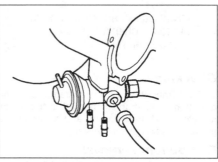

9.21 EGR valve connections and mountings

5 On refitting, clean the sealing washer (where fitted) and renew it if it is damaged or worn. Apply a smear of anti-seize compound to the sensor's threads, then refit the sensor, tightening it to the specified torque. Reconnect the wiring and secure with cable-ties where applicable.

Catalytic converter

6 The catalytic converter is part of the exhaust system front section. Refer to Sections 2 and 3 for renewal procedures and additional information.

EGR controller

7 The EGR controller is mounted on the relay panel above the radiator.
8 Disconnect the two hoses at the EGR controller, noting their locations.
9 Undo the outer bolt from the EGR controller mounting bracket.
10 Remove the controller and bracket, disconnect the wiring connector, then remove the controller from the bracket.
11 Refitting is a reversal of removal.

EGR valve

12 Disconnect the battery negative lead.
13 Undo the screw and remove the cover over the accelerator cable drum.
14 Detach the air cleaner inlet duct and the ECU module box air duct from each side of the radiator fan shroud.
15 Undo the two bolts each side securing the fan shroud and relay carrier to the front body panel.
16 Lift up the relay carrier and disconnect the fan wiring connectors, EGR controller wiring connector and EGR vacuum hoses. Lay the carrier to one side, clear of the fan shroud.
17 Lift the shroud upwards to release the two lower locating pegs, and remove the shroud and fan from the car.
18 Disconnect the air inlet duct at the throttle housing, and the crankcase ventilation and carbon canister hoses.
19 Remove the starter motor as described in Chapter 5A.
20 Disconnect the EGR temperature sensor

wiring at the connector, and release the connector from its clip.
21 Disconnect the EGR pipe from the valve (see illustration).
22 Undo the two bolts, remove the valve and recover the gasket.
23 If required, the EGR temperature sensor can be unscrewed from the side of the valve.
24 Refitting is a reversal of removal, but use a new gasket and tighten all nuts and bolts to the specified torque.

Secondary air injection system

25 To remove the air pump fitted in the air inlet duct, disconnect the wiring plug and the air hose, then remove the securing screws and withdraw the pump (see illustration).
26 To remove the secondary air injection manifold, first remove the fuel rail as described in Chapter 4A, Section 10. Disconnect the air supply hose from the manifold, then pull the manifold from its location (see illustrations).
27 Refitting the secondary air injection system components is a reversal of removal.

9.25 Secondary air injection pump securing screws (arrowed)

9.26a Disconnect the air supply hose . . .

9.26b . . . then pull the secondary air injection manifold from its location

Chapter 5 Part A:
Starting and charging systems

Contents

Degrees of difficulty

Easy, suitable for novice with little experience	**Fairly easy,** suitable for beginner with some experience	**Fairly difficult,** suitable for competent DIY mechanic	**Difficult,** suitable for experienced DIY mechanic	**Very difficult,** suitable for expert DIY or professional

Specifications

System type .... 12-volt, negative earth

Battery
Type .... Low-maintenance or maintenance-free sealed for life
Capacity .... 45 to 60 Ah (depending on model)
Charge condition:
    Poor .... 12.5 volts
    Normal .... 12.6 volts
    Good .... 12.7 volts

Alternator
Type .... Bosch or Nippon-Denso

Starter motor
Type .... Bosch

Torque wrench setting	**Nm**	**lbf ft**
Starter motor mounting bolts	40	30

---

1 General information and precautions

General information

The engine electrical system consists mainly of the charging and starting systems. Because of their engine-related functions, these components are covered separately from the body electrical devices such as the lights, instruments, etc (which are covered in Chapter 12). Information on the ignition system is covered in Part B of this Chapter.

The electrical system is of the 12-volt negative earth type.

The battery is of the low-maintenance or maintenance-free (sealed for life) type, and is charged by the alternator, which is belt-driven from the crankshaft pulley.

The starter motor is of the pre-engaged type, incorporating an integral solenoid. On starting, the solenoid moves the drive pinion into engagement with the flywheel ring gear before the starter motor is energised. Once the engine has started, a one-way clutch prevents the motor armature being driven by the engine until the pinion disengages from the flywheel.

Further details of the various systems are given in the relevant Sections of this Chapter. While some repair procedures are given, the usual course of action is to renew the component concerned. The owner whose interest extends beyond mere component renewal should obtain a copy of the *Automobile Electrical & Electronic Systems Manual*, available from the publishers of this manual.

Precautions

⚠️ *Warning: It is necessary to take extra care when working on the electrical system to avoid damage to semi-conductor devices (diodes and transistors), and to avoid the risk of personal injury. In addition to the precautions given in Safety first!, observe the following when working on the system:*

Always remove rings, watches, etc before working on the electrical system. Even with the battery disconnected, capacitive discharge could occur if a component's live terminal is earthed through a metal object. This could cause a shock or nasty burn.

Do not reverse the battery connections. Components such as the alternator, electronic control units, or any other components having semi-conductor circuitry could be irreparably damaged.

Never disconnect the battery terminals, the alternator, any electrical wiring or any test instruments when the engine is running.

Do not allow the engine to turn the alternator when the alternator is not connected.

Never test for alternator output by 'flashing' the output lead to earth.

Always ensure that the battery negative lead is disconnected when working on the electrical system.

If the engine is being started using jump leads and a slave battery, connect the batteries *positive-to-positive* and *negative-to-negative* (see *Jump starting*). This also applies when connecting a battery charger.

Never use an ohmmeter of the type incorporating a hand-cranked generator for circuit or continuity testing.

Before using electric-arc welding equipment on the car, *disconnect the battery, alternator and components such as the electronic control units* (where applicable) to protect them from the risk of damage.

Caution: Certain radio/cassettes fitted as standard equipment by Volvo have a built-in security code, to deter thieves. If the power source to the unit is cut, the anti-theft system will activate. Even if the power source is immediately reconnected, the radio/cassette unit will not function until the correct security code has been entered. The radio code should be supplied with the car when new, and may be found with the handbook in the glovebox. If you do not know the correct security code for the radio/cassette unit, do not disconnect the battery negative terminal, or remove the radio/cassette unit from the vehicle. Refer to your Volvo dealer for further information on whether the unit fitted to your car has a security code.

2 Battery - testing and charging

Standard and low-maintenance battery - testing

1 If the vehicle covers a small annual mileage, it is worthwhile checking the specific gravity of the electrolyte every three months to determine the state of charge of the battery. Use a hydrometer to make the check, and compare the results with the following table. Note that the specific gravity readings assume an electrolyte temperature of 15°C (60°F); for every 10°C (18°F) below 15°C (60°F) subtract 0.007. For every 10°C (18°F) above 15°C (60°F) add 0.007.

	Above 25°C	Below 25°C
Fully charged	1.210 to 1.230	1.270 to 1.290
70% charged	1.170 to 1.190	1.230 to 1.250
Discharged	1.050 to 1.070	1.110 to 1.130

2 If the battery condition is suspect, first check the specific gravity of electrolyte in each cell. A variation of 0.040 or more between any cells indicates loss of electrolyte or deterioration of the internal plates.
3 If the specific gravity variation is 0.040 or more, the battery should be renewed. If the cell variation is satisfactory but the battery is discharged, it should be charged as described later in this Section.

Maintenance-free battery - testing

4 In cases where a sealed for life maintenance-free battery is fitted, topping-up and testing of the electrolyte in each cell may not be possible (see Chapter 1, Section 10). The condition of the battery can therefore only be tested using a battery condition indicator or a voltmeter.
5 Certain models my be fitted with a maintenance-free battery, with a built-in charge condition indicator. The indicator is located in the top of the battery casing, and indicates the condition of the battery from its colour. The charge conditions denoted by the colour of the indicator should be printed on a label attached to the battery - if not, consult a Volvo dealer or automotive electrician for advice.
6 If testing the battery using a voltmeter, connect the voltmeter across the battery and note the voltage. The test is only accurate if the battery has not been subjected to any kind of charge for the previous six hours. If this is not the case, switch on the headlights for 30 seconds, then wait four to five minutes before testing the battery after switching off the headlights. All other electrical circuits must be switched off, so check that the doors and tailgate are fully shut when making the test.
7 If the voltage reading is less than 12.2 volts, then the battery is discharged, whilst a reading of 12.2 to 12.4 volts indicates a partially-discharged condition.

8 If the battery is to be charged, remove it from the vehicle and charge it as described later in this Section.

Standard and low-maintenance battery - charging

Note: *The following is intended as a guide only. Always refer to the manufacturer's recommendations (often printed on a label attached to the battery) before charging a battery.*

9 Charge the battery at a rate equivalent to 10% of the battery capacity (eg for a 45 Ah battery charge at 4.5 A) and continue to charge the battery at this rate until no further rise in specific gravity is noted over a four-hour period.
10 Alternatively, a trickle charger charging at the rate of 1.5 amps can safely be used overnight.
11 Specially rapid boost charges which are claimed to restore the power of the battery in 1 to 2 hours are not recommended, as they can cause serious damage to the battery plates through overheating. If the battery is completely flat, recharging should take at least 24 hours.
12 While charging the battery, note that the temperature of the electrolyte should never exceed 37.8°C (100°F).

Maintenance-free battery - charging

Note: *The following is intended as a guide only. Always refer to the manufacturer's recommendations (often printed on a label attached to the battery) before charging a battery.*

13 This battery type takes considerably longer to fully recharge than the standard type, the time taken being dependent on the extent of discharge, but it can take anything up to three days.
14 A constant voltage type charger is required, to be set, when connected, to 13.9 to 14.9 volts with a charger current below 25 amps. Using this method, the battery should be useable within three hours, giving a voltage reading of 12.5 volts, but this is for a partially-discharged battery and, as mentioned, full charging can take far longer.
15 If the battery is to be charged from a fully-discharged state (condition reading less than 12.2 volts), have it recharged by your Volvo dealer or local automotive electrician, as the charge rate is higher, and constant supervision during charging is necessary.

3 Battery - removal and refitting

Note: *Make sure that you have a copy of the radio/cassette unit security code number before disconnecting the battery. Also, ensure that the unit is switched off before battery disconnection, to avoid damage to the radio microprocessor circuitry.*

Removal

1 The battery is located in the front left-hand corner of the engine compartment. Where applicable, unclip and remove the cover from the top of the battery.

2 Slacken the clamp bolt and disconnect the clamp from the battery negative (earth) terminal.

3 Remove the insulation cover (where fitted) and disconnect the positive terminal lead(s) in the same way **(see illustration)**.

4 Unscrew the bolt and remove the battery retaining clamp bolt. Lift the battery out of the engine compartment.

Refitting

5 Refitting is a reversal of removal, but smear petroleum jelly on the terminals when reconnecting the leads, and always reconnect the positive lead first, and the negative lead last. Where applicable, refit the battery cover.

4 Charging system - testing

Note: *Refer to the warnings given in Safety first! and in Section 1 of this Chapter before starting work.*

1 If the ignition/no-charge warning light fails to illuminate when the ignition is switched on, first check the alternator wiring connections for security **(see illustration)**. If satisfactory, check that the warning light bulb has not blown, and that the bulbholder is secure in its location in the instrument panel. If the light still fails to illuminate, check the continuity of the warning light feed wire from the alternator to the bulbholder. If all is satisfactory, the alternator is at fault and should be renewed or taken to an auto-electrician for testing and repair.

2 If the ignition warning light illuminates when the engine is running, stop the engine and check that the drivebelt is correctly tensioned (see Chapter 1) and that the alternator connections are secure. If all is so far satisfactory, have the alternator checked by an auto-electrician for testing and repair.

3 If the alternator output is suspect even though the warning light functions correctly, the regulated voltage may be checked as follows.

4 Connect a voltmeter across the battery terminals and start the engine.

5 Increase the engine speed until the voltmeter reading remains steady; the reading should be between 13.5 and 14.8 volts.

6 Switch on as many electrical accessories (eg, the headlights, heated rear window and heater blower) as possible, and check that the alternator maintains the regulated voltage between 13.5 and 14.8 volts.

7 If the regulated voltage is not as stated, the fault may be due to worn brushes, weak brush springs, a faulty voltage regulator, a faulty

3.3 Lift up the cover for access to the battery positive terminal clamp

diode, a severed phase winding, or worn or damaged slip rings. The alternator should be renewed or taken to an auto-electrician for testing and repair.

5 Alternator - removal and refitting

Removal

1 Disconnect the battery negative lead.

2 Remove the auxiliary drivebelt as described in Chapter 1.

3 Disconnect the wiring multi-plugs and the leads from the terminal studs at the rear of the alternator **(see illustration)**.

4 Unscrew and remove the mounting nuts and bolts at the front and rear, and lift the alternator from its mounting bracket.

Refitting

5 Refitting is a reversal of removal. Refit the auxiliary drivebelt as described in Chapter 1.

6 Alternator - testing and overhaul

If the alternator is thought to be suspect, it should be removed from the vehicle and taken to an auto-electrician for testing. Most auto-electricians will be able to supply and fit brushes at a reasonable cost. However, check on the cost of repairs before proceeding, as it

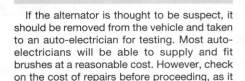

5.3 Typical alternator wiring connections (A) and rear mounting bolts (B)

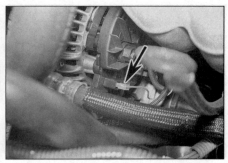

4.1 Warning light wire connection (arrowed) on rear of alternator

may prove more economical to obtain a new or exchange alternator.

7 Starting system - testing

Note: *Refer to the precautions given in Safety first! and in Section 1 of this Chapter before starting work.*

1 If the starter motor fails to operate when the ignition key is turned to the appropriate position, the following possible causes may be to blame:

a) *The battery is faulty.*

b) *The electrical connections between the switch, solenoid, battery and starter motor are somewhere failing to pass the necessary current from the battery through the starter to earth.*

c) *The solenoid is faulty.*

d) *The starter motor is mechanically or electrically defective.*

2 To check the battery, switch on the headlights. If they dim after a few seconds, this indicates that the battery is discharged - recharge (see Section 2) or renew the battery. If the headlights glow brightly, operate the ignition switch and observe the lights. If they dim, then this indicates that current is reaching the starter motor, therefore the fault must lie in the starter motor. If the lights continue to glow brightly (and no clicking sound can be heard from the starter motor solenoid), this indicates that there is a fault in the circuit or solenoid - see following paragraphs. If the starter motor turns slowly when operated, but the battery is in good condition, then this indicates that either the starter motor is faulty, or there is considerable resistance somewhere in the circuit.

3 If a fault in the circuit is suspected, disconnect the battery leads (including the earth connection to the body), the starter/ solenoid wiring and the engine/transmission earth strap. Thoroughly clean the connections, and reconnect the leads and wiring, then use a voltmeter or test light to check that full battery voltage is available at the battery positive lead connection to the solenoid, and that the earth is sound. Smear

5A

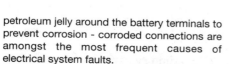

8.2 Wiring connections at the rear of the starter solenoid

8.3 Starter motor rear support bracket retaining bolt (arrowed)

8.4 Removing the starter motor from the bellhousing. Note the location of the dowel (arrowed)

petroleum jelly around the battery terminals to prevent corrosion - corroded connections are amongst the most frequent causes of electrical system faults.

4 If the battery and all connections are in good condition, check the circuit by disconnecting the wire from the solenoid blade terminal. Connect a voltmeter or test light between the wire end and a good earth (such as the battery negative terminal), and check that the wire is live when the ignition switch is turned to the start position. If it is, then the circuit is sound - if not, the circuit wiring can be checked as described in Chapter 12.

5 The solenoid contacts can be checked by connecting a voltmeter or test light between the battery positive feed connection on the starter side of the solenoid, and earth. When the ignition switch is turned to the start position, there should be a reading or lighted bulb, as applicable. If there is no reading or lighted bulb, the solenoid is faulty and should be renewed.

6 If the circuit and solenoid are proved sound, the fault must lie in the starter motor. In this event, it may be possible to have the starter motor overhauled by a specialist, but check on the cost of spares before proceeding, as it may prove more economical to obtain a new or exchange motor.

8 Starter motor - removal and refitting

Removal

1 Disconnect the battery negative lead.
2 Disconnect the wiring from the starter motor solenoid **(see illustration)**.
3 Unbolt the starter motor rear support bracket from the engine **(see illustration)**.
4 Undo the bolts securing the starter motor to the transmission bellhousing, and manoeuvre the unit from its location. Note the position of the locating dowel, and ensure it is in place when refitting **(see illustration)**.

Refitting

5 Refitting is a reversal of removal. Tighten all fixings securely.

9 Starter motor - testing and overhaul

If the starter motor is thought to be suspect, it should be removed from the vehicle and taken to an auto-electrician for testing. Most auto-electricians will be able to supply and fit brushes at a reasonable cost. However, check on the cost of repairs before proceeding, as it may prove more economical to obtain a new or exchange motor.

10 Ignition switch - removal and refitting

Refer to Chapter 12, Section 4.

Chapter 5 Part B:
Ignition system

Contents

Degrees of difficulty

Easy, suitable for novice with little experience		Fairly easy, suitable for beginner with some experience		Fairly difficult, suitable for competent DIY mechanic		Difficult, suitable for experienced DIY mechanic		Very difficult, suitable for expert DIY or professional	

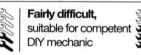

Specifications

General
System type:

B5202 S and B5252 S (10-valve) engines	Fenix 5.2 engine management system
B5254 S engines	EZ-129K ignition system with Bosch LH3.2-Jetronic fuel injection system, or Motronic 4.4/Denso engine management system (according to market/territory)
All other engines:	
Up to 1998 model year	Bosch Motronic 4.3 or 4.4 engine management system
1999 model year onwards	Bosch ME7 distributorless engine management system
Firing order	1-2-4-5-3 (No. 1 cylinder at timing belt end of engine)

Spark plugs
Type . . . .   See Chapter 1 Specifications

Ignition timing*

B5202 S and B5252 S (10-valve) engines	10° ± 2° BTDC @ 850 rpm
B5234 S engines	5° ± 2° BTDC @ 850 rpm
B5254 S engines:	
With EZ-129K ignition system	10° ± 2° BTDC @ 850 rpm
With Motronic engine management system	5° ± 2° BTDC @ 850 rpm
All other engines	6° ± 2° BTDC @ 850 rpm

Values given are for checking purposes only - no adjustment is possible

Ignition coil

Primary resistance	0.5 to 1.5 ohms
Secondary resistance	8000 to 9000 ohms

Torque wrench setting

	Nm	lbf ft
Knock sensors	20	15

1.9a Prise up the panel in the storage compartment to access the OBD terminal

1 General information

The ignition system is responsible for igniting the compressed fuel/air charge in each cylinder in turn at precisely the right moment for the prevailing engine speed and load. This is achieved by using a sophisticated engine management system, which utilises computer technology and electro-magnetic circuitry to achieve the required ignition characteristics.

Several systems are used on the models covered by this manual, dependent on engine size and type. On the Fenix 5.2 and Bosch Motronic/ME7 systems, a single electronic control unit (ECU) is used to control the complete engine management system, integrating the fuel and ignition functions. The only difference on the LH3.2-Jetronic system is that two ECUs are used, one for the fuel system and one for the EZ-129 K ignition system. However, both ECUs work in conjunction with each other to form one inter-related engine management package. The operation of all systems in terms of ignition control is virtually identical, with only minor differences in component arrangement.

The main components of the ignition side of the system are the ECU, the ignition power stage, the ignition coil, the distributor, the spark plugs and HT leads, and the various sensors that supply information to the ECU on engine operating conditions. The operation of the system is as follows.

1.9b Connecting a fault code reader to the OBD terminal

The ECU computes engine speed and crankshaft position from a series of holes drilled in the periphery of the engine flywheel, with an RPM sensor whose inductive head runs just above the drilled flywheel periphery. As the crankshaft rotates, the land (or 'teeth') between the drilled holes in the flywheel, passes the RPM sensor, which transmits a pulse to the ECU every time a tooth passes it. There is one missing hole in the flywheel periphery, which allows the land (or tooth) at that point to be twice as wide as the others. The ECU recognises the absence of a pulse from the RPM sensor at this point, and uses it to establish the TDC position for No 1 piston. The time interval between pulses, and the location of the missing pulse, allow the ECU to accurately determine the position of the crankshaft and its speed. The camshaft position sensor enhances this information by detecting whether a particular piston is on an inlet or an exhaust cycle.

Information on engine load is supplied to the ECU via the mass air flow sensor (or via the manifold absolute pressure sensor and inlet air temperature sensor on the Fenix 5.2 system). The engine load is determined by computation based on the quantity of air being drawn into the engine. Further information is sent to the ECU from two knock sensors. These sensors are sensitive to vibration, and detect the knocking which occurs when the engine starts to pink (pre-ignite). Sensors monitoring coolant temperature, throttle position, road speed, automatic transmission gear position (where applicable) and air conditioning system operation, provide additional input signals to the ECU on vehicle operating conditions.

From this constantly-changing data, the ECU selects, and if necessary modifies, a particular ignition advance setting from a map of ignition characteristics stored in its memory.

With the firing point established, the ECU sends a signal to the ignition power stage, which is an electronic switch controlling the current to the ignition coil primary windings. On receipt of the signal from the ECU, the power stage interrupts the primary current to the ignition coil, which induces a high-tension voltage in the coil secondary windings. This HT voltage is passed to the distributor cap, and then on to the spark plugs, via the distributor rotor arm and HT leads. The cycle is then repeated many times a second for each cylinder in turn.

The Motronic ME7 system does away with the conventional distributor cap, rotor arm and HT leads. Instead, each cylinder has its own small ignition coil, attached directly to each spark plug, and wired back to the ECU. When the firing point has been established, the ECU induces the HT voltage in the next coil in the firing order. In this way, there are no moving parts to fail or wear out - the system is also theoretically less susceptible to starting problems in damp conditions.

In the event of a fault in the system due to loss of a signal from one of the sensors, the ECU reverts to an emergency (limp-home) program. This will allow the car to be driven, although engine operation and performance will be limited. A warning light on the instrument panel will illuminate if the fault is likely to cause an increase in harmful exhaust emissions.

To facilitate fault diagnosis, the ignition system is provided with an on-board diagnostic facility, which can be interrogated using suitable diagnostic equipment (fault code reader). The OBD connector plug is accessed by opening the centre console compartment lid, and prising up the access panel **(see illustrations)**.

In addition to the above operations, many of the ignition system components have a second function in the control and operation of the fuel injection system. Further details will be found in Part A of Chapter 4.

2 Ignition system - testing

⚠ **Warning: Voltages produced by an electronic ignition system are considerably higher than those produced by conventional ignition systems. Extreme care must be taken when working on the system if the ignition is switched on. Persons with surgically-implanted cardiac pacemaker devices should keep well clear of the ignition circuits, components and test equipment.**

General

1 The components of the ignition system are normally very reliable; most faults are far more likely to be due to loose or dirty connections, or to tracking of HT voltage due to dirt, dampness or damaged insulation, than to the failure of any of the system's components. **Always** check all wiring thoroughly before condemning an electrical component, and work methodically to eliminate all other possibilities before deciding that a particular component is faulty.

2 The old practice of checking for a spark by holding the live end of an HT lead a short distance away from the engine is **not** recommended; not only is there a high risk of a powerful electric shock, but the ECU, HT coil, or power stage may be damaged. Similarly, **never** try to diagnose misfires by pulling off one HT lead at a time.

3 The following tests should be carried out when an obvious fault such as non-starting or a clearly detectable misfire exists. Some faults, however, are more obscure and are often disguised by the fact that the ECU will adopt an emergency program (limp-home) mode to maintain as much driveability as possible. Faults of this nature usually appear in the form of excessive fuel consumption, poor idling characteristics, lack of performance, knocking or pinking noises from the engine under certain conditions, or a combination of these conditions. Where problems such as this are experienced, the best course is to refer the car to a suitably-equipped garage for diagnostic testing using dedicated test equipment.

Engine will not start

Note: *Remember that a fault with the anti-theft alarm or immobiliser will give rise to apparent starting problems. Make sure that the alarm or immobiliser has been deactivated, referring to the vehicle handbook for details.*

4 If the engine either will not turn over at all, or only turns very slowly, check the battery and starter motor. Connect a voltmeter across the battery terminals (meter positive probe to battery positive terminal) then note the voltage reading obtained while turning the engine over on the starter for (no more than) ten seconds. If the reading obtained is less than approximately 9.5 volts, first check the battery, starter motor and charging system as described in Part A of this Chapter.

5 Further checking of the Motronic ME7 system is not possible without dedicated equipment

Except Motronic ME7 system

6 If the engine turns over at normal speed but will not start, check the HT circuit.

7 Connect a timing light (following its manufacturer's instructions) and turning the engine over on the starter motor; if the light flashes, voltage is reaching the spark plugs, so these should be checked first. If the light does not flash, check the HT leads themselves, followed by the distributor cap, carbon brush and rotor arm, using the information given in Chapter 1. If there is a spark, continue with the checks described in Section 3 of this Chapter.

8 If there is still no spark, check the condition of the coil, if possible by substitution with a known good unit, or by checking the primary and secondary resistances. If the fault persists, the problem lies elsewhere; if the fault is now cleared, a new coil is the obvious cure. However, check carefully the condition of the LT connections themselves before doing so, to ensure that the fault is not due to dirty or poorly-fastened connectors.

9 If the coil is in good condition, the fault is probably within the power stage, one of the system sensors, or related components (as applicable). In this case, a fault code should be logged in the diagnostic unit, which could be read using a fault code reader.

10 Fault codes can only be extracted from the ECU using a dedicated fault code reader. A Volvo dealer will obviously have such a reader, but they are also available from other suppliers, including Haynes. It is unlikely to be cost-effective for the private owner to purchase a fault code reader, but a well-equipped local garage or auto electrical specialist will have one.

Engine misfires

Except Motronic ME7 system

11 An irregular misfire suggests either a loose connection or intermittent fault on the primary circuit, or an HT fault on the coil side of the rotor arm.

12 With the ignition switched off, check carefully through the system, ensuring that all connections are clean and securely fastened. If the equipment is available, check the LT circuit as described above.

13 Check that the ignition coil, the distributor cap and the HT leads are clean and dry. Check the leads themselves and the spark plugs (by substitution if necessary), then check the distributor cap, carbon brush and rotor arm as described in Chapter 1.

14 Regular misfiring is almost certainly due to a fault in the distributor cap, HT leads or spark plugs. Use a timing light (paragraph 5 above) to check whether HT voltage is present at all leads.

15 If HT voltage is not present on any particular lead, the fault will be in that lead, or in the distributor cap. If HT is present on all leads, the fault will be in the spark plugs; check and renew them if there is any doubt about their condition.

16 If no HT is present, check the ignition coil; its secondary windings may be breaking down under load.

17 Any further checking of the system components should be carried out after first checking the ECU for fault codes - see paragraph 9.

Motronic ME7 system

18 An irregular misfire is probably due to a loose connection to one of the ignition coils or system sensors.

19 With the ignition switched off, check carefully through the system, ensuring that all connections are clean and securely fastened **(see illustration)**.

20 Regular misfiring indicates a problem with one of the ignition coils or spark plugs. Testing the coils is best left to a Volvo dealer.

21 Any further checking of the system components should be carried out after first checking the ECU for fault codes - see paragraph 9.

2.19 Check the security of the ignition coil connections

3 Fault-finding - general information and preliminary checks

Note: *Both the ignition and fuel systems must ideally be treated as one inter-related engine management system. Although the contents of this section is mainly concerned with the ignition side of the system, many of the components perform dual functions, and some of the following procedures of necessity relate to the fuel system.*

General information

1 The fuel and ignition systems on all engines covered by this manual incorporate an on-board diagnostic system to facilitate fault finding and system testing. Should a fault occur, the ECU stores a series of signals (or fault codes) for subsequent read-out via the OBD plug located under the centre console compartment lid.

2 If driveability problems have been experienced and engine performance is suspect, the on-board diagnostic system can be used to pinpoint any problem areas, but this requires special test equipment. Once this has been done, further tests may often be necessary to determine the exact nature of the fault; ie, whether a component itself has failed, or whether it is a wiring or other inter-related problem.

3 Apart from visually checking the wiring and connections, any testing will require the use of a fault code reader at least. A Volvo dealer will obviously have such a reader, but they are also available from other suppliers, including Haynes. It is unlikely to be cost-effective for the private owner to purchase a fault code reader, but a well-equipped local garage or auto electrical specialist will have one.

Preliminary checks

Note: *When carrying out these checks to trace a fault, remember that if the fault has appeared only a short time after any part of the vehicle has been serviced or overhauled, the first place to check is where that work was carried out, however unrelated it may appear, to ensure that no carelessly-refitted components are causing the problem.*

If you are tracing the cause of a partial engine fault, such as lack of performance, in addition to the checks outlined below, check the compression pressures. Check also that the fuel filter and air cleaner element have been renewed at the recommended intervals. Refer to Chapters 1 and 2A for details of these procedures.

Remember that any fault codes which have been logged will have to be cleared from the ECU memory using a dedicated fault code reader (see paragraph 3) before you can be certain the cause of the fault has been fixed.

4 Open the bonnet and check the condition of the battery connections - remake the connections or renew the leads if a fault is found. Use the same techniques to ensure that all earth points in the engine compartment provide good electrical contact through clean, metal-to-metal joints, and that all are securely fastened.

5 Next work methodically around the engine compartment, checking all visible wiring, and the connections between sections of the wiring loom. What you are looking for at this stage is wiring that is obviously damaged by chafing against sharp edges, or against moving suspension/transmission components and/or the auxiliary drivebelt, by being trapped or crushed between carelessly-refitted components, or melted by being forced into contact with hot engine castings, coolant pipes, etc. In almost all cases, damage of this sort is caused in the first instance by incorrect routing on reassembly after previous work has been carried out (see the note at the beginning of this sub-Section).

6 Obviously wires can break or short together inside the insulation so that no visible evidence betrays the fault, but this usually only occurs where the wiring loom has been incorrectly routed so that it is stretched taut or kinked sharply; either of these conditions should be obvious on even a casual inspection. If this is thought to have happened and the fault proves elusive, the suspect section of wiring should be checked very carefully during the more detailed checks which follow.

7 Depending on the extent of the problem, damaged wiring may be repaired by rejoining the break or splicing-in a new length of wire, using solder to ensure a good connection, and remaking the insulation with adhesive insulating tape or heat-shrink tubing, as desired. If the damage is extensive, given the implications for the vehicle's future reliability, the best long-term answer may well be to renew that entire section of the loom, however expensive this may appear.

8 When the actual damage has been repaired, ensure that the wiring loom is re-routed correctly, so that it is clear of other components, is not stretched or kinked, and is secured out of harm's way using the plastic clips, guides and ties provided.

9 Check all electrical connectors, ensuring that they are clean, securely fastened, and that each is locked by its plastic tabs or wire clip, as appropriate. If any connector shows external signs of corrosion (accumulations of white or green deposits, or streaks of 'rust'), or if any is thought to be dirty, it must be unplugged and cleaned using electrical contact cleaner. If the connector pins are severely corroded, the connector must be renewed; note that this may mean the renewal of that entire section of the loom.

10 If the cleaner completely removes the corrosion to leave the connector in a satisfactory condition, it would be wise to pack the connector with a suitable material which will exclude dirt and moisture, and prevent the corrosion from occurring again; a

Volvo dealer may be able to recommend a suitable product.

11 Working methodically around the engine compartment, check carefully that all vacuum hoses and pipes are securely fastened and correctly routed, with no signs of cracks, splits or deterioration to cause air leaks, or of hoses that are trapped, kinked, or bent sharply enough to restrict air flow. Check with particular care at all connections and sharp bends, and renew any damaged or deformed lengths of hose.

12 Working from the fuel tank, via the filter, to the fuel rail (and including the feed and return), check the fuel lines, and renew any that are found to be leaking, trapped or kinked. Check particularly the ends of the hoses - these can crack and perish sufficiently to allow leakage.

13 Check that the accelerator cable is correctly secured and adjusted, and that it is routed with as few sharp turns as possible. Renew the cable if there is any doubt about its condition, or if it appears to be stiff or jerky in operation. Refer to Chapter 4A for further information, if required.

14 Unclip the air cleaner cover, and check that the air filter is not clogged or soaked. A clogged air filter will obstruct the inlet air flow, causing a noticeable effect on engine performance. Renew the filter if necessary; refer to the relevant Sections of Chapter 1 for further information, if required.

15 Start the engine and allow it to idle.

Caution: Working in the engine compartment while the engine is running requires great care if the risk of personal injury is to be avoided; among the dangers are burns from contact with hot components, or contact with moving components such as the radiator cooling fan or the auxiliary drivebelt. Refer to Safety first! at the front of this manual before starting, and ensure that your hands, and any long hair or loose clothing, are kept well clear of hot or moving components at all times.

16 Working from the air inlet, via the air cleaner assembly and the mass air flow sensor (or inlet air temperature sensor) to the throttle housing and inlet manifold (and including the various vacuum hoses and pipes connected to these), check for air leaks. Usually, these will be revealed by sucking or hissing noises, but minor leaks may be traced by spraying a solution of soapy water on to the suspect joint; if a leak exists, it will be shown by the change in engine note and the accompanying air bubbles (or sucking-in of the liquid, depending on the pressure difference at that point). If a leak is found at any point, tighten the fastening clamp and/or renew the faulty components, as applicable.

17 Similarly, work from the cylinder head, via the manifold to the tailpipe, to check that the exhaust system is free from leaks. The simplest way of doing this, if the vehicle can

be raised and supported safely and with complete security while the check is made, is to temporarily block the tailpipe while listening for the sound of escaping exhaust gases; any leak should be evident. If a leak is found at any point, tighten the fastening clamp bolts and/or nuts, renew the gasket, and/or renew the faulty section of the system, as necessary, to seal the leak.

18 It is possible to make a further check of the electrical connections by wiggling each electrical connector of the system in turn as the engine is idling; a faulty connector will be immediately evident from the engine's response as contact is broken and remade. A faulty connector should be renewed to ensure that the future reliability of the system; note that this may mean the renewal of that entire section of the loom.

19 If the preliminary checks have failed to reveal the fault, the car must be taken to a Volvo dealer or suitably-equipped garage for diagnostic testing using electronic test equipment.

4 Ignition HT coil - removal and refitting

Except Motronic ME7 system

1 Disconnect the battery negative lead.

2 Disconnect the HT king lead from the centre of the coil, and the wiring connector from the ignition power stage just below the coil.

3 Undo the bolts securing the coil and power stage mounting bracket to the side of the suspension strut tower, and remove the assembly from the engine compartment **(see illustration)**. Note that the ignition coil and power stage are an integrated assembly, and the two components cannot be separated.

4 Inspect the coil visually for cracks, leakage of insulating oil or other obvious damage. Renew it if such damage is evident.

5 Refitting is a reversal of removal.

Motronic ME7 system

6 Refer to Chapter 1, Section 24.

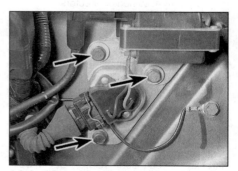

4.3 Ignition coil and power stage mounting bracket bolts (arrowed)

6.4 Removing the distributor cap from the rear of the cylinder head

6.5a Remove the flash shield . . .

6.5b . . . then undo the three screws and remove the rotor arm

5 Ignition system power stage - removal and refitting

The power stage and ignition coil are an integrated assembly, and the two components cannot be separated. Removal and refitting procedures are as for the ignition coil described in Section 4.

6 Distributor cap and rotor arm - removal and refitting

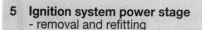

Note: *This Section does not apply to models with the Motronic ME7 system.*

Removal

1 Undo the screws and lift off the spark plug HT lead cover from the centre of the cylinder head.
2 Pull the HT leads off the spark plugs and release them from the retaining clips. Mark the leads if necessary to avoid confusion when refitting.
3 Undo the three screws which secure the distributor cap. The screws are captive, so do not attempt to remove them from the cap. Access can be improved, if necessary, by releasing the clips and moving the air cleaner lid to one side.
4 Lift off the distributor cap and HT leads complete **(see illustration)**. It is not advisable to remove the HT leads from the distributor

cap, unless absolutely necessary - if this must be done, make sure that the cap and leads are marked for position, so that there is no way the firing order can be lost.
5 Remove the flash shield, then mark the position of the rotor arm relative to the distributor, for use when refitting. Alternatively (or if a new rotor arm is being fitted), set the engine to TDC on No 1 cylinder, so that the rotor arm points to the notch mark on the distributor body. Undo the three screws and remove the rotor arm **(see illustrations)**.

Refitting

6 Refitting is a reversal of removal. Ensure that the HT leads are secured by their clips and not trapped when the cover is refitted.

7 Ignition system sensors - removal and refitting

RPM sensor

Removal

1 The RPM sensor is located on the top of the transmission bellhousing.
2 Trace the sensor wiring back from the sensor, and disconnect it at the wiring plug.
3 Remove the sensor retaining bolt, and withdraw the sensor from its mounting bracket on the bellhousing **(see illustration)**.

Refitting

4 Refit by reversing the removal operations.

Knock sensors

Removal

5 The two knock sensors are located on the front facing side of the cylinder block under the inlet manifold.
6 Refer to Chapter 4A and remove the inlet manifold.
7 Disconnect the wiring connector from the front or rear knock sensor as applicable.
8 Undo the retaining bolt and remove the sensor **(see illustration)**.

Refitting

9 Locate the sensor on the cylinder block, and refit and tighten the retaining bolt to the specified torque. When tightening the bolt, hold the front sensor (nearest the timing belt) with its connector at the 3 o'clock position, and the rear sensor with its connector at the 5 o'clock position.
10 Refit the inlet manifold as described in Chapter 4A.

Camshaft position sensor

Removal

11 On early models, the camshaft position sensor is located on the left-hand rear of the cylinder head, and operates from the exhaust camshaft. Later models have the sensor fitted to the inlet camshaft.
12 Trace the sensor wiring back from the sensor, and disconnect it at the wiring plug **(see illustration)**.
13 On early models, undo the two screws, and manipulate the sensor from its location on

5B

7.3 RPM sensor location and retaining bolt (arrowed)

7.8 Rear knock sensor location and retaining bolt (arrowed)

7.12 Camshaft position sensor wiring connector (arrowed) - early models

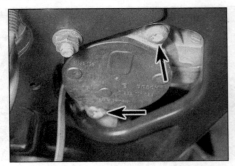

7.13 Camshaft position sensor retaining screws (arrowed) - early models

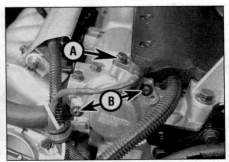

7.14 Camshaft position sensor retaining bolt (A) and end cover screws (B) - later models

the cylinder head, behind the engine tie-bar support bracket **(see illustration)**.

14 On later models, unscrew the retaining bolt and lift out the camshaft sensor from the inlet camshaft. If required, remove the two screws and take off the camshaft end cover **(see illustration)**.

Refitting

15 Refit by reversing the removal operations.

Coolant temperature sensor

16 Refer to Chapter 3, Section 6.

Vehicle speed sensor

17 Refer to Chapter 12, Section 7.

Throttle position sensor

18 Refer to Chapter 4A, Section 10.

8 Electronic control unit (ECU) - removal and refitting

Note: *The fuel and ignition ECUs, together with the automatic transmission ECU (where applicable), are all located in the ECU box situated at the front right-hand side of the engine compartment, in front of the cooling system expansion tank. Note that only the*
LH3.2-Jetronic/EZ-129 K system has a separate ignition ECU.

Removal

1 Ensure that the ignition is switched off.

2 Clean off the top of the ECU box lid, to make sure no debris falls inside when it is removed. Release the catch on the side of the ECU module box lid. Lift off the lid and place it to one side.

3 Pull the locking lever on top of the ECU forward, and withdraw the ECU from its location. The ignition system ECU is located in slot one of the module box, nearest to the engine.

Refitting

4 Locate the ECU in the box, engaging it with the connector in the base.

5 Push the locking lever down to secure the ECU, and refit the ECU box lid.

9 Ignition timing - checking

Note: *The ignition timing cannot be adjusted, but on early models it can be checked if wished.*

1 Bring the engine to operating temperature with the air conditioning switched off. With the
engine stopped, connect a timing light (stroboscope) as instructed by the manufacturers.

2 Undo the retaining bolt and remove the timing belt outer cover. The ignition timing marks (where present) consist of a scale on the timing belt inner cover, above the inlet camshaft sprocket, and a faint line on the inlet camshaft sprocket tooth. Note that many later models do not have any ignition timing marks at all.

3 Highlight the notch on the sprocket and the desired mark on the timing scale with white paint or typist's correction fluid (see *Specifications* for the desired values).

4 Run the engine at idle speed and shine the timing light on the timing scale. The sprocket notch will appear stationary and (if the timing is correct) in alignment with the appropriate mark on the timing scale.

Caution: Take great care not to get electrical leads, clothing, long hair etc, caught in the timing belt or auxiliary drivebelt.

5 Stop the engine, disconnect the timing light and refit the timing belt cover.

6 If the timing is incorrect, there is likely to be a fault in the RPM sensor, the fuel/ignition system ECU or associated wiring (see Section 3).

Chapter 6
Clutch

Contents

Degrees of difficulty

| Easy, suitable for novice with little experience | | Fairly easy, suitable for beginner with some experience | | Fairly difficult, suitable for competent DIY mechanic | | Difficult, suitable for experienced DIY mechanic | | Very difficult, suitable for expert DIY or professional | |

Specifications

General
Clutch type . . . . Single dry plate, diaphragm spring, hydraulic actuation

Driven plate
Diameter:
   B5204 T3, B5234 T and B5254 T engines . . . . 241 mm
   All other engines . . . . 230 mm

Pressure plate
Warp limit . . . . 0.2 mm

Torque wrench settings

	Nm	lbf ft
Master cylinder retaining nuts	25	18
Pressure plate retaining bolts	25	18
Release bearing and slave cylinder mounting bolts (later models)	10	7

1 General information

A single dry plate diaphragm spring clutch is fitted to all manual transmission models. The clutch is hydraulically operated via a master and slave cylinder. Early models have the slave cylinder mounted externally on the transmission housing, with a separate clutch release bearing attached to the release fork. Later models have an internally-mounted slave cylinder and release bearing combined into one unit.

The main components of the clutch are the pressure plate, the driven plate (sometimes called the friction plate or disc) and the release bearing. The pressure plate is bolted to the flywheel, with the driven plate sandwiched between them. The centre of the driven plate carries female splines which mate

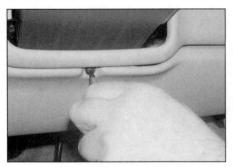

2.2a Remove the single screw . . .

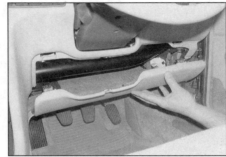

2.2b . . . then pull out the driver's lower trim panel . . .

2.2c . . . and disconnect the wiring plug from the footwell light

with the splines on the transmission input shaft. The release bearing acts on the diaphragm spring fingers of the pressure plate.

When the engine is running and the clutch pedal is released, the diaphragm spring clamps the pressure plate, driven plate and flywheel firmly together. Drive is transmitted through the friction surfaces of the flywheel and pressure plate to the linings of the driven plate, and thus to the transmission input shaft.

On early models, when the clutch pedal is depressed, the pedal movement is transmitted hydraulically to the release fork, and the fork moves the bearing to press on the diaphragm spring fingers. On later models, the slave cylinder is incorporated into the release bearing - when the slave cylinder operates, the release bearing moves against the diaphragm spring fingers. As the spring pressure on the pressure plate is relieved, the flywheel and pressure plate spin without moving the driven plate. As the pedal is released, spring pressure is restored and the drive is gradually taken up.

The clutch hydraulic system consists of a master cylinder, a slave cylinder and the associated pipes and hoses. The fluid reservoir is shared with the brake master cylinder.

Wear in the driven plate linings is compensated for automatically by the hydraulic system components, and no adjustment is necessary.

2 Clutch pedal - removal and refitting

Removal

1 Disconnect the battery negative lead.
2 Remove the trim panel under the facia on the driver's side, which is secured by a single screw, and is then pulled out of its locating slots at the top. Disconnect the wiring plug from the footwell light (see illustrations).
3 Fold back the carpet, then release the clip securing the master cylinder pushrod to the clutch pedal (see illustration).
4 Hold the pedal to prevent it moving upward under spring pressure, then release the pushrod from the pedal. Push the pedal down and disconnect the assistance spring from the pedal.
5 Extract the pedal retaining circlip, and slide the pedal off the pivot shaft (see illustration).
6 With the pedal removed, check the

condition of the pivot bushes and renew as necessary.

Refitting

7 Refit by reversing the removal operations. Apply grease to the pedal bushes, and use a new circlip to secure the pedal if the old one is in any way damaged or distorted.

3 Clutch master cylinder - removal and refitting

⚠️ *Warning: Hydraulic fluid is poisonous; wash off immediately and thoroughly in the case of skin contact, and seek immediate medical advice if any fluid is swallowed or gets into the eyes. Certain types of hydraulic fluid are inflammable, and may ignite when allowed into contact with hot components; when servicing any hydraulic system, it is safest to assume that the fluid IS inflammable, and to take precautions against the risk of fire as though it is petrol that is being handled. Hydraulic fluid is also an effective paint stripper, and will attack plastics; if any is spilt, it should be*

2.3 Master cylinder pushrod-to-clutch pedal retaining clip (arrowed)

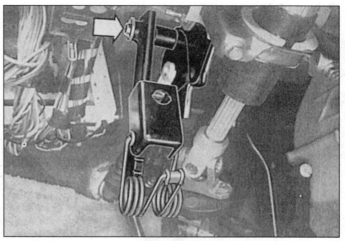

2.5 Extract the pedal retaining circlip (arrowed) and slide the pedal off the shaft

panel will flash; the ECU will revert to an emergency (limp-home) program which ensures that two forward gears and reverse will always be available, but gear changing must be performed manually. If a fault of this nature does occur, the ECU stores a series of signals (or fault codes) which can be read and interpreted using suitable diagnostic equipment, for quick and accurate fault diagnosis (see Section 11).

The automatic transmission is a complex unit, but if it is not abused, it is reliable and long-lasting. Repair or overhaul operations are beyond the scope of many dealers, let alone the home mechanic; specialist advice should be sought if problems arise which cannot be solved by the procedures given in this Chapter.

2 Automatic transmission fluid - draining and refilling

1 Renewal of the automatic transmission fluid is not a service requirement, and will normally only be necessary in the following circumstances:
   a) If the on-board diagnostic system has logged a fault code (see Sections 1 and 11).
   b) If the fluid is discoloured or has a burnt smell, resulting from hard and continuous operation of the transmission.
   b) If the car is continuously used for taxi work or extended periods of trailer towing, the fluid should be changed at the 40 000 mile (64 000 km) service interval.

2 Raise and securely support the front of the car (see Jacking and vehicle support).
3 Remove the splash guard under the radiator and, where applicable, the large splash guard under the engine.
4 Remove the drain plug located on the right-hand side of the casing, below and just forward of the driveshaft. Allow the contents of the transmission to drain into a suitable draining container. Refit and tighten the drain plug, using a new seal if necessary.
Caution: If the vehicle has just been run, the transmission fluid may be very hot
5 Refit the splash guard(s) and lower the car to the ground.
6 Refer to Chapter 5A if necessary, and remove the battery and battery tray.
7 Clean the fluid cooler return hose union on the transmission, then disconnect the hose at the transmission union. Plug or cap the open union on the transmission.
8 Attach a clear plastic hose to the end of the fluid cooler return hose. Lead the hose into the draining container.
9 Temporarily refit the battery tray and battery.
10 Apply the handbrake and move the gear selector lever to the P (Park) position.
11 Add 2.0 litres of fresh automatic transmission fluid of the specified type via the dipstick tube.

12 Start the engine and allow it to idle. Fluid will flow into the draining container. When bubbles appear in the fluid, stop the engine.
13 Add a further 2.0 litres of fresh automatic transmission fluid of the specified type via the dipstick tube.
14 Repeat paragraph 12, then remove the battery and battery tray. Remove the plastic hose, and reconnect the fluid cooler return hose to the transmission.
15 Refit the battery tray and battery securely.
16 Add a further 2.0 litres of fresh automatic transmission fluid.
17 Start the engine and allow it to idle. Move the gear selector lever through all the gear positions, stopping for four to five seconds in each position. Return the selector lever to the P position, wait for two minutes, then check the fluid level as described in Chapter 1, using the COLD markings on the dipstick. Top-up as necessary.
18 Dispose of the old fluid safely (see General repair procedures).
19 For a more accurate check of the fluid level, the transmission and fluid must be at operating temperature. The next time the car has been driven for more than 30 minutes, re-check the fluid level using the HOT markings on the dipstick, as described in Chapter 1.

3 Selector cable - removal, refitting and adjustment

Removal

1 Park the car on a level surface, then refer to Chapter 4A and remove the air cleaner assembly.
2 Refer to Chapter 5A and remove the battery and battery tray.
3 Working in the engine compartment, extract the locking clip and washer securing the selector inner cable to the transmission selector lever **(see illustration)**.
4 Undo the two nuts and remove the washers (where fitted) securing the selector outer cable bracket to the transmission. Lift the bracket off the mounting studs, and release the inner cable end from the selector lever.
5 Remove the centre console as described in Chapter 11.
6 Extract the retaining clip securing the selector inner cable to the gear selector lever, and the clip securing the selector outer cable to the gear selector housing.
7 Undo the screws and remove the trim/sound proofing panel from under the facia on the left-hand side.
8 Undo the screws and remove the carpet support plate under the centre of the facia on the left-hand side. Bend back the carpet to allow the support plate to be withdrawn.
9 Undo the bolts securing the cable entry cover plate to the bulkhead. Where applicable, release the shift lock cable from the selector cable.

3.3 Selector inner cable locking clip (lower arrow) and outer cable bracket nuts (right arrow)

10 Note the routing of the cable under the facia, and in the engine compartment, as an aid to refitting. Release any adjacent components as necessary, then pull the cable into the passenger compartment and remove it from the car.

Refitting and adjustment

11 From inside the car, carefully feed the cable through into the engine compartment, ensuring that it is correctly routed.
12 Reconnect the cable to the selector lever and housing, and secure with the retaining clips.
13 Refit the cable entry cover plate, carpet support plate and the trim/sound proofing panel.
14 Refit the centre console as described in Chapter 11.
15 Move the gear selector lever to position R (Reverse). Ensure that the gear lever and cable position do not move during subsequent operations.
16 Move the selector lever on the transmission as far forward as it will go to the P (Park) position. Ensure that P is selected by releasing the handbrake and trying to roll the car; the transmission should be locked. Re-apply the handbrake.
17 Move the transmission selector lever rearward one position to R (Reverse) **(see illustration)**.

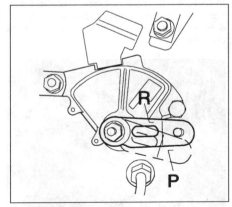

3.17 Move transmission selector lever forward to (P) then rearward one position to (R)

7B

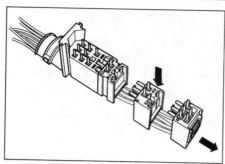

5.7 Separate the main wiring connector for access to the RPM sensor socket and pins

18 Without moving the selector cable or transmission selector lever position, locate the inner cable on the selector lever, and position the outer cable bracket on the transmission studs. Secure the bracket with the nuts and washers (where fitted), and tighten the nuts to the specified torque.
19 Refit the locking clip and washer securing the cable to the transmission selector lever.
20 Check the adjustment by moving the gear selector lever inside the car to the N (neutral) position. Without touching the locking button, move the lever forward slightly then backwards slightly. Play should be felt in both directions.
21 On completion, refit the air cleaner assembly (Chapter 4A), battery tray and battery.

4 Selector housing - removal and refitting

Removal

1 Disconnect the battery negative lead.
2 Grasp the selector lever gaiter around the internal retaining clip, turn the gaiter and clip through 90° and pull the gaiter down. Ensure that the retaining clip returns to its original position after releasing the gaiter.
3 Pull the selector lever knob firmly upwards to remove it from the selector lever. Note that considerable force is necessary to release it.
4 Refer to Chapter 11 and remove the centre console.

6.5 Transmission oil temperature sensor location

5 Extract the retaining clip securing the selector inner cable to the gear selector lever.
6 Extract the retaining clip securing the selector outer cable to the gear selector housing.
7 Remove the selector illumination bulbholder from the base of the indicator panel.
8 Where applicable, disconnect the shift lock solenoid wiring connector.
9 On later models, undo the two bolts and release the cross plate at the rear of the housing from the side reinforcement members on each side.
10 Undo the bolts securing the housing to the floor and remove it from the car.

Refitting

11 Refitting is a reversal of removal. When refitting the selector lever knob, push the retaining clip into the gaiter slightly, then push the gaiter over the catches against the edge of the knob. Press up the retaining clip, ensuring that it engages with the knob catches.

5 RPM sensor - removal and refitting

Removal

1 Refer to Chapter 5A and remove the battery.
2 Refer to Chapter 4A and remove the air cleaner assembly and inlet ducting.
3 Remove the battery tray and detach the air cleaner bracket.
4 Disconnect the transmission main wiring connector on the top of the transmission housing. Note the rubber gasket.
5 Remove the cable clamps around the cable harness and rubber grommet.
6 Insert a thin screwdriver into the end of the wiring connector housing, and depress the retaining catch. Lift the cables and sockets out of the connector housing.
7 Pull the wiring connector sockets apart, and remove the two-pin socket containing pins 16 and 17 **(see illustration)**.
8 Wipe clean the area around the sensor, then undo the retaining bolt and remove the RPM sensor from the top of the transmission housing.

Refitting

9 Smear some petroleum jelly on the sensor O-ring seal, locate the sensor in position and secure with the retaining bolt.
10 Reconnect the wiring sockets, and refit the cables and sockets into the connector housing.
11 Refit the rubber grommet and cable clamps to the cable harness, then reconnect the wiring connector.
12 Refit the battery tray, battery, and air cleaner assembly with reference to Chapters 4A and 5A.

6 Fluid temperature sensor - removal and refitting

Removal

1 Carry out the operations described in Section 5, paragraphs 1 to 6.
2 Pull the wiring connector sockets apart, and remove the two-pin socket containing pins 12 and 13.
3 Depress the locking device at the base of the socket, and push out the red locking lug slightly. Remove the two pins from the socket.
4 Drain the transmission fluid as described in Section 2.
5 Wipe clean the area around the sensor, then unscrew it from the front of the transmission housing **(see illustration)**. Place a container beneath the sensor as it is unscrewed, as there will be fluid spillage.
6 Note the routing of the sensor wiring and carefully pull it clear. Remove the sensor from the car.

Refitting

7 Smear some petroleum jelly on the sensor O-ring seal, then locate the sensor in position and tighten to the specified torque.
8 Route the sensor cables in their original positions, then push the connector pins into their locations in the wiring socket. Note that pin 12 is the blue/red cable and pin 13 is the blue/black cable. Re-attach the connector sockets.
9 Refit the cables and sockets into the connector housing.
10 Refit the rubber grommet and cable clamps to the cable harness, then reconnect the wiring connector.
11 Refit the battery tray, battery, and air cleaner assembly with reference to Chapters 4A and 5A.
12 Refill the transmission with fresh fluid as described in Section 2.

7 Kickdown switch - removal and refitting

The kickdown switch is an integral part of the accelerator cable. Refer to Chapter 4A for removal and refitting procedures.

8 Electronic control unit (ECU) - removal and refitting

Note: *The automatic transmission ECU, together with the fuel and ignition ECUs, are all located in the ECU box, situated at the front right-hand side of the engine compartment in front of the cooling system expansion tank.*

Removal

1 Ensure that the ignition is switched off.

2 Clean off the top of the ECU box lid, to make sure no debris falls inside when it is removed. Release the catch on the side of the ECU module box lid. Lift off the lid and place it to one side.

3 Pull the locking lever on top of the ECU forwards, and withdraw the ECU from its location in slot three of the box, nearest to the right-hand wheel arch.

Refitting

4 Locate the ECU in the box, engaging it with the connector in the base.

5 Push the locking lever down to secure the ECU, and refit the module box lid.

6 If a new ECU has been fitted, it will be necessary to adapt the throttle position sensor signal as follows.

> ⚠ *Warning: Take all the precautions described below against the car moving, and be sure to carry out this procedure in a location where the car will not be damaged, should it accidentally move forwards. If you are not confident about carrying out this procedure, take the car to a Volvo dealer (the car should be driveable, even though the kickdown function may not be available).*

7 Chock all four wheels and apply the handbrake fully.

8 Start the engine and move the selector lever to the D (Drive) position.

9 Depress the brake pedal, and hold it hard down during the following operations.

10 Depress the accelerator pedal fully, so that the kickdown switch closes, and hold it down for five seconds.

11 Release the accelerator pedal, and move the selector lever to the P (Park) position. The new throttle position sensor signal will now be stored in the ECU memory.

12 Switch off the engine and remove the wheel chocks.

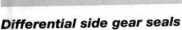

9 Fluid seals - renewal

Differential side gear seals

1 The procedure is the same as that described for the manual transmission in Chapter 7A, Section 4.

Input shaft/torque converter seal

2 Remove the transmission (see Section 10).

3 Pull the torque converter squarely out of the transmission. Be careful, as it is full of fluid.

4 Pull or lever out the old seal. Clean the seat and inspect the seal rubbing surface on the torque converter.

5 Lubricate the new seal with transmission fluid and fit it, lips inwards. Seat it with a piece of tube.

6 Lubricate the torque converter sleeve with transmission fluid, and slide the converter into place, pushing it in as far as it will go.

7 Check that the torque converter is fully seated by measuring the distance from the edge of the transmission housing face to the retaining bolt tabs on the converter. The dimension should be approximately 14 mm.

8 Refit the transmission as described in Section 10.

All seals

9 Check the transmission fluid level as described in Chapter 1 on completion.

10 Automatic transmission - removal and refitting

Note: *Arrangements must be made to support the engine from above, to allow the subframe to be detached on the left-hand side. The best way to support the engine is with a bar resting in the bonnet channels with an adjustable hook appropriately placed. Trolley jacks and the help of an assistant will also be required throughout the procedure.*

Removal

1 Set the steering wheel and roadwheels in the straight-ahead position. Release the steering column adjuster, and push the steering wheel in and upwards as far as it will go. Lock it in this position.

2 Move the gear selector lever to N (neutral).

3 Refer to Section 2 and drain the transmission fluid. This is not absolutely essential, but will remove the potential problem of fluid spillage when the driveshafts are removed, or when the transmission is moved out of the car.

4 Refer to Chapter 5A and remove the battery, then undo the bolts and remove the battery tray.

5 Refer to Chapter 4A and remove the air cleaner assembly and all relevant inlet ducting around the left-hand side of the engine.

6 On turbo models, remove the cover over the throttle housing and disconnect the air inlet pipe to the throttle housing. Move the pipe clear and secure it with a cable-tie. Also disconnect the upper oil cooler hose at the engine oil cooler.

7 Additionally on turbo models, disconnect the accelerator cable from the control pulley and mounting bracket. Remove the inlet ducts between the turbocharger and radiator/intercooler, and between the air cleaner and turbocharger.

8 Disconnect the selector cable at the transmission end as described in Section 3.

9 Disconnect the main wiring harness connector on top of the transmission casing.

10 Remove the cable clamps securing the wiring harness and earth lead.

11 Detach the cable conduit from the transmission, and release the oxygen sensor connector from the transmission bracket.

12 Disconnect the transmission fluid cooler inlet hose from the upper quick-release

connector on the side of the radiator. Disconnect the fluid cooler return hose at the transmission union. Cover or seal the disconnected hoses and unions.

13 Remove the fluid dipstick tube, and seal the opening.

14 Refer to Chapter 5A and remove the starter motor.

15 Lift the coolant expansion tank out of its mounting, and move it to one side.

16 Where exhaust gas recirculation is fitted, disconnect the hoses at the EGR controller above the radiator.

17 Undo the nut and remove the bolt securing the engine upper steady bar to the bracket on the engine. Note that a new nut and bolt will be required for refitting.

18 Undo the earth lead retaining bolt on the bulkhead, adjacent to the steady bar body bracket.

19 Undo all the transmission-to-engine retaining bolts that are accessible from above.

20 Referring to Chapter 8, remove the left-hand driveshaft completely, but only remove the right-hand driveshaft from the transmission, leaving it connected at the steering knuckle end.

21 Remove the splash guard under the radiator and, on early models, the large splash guard under the engine.

22 Remove the clips and release the pipe(s) running under the front of the subframe.

23 Release the cable-ties and lift the charcoal canister from its location on the left-hand side of the subframe. Support the canister clear of the subframe using a cable-tie.

24 Release the exhaust system from its mounting at the rear of the catalytic converter.

25 Undo the steering gear fluid pipe retaining clip bolts at the front and rear of the subframe.

26 Undo the two bolts securing the engine lower steady bar bracket to the transmission.

27 On right-hand-drive models, undo the two steering gear crash guard bolts at the rear of the subframe, and the nut securing the crash guard base to the subframe.

28 With reference to the note at the beginning of this Section, suitably support the engine from above, and adjust the support so that the load is just taken off the engine mountings.

29 Undo the bolt securing the engine front mounting to the subframe.

30 Slacken the bolt securing the engine rear mounting to the steering gear, then undo the five nuts securing the steering gear to the subframe. Note that new nuts will be required for refitting.

31 Position a sturdy trolley jack beneath, and in contact with, the left-hand side of the subframe. Ensure that the engine is securely supported from above.

32 Undo the two bolts each side securing the subframe rear mounting brackets to the body.

33 Slacken the two subframe mounting bolts on the right-hand side by approximately 15 mm. Note that new bolts will be required for refitting.

34 Undo the two subframe mounting bolts on the left-hand side. Collect the mounting bracket when the rear bolt is removed. Note that new bolts will be required for refitting.

35 Carefully lower the jack, and allow the subframe to drop on the left-hand side by approximately 100 mm. Ensure that the steering gear mounting bolts clear the subframe as it is lowered.

36 On right-hand-drive models, undo the bolts securing the anti-roll bar clamps on the left-hand side of the subframe, and slacken the right-hand side clamp bolts until they are only held by a few turns. Secure the left-hand side of the anti-roll bar to the steering gear using a cable-tie.

37 Lower the jack completely, and allow the subframe to hang free from the right-hand side mountings.

38 Remove the earth strap from the transmission.

39 Secure the left-hand side of the steering gear to a convenient place on the underbody, using strong wire.

40 Undo the nut and bolt, and remove the engine rear mounting from the steering gear and the transmission bracket.

41 Release the oxygen sensor wiring from the engine rear mounting bracket cover. Remove the cover, then remove the mounting bracket from the transmission.

42 Rotate the crankshaft, using a socket on the pulley nut, until one of the torque converter-to-driveplate retaining bolts becomes accessible through the opening on the rear facing side of the engine **(see illustration)**. Working through the opening, undo the bolt. Rotate the crankshaft as necessary and remove the remaining bolts in the same way. Note that new bolts will be required for refitting.

43 Lower the engine/transmission by means of the overhead support, until sufficient clearance exists to enable the transmission to be withdrawn. Take care not to lower the unit too far, or the exhaust downpipe will foul the steering gear. Also, make sure that the engine oil dipstick tube clears the radiator fan, and that no hoses or leads are trapped.

44 Securely and safely support the transmission from below on a trolley jack.

10.42 Removing the torque converter retaining bolts. Access hole in transmission housing (arrowed)

45 Undo the remaining bolts securing the transmission to the engine. Withdraw the transmission squarely off the engine dowels, making sure that the torque converter remains in position on the transmission. Use the access hole in the transmission housing to hold the converter in place.

46 Lower the jack and remove the unit from under the car.

Refitting

47 Before refitting the transmission, flush out the fluid cooler with fresh transmission fluid. To do this, attach a hose to the upper union, pour transmission fluid through the hose, and collect it in a container positioned beneath the return hose.

48 Clean the contact surfaces on the torque converter and driveplate, and the transmission and engine mating faces. Lightly lubricate the torque converter guide projection and the engine/transmission locating dowels with grease.

49 Check that the torque converter is fully seated by measuring the distance from the edge of the transmission housing face to the retaining bolt tabs on the converter. The dimension should be approximately 14 mm.

50 Manoeuvre the transmission squarely into position, and engage it with the engine dowels. Refit the lower bolts securing transmission to the engine, and tighten lightly first in a diagonal sequence, then again to the specified torque.

51 Attach the torque converter to the driveplate using new bolts. Rotate the crankshaft for access to the bolts as was done for removal, then rotate the torque converter by means of the access hole in transmission housing. Fit and tighten all the bolts hand-tight first, then tighten again to the specified torque.

52 Raise the engine to its approximate fitted position. Refit the rear engine mounting bracket and cover, and secure with the three bolts tightened to the specified torque.

53 Refit the engine rear mounting to the transmission bracket and steering gear, but do not fully tighten the nut and bolt at this stage.

54 Secure the oxygen sensor wiring to the mounting bracket cover.

55 On right-hand drive models, raise the subframe to within 100 mm of the body, align the steering gear and crash guard with their subframe locations, then refit the anti-roll bar clamps. Tighten all the clamp bolts to the specified torque.

56 Raise the subframe to its fitted position, ensuring that the steering gear bolts engage in their locations.

57 Fit the new subframe mounting bolts and rear mounting bracket and bolts on the left-hand side. Tighten the subframe bolts to the specified torque, then further, through the specified angle, using an angle-tightening gauge. Tighten the mounting bracket bolts to the specified torque.

58 Support the right-hand side of the subframe on the jack, and remove the two previously-slackened subframe bolts. Fit the new bolts and the two mounting bracket bolts, and tighten them as described in the previous paragraph.

59 Secure the steering gear to the subframe using five new nuts tightened to the specified torque.

60 Refit the engine front mounting bolt, then tighten the engine front and rear mountings to the specified torque.

61 On right-hand drive models, refit the two steering gear crash guard bolts at the rear of the subframe, and the nut securing the crash guard base to the subframe. Tighten to the specified torque.

62 Refit the engine lower steady bar bracket to the transmission, and tighten the bolts to the specified torque, then further, through the specified angle, using an angle-tightening gauge.

63 Refit the steering gear fluid pipe retaining clip bolts at the front and rear of the subframe, and reconnect the exhaust system mounting.

64 Reconnect the charcoal canister and the pipe clips at the front of the subframe.

65 Refit the driveshafts as described in Chapter 8.

66 Refit the splash guard under the radiator and where applicable, under the engine.

67 Refit the starter motor and all the transmission-to-engine upper bolts. Tighten the bolts to the specified torque.

68 Attach the cable conduit to the transmission, and secure the oxygen sensor connector to the transmission bracket.

69 Reconnect the transmission fluid cooler inlet and return hoses.

70 Refit the fluid dipstick tube with a new O-ring seal.

71 Refit the cable clamps securing the wiring harness and earth lead.

72 Reconnect the main wiring harness connector on top of the transmission casing.

73 Reconnect the earth lead to the bulkhead.

74 Secure the engine upper steady bar to its bracket, using a new nut and bolt. Tighten to the specified torque, then further, through the specified angle, using an angle-tightening gauge.

75 Where applicable, reconnect the EGR controller hoses.

76 Refit the coolant expansion tank, the engine oil cooler hose and air inlet pipe (where applicable).

77 Reconnect and adjust the selector cable as described in Section 3.

78 Refit the battery tray, battery, air cleaner assembly and all relevant inlet ducting, referring to Chapters 4A and 5A as necessary.

79 Where applicable, reconnect the accelerator cable to the control pulley and mounting bracket.

80 Check and if necessary refill or top-up the transmission fluid level.

11 Automatic transmission - fault diagnosis

The automatic transmission electronic control system incorporates an on-board diagnostic facility as an aid to fault finding and system testing. The diagnostic system is a feature of the electronic control unit (ECU) which continually monitors the system components and their operation. Should a fault occur, the ECU stores a series of signals (or fault codes) for subsequent read-out.

If a fault occurs, indicated by the flashing of the warning light on the instrument panel, the on-board diagnostics can be accessed using a fault code reader, for quick and accurate diagnosis. A Volvo dealer will obviously have such a reader, but they are also available from other suppliers, including Haynes. It is unlikely to be cost-effective for the private owner to purchase a fault code reader, but a well-equipped local garage or auto electrical specialist will have one.

In many instances, the fault may be nothing more serious than a corroded, trapped or loose wiring connection, or a loose, dirty, or badly-fitted component. Remember that if the fault has appeared only a short time after any part of the vehicle has been serviced or overhauled, the first place to check is where that work was carried out, however unrelated it may appear, to ensure that no carelessly-refitted components are causing the problem.

Even if the source of the problem is found and fixed, diagnostic equipment may still be required, to erase the fault code from the ECU memory, and stop the warning light flashing.

If the fault cannot be easily cured, the only alternatives possible at this time are the substitution of a suspect component with a known good unit (where possible), or entrusting further work to a Volvo dealer.

Chapter 8
Driveshafts

Contents

Degrees of difficulty

Easy, suitable for novice with little experience	Fairly easy, suitable for beginner with some experience	Fairly difficult, suitable for competent DIY mechanic	Difficult, suitable for experienced DIY mechanic	Very difficult, suitable for expert DIY or professional

Specifications

General

Driveshaft type . . . . Equal-length solid-steel shafts, splined to inner and outer constant velocity joints. Intermediate shaft incorporated in right-hand driveshaft assembly.

Outer constant velocity joint type . . . . Ball-and-cage

Inner constant velocity joint type:
  Manual transmission models . . . . Ball-and-cage
  Automatic transmission models . . . . Tripod

Lubrication

Lubricant type . . . . Special grease supplied in repair kit, or suitable molybdenum disulphide grease - consult a Volvo dealer

Quantity:
  Outer CV joint:
    Non-turbo models . . . . 80 g
    Turbo models . . . . 120 g
  Inner CV joint:
    Manual transmission models . . . . 120 g
    Automatic transmission models . . . . 190 g

Torque wrench settings

	Nm	lbf ft
Driveshaft nut:		
Stage 1	120	89
Stage 2	Angle-tighten a further 60°	
Right-hand driveshaft support bearing cap bolts	25	18
Roadwheel bolts	110	81

2.3 Driveshaft retaining nut (arrowed) - seen with wheel removed

2.6 Removing the ABS wheel sensor from the steering knuckle

2.10 Releasing the control arm balljoint from the steering knuckle (arrowed)

1 General information

Drive is transmitted from the differential to the front wheels by means of two solid-steel, equal-length driveshafts equipped with constant velocity (CV) joints at their inner and outer ends. Due to the position of the transmission, an intermediate shaft and support bearing are incorporated into the right-hand driveshaft assembly.

A ball-and-cage type CV joint is fitted to the outer end of each driveshaft. The joint has an outer member, which is splined at its outer end to accept the wheel hub, and is threaded so that it can be fastened to the hub by a large nut. The joint contains six balls within a cage, which engage with the inner member. The complete assembly is protected by a flexible gaiter secured to the driveshaft and joint outer member.

At the inner end, the driveshaft is splined to engage with a ball-and-cage type CV joint on manual transmission models, or a tripod type CV joint, containing needle roller bearings and cups, on automatic transmission versions. On the left-hand side, the driveshaft inner CV joint engages directly with the differential sun wheel. On the right-hand side, the inner joint is integral with the intermediate shaft, the inner end of which engages with the differential sun wheel. As on the outer joints, a flexible gaiter secured to the driveshaft and CV joint outer member protects the complete assembly.

2 Driveshafts - removal and refitting

Removal

1 Firmly apply the handbrake and chock the rear wheels. When the driveshaft nut is to be loosened (or tightened), it is preferable to do so with the car resting on its wheels. If the car is jacked up, this places a high load on the jack, and the car could slip off.

2 If the car has steel wheels, remove the wheel trim on the side being worked on - the driveshaft nut can then be loosened with the wheel on the ground. On models with alloy wheels, the safest option is to remove the wheel on the side being worked on, and to fit the temporary spare (see *Wheel changing* at the front of this Manual) - this wheel allows access to the driveshaft nut (refer to illustration 2.14b).

3 With an assistant firmly depressing the brake pedal, slacken the driveshaft retaining nut using a socket and a long extension bar **(see illustration)**. Note that this nut is extremely tight - ensure that the tools used to loosen it are of good quality, and a good fit.

4 Loosen the front wheel bolts, then jack up the front of the car and support it on axle stands (see *Jacking and vehicle support*). Remove the appropriate front roadwheel.

5 Remove the previously-slackened driveshaft retaining nut. Check the condition of the nut threads - although Volvo state that

the nut can be re-used, consider fitting a new one if the nut is known to have been removed and refitted several times.

6 Remove the ABS wheel sensor from the steering knuckle, and release the sensor wiring from the suspension strut bracket **(see illustration)**.

7 Undo the bolt securing the brake hose and ABS wiring bracket to the inner wheel arch.

8 Free the driveshaft CV joint from the hub flange by tapping it inwards approximately 10 to 15 mm with a plastic or copper mallet.

9 If removing the right-hand driveshaft, remove the splash guard under the engine (where fitted).

10 Undo the nut and remove the clamp bolt securing the suspension control arm balljoint to the steering knuckle. Push down on the suspension arm using a stout bar if necessary, to release the balljoint shank from the knuckle **(see illustration)**. If the balljoint is tight, spread the slot in the steering knuckle with a chisel or large screwdriver. Take care not to damage the balljoint dust cover during and after disconnection.

11 Swivel the suspension strut and steering knuckle assembly outwards, and withdraw the driveshaft CV joint from the hub flange **(see illustration)**.

12 If removing the left-hand driveshaft, free the inner CV joint from the transmission by levering between the edge of the joint and the transmission casing with a large screwdriver or similar tool. Take care not to damage the transmission oil seal or the inner CV joint gaiter. Withdraw the driveshaft from under the wheel arch.

13 If removing the right-hand driveshaft, undo the two bolts and remove the cap from the intermediate shaft support bearing **(see illustration)**. Pull the intermediate shaft out of the transmission, and remove the driveshaft assembly from under the wheel arch.

Refitting

14 Refitting is a reversal of removal, but observe the following points.

 a) *Prior to refitting, remove all traces of metal adhesive, rust, oil and dirt from the splines and threads of the outer CV joint.*

 b) *If working on the left-hand driveshaft, ensure that the inner CV joint is pushed*

2.11 Swivel the suspension strut and steering knuckle outwards to withdraw the CV joint

2.13 Removing the intermediate shaft support bearing cap from the right-hand driveshaft

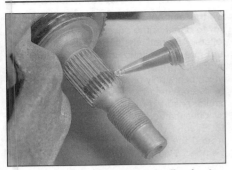

2.14a Apply a bead of metal adhesive to the CV joint splines before engaging the joint into the hub flange

2.14b Tighten the driveshaft nut using a torque wrench . . .

2.14c . . . then with an angle-tightening gauge

fully into the transmission, so that the retaining circlip locks into place in the differential gear.
c) Apply a 3 to 4 mm wide bead of metal adhesive (obtainable from Volvo dealers) to the splines of the outer CV joint before engaging the joint into the hub flange **(see illustration)**.
d) Lubricate the threads of the CV joint and the driveshaft retaining nut with engine oil before refitting the nut. A new nut should be used if there is any doubt about the old one's condition, or if it is known to have been removed and refitted several times.
e) Fit the same wheel as was used for loosening the driveshaft nut, and lower the car to the ground.
f) Tighten all nuts and bolts to the specified torque (see Chapters 9 and 10 for brake

3.3a Expand the CV joint internal circlip using a screwdriver . . .

3.3b . . . then tap off the joint using a hammer and drift

and suspension component torque settings). When tightening the driveshaft nut, tighten first using a torque wrench, then further, through the specified angle, using an angle-tightening gauge **(see illustrations)**.
g) Ensure that the ABS sensor, and sensor location in the steering knuckle, are perfectly clean before refitting.
h) Where applicable, refit the alloy wheel on completion. Tighten the roadwheel bolts to the specified torque.

3 Outer constant velocity joint gaiter - renewal

1 Remove the driveshaft (Section 2).
2 Cut off the gaiter retaining clips, then slide the gaiter down the shaft to expose the outer constant velocity joint.
3 Scoop out as much grease as possible from the joint, then expand the joint internal circlip using a screwdriver inserted between the circlip legs. At the same time, tap the exposed face of the ball hub with a hammer and drift to separate the joint from the driveshaft **(see illustrations)**. Slide the gaiter off the driveshaft.
4 With the constant velocity joint removed from the driveshaft, clean the joint using paraffin, or a suitable solvent, and dry it thoroughly. This is especially important if the old gaiter was badly split, as dust and grit may be embedded in the lubricating grease, which

3.8a Fit a new internal circlip to the CV joint before fitting

will otherwise cause rapid wear of the joint. Remove the internal retaining circlip, and obtain a new one for reassembly.
5 Move the inner splined driving member from side to side, to expose each ball in turn at the top of its track. Examine the balls for cracks, flat spots or signs of surface pitting.
6 Inspect the ball tracks on the inner and outer members. If the tracks have widened, the balls will no longer be a tight fit. At the same time, check the ball cage windows for wear or cracking between the windows. Obtain a new outer joint if any wear is apparent.
7 If the joint is in satisfactory condition, obtain a repair kit from your Volvo dealer, consisting of a new gaiter and retaining clips. The correct type and quantity of the special lubricating grease will usually be supplied with the kit; if not, your dealer will be able to supply it separately.
8 Fit the new internal circlip, then pack the joint with the grease supplied, working it well into the ball tracks, and into the driveshaft opening in the inner member **(see illustrations)**.
9 Slide the rubber gaiter onto the shaft, and locate its inner end in the driveshaft groove.
10 Engage the constant velocity joint with the driveshaft splines, and tap it onto the shaft until the internal circlip locates in the driveshaft groove.
11 Check that the circlip holds the joint securely on the driveshaft, then apply any remaining grease to the joint and the inside of the gaiter.

8

3.8b Pack the joint and gaiter with the special grease

3.12a Fit the gaiter retaining clip . . .

12 Locate the outer lip of the gaiter in the groove on the joint outer member, then fit the two retaining clips. Remove any slack in the clips by carefully compressing the raised section using a pair of pincers **(see illustrations)**.

13 Check that the constant velocity joint moves freely in all directions, then refit the driveshaft as described in Section 2.

4 Inner constant velocity joint gaiter - renewal

Manual transmission models

1 The procedure is the same as described in Section 3 for the outer joint gaiter. If the outer CV joint has already been removed, then it will not be necessary to remove the inner joint to renew the gaiter; it can simply be withdrawn from the outer end of the driveshaft.

Automatic transmission models

Non-turbo models

2 Remove the driveshaft as described in Section 2.

3 Release the gaiter retaining clips, then slide the gaiter down the shaft to expose the joint.

4 Mark the position of the CV joint relative to the driveshaft as an aid to reassembly.

5 Using a screwdriver, carefully bend up the anti-separation plate tangs at their corners **(see illustration)**. Slide the outer member off the tripod joint.

4.5 On non-turbo models, bend up the inner joint anti-separation plate tangs with a screwdriver

3.12b . . . and compress the raised section with pincers

6 Using circlip pliers, extract the circlip securing the tripod joint to the driveshaft. Mark the position of the tripod in relation to the driveshaft, using a dab of paint or a punch.

7 The tripod joint can now be removed. If it is tight, draw the joint off the driveshaft end using a puller. Ensure that the legs of the puller are located behind the joint inner member, and not in contact with the joint rollers. Alternatively, support the inner member of the tripod joint, and press the shaft out using a hydraulic press, again ensuring that no load is applied to the joint rollers.

8 With the tripod joint removed, slide the gaiter off the end of the driveshaft.

9 Wipe clean the joint components, taking care not to remove the alignment marks made on dismantling. **Do not** use paraffin or other solvents to clean this type of joint.

10 Examine the tripod joint, rollers and outer member for any signs of scoring or wear. Check that the rollers move smoothly on the tripod stems. If wear is evident, the joint must be renewed.

11 If the inner joint is in satisfactory condition, obtain a repair kit from your Volvo dealer consisting of a new gaiter and retaining clips. The correct type and quantity of the special lubricating grease will usually be supplied with the kit; if not, your dealer will be able to supply it separately.

12 Carefully slide the new gaiter onto the driveshaft.

13 Aligning the marks made on dismantling, engage the tripod joint with the driveshaft splines. Use a hammer and soft metal drift to

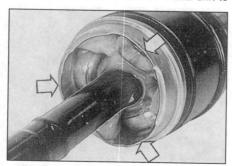

4.24 On turbo models, bend up the inner joint folded collar (arrowed) using pliers

tap the joint onto the shaft, taking great care not to damage the driveshaft splines or joint rollers. Alternatively, support the driveshaft, and press the joint into position using a hydraulic press and suitable tubular spacer which bears only on the joint inner member.

14 Secure the tripod joint in position with the circlip, ensuring that it is correctly located in the driveshaft groove.

15 Evenly distribute the special grease around the tripod joint and inside the outer member. Pack the gaiter with any excess grease.

16 Slide the outer member into position over the tripod joint, ensuring that the marks made on removal are aligned.

17 Carefully tap the anti-separation plate tangs back into their original shape using a mallet.

18 Slide the gaiter up the driveshaft, and locate it in the grooves on the driveshaft and joint outer member.

19 Fit the retaining clips to the gaiter. Remove any slack in the clips by carefully compressing the raised section using a pair of pincers.

20 Check that the constant velocity joint moves freely in all directions, then refit the driveshaft as described in Section 2.

Turbo models

21 Remove the driveshaft as described in Section 2.

22 Release the gaiter retaining clips, then slide the gaiter down the shaft to expose the joint.

23 Mark the position of the CV joint relative to the driveshaft as an aid to reassembly.

24 Using pliers, carefully bend up the folded collar of the joint outer member sufficiently to allow the tripod joint rollers to slide out **(see illustration)**. Withdraw the outer member off the tripod joint. Be prepared to hold the rollers in place, otherwise they may fall off the tripod ends as the outer member is withdrawn. If necessary, secure the rollers in place using tape after removal of the outer member. The rollers are matched to the tripod joint stems, and it is important that they are not interchanged.

25 Using circlip pliers, extract the circlip securing the tripod joint to the driveshaft.

26 The tripod joint can now be removed. If it is tight, draw the joint off the driveshaft end using a puller. Ensure that the legs of the puller are located behind the joint inner member, and not in contact with the joint rollers. Alternatively, support the inner member of the tripod joint, and press the shaft out using a hydraulic press, again ensuring that no load is applied to the joint rollers.

27 With the tripod joint removed, slide the gaiter off the end of the driveshaft.

28 Wipe clean the joint components, taking care not to remove the alignment marks made on dismantling. **Do not** use paraffin or other solvents to clean this type of joint.

29 Examine the tripod joint, rollers and outer member for any signs of scoring or wear. Check that the rollers move smoothly on the tripod stems. If wear is evident, the joint must be renewed.

30 If the inner joint is in satisfactory condition, obtain a repair kit from your Volvo dealer consisting of a new gaiter and retaining clips. The correct type and quantity of the special lubricating grease will usually be supplied with the kit; if not, your dealer will be able to supply it separately.

31 Carefully slide the new gaiter onto the driveshaft.

32 Engage the tripod joint with the driveshaft splines. Use a hammer and soft metal drift to tap the joint onto the shaft, taking great care not to damage the driveshaft splines or joint rollers. Alternatively, support the driveshaft, and press the joint into position using a hydraulic press and suitable tubular spacer which bears only on the joint inner member.

33 Secure the tripod joint in position with the circlip, ensuring that it is correctly located in the driveshaft groove.

34 Evenly distribute the special grease around the tripod joint and inside the outer member. Pack the gaiter with any excess grease.

35 Slide the outer member into position over the tripod joint, ensuring that the marks made on removal are aligned.

36 Carefully return the outer member folded collar back to its original shape.

37 Slide the gaiter up the driveshaft, and locate it in the grooves on the driveshaft and joint outer member.

38 Fit the retaining clips to the gaiter. Remove any slack in the clips by carefully compressing the raised section using a pair of pincers.

39 Check that the constant velocity joint moves freely in all directions, then refit the driveshaft as described in Section 2.

5 Right-hand driveshaft support bearing - removal and refitting

Note: *A hydraulic press and suitable mandrels will be required for this operation. If these are not available, remove the right-hand driveshaft and intermediate shaft as described, then take the intermediate shaft to a Volvo dealer or engineering works to have the support bearing changed.*

Removal

1 Remove the driveshaft (see Section 2).

2 Remove the inner constant velocity joint and gaiter from the driveshaft as described in Section 4.

3 Using circlip pliers, extract the support bearing retaining circlip from the intermediate shaft.

4 Position the support bearing on a press bed with the intermediate shaft uppermost. Press the intermediate shaft out of the support bearing.

Refitting

5 Place the new support bearing on the pressbed, and insert the intermediate shaft through its centre. Press the shaft and constant velocity joint into the bearing until the bearing is against the stop on the shaft.

6 Refit the circlip, ensuring that it locates fully into its groove.

7 Refit the inner constant velocity joint and gaiter to the driveshaft, then refit the driveshaft to the car as described in Sections 4 and 2 respectively.

6 Driveshaft overhaul - general information

Road test the car, and listen for a metallic clicking from the front as the car is driven slowly in a circle with the steering on full-lock. Repeat the check on full-left and full-right lock. This noise may also be apparent when pulling away from a standstill with lock applied. If a clicking noise is heard, this indicates wear in the outer constant velocity joints.

If vibration, consistent with road speed, is felt through the car when accelerating, there is a possibility of wear in the inner constant velocity joints.

Constant velocity joints can be dismantled and inspected for wear as described in Sections 3 and 4. If wear is apparent, the joints should be renewed. It is unclear at the time of writing whether the driveshaft joints are available separately, or whether a complete driveshaft must be obtained. Consult your Volvo dealer or parts supplier for more information.

8

Chapter 9
Braking system

Contents

Degrees of difficulty

Easy, suitable for novice with little experience	**Fairly easy,** suitable for beginner with some experience	**Fairly difficult,** suitable for competent DIY mechanic ⚒

Difficult, suitable for experienced DIY mechanic ⚒	**Very difficult,** suitable for expert DIY or professional ⚒

Specifications

General

System type:

Footbrake . . . . Dual-circuit hydraulic with servo assistance. Disc brakes front and rear. Anti-lock braking (ABS) on all models

Handbrake . . . . Mechanical to drums incorporated in rear brake discs

Front brakes

Type . . . . Ventilated disc, with single-piston sliding calipers
Brake pad minimum lining thickness . . . . 3.0 mm
Disc diameter . . . . 280 mm
Disc thickness:
New . . . . 26.0 mm
Wear limit . . . . 23.0 mm
Maximum disc run-out . . . . 0.04 mm
Maximum disc thickness variation . . . . 0.008 mm

Rear brakes

Type . . . . Solid disc, with twin-piston fixed calipers
Brake pad minimum lining thickness . . . . 2.0 mm
Disc diameter . . . . 295 mm
Disc thickness:
New . . . . 9.6 mm
Wear limit . . . . 8.4 mm
Maximum disc run-out . . . . 0.08 mm
Maximum disc thickness variation . . . . 0.008 mm

Handbrake

Drum diameter . . . . 178 mm
Maximum drum run-out . . . . 0.15 mm
Maximum drum out-of-round . . . . 0.15 mm

Torque wrench settings	Nm	lbf ft
ABS ECU mounting bolts	5	4
ABS wheel sensor mounting bolts	10	7
Flexible hose unions	18	13
Front caliper bracket bolts*	100	74
Front caliper guide pin bolts	30	22
Master cylinder mounting nuts	25	18
Rear caliper mounting bolts*	50	37
Rigid pipe unions	14	10
Roadwheel bolts	110	81
Vacuum servo unit mounting nuts	25	18

Use new bolts every time

1 General information

The brake pedal operates disc brakes on all four wheels by means of a dual circuit hydraulic system with servo assistance. The handbrake operates separate drum brakes on the rear wheels by means of cables. An anti-lock braking system (ABS) is fitted to all models, and is described in further detail in Section 18.

The hydraulic system is split into two circuits, so that in the event of failure of one circuit, the other will still provide adequate braking power (although pedal travel and effort may increase). An axle-split system is employed, in which one circuit serves the front brakes and the other circuit the rear brakes.

The brake servo is of the direct-acting type, being interposed between the brake pedal and the master cylinder. The servo magnifies the effort applied by the driver. It is vacuum-operated, the vacuum being derived from the inlet manifold.

Instrument panel warning lights alert the driver to low fluid level by means of a level sensor in the master cylinder reservoir. Other warning lights remind when the handbrake is applied, and indicate the presence of a fault in the ABS system.

Note: *When servicing any part of the system, work carefully and methodically; also observe scrupulous cleanliness when overhauling any part of the hydraulic system. Always renew components (in axle sets, where applicable) if in doubt about their condition, and use only genuine Volvo replacement parts, or at least those of known good quality. Note the warnings given in Safety first and at relevant points in this Chapter concerning the dangers of asbestos dust and hydraulic fluid.*

2 Hydraulic system - bleeding

⚠️ *Warning: Hydraulic fluid is poisonous; wash off immediately and thoroughly in the case of skin contact, and seek immediate medical advice if any fluid is swallowed or gets into the eyes. Certain types of hydraulic fluid*

are inflammable, and may ignite when allowed into contact with hot components; when servicing any hydraulic system, it is safest to assume that the fluid IS inflammable, and to take precautions against the risk of fire as though it is petrol that is being handled. Hydraulic fluid is also an effective paint stripper, and will attack plastics; if any is spilt, it should be washed off immediately, using copious quantities of clean water. Finally, it is hygroscopic (it absorbs moisture from the air). The more moisture is absorbed by the fluid, the lower its boiling point becomes, leading to a dangerous loss of braking under hard use. Old fluid may be contaminated and unfit for further use. When topping-up or renewing the fluid, always use the recommended type, and ensure that it comes from a freshly-opened sealed container.

General

1 The correct functioning of the brake hydraulic system is only possible after removing all air from the components and circuit; this is achieved by bleeding the system.

2 During the bleeding procedure, add only clean, fresh hydraulic fluid of the specified type; never re-use fluid that has already been bled from the system. Ensure that sufficient fluid is available before starting work.

3 If there is any possibility of incorrect fluid being used in the system, the brake lines and components must be completely flushed with uncontaminated fluid and new seals fitted to the components.

4 If brake fluid has been lost from the master cylinder due to a leak in the system, ensure that the cause is traced and rectified before proceeding further.

5 Park the car on level ground, apply the handbrake, and switch off the ignition.

6 Check that all pipes and hoses are secure, unions tight, and bleed screws closed. Remove the dust caps and clean any dirt from around the bleed screws.

7 Unscrew the master cylinder reservoir cap, and top-up the reservoir to the MAX level line. Refit the cap loosely, and remember to maintain the fluid level at least above the MIN level line throughout the procedure, otherwise there is a risk of further air entering the system.

8 There are a number of one-man, do-it-yourself, brake bleeding kits currently available from motor accessory shops. It is recommended that one of these kits is used wherever possible, as they greatly simplify the bleeding operation, and also reduce the risk of expelled air and fluid being drawn back into the system. If such a kit is not available, the basic (two-man) method must be used, which is described in detail below.

9 If a kit is to be used, prepare the car as described previously, and follow the kit manufacturer's instructions, as the procedure may vary slightly according to the type being used; generally, they are as outlined below in the relevant sub-section.

10 Whichever method is used, the same sequence must be followed (paragraphs 11 and 12) to ensure the removal of all air from the system.

Bleeding sequence

11 If the hydraulic system has only been partially disconnected and suitable precautions were taken to minimise fluid loss, it should only be necessary to bleed that part of the system (ie the primary or secondary circuit).

12 If the complete system is to be bled, then it should be done in the following sequence:

   a) *Rear brakes (in either order).*
   b) *Right-hand front brake.*
   c) *Left-hand front brake.*

Bleeding - basic (two-man) method

13 Collect a clean glass jar of reasonable size and a suitable length of plastic or rubber tubing, which is a tight fit over the bleed screw, and a ring spanner to fit the screws. The help of an assistant will also be required.

14 If not already done, remove the dust cap from the bleed screw of the first wheel to be bled **(see illustration)**, and fit the spanner and bleed tube to the screw. Place the other end of the tube in the jar, and pour in sufficient fluid to cover the end of the tube.

15 Ensure that the master cylinder reservoir fluid level is maintained at least above the MIN level line throughout the procedure.

16 Have the assistant fully depress the brake pedal several times to build up pressure, then maintain it on the final downstroke.

17 While pedal pressure is maintained, unscrew the bleed screw (approximately one turn) and allow the compressed fluid and air to flow into the jar. The assistant should maintain pedal pressure, following it down to the floor if necessary, and should not release it until instructed to do so. When the flow stops, tighten the bleed screw again have the assistant release the pedal slowly, and recheck the reservoir fluid level.

18 Repeat the steps given in paragraphs 16 and 17 until the fluid emerging from the bleed screw is free from air bubbles. If the master cylinder has been drained and refilled, and air is being bled from the first screw in the sequence, allow approximately five seconds between cycles for the master cylinder passages to refill.

19 When no more air bubbles appear, tighten the bleed screw securely, remove the tube and spanner, and refit the dust cap. Do not overtighten the bleed screw.

20 Repeat these procedures on the remaining calipers in sequence until all air is removed from the system and the brake pedal feels firm again.

Bleeding - using a one-way valve kit

21 As their name implies, these kits consist of a length of tubing with a one-way valve fitted, to prevent expelled air and fluid being drawn back into the system; some kits include a translucent container, which can be positioned so that the air bubbles can be more easily seen flowing from the end of the tube.

22 The kit is connected to the bleed screw, which is then opened **(see illustration)**. The user returns to the driver's seat, depresses the brake pedal with a smooth steady stroke, and slowly releases it; this is repeated until the expelled fluid is clear of air bubbles.

23 Note that these kits simplify work so much that it is easy to forget the master cylinder fluid level; ensure that this is maintained at least above the MIN level line at all times.

Bleeding - using a pressure-bleeding kit

24 These kits are usually operated by the reserve of pressurised air contained in the spare tyre. However, note that it will probably be necessary to reduce the pressure to a lower level than normal; refer to the instructions supplied with the kit.

25 By connecting a pressurised, fluid-filled container to the master cylinder reservoir, bleeding is then carried out by simply opening each bleed screw in turn (in the specified sequence) and allowing the fluid to run out, until no more air bubbles can be seen in the expelled fluid.

26 This method has the advantage that the large reservoir of fluid provides an additional safeguard against air being drawn into the system during bleeding.

27 Pressure-bleeding is particularly effective when bleeding difficult systems, or when

2.14 Bleed screw (arrowed) on rear brake caliper

bleeding the complete system at the time of routine fluid renewal. It is also the method recommended by Volvo if the hydraulic system has been drained either wholly or partially.

All methods

28 When bleeding is complete, and firm pedal feel is restored, wash off any spilt fluid, tighten the bleed screws securely, and refit their dust caps.

29 Check the hydraulic fluid level in the master cylinder reservoir, and top-up if necessary.

30 Discard any hydraulic fluid that has been bled from the system; it will not be fit for re-use.

31 Check the feel of the brake pedal. If it feels at all spongy, air must still be present in the system, and further bleeding is required. Failure to bleed satisfactorily after a reasonable repetition of the bleeding operations may be due to worn master cylinder seals.

32 Check the operation of the clutch. Any problems noted would indicate a need to bleed the clutch system also - see Chapter 6, Section 5.

3 Hydraulic pipes and hoses - renewal

Note: *Before starting work, refer to the warning at the beginning of Section 2 concerning the dangers of hydraulic fluid.*

3.2a Brake flexible hose connections at rear axle . . .

2.22 Bleeding the brakes using a one-man kit

1 If any pipe or hose is to be renewed, minimise hydraulic fluid loss by removing the master cylinder reservoir cap, placing a piece of plastic film over the reservoir and sealing it with an elastic band. Alternatively, flexible hoses can be sealed, if required, using a proprietary brake hose clamp; metal brake pipe unions can be plugged (if care is taken not to allow dirt into the system) or capped immediately they are disconnected. Place a wad of rag under any union that is to be disconnected, to catch any spilt fluid.

2 If a flexible hose is to be disconnected, unscrew the brake pipe union nut before removing the spring clip which secures the hose to its mounting, where applicable. Some of the flexible hose unions are protected by a rubber cover - in this case, the pipe will have to be removed from its mounting bracket first, and the cover slid down the pipe, before the nut can be unscrewed **(see illustrations)**.

3 To unscrew the union nuts, it is preferable to obtain a brake pipe spanner of the correct size; these are available from most large motor accessory shops. Failing this, a close-fitting open-ended spanner will be required, though if the nuts are tight or corroded, their flats may be rounded-off if the spanner slips. In such a case, a self-locking wrench is often the only way to unscrew a stubborn union, but it follows that the pipe and the damaged nuts must be renewed on reassembly.

4 Always clean a union and surrounding area before disconnecting it. If disconnecting a component with more than one union, make a careful note of the connections before disturbing any of them.

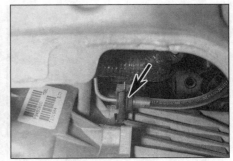
3.2b . . . and on transmission housing - note rubber cover (arrowed)

9

4.2 Extract the brake pad retaining spring clip

4.3a Remove the guide pin protective caps . . .

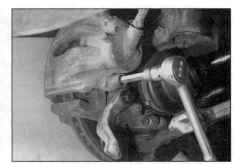

4.3b . . . then unscrew both guide pins

5 If a brake pipe is to be renewed, it can be obtained, cut to length and with the union nuts and end flares in place, from Volvo dealers. All that is then necessary is to bend it to shape, following the line of the original, before fitting it to the car. Alternatively, most motor accessory shops can make up brake pipes from kits, but this requires very careful measurement of the original, to ensure that the replacement is of the correct length. The safest answer is usually to take the original to the shop as a pattern.

6 Before refitting, blow through the new pipe or hose with dry compressed air. Do not overtighten the union nuts. It is not necessary to exercise brute force to obtain a sound joint.

7 If flexible rubber hoses are renewed, ensure that the pipes and hoses are correctly routed, with no kinks or twists, and that they are secured in the clips or brackets provided. Original equipment flexible hoses have white lines along their length which clearly show if the hose is twisted.

8 After fitting, bleed the hydraulic system as described in Section 2, wash off any spilt fluid, and check carefully for fluid leaks.

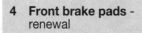

4 Front brake pads -
renewal

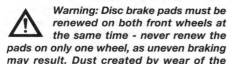

⚠ *Warning: Disc brake pads must be renewed on both front wheels at the same time - never renew the pads on only one wheel, as uneven braking may result. Dust created by wear of the*

pads may contain asbestos, which is a health hazard. Never blow it out with compressed air and do not inhale any of it. DO NOT use petroleum-based solvents to clean brake parts. Use brake cleaner or methylated spirit only. DO NOT allow any brake fluid, oil or grease to contact the brake pads or disc. Also refer to the warning at the start of Section 2 concerning the dangers of hydraulic fluid.

1 Loosen the front wheel bolts and chock the rear wheels. Jack up the front of the car and support it on axle stands (see *Jacking and vehicle support*). Remove the front roadwheels, noting how the locating peg fits into the back of the wheel.

2 Using a screwdriver, carefully extract the brake pad retaining spring clip, noting its fitted location and taking care not to deform it **(see illustration)**.

3 Remove the protective caps over the two caliper guide pins, then unscrew both pins using a 7 mm hexagonal socket **(see illustrations)**.

4 Withdraw the caliper off the brake pads and caliper bracket, taking care not to stretch the brake hose **(see illustration)**.

5 Remove the inboard pad with spring clip retainer from the caliper piston, and the outboard brake pad from the caliper bracket **(see illustrations)**. Suspend the caliper using string or wire tied to a convenient suspension component. Do not press the brake pedal whilst the caliper is removed.

6 Measure the thickness of the pad friction linings. If any one pad lining has worn down to

the specified minimum, all four front pads must be renewed. Do not interchange pads in an attempt to even out wear. (Uneven pad wear may be due to the caliper sticking on the guide pins).

7 Clean the caliper and bracket with a damp rag or an old paintbrush. Inspect the caliper piston and dust boot for signs of fluid leakage. Also inspect the guide pin rubber bushes. Repair or renew as necessary (see Section 8).

8 Remove any scale or rust from the outer rim of the brake disc with a wire brush or file. Inspect the visible surface of the brake disc. If deep scoring, cracks or grooves are evident, or if brake judder or snatch has been a problem, carry out a more thorough inspection (see Section 6).

9 If new pads are to be fitted, press the caliper piston back into its bore with a pair of pliers, being careful not to damage the dust boot. Remove some fluid from the master cylinder reservoir to prevent overflowing as the piston is pressed back.

> **HAYNES HiNT** *An ideal way to remove fluid from the master cylinder reservoir is to use a clean syringe or an old poultry baster.*

10 Position the outboard pad in the caliper bracket with the friction surface towards the disc. Engage the spring clip retainer of the inboard pad with the caliper piston and push the pad fully into contact with the piston. Place the caliper over the disc and onto the caliper bracket.

4.4 Withdraw the caliper off the brake pads

4.5a Remove the inboard pad from the caliper piston . . .

4.5b . . . and the outboard pad from the caliper bracket

5.2a Tap out the two rear brake pad retaining pins . . .

5.2b . . . and remove the anti-rattle spring

5.4 Withdraw the brake pads and anti-squeal shims

11 Lubricate the guide pins with silicone grease, insert them into the caliper and tighten both to the specified torque. Refit the protective caps to the guide pins.
12 Refit the brake pad retaining spring clip.
13 Press the brake pedal several times to bring the pads up to the disc.
14 Repeat the operations on the other front brake.
15 Refit the roadwheels, lower the car and tighten the wheel bolts in a diagonal sequence to the specified torque.
16 Check the brake fluid level and top-up if necessary.
17 If new pads have been fitted, avoid hard braking as far as possible for the first few hundred miles to allow the linings to bed-in.

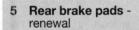

5 Rear brake pads - renewal

⚠️ *Warning: Disc brake pads must be renewed on both rear wheels at the same time - never renew the pads on only one wheel as uneven braking may result. Dust created by wear of the pads may contain asbestos, which is a health hazard. Never blow it out with compressed air and do not inhale any of it. DO NOT use petroleum-based solvents to clean brake parts. Use brake cleaner or methylated spirit only. DO NOT allow any brake fluid, oil or grease to contact the brake pads or disc. Also refer to the warning at the start of Section 2 concerning the dangers of hydraulic fluid.*

1 Loosen the rear wheel bolts and chock the front wheels. Jack up the rear of the car and support it on axle stands (see *Jacking and vehicle support*). Remove the rear roadwheels, noting how the locating peg fits into the back of the wheel.
2 Drive the two retaining pins out of the caliper using a hammer and punch. Recover the anti-rattle spring, noting how it fits **(see illustrations)**. Obtain a new spring for reassembly.
3 Press each pad away from the disc, using pliers. Do not lever between the pads and the disc.

4 Pull the pads out of the caliper, along with the anti-squeal shims (if fitted) **(see illustration)**. Identify their position if they are to be re-used. Do not press the brake pedal with the pads removed.
5 Measure the thickness of the pad friction linings. If any one pad lining has worn down to the specified minimum, all four rear pads must be renewed. Do not interchange pads in an attempt to even out wear.
6 Clean the caliper with a damp rag or an old paintbrush. Inspect the caliper pistons and dust boots for signs of fluid leakage. Repair or renew as necessary (see Section 9).
7 Inspect the visible surface of the brake disc. If deep scoring, cracks or grooves are evident, or if brake judder or snatch has been a problem, carry out a more thorough inspection (see Section 7). Remove the caliper if necessary for access to the inboard face of the disc.
8 If new pads are to be fitted, press the caliper pistons back into their bores using pliers. Remove some fluid from the master cylinder reservoir to prevent overflowing as the pistons are pressed back.

 HAYNES HiNT *An ideal way to remove fluid from the master cylinder reservoir is to use a clean syringe or an old poultry baster.*

9 Fit the pads and shims into the jaws of the caliper with the friction surfaces towards the disc.

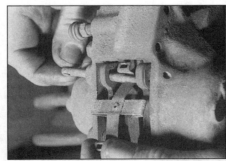

5.10a Refit the upper brake pad retaining pin and anti-rattle spring . . .

10 Insert the upper pad retaining pin together with the anti-rattle spring, and tap the retaining pin fully home. Fit the lower pad retaining pin in the same way, making sure that the pin passes over the tongue of the spring **(see illustrations)**.
11 Pump the brake pedal several times to bring the new pads up to the discs.
12 Repeat the operations on the other rear brake.
13 Refit the roadwheels, lower the car and tighten the wheel bolts in a diagonal sequence to the specified torque.
14 Check the brake fluid level and top-up if necessary.
15 If new pads have been fitted, avoid harsh braking as far as possible for the first few hundred miles to allow the linings to bed in.

6 Front brake disc - inspection, removal and refitting

Note: *Before starting work, refer to the warning at the beginning of Section 4 concerning the dangers of asbestos dust.*

Inspection

Note: *If either disc requires renewal, BOTH should be renewed at the same time, to ensure even and consistent braking. New brake pads should also be fitted.*

1 Remove the front brake pads as described in Section 4.
2 Inspect the disc friction surfaces for cracks or deep scoring (light grooving is normal and

5.10b . . . then refit the lower pin, passing it over the tongue of the spring

9

6.5 Removing the front brake caliper bracket

6.6a Undo the front disc retaining spigot pin . . .

6.6b . . . then remove the disc

may be ignored). A cracked disc must be renewed; a scored disc can be reclaimed by machining, provided that the thickness is not reduced below the specified minimum.

3 Check the disc run-out using a dial test indicator with its probe positioned near the outer edge of the disc. If the run-out exceeds the figures given in the *Specifications*, machining may be possible, otherwise disc renewal will be necessary.

If a dial test indicator is not available, check the run-out by positioning a fixed pointer near the outer edge, in contact with the disc face. Rotate the disc and measure the maximum displacement of the pointer with feeler blades.

4 Excessive disc thickness variation can also cause judder. Check this using a micrometer.

Removal

5 With the brake pads and caliper removed (Section 4), undo the two mounting bolts and remove the brake caliper bracket **(see illustration)**. Note that new bolts will be required for refitting.

6 Check whether the position of the disc in relation to the hub is marked, and if not, make your own mark as an aid to refitting. Remove the spigot pin which holds the disc to the hub, and lift off the disc **(see illustrations)**.

Refitting

7 Ensure that the hub and disc mating faces are spotlessly clean. Clean any rustproofing compound off a new disc with methylated spirit and a rag.

8 Locate the disc on the hub with the orientation marks aligned, and refit the retaining spigot pin.

9 Refit the brake caliper bracket, and tighten the new bolts to the specified torque.

10 Refit the brake pads as described in Section 4.

7 Rear brake disc -
inspection, removal and refitting

Note: *Before starting work, refer to the warning at the beginning of Section 5 concerning the dangers of asbestos dust.*

Inspection

Note: *If either disc requires renewal, BOTH should be renewed at the same time, to ensure even and consistent braking. New brake pads should also be fitted.*

1 With the rear brake pads removed (Section 5), the inspection procedures are the same as for the front brake disc, and reference should be made to Section 6, paragraphs 2 to 4 inclusive. Additionally, after removal, check the condition of the handbrake drums. Refinishing, run-out and out-of-round limits

are given in the *Specifications*. The drums are unlikely to wear, unless the handbrake is habitually used to stop the car.

Removal

2 If not already done, remove the rear brake pads as described in Section 5.

3 Release the caliper brake pipe from the retaining clip on the suspension trailing arm and, if working on the left-hand caliper, undo the brake pipe three-way connector mounting bolt.

4 Undo the two caliper mounting bolts, and withdraw the caliper without straining the brake pipe **(see illustration)**. Note that new bolts will be required for refitting. Suitably support the caliper, or suspend it using string or wire tied to a convenient suspension component.

5 Unscrew the wheel locating spigot pin from the disc **(see illustration)**.

6 Mark the position of the disc in relation to the hub, then pull off the disc **(see illustration)**. Tap it with a soft-faced mallet if necessary to free it. If it is not possible to remove the disc due to it binding on the handbrake shoes, proceed as follows.

7 From inside the car, lift up the centre console armrest and carefully prise out the rectangular cover panel from the base of the console.

8 Working through the cover panel aperture, and using a cranked hexagonal key, turn the adjuster bolt on the rear of the handbrake lever until there is slack in the handbrake cables.

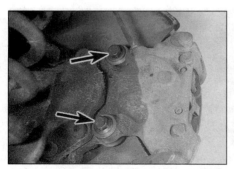

7.4 Rear brake caliper mounting bolts (arrowed)

7.5 Undo the rear disc spigot pin . . .

7.6 . . . then remove the disc

7.9 Releasing the handbrake shoe internal adjuster wheel

9 Turn the rear brake disc until the handbrake adjustment hole is positioned over the handbrake shoe internal adjuster wheel. Insert a screwdriver through the hole, and turn the adjuster wheel as necessary to back off the handbrake shoes **(see illustration)**.

Refitting

10 Ensure that the hub and disc mating faces are spotlessly clean. Clean any rustproofing compound off a new disc with methylated spirit and a rag.
11 Locate the disc on the hub with the orientation marks aligned, and refit the retaining spigot pin.
12 Refit the brake caliper and tighten the new bolts to the specified torque. Secure the brake pipe in the support clips or refit the three-way connector bolt, as applicable.
13 Refit the brake pads as described in Section 5.
14 Adjust the handbrake as described in Section 13.

8 Front brake caliper - removal, overhaul and refitting

Note: Before starting work, refer to the warning at the beginning of Section 2 concerning the dangers of hydraulic fluid, and to the warning at the beginning of Section 4 concerning the dangers of asbestos dust.

Removal

1 Apply the handbrake and chock the rear wheels. Loosen the front wheel bolts, then jack up the front of the car and support it on axle stands (see Jacking and vehicle support). Remove the roadwheel.
2 To minimise fluid loss, unscrew the master cylinder reservoir filler cap and place a piece of polythene over the filler neck. Secure the polythene with an elastic band ensuring that an airtight seal is obtained. Alternatively, use a brake hose clamp, a G-clamp, or a similar tool with protected jaws, to clamp the front flexible hydraulic hose.
3 Clean the area around the hydraulic hose-to-caliper union, then slacken the hose union half a turn. Be prepared for fluid spillage.

4 Remove the brake pads as described in Section 4.
5 Unscrew the caliper from the hydraulic hose, and wipe up any spilled brake fluid immediately. Plug or cap the open unions.
6 If it is wished to remove the caliper bracket, undo the two bolts which secure it to the steering knuckle. Note that new bolts will be required for refitting.

Overhaul

7 With the brake caliper removed, clean it externally with methylated spirit and a soft brush.
8 Remove the bleed screw and empty any remaining hydraulic fluid out of the caliper.
9 Remove the piston dust boot and pull the piston out of the caliper bore. If the caliper piston is reluctant to move, refit the bleed screw and apply low air pressure (eg from a foot pump) to the fluid inlet, but note that the piston may be ejected with some force.
10 Hook out the piston seal from the bore using a blunt instrument.
11 Withdraw the two guide pin rubber bushes from their locations.
12 Clean the piston and caliper bore with a lint-free rag and some clean brake fluid or methylated spirit. Slight imperfections may be polished out with steel wool. If any pitting, scoring or wear ridges are evident, the caliper must be renewed.
13 Renew all rubber components (seal, dust boot and guide pin bushes) as a matter of course. Blow through the fluid inlet and bleed screw hole with compressed air.
14 Lubricate the new piston seal with clean brake fluid. Insert the seal into the groove in the bore, using your fingers only.
15 Fit a new dust boot to the piston, ensuring that it is properly seated in the piston groove. Extend the dust boot ready for fitting.
16 Lubricate the piston and bore with clean brake fluid.
17 Offer the piston and dust boot to the caliper. Engage the dust boot with the groove in the caliper, then push the piston through the dust boot into the caliper bore.
18 Fit the new guide pin rubber bushes, then refit the caliper bleed screw.

Refitting

19 If removed, refit the caliper bracket using new bolts tightened to the specified torque.
20 Refit the brake pads as described in Section 4, but screw the caliper onto the flexible hose before refitting it to the caliper bracket.
21 Tighten the flexible hose union ensuring that the hose is not kinked.
22 Remove the brake hose clamp or polythene, where fitted, and bleed the hydraulic system as described in Section 2.
23 Apply the footbrake two or three times to settle the pads, then refit the roadwheel and lower the car. Tighten the wheel bolts in a diagonal sequence to the specified torque.

9 Rear brake caliper - removal, overhaul and refitting

Note: Before starting work, refer to the warning at the beginning of Section 2 concerning the dangers of hydraulic fluid, and to the warning at the beginning of Section 5 concerning the dangers of asbestos dust.

Removal

1 To minimise fluid loss, unscrew the master cylinder reservoir filler cap, and place a piece of polythene over the filler neck. Secure the polythene with an elastic band, ensuring that an airtight seal is obtained. Alternatively, use a brake hose clamp, a G-clamp, or a similar tool with protected jaws, to clamp the rear flexible hydraulic hose.
2 Remove the rear brake pads as described in Section 5.
3 Clean around the hydraulic union on the caliper, then undo the pipe union. Be prepared for fluid spillage, and plug or cap the open unions.
4 Undo the two retaining bolts and remove the caliper. Note that new bolts will be required for refitting.

Overhaul

5 This is essentially the same procedure as that described for the front caliper (see Section 8), except that there are two pistons in each caliper. Do not attempt to separate the caliper halves to facilitate removal of the pistons.

Refitting

6 Fit the caliper over the disc and secure it to the stub axle bracket with two new bolts. Tighten the bolts to the specified torque.
7 Refit the brake pipe to the caliper, and tighten the union securely.
8 Refit the brake pads as described in Section 5.
9 Remove the brake hose clamp or polythene, where fitted, and bleed the hydraulic system as described in Section 2.
10 Apply the footbrake two or three times to settle the pads, then refit the roadwheel and lower the car. Tighten the wheel bolts in a diagonal sequence to the specified torque.

10 Brake master cylinder - removal and refitting

Note: Before starting work, refer to the warning at the beginning of Section 2 concerning the dangers of hydraulic fluid.
Note: Overhaul of the master cylinder is not possible, and internal components are not available separately. In the event of a fault in the master cylinder, the unit must be renewed.

Removal

1 Disconnect the battery negative lead.

9

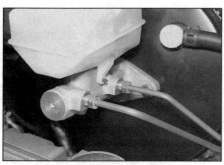

10.5 Brake pipe attachments at the master cylinder

2 Syphon as much fluid as possible from the master cylinder reservoir, using a hydrometer or old poultry baster.
Caution: Do not syphon the fluid by mouth - it is poisonous.
3 Disconnect the warning light wiring connector from the reservoir cap.
4 Release the spring clip and disconnect the clutch master cylinder fluid hose from the side of the reservoir. Be prepared for fluid spillage. Plug the open end of the hose and the reservoir orifice.
5 Disconnect the hydraulic pipe unions from the master cylinder **(see illustration)**. Be prepared for further fluid spillage. Cap the open unions to keep dirt out.
6 Remove the nuts which secure the master cylinder to the servo. Pull the master cylinder off the servo studs and remove it. Be careful not to spill hydraulic fluid on the paintwork.

Refitting

7 Place the master cylinder in position on the servo unit, and secure with the nuts tightened to the specified torque.
8 Refit the brake pipes, but do not tighten the union nuts fully at this stage.
9 Refit the fluid hose to the reservoir. Lubricate the hose end with brake hydraulic fluid to ease fitting.
10 Reconnect the warning light connector to the reservoir cap then reconnect the battery.
11 Place absorbent rags under the brake pipe unions on the master cylinder, then fill the reservoir with clean hydraulic fluid of the specified type.

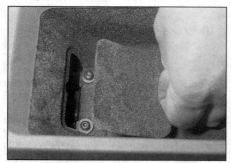

13.5 Prise up the cover panel from the base of the centre console for access to the handbrake lever adjuster bolt

12 Tighten the brake pipe unions securely when hydraulic fluid can be seen seeping out.
13 Bleed the hydraulic system as described in Section 2 on completion. On manual transmission models, bleed the clutch hydraulic system as described in Chapter 6.
14 After the system has been bled, pressure test the master cylinder by depressing the brake pedal hard and holding it down for 30 seconds. Release the pedal and check for leaks around the master cylinder pipe unions.

11 Brake pedal - removal and refitting

The procedure for removal and refitting of the brake pedal is the same as for the clutch pedal. Refer to Chapter 6, Section 2.

12 Vacuum servo unit - removal and refitting

Removal

1 Disconnect the battery negative lead, then depress the brake pedal several times to dissipate any vacuum in the servo unit.
2 On left-hand-drive models, remove the ABS hydraulic modulator as described in Section 19.
3 Remove the brake master cylinder as described in Section 10.
4 Disconnect the servo vacuum feed by levering out the non-return valve on the front of the servo unit.
5 Disconnect the wiring connector from the brake pedal position sensor.
6 Release the wiring loom and ducting around the servo as necessary, for improved access.
7 Remove the trim panel under the facia on the driver's side, which is secured by a single screw, and is then pulled out of its locating slots at the top. Disconnect the wiring plug from the footwell light.
8 Disconnect the servo pushrod and linkage from the brake pedal by removing the retaining clip.

13.6 Handbrake lever adjuster bolt (arrowed) as seen with the centre console removed

9 Undo the four nuts, then remove the servo from the engine compartment. Recover the O-ring seal between the servo and the bulkhead.

Refitting

10 Refitting is a reversal of removal bearing in mind the following points:
  a) Ensure that the O-ring is in position before fitting the servo.
  b) Tighten all nuts and bolts to the specified torque.
  c) Refit the master cylinder as described in Section 10.
  d) On left-hand-drive models, refit the ABS hydraulic modulator as described in Section 19.
  e) Bleed the hydraulic system as described in Section 2 on completion.

13 Handbrake - adjustment

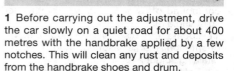

1 Before carrying out the adjustment, drive the car slowly on a quiet road for about 400 metres with the handbrake applied by a few notches. This will clean any rust and deposits from the handbrake shoes and drum.
2 Loosen the rear wheel bolts and chock the front wheels. Jack up the rear of the car and support it on axle stands (see *Jacking and vehicle support*). Remove the rear roadwheels.
3 With the handbrake fully released, turn one of the rear brake discs until the handbrake adjustment hole is positioned over the handbrake shoe internal adjuster wheel. Insert a screwdriver through the hole and turn the adjuster wheel as necessary until the disc is locked (see illustration 7.9). Now back off the adjuster wheel by about 4 to 5 notches until the disc is again free to turn without any trace of binding. Repeat this procedure on the other rear brake.
4 From inside the car, pull up the handbrake lever and check that full braking effect is achieved on the rear wheels between 3 and 5 clicks of the handbrake lever ratchet. If this is not the case, proceed as follows.
5 Lift up the centre console armrest, and carefully prise out the rectangular cover panel from the base of the console **(see illustration)**.
6 Working through the cover panel aperture and using a cranked hexagonal key, turn the adjuster bolt on the rear of the handbrake lever until the conditions described in paragraph 4 are met **(see illustration)**. Release the handbrake lever, and check that the rear wheels are both free to turn without binding. Refit the centre console cover panel.
7 When adjustment is correct, refit the roadwheels and lower the car. Tighten the wheel bolts in a diagonal sequence to the specified torque.

14.4a Unhook the handbrake shoe lower return spring . . .

14.4b . . . and upper return spring . . .

14.4c . . . then separate the shoes, noting the fitted position of the adjuster

14 Handbrake shoes - inspection and renewal

Inspection

1 Remove the rear brake disc (Section 7).
2 Inspect the shoes for wear, damage or oil/fluid contamination. Renew them if necessary as described below. As with the brake pads, the shoes must be renewed in axle sets.
3 If the shoes are contaminated, identify and rectify the source of any contamination before the new shoes are fitted; one possible problem area could be the hub bearing grease seal. Unfortunately, if this has failed, the hub assembly must be renewed complete (See Chapter 10).

Renewal

4 Unhook the handbrake shoe lower return spring, prise the shoes apart and remove them from the backplate. Unhook the upper return spring and separate the shoes. Note the correct fitted position of the adjuster mechanism as it is removed **(see illustrations)**.
5 Clean the backplate, the inside of the brake disc and the adjuster mechanism. Make sure that the adjuster wheel turns freely on its threads.
6 Apply a smear of high melting-point grease to the shoe contact areas on the brake backplate, and to the threads of the adjuster mechanism.
7 Refitting is a reversal of removal. Take care not to get grease or oil onto the brake linings or the disc friction surface.
8 Refit the brake disc as described in Section 7, then adjust the handbrake as described in Section 13.

15 Handbrake cable - removal and refitting

Removal

1 Loosen the rear wheel bolts and chock the front wheels. Jack up the rear of the car and support it on axle stands (see *Jacking and vehicle support*). Remove the rear roadwheels.

2 Refer to Chapter 11 and remove the centre console. Also remove the rear seat and carpets as necessary to gain access to the cable entry in the floorpan.
3 Ensure that the handbrake is released, then slacken the handbrake adjuster bolt at the rear of the lever until there is slack in the cables (refer to illustration 13.6).
4 Extract the circlip and withdraw the handbrake cable operating segment from the handbrake lever shaft, then disconnect the handbrake inner cable end piece from the segment **(see illustrations)**.
5 Drill out the rivet securing the handbrake cable to the suspension trailing arm on each side. Undo the screw and release the cable support bracket from the trailing arm mounting just forward of the rear wheel arch **(see illustrations)**.
6 At each handbrake outer cable end, twist the cable plastic guide sleeve back and forth to release it from the stub axle. Disconnect the inner cable from the handbrake shoe expander by sliding the cable end piece out of the expander sleeve **(see illustrations overleaf)**.
7 Release any remaining cable clips, and withdraw the cable out from inside the car.

Refitting

8 Attach the end of the inner cable to the handbrake shoe expander, and pull it fully into place so that it locks in the expander sleeve.
9 Push the guide sleeve back into position on the stub axle.

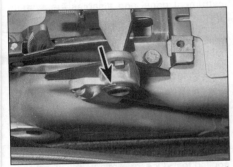

15.4a Extract the cable operating segment circlip (arrowed)

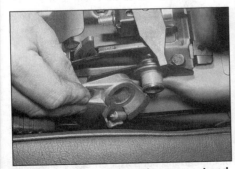

15.4b . . . then withdraw the segment and disconnect the cable

15.5a Drill out the rivet securing the handbrake cable to the suspension arm . . .

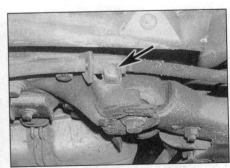

15.5b . . . and undo the support bracket screw (arrowed)

9

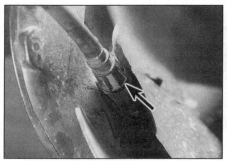
15.6a Twist the guide sleeve (arrowed) back and forth . . .

15.6b . . . to release it from the stub axle

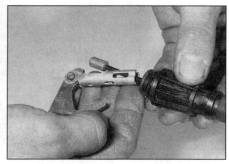
15.6c Slide the inner cable end piece out of the expander sleeve

10 Feed the cable through to the inside of the car, and reconnect the inner cable end to the handbrake lever segment. Engage the segment with the handbrake lever mechanism, and secure with the circlip. Ensure that the circlip locates fully into its groove.

11 Refit the cable support bracket to the trailing arm mounting.

12 Secure the cable to the suspension trailing arm with a new pop rivet. Alternatively, the cable could be attached to the trailing arm using a suitable cable-tie, or using a self-tapping screw to secure the clip.

13 Refit any remaining cable clips, then refit the centre console as described in Chapter 11. Refit the rear seat and carpets.

14 Operate the handbrake two or three times to settle the cable, then adjust the handbrake as described in Section 13.

16 Handbrake lever - removal and refitting

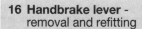

Removal

1 Remove the centre console as described in Chapter 11.

2 Disconnect the wiring connector from the handbrake warning light switch.

3 Undo the warning light switch mounting bolt and remove the switch.

4 Undo the three bolts securing the lever assembly to the floor.

5 Disconnect the handbrake cables and remove the lever assembly from the car.

Refitting

6 Refitting is a reversal of removal. Adjust the handbrake as described in Section 13 on completion.

17 Stop-light switch - removal and refitting

Removal

1 Disconnect the battery negative lead.

2 Remove the trim panel under the facia on the driver's side, which is secured by a single

screw, and is then pulled out of its locating slots at the top. Disconnect the wiring plug from the footwell light.

3 Depress the brake pedal slightly, then push the stop-light switch towards the pedal to release the locking sleeve.

4 Pull the locking sleeve towards the switch plunger as far as it will go.

5 Compress the switch side retaining catches and withdraw the switch from the pedal bracket. Disconnect the wiring connector(s) and remove the switch **(see illustration)**.

Refitting

6 Make sure that the switch locking sleeve is fully extended towards the switch plunger.

7 Reconnect the wiring then, with the brake pedal depressed, locate the switch in the pedal bracket. Push the switch into the bracket until a click is heard as the retaining catches clip into the bracket.

8 Pull the brake pedal up as far as it will go; this will automatically adjust the switch.

9 Gently rock the switch to ensure that it is securely in place, then reconnect the battery and check the operation of the stop-lights.

10 Refit the panels removed for access.

18 Anti-lock braking system (ABS) - general information

The anti-lock braking system fitted as standard equipment on all models, monitors the rotational speed of the wheels under braking. Sudden deceleration of one wheel,

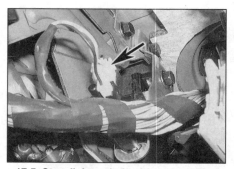
17.5 Stop-light switch wiring connector (arrowed)

indicating that lock-up is occurring, causes the hydraulic pressure to that wheel's brake to be reduced or interrupted momentarily.

The main components of the system are the wheel sensors, the electronic control unit (ECU) and the hydraulic modulator assembly.

One sensor is fitted to each wheel, together with a pulse wheel carried on the wheel hub. The sensors monitor the rotational speeds of the wheels, and are able to detect when there is a risk of wheel locking (low rotational speed). The wheel sensors also provide vehicle speed information to the speedometer.

Information from the sensors is fed to the ECU, which operates solenoid valves in the hydraulic modulator. The solenoid valves restrict the hydraulic fluid supply to any caliper detected to be on the verge of locking.

Should a fault develop in the system, the ECU illuminates a warning light on the instrument panel and disables the system. Normal braking will still be available, but without the anti-lock function. In the event of a fault, the ECU stores a series of signals (or fault codes) for subsequent read-out using diagnostic equipment (see Section 20).

On cars equipped with a traction control system (TRACS), the ABS system performs a dual role. In addition to detecting when a wheel is locking under braking, the system also detects a wheel that is spinning under acceleration. When this condition is detected, the brake on that wheel is momentarily applied to reduce, or eliminate the wheel spin. When the rotational speed of the spinning wheel is detected to be equal to the other wheels, the brake is released.

19 Anti-lock braking system (ABS) components - removal and refitting

Removal

Front wheel sensor

1 Loosen the appropriate front wheel bolts and chock the rear wheels. Jack up the front of the car and support it on axle stands (see *Jacking and vehicle support*). Remove the roadwheel.

19.2a ABS wheel sensor wiring connector (arrowed) - left-hand . . .

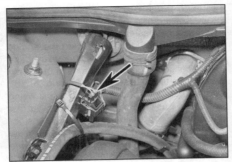
19.2b . . . and right-hand side

19.3a Remove the wheel sensor from the steering knuckle . . .

2 Disconnect the wiring plug for the wheel sensor - the plugs are located in each rear corner of the engine compartment **(see illustrations)**. Once the plug is disconnected, feed the wiring down into the wheel arch.

3 Undo the bolt which secures the sensor to the steering knuckle. Withdraw the sensor, and unclip the wiring from the brackets on the suspension strut and inner wing **(see illustrations)**.

Front pulse wheel

4 The front pulse wheel is a press fit on the driveshaft constant velocity joint, and special tools are required for removal. This work should be entrusted to a Volvo dealer.

Rear wheel sensor

5 Loosen the appropriate rear wheel bolts and chock the front wheels. Jack up the rear of the car and support it on axle stands (see *Jacking and vehicle support*). Remove the roadwheel.

6 Undo the bolt which secures the sensor to the stub axle. Withdraw the sensor and disconnect the wiring connector. On certain models, it will be necessary to trace the wiring back until the connector is located and can then be disconnected. This may entail removal of the rear seats or luggage compartment trim panels (see Chapter 11).

Electronic control unit (ECU)

7 The ECU is attached to the main modulator, and can only be separated once the modulator is removed, as described later in this Section.

Hydraulic modulator

Note: *Before starting work, refer to the warning at the beginning of Section 2 concerning the dangers of hydraulic fluid.*

8 Disconnect the battery negative lead.

9 Drain the hydraulic fluid from the braking system. This is essentially the same operation as bleeding the system (see Section 2), but no fluid is added to the master cylinder reservoir during the procedure. Note, however that when the system is bled on completion, pressure-bleeding equipment will be necessary.

10 Remove the complete air cleaner assembly as described in Chapter 4A. Additionally, on turbo models, remove the inlet duct between the air cleaner assembly and the turbocharger.

11 Wipe clean all the brake pipe unions at the hydraulic modulator. Place absorbent rags beneath the pipe unions to catch any spilt fluid.

12 Before disconnecting the fluid pipes from the hydraulic modulator, mark them for position (e.g. by wrapping labels around the pipes). Undo the union nuts on the brake pipes on the side of the hydraulic modulator. Carefully withdraw the pipes, and cover the open unions and pipe ends **(see illustration)**.

13 Unclip the cover from the large wiring connector at the side of the modulator. Release the connector locking clip and disconnect the wiring plug.

14 Disconnect the ABS pump motor wiring connector.

15 Undo the bolts securing the hydraulic modulator mounting bracket to the inner wing.

Move the wiring aside, and lift out the modulator assembly and bracket.

16 If required (such as for renewal of the ECU), the modulator can be separated from the mounting bracket by removing the four mounting bolts.

17 Note that the modulator is a sealed precision assembly, and must not under any circumstances be dismantled.

Brake pedal position sensor

18 Depress the brake pedal two or three times to dissipate any vacuum remaining in the servo unit.

19 Disconnect the wiring connector from the pedal sensor located on the front face of the vacuum servo unit **(see illustration)**.

20 Open the circlip and withdraw the sensor from the servo. Recover the O-ring and spacer sleeve from the sensor.

Refitting

21 In all cases, refitting is a reversal of the removal operations but note the following points:

a) *Clean off all dirt from the wheel sensors and mounting locations before refitting, and also clean the pulse wheels with a stiff brush.*

b) *Bleed the hydraulic system as described in Section 2 after refitting the hydraulic modulator.*

c) *Use a new O-ring on the brake pedal position sensor, and ensure that the colour-coded spacer sleeve matches the colour code of the servo unit.*

19.3b . . . and prise out the wiring grommets (arrowed) from the clips under the wheel arch

19.12 ABS hydraulic modulator

19.19 Brake pedal position sensor on the front of the servo unit

9

20 Anti-lock braking system (ABS) - fault diagnosis

General information

1 The anti-lock braking system incorporates an on-board diagnostic system to facilitate fault finding and system testing. Should a fault occur, the ECU stores a series of signals (or fault codes) for subsequent read-out via the OBD plug located under the centre console compartment lid.

2 If problems have been experienced, the on-board diagnostic system can be used to pinpoint any problem areas, but this requires special test equipment. Once this has been done, further tests may often be necessary to determine the exact nature of the fault; ie, whether a component itself has failed, or whether it is a wiring or other inter-related problem. Apart from visually checking the wiring and connections, any testing will require the use of a fault code reader at least. A Volvo dealer will obviously have such a reader, but they are also available from other suppliers, including Haynes. It is unlikely to be cost-effective for the private owner to purchase a fault code reader, but a well-equipped local garage or auto electrical specialist will have one.

Preliminary checks

Note: *When carrying out these checks to trace a fault, remember that if the fault has appeared only a short time after any part of the vehicle has been serviced or overhauled, the first place to check is where that work was carried out, however unrelated it may appear, to ensure that no carelessly-refitted components are causing the problem.*

Remember that any fault codes which have been logged will have to be cleared from the ECU memory using a dedicated fault code reader (see paragraph 2) before you can be certain the cause of the fault has been fixed.

3 Open the bonnet and check the condition of the battery connections - remake the connections or renew the leads if a fault is found. Use the same techniques to ensure that all earth points in the engine compartment provide good electrical contact through clean, metal-to-metal joints, and that all are securely fastened.

4 Next work methodically around the engine compartment, checking all visible wiring, and the connections between sections of the wiring loom (refer to illustrations 20.2a and 20.2b). What you are looking for at this stage is wiring that is obviously damaged by chafing against sharp edges, or against moving suspension/transmission components and/or the auxiliary drivebelt, by being trapped or crushed between carelessly-refitted components, or melted by being forced into contact with hot engine castings, coolant pipes, etc. In almost all cases, damage of this sort is caused in the first instance by incorrect routing on reassembly after previous work has been carried out (see the note at the beginning of this sub-Section).

5 Obviously wires can break or short together inside the insulation so that no visible evidence betrays the fault, but this usually only occurs where the wiring loom has been incorrectly routed so that it is stretched taut or kinked sharply; either of these conditions should be obvious on even a casual inspection. If this is thought to have happened and the fault proves elusive, the suspect section of wiring should be checked very carefully during the more detailed checks which follow.

6 Depending on the extent of the problem, damaged wiring may be repaired by rejoining the break or splicing-in a new length of wire, using solder to ensure a good connection, and remaking the insulation with adhesive insulating tape or heat-shrink tubing, as desired. If the damage is extensive, given the implications for the vehicle's future reliability, the best long-term answer may well be to renew that entire section of the loom, however expensive this may appear.

7 When the actual damage has been repaired, ensure that the wiring loom is re-routed correctly, so that it is clear of other components, is not stretched or kinked, and is secured out of harm's way using the plastic clips, guides and ties provided.

8 Check all electrical connectors, ensuring that they are clean, securely fastened, and that each is locked by its plastic tabs or wire clip, as appropriate. If any connector shows external signs of corrosion (accumulations of white or green deposits, or streaks of 'rust'), or if any is thought to be dirty, it must be unplugged and cleaned using electrical contact cleaner. If the connector pins are severely corroded, the connector must be renewed; note that this may mean the renewal of that entire section of the loom.

9 If the cleaner completely removes the corrosion to leave the connector in a satisfactory condition, it would be wise to pack the connector with a suitable material which will exclude dirt and moisture, and prevent the corrosion from occurring again; a Volvo dealer may be able to recommend a suitable product.

10 Working methodically around the engine compartment, check carefully that all vacuum hoses and pipes are securely fastened and correctly routed, with no signs of cracks, splits or deterioration to cause air leaks, or of hoses that are trapped, kinked, or bent sharply enough to restrict air flow. Check with particular care at all connections and sharp bends, and renew any damaged or deformed lengths of hose.

11 Check the brake lines, and renew any that are found to be leaking, corroded or crushed. Check particularly the flexible hoses at the brake calipers.

12 It is possible to make a further check of the electrical connections by wiggling each electrical connector of the system in turn as the engine is idling; a faulty connector will be immediately evident from the engine's response (or that of the warning light) as contact is broken and remade. A faulty connector should be renewed to ensure that the future reliability of the system; note that this may mean the renewal of that entire section of the loom.

13 Ensure that the wiring and connections to the wheel sensors are thoroughly checked - the wheel sensors are subjected to water, road salt and general dirt, and are often responsible for the ABS warning light coming on.

14 If the preliminary checks have failed to reveal the fault, the car must be taken to a Volvo dealer or suitably-equipped garage for diagnostic testing using electronic test equipment.

Chapter 10
Suspension and steering

Contents

Degrees of difficulty

Easy, suitable for novice with little experience	Fairly easy, suitable for beginner with some experience	Fairly difficult, suitable for competent DIY mechanic	Difficult, suitable for experienced DIY mechanic	Very difficult, suitable for expert DIY or professional

Specifications

Front suspension
Type . . . . Independent, with MacPherson struts incorporating coil springs and telescopic shock absorbers. Anti-roll bar fitted to all models

Rear suspension
Type . . . . Semi-independent Delta Link, comprising two longitudinal trailing arms and integrated transverse arms, with coil springs and telescopic shock absorbers. Anti-roll bar fitted to all models

Steering
Type . . . . Power-assisted rack-and-pinion
Steering fluid type . . . . See end of Weekly checks on page 0•16

Wheel alignment and steering angles
Front wheel:
  Camber angle . . . . 0° ± 1.0°
  Maximum difference between sides . . . . 1.0°
  Castor angle . . . . 3°20' ± 1.0°
  Maximum difference between sides . . . . 1.0°
  Toe setting (measured at wheel rims) . . . . 20' ± 6' toe-in
Rear wheel:
  Camber angle . . . . -1.0° ± 30'
  Toe setting (measured at wheel rims) . . . . 4' ± 10' toe -n

Roadwheels
Type . . . . Pressed-steel or aluminium alloy (depending on model)
Size . . . . 6J x 15, 6.5J x 15, 6.5J x 16, 7J x 17
Lateral run-out (maximum):
  Steel wheel . . . . 0.8 mm
  Aluminium wheel . . . . 0.6 mm
Radial run-out (maximum):
  Steel wheel . . . . 1.0 mm
  Aluminium wheel . . . . 0.6 mm

10

Tyres

Tyre pressures	See end of *Weekly checks* on page 0•17
Tyre sizes (dependent on model, market and territory):	
Non-turbo models	185/65 R 15, 195/60 R 15, 205/55 R 15, 205/50 R 16, T115/70 R15 (temporary spare)
Turbo models	185/65 R 15 (winter tyres), 205/55 R 15, 205/50 R 16, 205/45 R 17, T115/70 R15 (temporary spare)

Torque wrench settings

	Nm	lbf ft
Front suspension		
Anti-roll bar clamp bolts	50	37
Anti-roll bar connecting link nuts	50	37
Control arm balljoint clamp bolt nut	50	37
Control arm-to-subframe mounting nuts:*		
Stage 1	65	48
Stage 2	Angle-tighten a further 120°	
Driveshaft nut:		
Stage 1	120	89
Stage 2	Angle-tighten a further 60°	
Hub carrier to steering knuckle:*		
Stage 1	20	15
Stage 2	45	33
Stage 3	Angle-tighten a further 60°	
Shock absorber retaining nut	70	52
Subframe rear mounting brackets to body	50	37
Subframe front and rear mounting bolts:*		
Stage 1	105	77
Stage 2	Angle-tighten a further 120°	
Suspension strut to steering knuckle:*		
Stage 1	65	48
Stage 2	Angle-tighten a further 90°	
Suspension strut to upper mounting nut	70	52
Suspension strut upper mounting to body	25	18
Rear suspension		
Anti-roll bar-to-trailing arm mountings:*		
M10 nut:		
Stage 1	50	37
Stage 2	Angle-tighten a further 90°	
M12 nut:		
Stage 1	65	48
Stage 2	Angle-tighten a further 90°	
Anti-roll bar-to-transverse arm mountings:		
M10 nut	50	37
M12 nut:		
Stage 1	65	48
Stage 2	Angle-tighten a further 90°	
Backplate to stub axle:		
Upper bolts	25	18
Lower bolts	20	15
Coil spring seat:		
Upper seat to body	50	37
Lower seat to trailing arm	40	30
Rear hub nut:		
Stage 1	120	89
Stage 2	Angle-tighten a further 35°	
Shock absorber lower mounting nut	80	59
Shock absorber upper mounting centre nut:		
Standard shock absorber	40	30
Nivomat shock absorber with M12 nut	40	30
Nivomat shock absorber with M10 nut:*		
Stage 1	20	15
Stage 2	Angle-tighten a further 90°	
Shock absorber upper mounting to body	25	18
Stub axle to trailing arm:*		
Stage 1	35	26
Stage 2	Angle-tighten a further 60°	

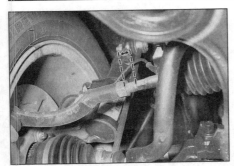

19.1 Count the number of threads showing on the track rod

33 On all models, refit the remaining fluid pipe clips, and tighten the bolts on all the clips securely.
34 On right-hand-drive models, refit the steering gear crash guard.
35 Refit the track rod ends to the steering arms, and secure with new nuts tightened to the specified torque.
36 Where applicable, refit the splash guard under the engine.
37 Reconnect the battery, refit the roadwheels then bleed the steering gear as described in Section 20.
38 With the car lowered, tighten the wheel bolts in a diagonal sequence to the specified torque.
39 Have the front wheel toe-in checked and adjusted by a Volvo dealer.

19 Steering gear gaiters - renewal

1 Count and record the number of exposed threads on the track rod, from the end of the rod to the track rod end locknut (see illustration).
2 Remove the track rod end on the side concerned as described in Section 22. Unscrew the locknut from the track rod.
3 Release the two clips and peel off the gaiter.
4 Clean out any dirt and grit from the inner end of the track rod and (when accessible) the rack.

5 Pack the new gaiter with 20 grams of steering gear grease obtainable from Volvo dealers, then fit and secure the new gaiter.
6 Refit the track rod end locknut, and position it so that the same number of threads counted on removal are visible.
7 Refit the track rod end as described in Section 22.

20 Steering gear - bleeding

1 On early models, the steering pump and combined fluid reservoir are mounted on the front-facing side of the engine at the timing belt end. Later models have the reservoir on the right-hand inner wing, in front of the cooling system expansion tank. Wipe clean the area around the reservoir filler neck, and unscrew the filler cap/dipstick from the reservoir.
2 The fluid level in the reservoir is checked by means of a dipstick in the filler cap. The dipstick has markings on both sides so that the fluid level can be checked with the engine cold, or hot after the car has been driven. Fluid level should not exceed the COLD or HOT mark as applicable, nor drop below the ADD mark.
3 If topping-up is necessary, use clean fluid of the specified type (see Weekly checks). Check for leaks if frequent topping-up is required. Do not run the engine without fluid in the reservoir.
4 After component renewal, or if the fluid level has been allowed to fall so low that air has entered the hydraulic system, bleeding must be carried out as follows.
5 Fill the reservoir to the correct level as described above.
6 Chock the rear wheels, then jack up the front of the vehicle and support it on axle stands (see Jacking and vehicle support).
7 Turn the steering wheel repeatedly from full lock one way, to full lock the other way, and top-up the fluid level as necessary.
8 Lower the car to the ground then start the engine and allow it to idle.

9 Turn the steering wheel slowly to the full right lock position, and hold it there for ten seconds.
10 Now turn the steering wheel slowly to the full left lock position, and hold it there for ten seconds.
11 Top-up the fluid level again if necessary.
12 Repeat paragraphs 9 and 10 ten times. Move the car forward slightly to avoid excessive wear on the tyres, and repeat paragraphs 9 and 10 a further ten times. Repeatedly check and if necessary top-up the fluid level during this operation.
13 On completion, stop the engine, recheck the fluid level then refit the reservoir filler cap.

21 Steering pump - removal and refitting

Removal

1 Remove the auxiliary drivebelt as described in Chapter 1.
2 Drain approximately three litres of coolant from the radiator as described in Chapter 1, Section 29.
3 Disconnect the radiator top hose from the thermostat housing.
4 To improve access, remove the cold air inlet duct from the ECU box (see illustration). Disconnect the fluid supply hose from the clip on the engine oil dipstick tube or above the pump pulley.

Models with remote-mounted (inner wing) reservoir

5 Lift the reservoir out of the mounting, and clamp the fluid hose to reduce fluid loss.
6 Slacken the fluid pressure pipe union nut one quarter of a turn (see illustration).
7 Undo the four mounting bolts at the rear of the pump (see illustration).

Models with pump-mounted reservoir

8 Undo the reservoir guard plate upper mounting bolt and remove the spacer sleeve, then slacken the guard plate lower mounting nut (see illustration).
9 Slacken the fluid pressure pipe union nut one quarter of a turn.

21.4 Disconnecting the ECU box air inlet duct - note the fluid supply hose clip (arrowed)

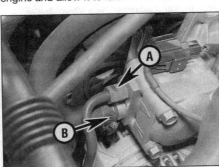

21.6 Pressure pipe union nut (A) and fluid supply hose (B)

21.7 Steering pump mounting bolts (arrowed)

10

21.8 Steering pump guard plate upper mounting bolt (arrowed)

10 Undo the five pump mounting bolts; three are accessible through the holes in the pump pulley, and two are at the rear of the pump.

11 Carefully lift the pump up and out of its location.

All models

12 Place absorbent rags below the pump. Unscrew the pressure pipe union, and recover the O-ring.

13 Separate the fluid supply hose from the pipe stub on the pump - do not use excessive force, or the hose may be damaged. If necessary, use a sharp knife to make a small cut lengthways in the hose, to enable the hose to be pulled off the pipe stub on the pump. Note that the hose must not be shortened beyond the marking stripe at the end.

14 Raise and support the front of the car so that the wheels are just clear of the ground.

15 Position a suitable container beneath the front of the car, and collect the fluid from the hoses as the steering is turned from lock to lock.

16 If a new pump is to be fitted, have the pulley and (where applicable) the reservoir transferred to it by a dealer, as special tools are required.

Refitting

17 Refitting is a reversal of removal, bearing in mind the following points:

a) Use a new O-ring on pressure pipe union.

b) If the return hose had to be cut for removal, trim off the end of the hose before reconnecting to the pipe stub.

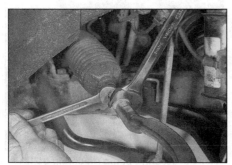

22.2 Slackening the track rod end locknut

c) Tighten the mounting and (where applicable) the guard plate bolts to the specified torque.

d) Refit the auxiliary drivebelt and top-up the cooling system as described in Chapter 1.

e) On models with the remotely-sited reservoir, remove the hose clamp and refit the reservoir into its mounting.

f) Refill/top-up the fluid reservoir, and bleed the system as described in Section 20.

22 Track rod end - removal and refitting

Removal

1 Loosen the appropriate front wheel bolts. Chock the rear wheels, then jack up the front of the vehicle and support it on axle stands (see *Jacking and vehicle support*). Remove the appropriate front roadwheel.

2 Counterhold the track rod, and slacken the track rod end locknut by half a turn **(see illustration)**. If the locknut is now left in this position, it will act as a further guide for refitting.

3 Unscrew the track rod end ballpin nut. Separate the ballpin from the steering arm with a proprietary balljoint separator, then remove the nut and disengage the ballpin from the arm **(see illustration)**.

4 Unscrew the track rod end from the track rod, counting the number of turns needed to remove it. Make a note of the number of turns, so that the tracking can be reset (or at least approximated) on refitting.

Refitting

5 Screw the track rod end onto the track rod by the same number of turns noted during removal.

6 Engage the ballpin in the steering arm. Fit a new nut and tighten it to the specified torque.

7 Counterhold the track rod and tighten the locknut.

8 Refit the front wheel, lower the car and tighten the wheel bolts in a diagonal sequence to the specified torque.

9 Have the front wheel toe-in (tracking) checked and adjusted by a Volvo dealer.

23 Wheel alignment and steering angles - general information

1 A car's steering and suspension geometry is defined in four basic settings - all angles are expressed in degrees (toe settings are also expressed as a measurement); the relevant settings are camber, castor, steering axis inclination, and toe setting. On the models covered by this manual, only the front camber and the front and rear wheel toe settings are adjustable.

2 Camber is the angle at which the front wheels are set from the vertical when viewed from the front or rear of the car. Negative camber is the amount (in degrees) that the wheels are tilted inward at the top from the vertical.

3 The front camber angle is adjusted by slackening the steering knuckle-to-suspension strut mounting bolts and repositioning the steering knuckle assemblies as necessary.

4 Castor is the angle between the steering axis and a vertical line when viewed from each side of the car. Positive castor is when the steering axis is inclined rearward at the top.

5 Steering axis inclination is the angle (when viewed from the front of the vehicle) between the vertical and an imaginary line drawn through the front suspension strut upper mounting and the control arm balljoint.

6 Toe setting is the amount by which the distance between the front inside edges of the roadwheels (measured at hub height) differs from the diametrically opposite distance measured between the rear inside edges of the roadwheels. Toe-in is when the roadwheels point inwards, towards each other at the front, while toe-out is when they splay outwards from each other at the front.

7 The front wheel toe setting is adjusted by altering the length of the steering track rods on both sides. This adjustment is normally referred to as the tracking.

8 The rear wheel toe setting is adjusted by altering the position of the rear suspension transverse arm-to-trailing arm mountings.

9 With the exception of the front and rear toe settings, and the front camber angles, all other suspension and steering angles are set during manufacture, and no adjustment is possible. It can be assumed, therefore, that unless the vehicle has suffered accident damage, all the preset angles will be correct.

10 Special optical measuring equipment is necessary to accurately check and adjust the front and rear toe settings and front camber angles, and this work should be carried out by a Volvo dealer or similar expert. Most tyre-fitting centres have the expertise and equipment to carry out at least a front wheel toe setting (tracking) check for a nominal charge.

22.3 Release the track rod end ballpin using a balljoint separator

Chapter 11
Bodywork and fittings

Contents

Degrees of difficulty

Easy, suitable for novice with little experience	**Fairly easy,** suitable for beginner with some experience	**Fairly difficult,** suitable for competent DIY mechanic	**Difficult,** suitable for experienced DIY mechanic	**Very difficult,** suitable for expert DIY or professional

Specifications

Torque wrench settings	Nm	lbf ft
Front seat belt inertia reels	40	30
Front seat belt tensioner bolt	6	4
Front seat to floor	40	30
Passenger airbag fasteners	10	7
Rear seat belt lower anchorages	48	35

1 General information

The bodyshell is made of pressed-steel sections, and is available in four-door Saloon, five-door Estate and two-door Coupe versions. Most components are welded together, but some use is made of structural adhesives. The doors and door pillars are reinforced against side impacts as part of the side impact protection system (SIPS).

A number of structural components and body panels are made of galvanised steel to provide a high level of protection against corrosion. Extensive use is also made of plastic materials, mainly in the interior, but also in exterior components. The front and rear bumpers are moulded from a synthetic material that is very strong and yet light. Plastic components such as wheel arch liners are fitted to the underside of the vehicle to further improve corrosion resistance.

2 Maintenance - bodywork and underframe

The general condition of a vehicle's bodywork is the one thing that significantly affects its value. Maintenance is easy but needs to be regular. Neglect, particularly after minor damage, can lead quickly to further deterioration and costly repair bills. It is important also to keep watch on those parts of the vehicle not immediately visible, for instance the underside, inside all the wheel arches and the lower part of the engine compartment.

The basic maintenance routine for the bodywork is washing preferably with a lot of water, from a hose. This will remove all the loose solids which may have stuck to the vehicle. It is important to flush these off in such a way as to prevent grit from scratching the finish. The wheel arches and underframe need washing in the same way to remove any accumulated mud which will retain moisture and tend to encourage rust. Oddly enough, the best time to clean the underframe and wheel arches is in wet weather when the mud is thoroughly wet and soft. In very wet weather the underframe is usually cleaned of large accumulations automatically and this is a good time for inspection.

Periodically, except on vehicles with a wax-based underbody protective coating, it is a good idea to have the whole of the underframe of the vehicle steam-cleaned, engine compartment included, so that a thorough inspection can be carried out to see what minor repairs and renovations are necessary. Steam-cleaning is available at many garages, and is necessary for removal of the accumulation of oily grime which sometimes is allowed to become thick in certain areas. If steam-cleaning facilities are not available, there are one or two excellent grease solvents available which can be brush applied; the dirt can then be simply hosed off. Note that these methods should not be used on vehicles with wax-based underbody

11

protective coating, or the coating will be removed. Such vehicles should be inspected annually, preferably just prior to winter, when the underbody should be washed down and any damage to the wax coating repaired using underseal. Ideally, a completely fresh coat should be applied. It would also be worth considering the use of such wax-based protection for injection into door panels, sills, box sections, etc, as an additional safeguard against rust damage where such protection is not provided by the vehicle manufacturer.

After washing paintwork, wipe off with a chamois leather to give an unspotted clear finish. A coat of clear protective wax polish will give added protection against chemical pollutants in the air. If the paintwork sheen has dulled or oxidised, use a cleaner/polisher combination to restore the brilliance of the shine. This requires a little effort, but such dulling is usually caused because regular washing has been neglected. Care needs to be taken with metallic paintwork, as special non-abrasive cleaner/polisher is required to avoid damage to the finish.

Always check that the door and ventilator opening drain holes and pipes are completely clear, so that water can be drained out. Brightwork should be treated in the same way as paintwork. Windscreens and windows can be kept clear of the smeary film which often appears by the use of a proprietary glass cleaner. Never use any form of wax or other body or chromium polish on glass, especially not on the windscreen or tailgate.

3 Maintenance -
upholstery and carpets

Mats and carpets should be brushed or vacuum cleaned regularly to keep them free of grit. If they are badly stained, remove them from the vehicle for scrubbing or sponging, and make quite sure they are dry before refitting. Seats and interior trim panels can be kept clean by wiping with a damp cloth and a proprietary upholstery cleaner. If they do become stained (which can be more apparent on light-coloured upholstery) use a little liquid detergent and a soft nail brush to scour the grime out of the grain of the material. Do not forget to keep the headlining clean in the same way as the upholstery. When using liquid cleaners inside the vehicle, do not over-wet the surfaces being cleaned. Excessive damp could get into the seams and padded interior causing stains, offensive odours or even rot.

> **HAYNES HiNT** *If the inside of the vehicle gets wet accidentally, it is worthwhile taking some trouble to dry it out properly, particularly where carpets are involved. Do not leave oil or electric heaters inside the vehicle for this purpose.*

4 Minor body damage -
repair

Repair of minor scratches in bodywork

If the scratch is very superficial, and does not penetrate to the metal of the bodywork, repair is very simple. Lightly rub the area of the scratch with a paintwork renovator, or a very fine cutting paste, to remove loose paint from the scratch, and to clear the surrounding bodywork of wax polish. Rinse the area with clean water.

In the case of metallic paint, the most commonly-found 'scratches' are not in the paint, but in the lacquer top coat, and appear white. If care is taken , these can sometimes be rendered less obvious by very careful use of paintwork renovator (which would otherwise not be used on metallic paintwork); otherwise, repair of these scratches can be achieved by applying lacquer with a fine brush.

Apply touch-up paint to the scratch using a fine paint brush; continue to apply fine layers of paint until the surface of the paint in the scratch is level with the surrounding paintwork. Allow the new paint at least two weeks to harden: then blend it into the surrounding paintwork by rubbing the scratch area with a paintwork renovator or a very fine cutting paste. Finally, apply wax polish.

Where the scratch has penetrated right through to the metal of the bodywork, causing the metal to rust, a different repair technique is required. Remove any loose rust from the bottom of the scratch with a penknife, then apply rust-inhibiting paint, to prevent the formation of rust in the future. Using a rubber or nylon applicator fill the scratch with bodystopper paste. If required, this paste can be mixed with cellulose thinners, to provide a very thin paste which is ideal for filling narrow scratches. Before the stopper-paste in the scratch hardens, wrap a piece of smooth cotton rag around the top of a finger. Dip the finger in cellulose thinners, and then quickly sweep it across the surface of the stopper-paste in the scratch; this will ensure that the surface of the stopper-paste is slightly hollowed. The scratch can now be painted over as described earlier in this Section.

Repair of dents in bodywork

When deep denting of the vehicle's bodywork has taken place, the first task is to pull the dent out, until the affected bodywork almost attains its original shape. There is little point in trying to restore the original shape completely, as the metal in the damaged area will have stretched on impact, and cannot be reshaped fully to its original contour. It is better to bring the level of the dent up to a point which is about 3 mm below the level of the surrounding bodywork. In cases where the dent is very shallow anyway, it is not worth trying to pull it out at all. If the underside of the dent is accessible, it can be hammered out gently from behind, using a mallet with a wooden or plastic head. Whilst doing this, hold a suitable block of wood firmly against the outside of the panel to absorb the impact from the hammer blows and thus prevent a large area of the bodywork from being 'belled-out'.

Should the dent be in a section of the bodywork which has a double skin or some other factor making it inaccessible from behind, a different technique is called for. Drill several small holes through the metal inside the area - particularly in the deeper section. Then screw long self-tapping screws into the holes just sufficiently for them to gain a good purchase in the metal. Now the dent can be pulled out by pulling on the protruding heads of the screws with a pair of pliers.

The next stage of the repair is the removal of the paint from the damaged area, and from an inch or so of the surrounding 'sound' bodywork. This is accomplished most easily by using a wire brush or abrasive pad on a power drill, although it can be done just as effectively by hand using sheets of abrasive paper. To complete the preparation for filling, score the surface of the bare metal with a screwdriver or the tang of a file, or alternatively, drill small holes in the affected area. This will provide a really good 'key' for the filler paste.

To complete the repair, see the Section on filling and re-spraying.

Repair of rust holes or gashes in bodywork

Remove all paint from the affected area, and from an inch or so of the surrounding 'sound' bodywork, using an abrasive pad or a wire brush on a power drill. If these are not available, a few sheets of abrasive paper will do the job just as effectively. With the paint removed, you will be able to gauge the severity of the corrosion, and therefore decide whether to renew the whole panel (if this is possible) or to repair the affected area. New body panels are not as expensive as most people think, and it is often quicker and more satisfactory to fit a new panel than to attempt to repair large areas of corrosion.

Remove all fittings from the affected area, except those which will act as a guide to the original shape of the damaged bodywork. Then, using tin snips or a hacksaw blade, remove all loose metal and any other metal badly affected by corrosion. Hammer the edges of the hole inwards in order to create a slight depression for the filler paste.

Wire-brush the affected area to remove the powdery rust from the surface of the remaining metal. Paint the affected area with rust-inhibiting paint; if the back of the rusted area is accessible treat this also.

Before filling can take place, it will be necessary to block the hole in some way. This can be achieved by the use of aluminium or plastic mesh, or aluminium tape.

Aluminium or plastic mesh or glass fibre matting is probably the best material to use for a large hole. Cut a piece to the approximate size and shape of the hole to be filled, then position it in the hole so that its edges are below the level of the surrounding bodywork. It can be retained in position by several blobs of filler paste around its periphery.

Aluminium tape should be used for small or very narrow holes. Pull a piece off the roll and trim it to the approximate size and shape required, then pull off the backing paper (if used) and stick the tape over the hole; it can be overlapped if the thickness of one piece is insufficient. Burnish down the edges of the tape with the handle of a screwdriver or similar, to ensure that the tape is securely attached to the metal underneath.

Bodywork repairs - filling and re-spraying

Before using this Section, see the Sections on dent, deep scratch, rust holes and gash repairs.

Many types of bodyfiller are available, but generally speaking those proprietary kits which contain a tin of filler paste and a tube of resin hardener are best for this type of repair; some can be used directly from the tube. A wide, flexible plastic or nylon applicator will be found invaluable for imparting a smooth and well contoured finish to the surface of the filler.

Mix up a little filler on a clean piece of card or board - measure the hardener carefully (follow the maker's instructions on the pack) otherwise the filler will set too rapidly or too slowly. Using the applicator, apply the filler paste to the prepared area; draw the applicator across the surface of the filler to achieve the correct contour and to level the filler surface. As soon as a contour that approximates to the correct one is achieved, stop working the paste - if you carry on too long the paste will become sticky and begin to 'pick up' on the applicator. Continue to add thin layers of filler paste at twenty-minute intervals until the level of the filler is just proud of the surrounding bodywork.

Once the filler has hardened, excess can be removed using a metal plane or file. From then on, progressively finer grades of abrasive paper should be used, starting with a 40-grade production paper and finishing with 400-grade wet-and-dry paper. Always wrap the abrasive paper around a flat rubber, cork, or wooden block - otherwise the surface of the filler will not be completely flat. During the smoothing of the filler surface the wet-and-dry paper should be periodically rinsed in water. This will ensure that a very smooth finish is imparted to the filler at the final stage.

At this stage the 'dent' should be surrounded by a ring of bare metal, which in turn should be encircled by the finely 'feathered' edge of the good paintwork. Rinse the repair area with clean water, until all of the dust produced by the rubbing-down operation has gone.

Spray the whole repair area with a light coat of primer - this will show up any imperfections in the surface of the filler. Repair these imperfections with fresh filler paste or bodystopper, and once more smooth the surface with abrasive paper. If bodystopper is used, it can be mixed with cellulose thinners to form a really thin paste which is ideal for filling small holes. Repeat this spray and repair procedure until you are satisfied that the surface of the filler, and the feathered edge of the paintwork are perfect. Clean the repair area with clean water and allow to dry fully.

The repair area is now ready for final spraying. Paint spraying must be carried out in a warm, dry, windless and dust free atmosphere. This condition can be created artificially if you have access to a large indoor working area, but if you are forced to work in the open, you will have to pick your day very carefully. If you are working indoors, dousing the floor in the work area with water will help to settle the dust which would otherwise be in the atmosphere. If the repair area is confined to one body panel, mask off the surrounding panels; this will help to minimise the effects of a slight mis-match in paint colours. Bodywork fittings (eg chrome strips, door handles etc) will also need to be masked off. Use genuine masking tape and several thicknesses of newspaper for the masking operations.

Before commencing to spray, agitate the aerosol can thoroughly, then spray a test area (an old tin, or similar) until the technique is mastered. Cover the repair area with a thick coat of primer; the thickness should be built up using several thin layers of paint rather than one thick one. Using 400 grade wet-and-dry paper, rub down the surface of the primer until it is really smooth. While doing this, the work area should be thoroughly doused with water, and the wet-and-dry paper periodically rinsed in water. Allow to dry before spraying on more paint.

Spray on the top coat, again building up the thickness by using several thin layers of paint. Start spraying in the centre of the repair area and then, with a single side-to-side motion, work outwards until the whole repair area and about 50 mm of the surrounding original paintwork is covered. Remove all masking material 10 to 15 minutes after spraying on the final coat of paint.

Allow the new paint at least two weeks to harden, then, using a paintwork renovator or a very fine cutting paste, blend the edges of the paint into the existing paintwork. Finally, apply wax polish.

Plastic components

With the use of more and more plastic body components by the vehicle manufacturers (eg bumpers, spoilers, and in some cases major body panels), rectification of more serious damage to such items has become a matter of either entrusting repair work to a specialist in this field, or renewing complete components. Repair of such damage by the DIY owner is not really feasible owing to the cost of the equipment and materials required for effecting such repairs. The basic technique involves making a groove along the line of the crack in the plastic using a rotary burr in a power drill. The damaged part is then welded back together by using a hot-air gun to heat up and fuse a plastic filler rod into the groove. Any excess plastic is then removed and the area rubbed down to a smooth finish. It is important that a filler rod of the correct plastic is used, as body components can be made of a variety of different types (eg polycarbonate, ABS, polypropylene).

Damage of a less serious nature (abrasions, minor cracks etc) can be repaired by the DIY owner using a two-part epoxy filler repair material. Once mixed in equal proportions, this is used in similar fashion to the bodywork filler used on metal panels. The filler is usually cured in twenty to thirty minutes, ready for sanding and painting.

If the owner is renewing a complete component himself, or if he has repaired it with epoxy filler, he will be left with the problem of finding a suitable paint for finishing which is compatible with the type of plastic used. At one time the use of a universal paint was not possible owing to the complex range of plastics encountered in body component applications. Standard paints, generally speaking, will not bond to plastic or rubber satisfactorily. However, it is now possible to obtain a plastic body parts finishing kit which consists of a pre-primer treatment, a primer and coloured top coat. Full instructions are normally supplied with a kit, but basically the method of use is to first apply the pre-primer to the component concerned and allow it to dry for up to 30 minutes. Then the primer is applied and left to dry for about an hour before finally applying the special coloured top coat. The result is a correctly-coloured component where the paint will flex with the plastic or rubber, a property that standard paint does not normally possess.

5 Major body damage - repair

Where serious damage has occurred or large areas need renewal due to neglect, completely new sections or panels will need welding in - this is best left to professionals. If the damage is due to impact, it will also be necessary to check completely the alignment of the body shell structure. Due to the principle of construction, the strength and shape of the whole can be affected by damage to a part. In such instances, the services of a Volvo agent with specialist checking jigs are essential. If a body is left misaligned, it is first of all dangerous as the car will not handle properly and secondly uneven stresses will be imposed on the steering, engine and transmission, causing abnormal wear or complete failure. Tyre wear may also be excessive.

11

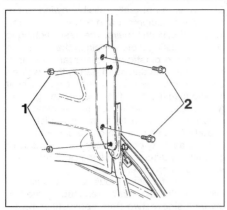

6.8a Bonnet adjustment details

1 Hinge nuts - vertical adjustment
2 Hinge bolts - fore and aft adjustment

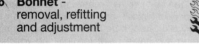

6 Bonnet -
removal, refitting
and adjustment

Removal

1 Open the bonnet, release the stud fasteners and remove the inner soundproofing panel.
2 Disconnect the washer tube from the bonnet at the T-piece. Unclip the tube and move it aside.
3 Mark around the bonnet-to-hinge retaining bolts with a felt tip pen for reference when refitting.
4 With the aid of an assistant, support the

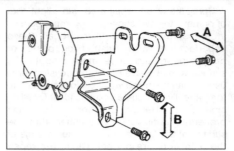
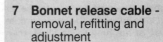

6.8b Bonnet lock adjustment points

A Lateral adjustment
B Vertical adjustment

bonnet and remove the hinge bolts. Lift off the bonnet and store it in a safe place.

Refitting and adjustment

5 Before refitting, place pads of rags under the corners of the bonnet near the hinges to protect the paintwork from damage.
6 Fit the bonnet and insert the hinge bolts. Just nip the bolts up in their previously marked positions.
7 Reconnect the washer tube and refit the soundproofing panel.
8 Shut the bonnet and check its fit. The two hinge bolts each side control the fore and aft adjustment; the two hinge nuts each side control the height of the bonnet at the rear. Front height is adjusted by altering the position of the bonnet lock mounting brackets on each side **(see illustrations)**.
9 Tighten the hinge nuts and bolts securely when adjustment is correct.

7 Bonnet release cable -
removal, refitting and adjustment

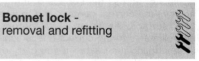

Removal

1 The release cable assembly is in two sections - one section runs from the release handle in the passenger compartment to the left-hand, or right-hand bonnet lock, as applicable, and the other section runs between the two bonnet locks.
2 Open the bonnet then from inside the car, disconnect the inner cable end from the release handle and remove the outer cable and adjuster from the support bracket **(see illustrations)**.
3 Pull the cable through the bulkhead grommet and disconnect the other end from the left-hand, or right-hand bonnet lock. Release the cable-ties and remove the cable.
4 Slacken the bonnet lock bolts and move the two locks toward each other to introduce some slack in the interconnecting cable.
5 Disconnect the cable ends from the lock levers, release the cable-ties and remove the cable.

Refitting and adjustment

6 Refit by reversing the removal operations. Adjust the threaded section of the cable at the release lever end, to take most of the slack out of the inner in the resting position. Adjust the interconnecting cable to remove the slack by moving the bonnet locks laterally. Tighten all the bolts securely on completion.

8 Bonnet lock -
removal and refitting

Removal

1 Open the bonnet and mark the position of the bonnet lock and lock mounting bracket on the side concerned, using a felt tip pen.
2 Undo the two bolts securing the relevant bonnet lock to the mounting bracket **(see illustration)**.
3 Where applicable, disconnect the wiring

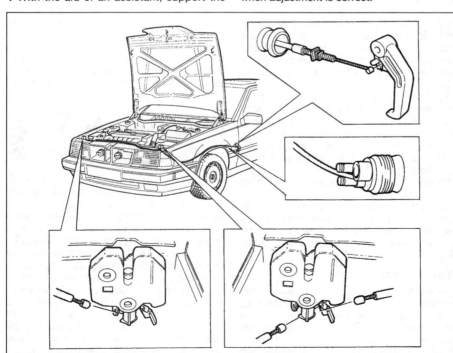

7.2a Bonnet release cable components and attachments - left-hand-drive model shown

7.2b Disconnect the inner cable (arrowed) from the release handle

plug from the alarm system bonnet lock switch **(see illustration)**.

4 Lift off the lock, disconnect the inter-connecting release cable and, depending to the side being worked on, the release cable leading from the release handle. Remove the lock.

Refitting

5 Refitting is a reversal of removal. Take up the slack in the interconnecting release cable by moving the lock(s) laterally in the mounting bracket. Adjust the height of the lock for correct fit and closure of the bonnet, by moving the mounting bracket up or down as necessary.

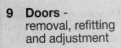

9 Doors -
removal, refitting and adjustment

Removal

1 Disconnect the battery negative lead.
2 Open the door and support it with a jack or axle stand, using rags to protect the paintwork.
3 Disconnect the front door electrical wiring. Loosen the grub screw, then turn the connector anti-clockwise and pull it out of the socket on the pillar **(see illustration)**. If removing a rear door, release the convoluted sleeve from the door pillar, and disconnect the connector located inside the sleeve.
4 Release the door check strap by undoing the bolt securing it to the pillar bracket.
5 Undo the grub screw that locks the hinge pin to the hinge bracket on the pillar **(see illustration)**.

8.2 Bonnet lock-to-bracket bolts (arrowed)

6 With the help of an assistant, lift the door upwards to disengage the hinge pins, then remove the door.

Refitting and adjustment

7 Refit the door by reversing the removal operations then adjust as follows.
8 Close the door and check the alignment with the surrounding body panels. The gap should be equal all round, and the door must be flush with the outside of the car. The rear edge of the front door should be 0 to 1.5 mm outside the front edge of the rear door (or rear wing on C70 models).
9 Fore and aft adjustment of the door at the top and bottom is by shims inserted between the hinges and the door. Shims are available in thicknesses of 0.3 and 0.5 mm, and can be slid into place after slackening the hinge retaining bolts.
10 Vertical and lateral adjustment is made by slackening the hinge retaining bolts slightly

8.3 Bonnet lock switch wiring plug - only fitted to left-hand lock assembly

and moving the door as necessary.
11 Once the correct door fit is obtained, adjust the striker plate so that the door opens and closes easily but firmly. With the door handle pulled out, shut the door and check that the lock slides over the striker plate without scraping.

10 Door interior trim panel -
removal and refitting

Removal

1 Disconnect the battery negative lead.
2 Prise off the screw cover inside the door pull, and remove the Torx screw beneath **(see illustrations)**.
3 Prise off the trim surrounding the door interior handle, and the trim panel from the door mirror **(see illustrations)**.

9.3 Turn the door wiring connector (arrowed) anti-clockwise to disconnect

9.5 Door hinge pin retaining grub screw (arrowed)

10.2a Taking care not to mark the trim, prise off the screw cover . . .

10.2b . . . and remove the Torx screw

10.3a Prise off the trim around the door handle . . .

10.3b . . . and from the door mirror

11

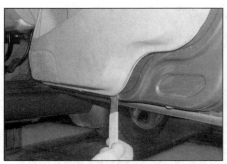

10.4 Use a wide-bladed tool to release the door trim panel lower clips

10.5a Lift the door trim panel over the door locking knob . . .

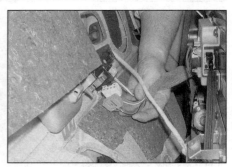

10.5b . . . then disconnect the wiring plugs from the trim panel switches

4 The door trim panel is further secured by seven push-fit clips around the base of the panel. Use a wide-bladed tool between the panel and the door to release these clips **(see illustration)**. Note that some force is necessary, and it is quite likely that the fasteners will break off during this operation. Be prepared to obtain new ones for refitting.

5 Lift the panel over the door lock knob, then pull the panel away from the door sufficiently to gain access to the various wiring plugs behind it. Noting their locations, disconnect the wiring from the window, door mirror and door locking switches, and from the boot/tailgate and fuel filler release control (as applicable) **(see illustrations)**.

6 Remove the door trim panel from the car.

7 If a new driver's door panel is being fitted, note that the new panel may not have a cut-out for the door mirror control switch. There is provision for one to be cut from the inside of

the panel, but it would be wise to consult your Volvo dealer before taking a knife to the panel.

Refitting

8 Refitting is a reversal of removal. Obtain and fit new fasteners for the base of the panel if any were broken during removal. Check the operation of all switches before finally fitting the trim panel into place.

> **11 Door handle and lock components -** removal and refitting

Outer handle

Removal

1 Slacken, but do not remove, the two Torx screws securing the door lock **(see illustration)**.

2 From the edge of the door, prise out the plastic cover plate over the outer handle retaining screws, and remove the two Torx screws beneath **(see illustration)**.

3 On C70 models, remove the door trim panel as described in Section 10. Working through the aperture in the inner door, press out the lock operating peg from the rear of the handle **(see illustration)**.

4 Press in the lock while removing the outer handle, disengaging the forward pivot from the location in the door, and the lock cylinder operating rod from the lock motor **(see illustrations)**.

Refitting

5 Refitting is a reversal of removal. On C70 models, check for correct operation before refitting the door trim.

Front door lock cylinder

Removal

6 Remove the outer handle as described previously. This definitely makes the job easier, but is not essential - once the plastic cover plate is removed as described in paragraph 2, the retaining clip can be accessed via the hole between the handle retaining screws.

7 Prise off the end cover which fits around the lock cylinder from the outer side of the handle, and recover the seal **(see illustrations)**.

8 Prise up the retaining clip located between the handle retaining screw holes, and pull or prise the lock cylinder out - the key is not

11.1 Slacken the two door lock retaining screws (arrowed)

11.2 Undo the two outer handle retaining screws from the edge of the door

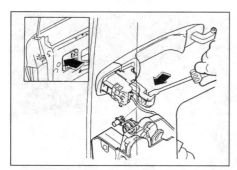

11.3 Press out the lock operating peg in the direction arrowed

11.4a Withdraw the handle from the lock assembly . . .

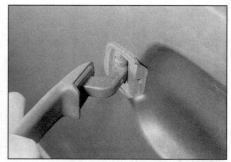

11.4b . . . then disengage the other end from the forward pivot

11.7a Prise off the outer handle end cover . . .

11.7b . . . and recover the seal

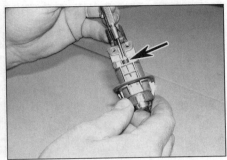

11.8a Prise up the retaining spring clip . . .

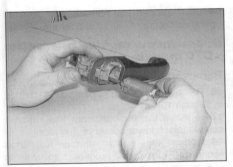

11.8b . . . and withdraw the lock cylinder

11.12a Undo the window guide channel lower retaining screw . . .

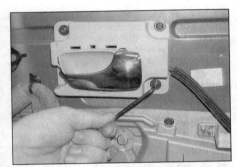

11.12b . . . and the four inner handle screws

required for this (see illustrations). Note which way round the lock cylinder fits - ie the fitted location of the slot for the retaining clip.

Refitting

9 Refitting is a reversal of removal, noting the following points:
  a) *Make sure the lock cylinder is inserted the correct way round.*
  b) *Do not insert the key in the lock cylinder when it is being refitted, or the cylinder may be installed in the wrong position.*
  c) *Check for correct operation before refitting the door trim.*

Front door lock assembly

Removal

10 Remove the door trim panel as described in Section 10. Where applicable, prise out the plastic cover from the access aperture at the rear of the door.

11 Remove the front door lock cylinder and outer handle as described previously. Remove the lock securing screws completely, however.

12 Undo the window guide channel lower retaining Torx screw, and the four screws securing the door inner handle (see illustrations).

13 Manoeuvre the lock assembly upwards and out of the door, disconnecting the lock button operating rod if required (see illustration).

14 Disconnect the lock assembly wiring connectors, noting their locations, and release the wiring from the door as necessary.

15 Unhook the interior handle operating cable from the lock, noting how the cable is routed (see illustrations). Remove the lock assembly from the car.

Refitting

16 Refitting is a reversal of the removal

procedure. Check for correct operation before refitting the door trim.

Rear door lock assembly (S70/V70)

Removal

17 Remove the door trim panel as described in Section 10.

18 Remove the outer handle as described previously. Remove the lock securing screws completely, however.

19 Slacken the window guide channel lower retaining Torx screw, but do not remove the guide channel.

20 Loosen and remove the screws securing the interior handle to the door, and lower the handle out of its location.

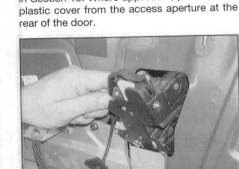

11.13 Removing the door lock assembly

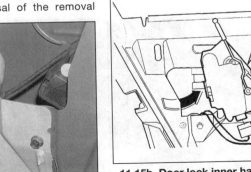

11.15a Inner handle cable is located by a rubber grommet

11.15b Door lock inner handle operating cable guide (A) - inset shows unhooking cable from lock

11

12.4 Removing the window regulator motor

12.8 Remove the plastic cover over the access panel at the rear of the door

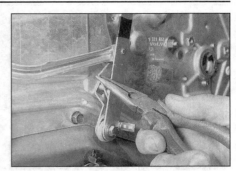

12.9 Release the inner door handle return spring from the handle lever

21 Unhook the interior handle operating cable from the lock, noting how the cable is routed. Prise off the outer cable mounting guide from the lock assembly.
22 Remove the lock assembly by bending the window guide channel out of the way, and pulling the lock downwards and out of the door.
23 Disconnect the lock assembly wiring connectors, noting their locations, and release the wiring from the door as necessary.

Refitting

24 Refitting is a reversal of the removal procedure. Check for correct operation before refitting the door trim.

12 Window regulator and glass - removal and refitting

Door window regulator motor - S70/V70 models

Removal

1 Remove the door interior trim panel as described in Section 10.
2 Raise the window, and secure it in the raised position with adhesive tape over the top of the door frame.
3 Disconnect the motor wiring at the connector.
4 Undo the three bolts and withdraw the motor from the regulator cassette **(see illustration)**.

Refitting

5 Refitting is a reversal of the removal procedure. Check for correct operation before refitting the door trim.

Door window regulator cassette - S70/V70 models

Removal

6 Remove the window regulator motor as described previously.
7 Remove the door speaker, and disconnect its wiring plug.
8 Remove the plastic cover over the access aperture at the rear of the door **(see illustration)**.
9 Using pliers, slip the inner door handle return spring off the handle lever **(see illustration)**.
10 Undo the pivot bolt at the handle lever base, and collect the return spring.
11 Undo the three bolts and remove the handle lever frame **(see illustration)**.
12 Lower the window glass until the front and rear glass carriages are accessible through the apertures in the door.
13 Extract the locking clips from the glass carriages, and release the lift arms from the slides **(see illustration)**.
14 Undo the eight bolts securing the cassette to the door. Support the window glass, then withdraw the cassette from the door **(see illustration)**.

Refitting

15 Refitting is a reversal of the relevant

removal procedure. Check for correct operation before refitting the door trim.

Door window regulator cassette - C70 models

Removal

16 Remove the door trim panel as described in Section 10.
17 Remove the locknut from the adjuster screw at each lower corner of the door.
18 Noting the exact number of turns required, turn the adjuster screws in completely.
19 Remove the door speaker, and disconnect its wiring plug.
20 Carefully remove the soundproofing panels behind the speaker aperture - note that these must be intact and properly attached on reassembly, or the speaker sound quality will be affected.
21 Remove the six screws (three each at the front and rear) securing the window cassette to the top of the door. Pull off the weatherstrip between the window and the top of the cassette.
22 Remove the screws securing the door interior handle to the door.
23 Reach inside the door and disconnect the window motor wiring connector.
24 Remove the three window motor securing nuts.
25 Remove the two screws securing the SIPS (side impact protection system) blocks to the base of the door, and remove the blocks.

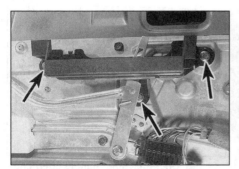

12.11 Undo the three handle lever frame retaining bolts (arrowed)

12.13 Extract the locking clips from the lift rail slides

12.14 Removing the window regulator cassette from the door

26 With the help of an assistant to support the glass, and taking care not to damage either the door or the glass, open the door and lift the window cassette out through the top of the door.

Refitting

27 Refitting is a reversal of removal, bearing in mind the following points:

   a) *Before finally tightening the six screws which secure the cassette to the top of the door, the door must be closed to ensure proper alignment.*

   b) *The lower adjustment screws control the side-to-side alignment of the window - these should be screwed out by the number of turns noted on removal (approximately 5 turns, typically).*

   c) *The window vertical alignment is controlled by the cable adjustment screws on the front and rear glass carriages. The vertical alignment should not require adjustment unless the motor and cables have been disturbed.*

   d) *To set the vertical alignment, fully close the window, and check that the adjustment screw at the rear of the glass touches the stop on the door; adjust if necessary. Check the fit at the front of the glass. Adjust if necessary by loosening the cable clamp screw on the front carriage, and moving the carriage relative to the cable until the fit is correct; tighten the clamp screw on completion.*

   e) *The fit of the window against the weatherstrip can be determined by trapping a single-folded piece of paper between the glass and the strip, by fully closing the door. When pulled out, the paper should not move easily, but it should not tear. Check the fit all around the glass, using this method.*

Door window regulator motor - C70 models

Removal

28 The regulator motor can only be effectively removed once the regulator cassette has first been removed as described previously.

29 The motor is secured to the cassette by three bolts. The control cables must be detached from the front and rear glass carriages, and from the motor itself. It is advisable to mark the fitted position of the cable to the front and rear glass carriages, and to use these marks when refitting, so that the proper fit of the window is retained.

Refitting

30 Refitting is a reversal of removal. Align the window as described in paragraph 27.

Front door window glass - S70/V70 models

Removal

31 Remove the window regulator cassette as described previously.

32 If not already done, carefully prise up the

12.32 Prise up the door inner weatherstrip

inner weatherstrip and remove it from the top edge of the door panel **(see illustration)**.

33 Move the glass down as far as it will go, tip it up at the rear and lift it out of the door **(see illustration)**.

Refitting

34 Refitting is a reversal of removal.

Rear door window glass - S70/V70 models

Removal

35 Remove the window regulator cassette as described previously.

36 Carefully prise up the inner weatherstrip and remove it from the top edge of the door panel.

37 Remove the wiring clamp at the bottom of the window rear guide channel, undo the two screws and pull the channel up and out.

38 Move the glass down as far as it will go, tip it up at the rear and lift it out of the door.

Refitting

39 Refitting is a reversal of removal.

Door window glass - C70 models

Removal

40 Remove the window regulator cassette as described previously.

41 The glass is secured to the front and rear carriages by a screw which passes through the glass, and a number of shim plates.

42 With the window lowered for access to the front and rear screws, have an assistant support the glass.

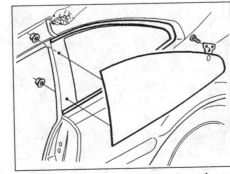

12.51 Remove the two front nuts and rear hinge bolt, and remove the side glass

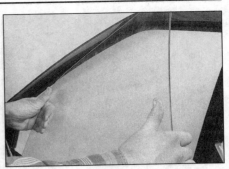

12.33 Lifting out the door window glass

43 Remove the screws and take off the shim plates, noting their fitted positions. Lift the glass out of the door.

Refitting

44 Refitting is a reversal of removal. Providing the motor and cables are not disturbed, the proper fit of the window should be retained, with no adjustment necessary. Adjustment details are given in paragraph 27.

Rear opening side window glass - C70 models

Removal

45 Prise off the cover over the seat belt upper mounting, and remove the seat belt upper mounting bolt.

46 Fold the seat belt to one side, and remove the screw securing the seat belt guide to the base of the B-pillar trim panel.

47 Lift the trim panel upwards and remove it.

48 Prise up the trim covers over the rear grab handle securing screws, and remove the screws beneath. Take off the rear grab handle.

49 Prise out the rear reading light from the rear window trim panel, and disconnect the wiring plug to remove the light unit.

50 Carefully prise off the rear window trim panel, which is secured by three clips. Use a wide-bladed tool, and take care not to damage the finish by protecting the blade with card or tape.

51 Have an assistant support the rear window from outside. From inside the car, loosen and remove the rear hinge bolt, then remove the two front mounting nuts, and remove the window glass **(see illustration)**.

Refitting

52 Refitting is a reversal of the removal procedure.

13 Tailgate interior trim panel - removal and refitting

Removal

1 Open the tailgate and remove the cover around the inner handle by inserting a spatula under the upper edge and forcing it down **(see illustration)**.

11

13.1 Remove the tailgate inner handle cover with a spatula

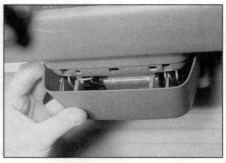

13.2 Pull off the high-level brake light cover

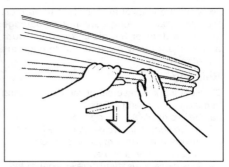

13.4 Pull the trim panel backwards and downwards to free the inner retainers

2 Remove the cover over the high-level brake light by grasping it on each side and pulling down **(see illustration)**. Take care not to break the fragile inner retaining catches.
3 Insert a strip of cardboard about 180 x 100 mm between the upper and lower panels on each side. The edges of the lower panel are quite sharp and will easily scratch the upper panel if not protected.
4 Grip between the tailgate weatherstrip and the trim panel along the lower edge, and pull the panel backwards and downwards to free the inner retainers **(see illustration)**.
5 Bend the lower edge of the panel down to clear the tailgate then push it forwards by striking it sharply on each side. Catch the panel as the upper retainers come free.
6 Remove the upper trim panel from around the glass by pulling both edges inward and the upper edge backwards.

Refitting

7 Refitting is a reversal of removal. Ensure that the cardboard strips are used to protect the upper panel when refitting the lower panel.

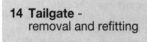

14 Tailgate - removal and refitting

Removal

1 Disconnect the battery negative lead.
2 Using a small screwdriver, carefully prise out the courtesy light in the centre of the rear

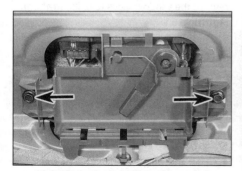

16.2 Undo the two bolts (arrowed) securing the inner handle to the tailgate

roof section trim. Disconnect the wiring and remove the light.
3 Prise out the plastic caps over the two rear roof section trim retaining screws. Undo the screws and remove the trim.
4 Prise out the caps over the combined roof sill and D-pillar trim panel and undo the screws on both sides. Release the panels by pulling them free of their retaining clips.
5 Lift up the removable floor panel at the right-hand rear of the load space area.
6 Disconnect the tailgate washer hose downstream of the in-line filter now exposed. Pull the hose from its location.
7 Disconnect the wiring connector on the left-hand side and push it through the hinge hole.
8 Undo the screws and remove the tailgate side trim rails on each side.
9 With the help of an assistant, undo the two hinge screws each side and lift away the tailgate.

Refitting

10 Refitting is a reversal of removal.

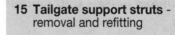

15 Tailgate support struts - removal and refitting

Removal

1 Using a small screwdriver, carefully prise out the courtesy light in the centre of the rear roof section trim. Disconnect the wiring and remove the light.

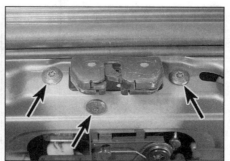

16.5 Undo the three lock retaining bolts (arrowed) and manipulate the assembly out of the tailgate

2 Prise out the plastic caps over the two rear roof section trim retaining screws. Undo the screws and remove the trim.
3 Prise out the caps over the combined roof sill and D-pillar trim panel and undo the screws on both sides. Release the panels by pulling them free of their retaining clips.
4 Support the tailgate in the open position using a suitable prop.
5 Disconnect the bracket securing the strut to the body.
6 Release the strut balljoints and remove the strut from the car.

Refitting

7 Refitting is a reversal of removal.

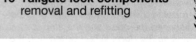

16 Tailgate lock components - removal and refitting

Removal

Lock assembly

1 Remove the tailgate interior trim panel as described in Section 13.
2 Undo the two bolts securing the inner handle to the tailgate **(see illustration)**.
3 Disconnect the central locking wiring connector.
4 Disconnect the link rods to the exterior handle and lock cylinder.
5 Undo the three Torx bolts securing the lock, and manipulate the assembly out of the tailgate aperture **(see illustration)**.

Exterior handle

6 Remove the tailgate wiper motor (Chapter 12).
7 Disconnect the link rods at the lock cylinder and exterior handle lever.
8 Disconnect the number plate light wiring connector, and release the cable clips.
9 Undo the four nuts (two near the centre and two at the edges) and carefully withdraw the exterior handle from the tailgate **(see illustrations)**. Feed the number plate light wiring out through the tailgate with the handle.

Lock cylinder

10 Remove the exterior handle as described previously.

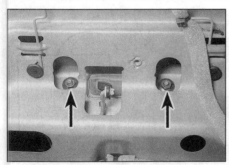

16.9a Undo the tailgate exterior handle retaining bolts (two centre bolts arrowed) . . .

16.9b . . . and withdraw the handle from the tailgate

16.11 Tailgate lock cylinder retaining circlip (arrowed)

11 Extract the circlip at the rear of the cylinder **(see illustration)**, and pull the cylinder out of the exterior handle assembly.

Refitting

12 Refitting is a reversal of the relevant removal procedure.

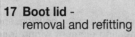

17 Boot lid - removal and refitting

Removal

S70 models

1 Open the boot and remove the soundproofing panel.
2 Disconnect the central locking system and number plate/tail light wiring so that the boot lid is free to be removed.
3 Extract the retaining clip securing the top of the strut to the boot lid hinge, and swing the strut out of the way.
4 Mark around the hinge bolts. With the aid of an assistant, undo the hinge bolts and lift away the lid.

C70 models

5 Open the boot lid, and have an assistant support it.
6 Prise off the left-hand side trim panel from inside the boot, and disconnect the wiring plug for the number plate lighting. Withdraw the wiring so that it can be removed with the boot lid.
7 Extract the retaining clip securing the top of

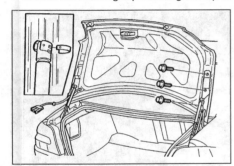

17.8 Boot lid removal details - C70 models

the strut to the boot lid hinge, and swing the strut out of the way.
8 Mark around the hinge plates as a guide to refitting, then unscrew and remove the three hinge-to-boot lid bolts each side, and remove the boot lid **(see illustration)**.

Refitting

9 Refit by reversing the removal operations. Check the fit and closure of the boot lid.
10 On S70 models, vertical and fore-and-aft adjustment of the front edge of the boot lid is carried out by turning the eccentric nut in the hinge below the parcel shelf (removing the parcel shelf as described in Section 26 will improve access).
11 On C70 models, vertical and fore-and-aft adjustment is carried out by repositioning the hinges relative to the boot lid and the rear wing. If the boot lid is accurately refitted using the marks made before removal, it should not require further adjustment.
12 On all models, vertical and lateral adjustment of the rear edge is carried out by repositioning the striker plate within the movement offered by the elongated bolt holes.

18 Boot lid support struts - removal and refitting

Removal

S70 models

1 Remove the B-pillar trim panel and the rear parcel shelf as described in Section 26.
2 Release the support strut front balljoint from the mounting stud.
3 Extract the retaining clip securing the strut to the boot lid hinge, and remove the strut.

C70 models

4 Support the boot lid, then extract the retaining clip securing the top of the strut to the boot lid hinge, and pull the top of the strut off its balljoint mounting. Remove the strut from the car.

Refitting

5 Refitting is a reversal of removal. Note that

the struts contain gas under pressure - if new ones have been fitted, the old ones should be disposed of safely, and should on no account be incinerated.

19 Boot lid lock components - removal and refitting

Removal

Lock assembly

1 Open the boot and remove the soundproofing panel.
2 Undo the three bolts and remove the cover plate.
3 Disconnect the link rod from the outer handle lever.
4 Disconnect the central locking motor wiring connector.
5 Open the plastic adjuster sleeve, disconnect the lock cylinder link rod, then manipulate the lock assembly out of the boot lid aperture **(see illustration)**.

Exterior handle - S70 models

6 Open the boot and remove the soundproofing panel.
7 Disconnect the link rods at the lock cylinder and exterior handle lever.

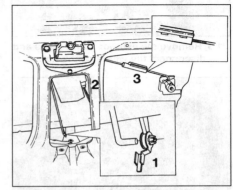

19.5 Boot lid lock removal details

1 Disconnect the exterior handle link rod
2 Disconnect the wiring connector
3 Disconnect the lock cylinder link rod at the adjuster sleeve

11

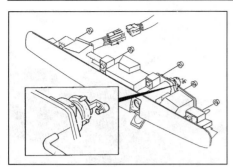

19.9 Boot exterior handle removal details - S70 models

Inset shoes disconnecting link rod from lock cylinder

8 Disconnect the number plate light wiring connector, and release the cable clips.

9 Undo the five nuts and carefully withdraw the exterior handle from the boot lid **(see illustration)**. Feed the number plate light wiring out through the boot lid with the handle.

Lock cylinder - S70 models

10 Remove the exterior handle as described previously.

11 Extract the lock cylinder retaining pin, and pull the cylinder out of the exterior handle assembly **(see illustration)**.

Lock cylinder - C70 models

12 Open the boot lid, and from outside, drill out the rivet which secures the lock cylinder retaining clip.

21.3 Remove the exterior mirror glass and disconnect the wiring connectors

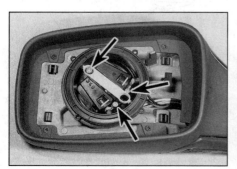

21.5 Mirror motor retaining screws (arrowed)

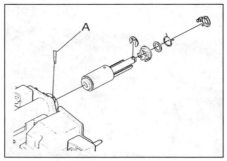

19.11 Remove the locking pin (A) and remove the lock cylinder - S70 models

13 Pull the link rod out of the lock cylinder.

14 Slide the retaining clip out of the lock cylinder, and withdraw the lock cylinder and sealing ring from the boot lid **(see illustration)**.

15 When refitting, if riveting equipment is not available, it may be possible to use a small self-tapping screw to secure the lock cylinder retaining clip.

Refitting

16 Refitting is a reversal of the relevant removal procedure.

20 Windscreen and other fixed glass - removal and refitting

Special equipment and techniques are needed for successful removal and refitting of the windscreen, rear window and side windows (other than the opening rear side window on C70 models, which is covered in Section 12). Have the work carried out by a Volvo dealer or a windscreen specialist.

21 Exterior mirrors and associated components - removal and refitting

⚠️ *Warning: If the mirror glass is broken, wear gloves to protect your hands. This is good advice, in fact, even if the glass is not broken, due to the risk of glass breakage.*

21.9 Disconnect the door mirror wiring connector . . .

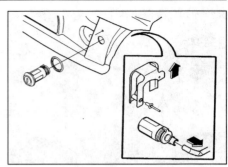

19.14 Lock cylinder removal details - C70 models

Removal

Mirror glass

1 Pivot the mirror glass into the mirror housing as far as possible on the inside edge.

2 Insert a thin flat-bladed screwdriver between the outer edge of the glass and the mirror housing, and release one of the glass retaining hooks.

3 Pull the mirror glass out of the housing, and disconnect the heating element wiring **(see illustration)**.

Mirror motor

4 Remove the mirror glass as described previously

5 Undo the three retaining screws and remove the motor **(see illustration)**, disconnecting the wiring connector as it becomes accessible.

Edge cover

6 Remove the mirror glass as described previously

7 Undo the four screws and remove the edge cover.

Mirror (complete unit)

8 Remove the door interior trim panel as described in Section 10.

9 Disconnect the motor wiring at the connector inside the door **(see illustration)**.

10 Support the mirror, then undo the three mounting screws and withdraw the mirror from the door **(see illustration)**. Release the rubber grommet from the door as the mirror is withdrawn.

21.10 . . . then unscrew the three mirror mounting screws, and withdraw the mirror

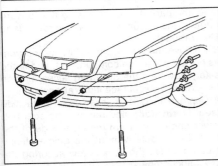

22.9 Front bumper removal details

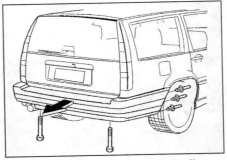

22.12 Rear bumper removal details -
S70 and V70 models

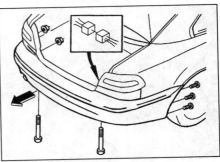

22.21 Rear bumper removal details -
C70 models

Refitting

11 Refitting is a reversal of the relevant removal procedure. Where applicable, ensure that the rubber grommet is correctly located in its hole in the door.

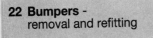

22 Bumpers -
removal and refitting

Note: *The bumpers consist of several sections, and once the bumper assembly has been removed as described below, the outer cover can be unclipped and the bumper dismantled. It is unclear at the time of writing whether the individual sections that make up the bumper are available separately.*

Front bumper -
S70 and V70 models

1 Open the bonnet.
2 Undo the retaining bolt each side, release the front edge clips and remove the splash guard under the radiator.
3 On models with headlight wipers, lift up the cover and remove the wiper arm securing nut on each side. Pull off the washer supply hose, and remove the wiper arms.
4 Disconnect the wiring plug from the outside temperature sensor at the base of the bumper. Where front foglights are fitted, disconnect the wiring plug at the rear of each light unit.

Turbo models
5 On turbo models, the air baffle inside the lower centre section of the bumper/spoiler must first be removed.
6 Remove the baffle cover clip inside of each headlight, and the two screws from below, and remove the cover panel.
7 Using a small flat-bladed screwdriver, release the ten clips (five above, five below) and remove the air baffle from the bumper.

All models
8 Remove the four rivets securing each plastic wheel arch liner to the edge of the bumper, either by drilling them out or cutting the heads off - either way, take care to avoid damaging the finish.
9 Remove the 14 mm bolt each side, just

below the headlight. With the help of an assistant, pull the bumper off the side mounting slides and lower it to the ground **(see illustration)**.
10 Refitting is a reversal of removal. Take care when offering the bumper into position that the side mounting slides engage correctly. If riveting equipment is not available, it may be possible to secure the bumper ends using suitable self-tapping screws.

Rear bumper -
S70 and V70 models

11 Remove the three rivets securing each plastic wheel arch liner to the edge of the bumper, either by drilling them out or cutting the heads off - either way, take care to avoid damaging the finish.
12 Remove the 14 mm bolt each side, just below the tail lights, then with the help of an assistant, pull the bumper off the side mounting slides and lower it to the ground **(see illustration)**.
13 Refitting is a reversal of removal. Take care when offering the bumper into position that the side mounting slides engage correctly. If riveting equipment is not available, it may be possible to secure the bumper ends using suitable self-tapping screws.

Front bumper -
C70 models

14 Follow the procedures in paragraphs 1 to 7.
15 Remove the three screws each side securing the wheel arch liner to the edge of the bumper.
16 Working directly below each headlight, prise out the cover over the bumper lower mounting bolt. Unscrew the mounting bolt each side, then with the help of an assistant, pull the bumper off the side mounting slides and lower it to the ground.
17 Refitting is a reversal of removal. Take care when offering the bumper into position that the side mounting slides engage correctly.

Rear bumper - C70 models

18 Open the boot lid, and remove the interior trim panels each side below the rear light units.
19 Unscrew the two nuts either side now exposed - these secure the outer trim panels

below the rear light units, which are integral with the rear bumper.
20 Disconnect the aerial wiring in-line connector plug next to the right-hand rear light unit.
21 Remove the 14 mm bolt each side, just below the tail lights, then with the help of an assistant, pull the bumper off the side mounting slides and lower it to the ground **(see illustration)**.
22 Refitting is a reversal of removal. Take care when offering the bumper into position that the side mounting slides engage correctly.

23 Front grille panel -
removal and refitting

Removal

1 Open the bonnet and remove the six plastic clips at the rear of the grille by sliding them sideways.
2 Remove the grille and recover the rubber seal.

Refitting

3 Refit by reversing the removal operations.

24 Front seat -
removal and refitting

Note: *All models are equipped with a SIPS airbag, fitted into the side of the front seat backrest, as part of the Side Impact Protection System. Various labels around the car will confirm whether the vehicle is so equipped; refer to Chapter 12 for further information on the SRS and SIPS systems.*

⚠️ **Warning: There is a risk of injury if the SIPS bag is triggered inadvertently when working on the front seat. Ensure that the safety device described in the following paragraphs is installed, and never apply external force to the side of the seat. It is strongly recommended that any work involving the front seat is entrusted to a Volvo dealer. Refer to Chapter 12 for further information on the SRS system.**

11

24.2a Use a screwdriver to release the manual seat adjuster knobs . . .

24.2b . . . then remove the seat side compartment

Removal

1 Ensure that the ignition is switched off, then disconnect the battery negative lead. Wait at least 10 minutes before proceeding.

2 Raise the seat base to its maximum height. On manually-adjusted seats, lift up each seat adjuster knob, and using a flat-bladed screwdriver, release the inner tabs and remove the plastic cover. Remove the seat

side compartment by releasing the forward edge and pushing backwards (see illustrations).

3 Remove the red plastic safety device from its holder in the side compartment, and fit the safety device to the SIPS bag sensor unit on the side of the seat (see illustrations).

4 Depress the quick-release catch at the side (see illustration), and remove the seat belt lower anchorage from the outer side of the seat. On models without the quick-release catch, remove the Torx screw securing the lower anchorage.

5 Move the seat forwards. Remove the single bolt from the inner and outer track - these are concealed by trim covers (see illustrations).

6 Move the seat rearwards. Remove the trim cover, then remove the single bolt from the front of each track (see illustrations).

7 Disconnect the seat heater and seat belt

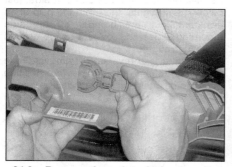

24.3a Remove the safety device from its storage location . . .

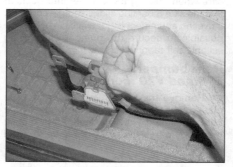

24.3b . . . and clip it into the SIPS sensor as shown

24.4 Release the seat belt catch (arrowed)

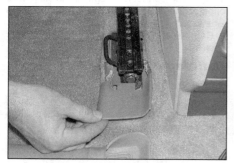

24.5a Remove the trim cover from the inner . . .

24.5b . . . and outer rear seat rail . . .

24.5c . . . then remove the inner . . .

24.5d . . . and outer rear seat rail bolt

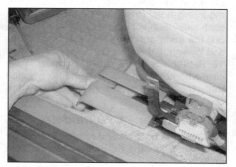

24.6a Remove the trim cover from the front of the seat rail . . .

24.6b . . . and remove the front bolt

switch wiring connectors (as applicable) from under the seat cushion **(see illustration)**. Note the location of each plug for use when refitting. On models with electric seats, disconnect the wiring plugs from the switch control panel.

8 Lift the seat upwards to release the front and rear guide pins, then remove the seat from the car.

Refitting

9 Locate the seat over the guide pins, reconnect the wiring, and insert the retaining bolts. Tighten the bolts to the specified torque in the following sequence - rear inner, front outer, front inner, rear outer. Refit the bolt covers.

10 Reconnect the seat belt lower anchorage, ensuring that the catch is fully engaged.

11 Remove the safety device from the SIPS bag sensor unit and return it to its holder in the side compartment. Refit the side compartment to the seat.

12 Make sure that no-one is inside the car. Switch on the ignition, then reconnect the battery negative lead. Switch the ignition off, then on again, and check that the SRS warning light comes on, then goes out within 15 seconds.

24.7 Disconnect the wiring plugs under the front of the seat

11 Press the backrest out and pull it up in its outer mounting. Lift the backrest up and out of the car.

C70 models

12 Free the seat cushion from its retaining clips by lifting the front edge, then remove the cushion.

13 Remove the two screws at the base of the backrest, then pull the base of the backrest forwards and lift upwards to release it.

14 Pull the rear seat belts around the sides of the backrest, and remove the backrest from the car.

Refitting

All models

15 Refit by reversing the removal operations.

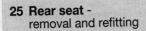

25 Rear seat -
removal and refitting

Removal

S70 models

1 Free the seat cushion from its retaining clips by lifting the front edge, then remove the cushion.

2 Ensure that the safety locking catches in the boot, on either side of the backrest, are up, then pull the release catch forward and fold down the backrest.

3 Move one side of the backrest towards the side of the car and at the same time lift up **(see illustration)**. Remove one side of the backrest, then remove the other side in the same way.

V70 models

4 If the seat is heated, disconnect the heater wiring at the connectors under the front of the cushion.

5 Use the loop provided to pull the cushion forwards, then pull the red catches upward.

6 Fold the cushion back almost all the way, then lift up to remove.

7 If the backrest is heated, disconnect the wiring at the connectors.

8 Remove the side padding and undo the seat belt anchorage retaining bolts in the floor. Remove the anchorages.

9 Release the catch and fold the backrest forward very slightly.

10 Remove the clip securing the backrest mounting to the wheel arch by pressing it in at the bottom with a screwdriver and lifting it up with a second screwdriver **(see illustration)**.

26 Interior trim -
removal and refitting

Note: *Refer to earlier Sections of this Chapter for specific procedures covering door and tailgate interior trim panels.*

Interior trim panels - general

1 The interior trim panels are secured using either screws or various types of trim fasteners, usually studs or clips.

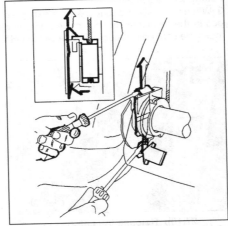

25.10 Rear seat removal on Estate models

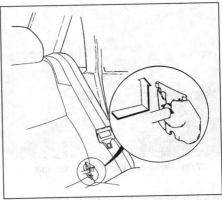

25.3 Rear seat removal on Saloon models

2 Check that there are no other panels overlapping the one to be removed, or other components hindering removal; usually there is a sequence that has to be followed, and this will only become obvious on close inspection. In the case of the rear side trim panels on C70 models, for instance, the rear seat must first be removed.

3 Some of the interior panels will additionally be retained by the screws which are used to secure other items, such as the grab handles.

4 Remove all visible retainers such as screws, noting that these may be hidden under small plastic caps. If the panel will not come free, it is held by internal clips or fasteners. These are usually situated around the edges of the panel, and can be prised up to release them; note, however that they can break quite easily, so replacements should be available. The best way of releasing such clips is to use a large flat-bladed screwdriver or other wide-bladed tool. Note that in many cases, the adjacent sealing strip must be prised back to release a panel.

5 When removing a panel, **never** use excessive force or the panel may be damaged; always check carefully that all fasteners or other relevant components have been removed or released before attempting to withdraw a panel.

6 Refitting is a reversal of removal; secure the fasteners by pressing them firmly into place and ensure that all disturbed components are correctly secured to prevent rattles.

Rear parcel shelf

S70 models

7 Free the seat cushion from its retaining clips by lifting the front edge, then remove the cushion.

8 Remove the side backrest padding by pulling it out and lifting up.

9 Undo the bolt securing the centre seat belt anchorage to the floor.

10 Ensure that the safety locking catches in the boot, on either side of the backrest, are up, then pull the release catch forward and fold down the backrest.

11 Release the parcel shelf from the two clips

11

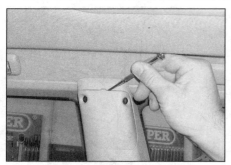

27.9a Prise out the ultrasonic unit . . .

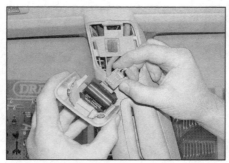

27.9b . . . and disconnect the wiring plug

at the front edge by inserting a screwdriver and carefully prising up.

12 Pull out the shelf, and thread the seat belt through the opening in the shelf.

13 If necessary, lift out the soundproofing panel under the parcel shelf.

14 Refitting is a reversal of removal. Tighten the seat belt anchorage to the specified torque.

C70 models

15 Remove the rear seat (see Section 25).

16 The parcel shelf is secured by two clips at the front edge. Prise out the clips using a suitable wide-bladed tool.

17 Thread the rear seat belts down through the slot in the shelf (one slot is provided for each belt), then lift the shelf at the rear and tip it forwards to remove, releasing it from the edges of the surrounding trim panels.

18 If necessary, recover the foam/rubber gaskets which sit on top of the rear shelf speakers.

19 Refitting is a reversal of removal. Check the condition of the speaker gaskets, and renew if necessary.

Carpets

20 The passenger compartment floor carpet is in three sections; front left, front right and rear, and is secured at the sides by the front and rear sill trim panels.

21 Carpet removal and refitting is reasonably straightforward, but is very time-consuming because all adjoining trim panels must be removed first, as must components such as the seats, centre console and seat belt lower anchorages.

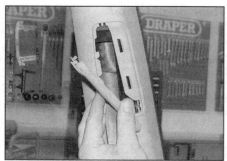

27.10a Prise out and remove the seat belt guide

Headlining

22 The headlining is clipped to the roof, and can be withdrawn only once all fittings such as grab handles, sun visors, sunroof (if fitted), fixed window glass, and related trim panels have been removed and the relevant sealing strips have been prised clear.

23 Note that headlining removal and refitting requires considerable skill and experience if it is to be carried out without damage, and is therefore best entrusted to a dealer or automotive upholstery specialist.

27 Seat belts - general information, removal and refitting

1 All models are equipped with pyrotechnical front seat belt tensioners as part of the Supplemental Restraint System (SRS). The system is designed to instantaneously take up any slack in the seat belt in the case of a sudden frontal impact, therefore reducing the possibility of injury to the front seat occupants. Each front seat is fitted with the system, the tensioner being situated behind the upper B-pillar trim panel.

2 The seat belt tensioner is triggered, with the driver's and passenger's airbag, by a frontal impact above a pre-determined force. Lesser impacts, including impacts from behind, will not trigger the system.

3 When the system is triggered, the explosive gas in the tensioner mechanism retracts and locks the seat belt through a cable which acts

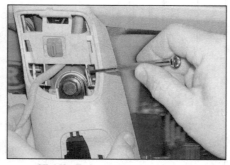

27.10b Release the catches . . .

on the inertia reel. This prevents the seat belt moving, and keeps the occupant firmly in position in the seat. Once the tensioner has been triggered, the seat belt will be permanently locked and the assembly must be renewed. If any abnormal rattling noises are heard when pulling out or retracting the belt, this also indicates that the tensioner has been triggered.

4 There is a risk of injury if the system is triggered inadvertently when working on the vehicle, and it is therefore strongly recommended that any work involving the seat belt tensioner system is entrusted to a Volvo dealer. Note the following warnings before contemplating any work on the front seat belts.

⚠ *Warning: Switch off the ignition, disconnect the battery negative lead, and wait for at least 10 minutes before starting work involving the front seat belts.*

Do not expose the tensioner mechanism to temperatures in excess of 100°C (212°F).

If the tensioner mechanism is dropped, it must be renewed, even it has suffered no apparent damage.

Do not allow any solvents to come into contact with the tensioner mechanism.

Do not attempt to open the tensioner mechanism, as it contains explosive gas.

Tensioners from other vehicles, even from the same model and year, must not be fitted as replacement parts.

Tensioners must be discharged before they are disposed of, but this task should be entrusted to a Volvo dealer.

Removal

Front seat belts - S70 and V70 models

5 Switch off the ignition, then disconnect the battery negative lead. Wait for at least 10 minutes before proceeding.

6 Raise the seat base to its maximum height. On manually-adjusted seats, lift up each seat adjuster knob, and using a flat-bladed screwdriver, release the inner tabs and remove the plastic cover. Remove the seat side compartment by releasing the forward edge and pushing backwards (refer to illustrations 24.2a and b).

7 Remove the safety device from its holder in the side compartment, and fit the safety device to the SIPS bag sensor unit on the side of the seat (refer to illustrations 24.3a and b).

8 Depress the quick-release catch at the side, and remove the seat belt lower anchorage from the outer side of the seat (refer to illustration 24.4). On models without the quick-release catch, remove the Torx screw securing the lower anchorage.

9 Prise out the alarm system ultrasonic unit from the top of the B-pillar trim panel, and disconnect the wiring plug **(see illustrations)**.

10 Prise out the belt guide from the B-pillar trim, and pass the seat belt through the slot in the guide. Remove the B-pillar trim panel by releasing the catches and pulling it off from the top of the panel **(see illustrations)**.

27.10c ... and pull away the B-pillar trim panel

27.11 Seat belt tensioner wiring plug (A) and retaining screw (B)

27.12a Seat belt inertia reel upper ...

27.12b ... and lower retaining bolt

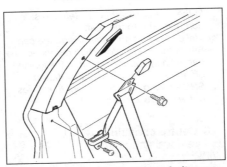

27.16 Removing the front seat belt upper components - C70 models

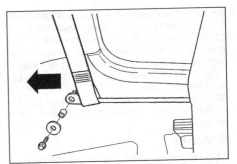

27.18 Removing the front seat belt from the slider rail - C70 models

11 Confirm that the battery is disconnected, then unplug the wiring connector from the seat belt tensioner **(see illustration)**. This wiring plug should never be disconnected (or reconnected) while the battery negative lead is connected.

12 Unscrew and remove the tensioner Torx retaining screw, then unscrew the two belt reel mounting bolts and remove the seat belt and tensioner from the car **(see illustrations)**.

13 To remove the belt buckle, it will probably be necessary to remove the seat first, as described in Section 24. The buckles are secured with a very large Torx bolt.

Front seat belts - C70 models

14 Proceed as described in paragraphs 1 to 4.

15 Prise off the cover over the seat belt upper mounting, and remove the seat belt upper mounting bolt.

16 Fold the seat belt to one side, and remove the screw securing the seat belt guide to the base of the B-pillar trim panel **(see illustration)**.

17 Locally remove the trim/carpet over the rear of the floor-mounted seat belt rail, for access to the rail mounting bolt at the rear.

18 Unscrew and remove the bolt, together with the washer and spacer, then pull the rail out slightly and slide the end of the seat belt off the rail **(see illustration)**.

19 Locally remove the trim/carpet at the base of the B-pillar, for access to the seat belt reel. To improve access further, it may also be necessary to remove the rear seat cushion as described in Section 25, and to partially remove the rear side trim panel by releasing the retaining clips around the panel edges.

20 Confirm that the battery is disconnected, then unplug the wiring connector from the seat belt tensioner. This wiring plug should never be disconnected (or reconnected) while the battery negative lead is connected.

21 Unscrew and remove the belt reel mounting bolt, and remove the seat belt and tensioner from the car **(see illustration)**.

22 To remove the belt buckle, it will probably be necessary to remove the seat first, as described in Section 24. The buckles are secured with a very large Torx bolt.

Rear seat belts - S70 models

23 Remove the parcel shelf as described in Section 26, then remove the side backrest padding by pulling it out and lifting up.

24 Remove the rear seat as described in Section 25.

25 Remove the soundproofing panel located under the parcel shelf. Undo the retaining

bolts securing the inertia reel assemblies and the lower anchorages and buckles on each side and in the centre.

26 Feed the belts through the apertures in the parcel shelf, and remove them from the car.

Rear seat belts - V70 models

27 Access to the buckles and floor anchorages is gained by tipping the seat cushion forwards **(see illustration)**.

28 Access to the inertia reels, located inside the seat backrests, entails removing the seat upholstery which can easily be damaged if done carelessly or without the correct special tools. For this reason, entrust this work to a Volvo dealer.

Rear seat belts - C70 models

29 Remove the rear seat and the rear parcel shelf as described in Sections 25 and 26.

27.21 Removing the front seat belt reel and tensioner - C70 models

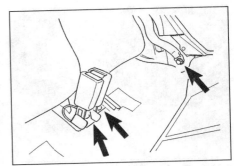

27.27 Rear seat belt buckle and lower anchorage bolts (V70 models) - arrowed

11

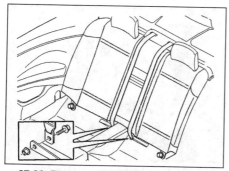

27.30 Rear seat belt lower anchorage details - C70 models

30 Unbolt the seat belt anchorages either side of the central floor tunnel (see illustration).
31 If both rear belts are being removed, mark them for position to aid refitting. Unscrew and remove the two belt reel mounting bolts each side, and remove the rear belts from the car (see illustration).
32 If required, the rear belt buckles can be unbolted and removed from the floor mountings.

Refitting

33 In all cases, refit by reversing the removal operations. Tighten the seat belt mountings to the specified torque. When refitting the front seat belts, note the following points:
a) *Reconnect the seat belt lower anchorage, ensuring that the catch is fully engaged.*
b) *Remove the safety device from the SIPS bag sensor unit, and return it to its holder*

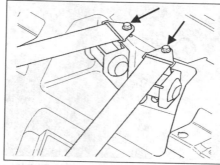

27.31 Rear seat belt reel mounting bolts (C70 models) - arrowed

in the side compartment. Refit the side compartment to the seat.
c) *Make sure that no-one is inside the car. Switch on the ignition, then reconnect the battery negative lead. Switch the ignition off, then on again, and check that the SRS warning light comes on, then goes out within 15 seconds.*

28 Centre console - removal and refitting

Removal

1 Disconnect the battery negative lead. Move the gear or selector lever to neutral - note that it may be necessary to move the gear or selector lever as the console is removed.

2 At the front of the console, prise out the coin holder tray (see illustration). Where applicable, push out the heated seat switches from below, and disconnect their wiring plugs.
3 Unclip and lift out the oddments tray. Remove the two screws now visible at the front of the console (see illustrations). Take care not to let the screws fall as they are removed, since they may be difficult to retrieve.
4 Apply the handbrake fully, then carefully prise free the trim panel below the handbrake lever. The panel must be moved sideways to disengage the main retaining clip. Unclip the panel at the top of the handbrake lever, then carefully work the gaiter over the lever and remove the trim panel (see illustrations).
5 Disconnect the wiring plugs visible below the handbrake lever (see illustration).
6 Working through the aperture below the handbrake lever, release the gear lever gaiter or selector panel from the console by first disengaging the clips at the rear (see illustration). Once the rear edge is released, prise up the rest of the gaiter or selector panel, then feed it down into the console, to allow the console to be lifted over.
7 Open the rear storage compartment lid, and prise up the cover panel in the compartment base. Undo the two screws now exposed (see illustrations).
8 On C70 models, remove the rear seat cushion as described in Section 25. Remove the two screws securing the rear of the console.

28.2 Prise out the coin holder tray from the front of the console

28.3a Prise out the oddments tray . . .

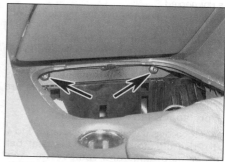

28.3b . . . for access to the console front screws (arrowed)

28.4a The handbrake trim panel must be prised sideways to release the main clip . . .

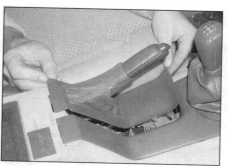

28.4b . . . and is then removed fully to the side and over the handbrake lever

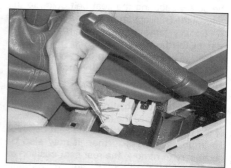

28.5 Disconnect the wiring plugs below the handbrake lever

28.6 Unclip the gear lever gaiter from the console

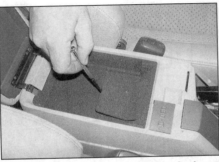

28.7a Prise up the cover panel in the base of the rear storage compartment . . .

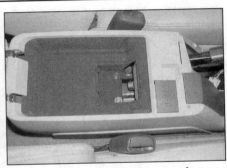

28.7b . . . for access to the console rear screws

9 Lift both sides of the console at the point where the cigar lighter fits, to disengage the locating peg on either side **(see illustration)**.
10 Slide the console rearwards to disengage it from under the facia at the front. Moving the gear or selector lever as necessary, check that the console is free to be removed, then lift the console over the gear/selector and handbrake levers, and remove it from the car **(see illustration)**.
11 The various sections of the console are held together by various nuts and screws, visible from beneath.

28.9 Lift up the console to disengage the front locating peg each side (one arrowed)

28.10 Removing the centre console

Refitting

12 Refitting is a reversal of removal.

29.2 Remove six screws, then pull the glovebox out of the facia

29 Facia -
removal and refitting

Note: *For access to the instrument panel and related components, only the facia top section need be removed.*

Facia top section

Removal

1 Disconnect the battery negative lead, and wait at least 10 minutes before proceeding.
2 Undo the six screws on the front face of the glovebox, then pull the box rearwards to disengage the retaining clips and remove it from the facia **(see illustration)**.

3 On cars equipped with a passenger's airbag, confirm that the battery is disconnected, then disconnect the wiring connector from the base of the airbag module. Undo the three screws securing the airbag module bracket above the glovebox, then remove the six nuts securing the module to the inside of the facia panel.
4 Open both front doors, and prise out the side air vents from the ends of the facia. Remove the four main facia air vents by prising them out using a screwdriver (use a piece of card to protect the facia) **(see illustrations)**.
5 Carefully prise up the speaker grilles on each side of the top section **(see illustration)**. The speakers themselves do not have to be removed, providing care is taken as the top section is removed.

29.4a Prise out the side air vents . . .

29.4b . . . and the main vents from the centre and each side

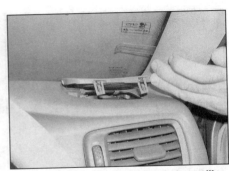

29.5 Prise up the facia top speaker grilles

8.2b Removing the outer (round) cover from behind the headlight

8.3 Pull the wiring plug from the bulb

8.4 Release the bulb retaining clip

8.5 Removing the dipped beam bulb

8.8 Removing the inner cover from behind the headlight

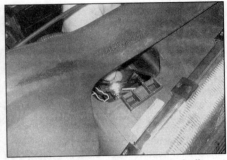

8.9 Removing the main beam bulb

3 Pull the wiring plug off the rear of the bulb **(see illustration)**.

4 Squeeze together the legs of the bulb retaining clip, and swing the clip to one side for access to the bulb **(see illustration)**.

5 Lift out the bulb, noting how it fits in the holder **(see illustration)**.

6 When fitting the new bulb, do not touch the glass (paragraph 1). Make sure that the lugs on the bulb flange engage with the slots in the holder.

7 Refitting is a reversal of removal.

Headlight main beam

8 Open the bonnet. Unclip the inner plastic cover on the rear of the light unit and lift off **(see illustration)**.

9 Proceed as described in paragraphs 3 to 7 **(see illustration)**.

Front sidelight

10 Open the bonnet. Turn the outer (round) plastic cover on the rear of the light unit anti-clockwise and lift off.

11 Pull the bulbholder (located inboard of the dipped beam bulb) from the rear of the headlight - there is no need to disconnect the wiring plug **(see illustration)**.

12 Pull the wedge-base bulb out of the holder **(see illustration)**.

13 Refitting is a reversal of removal.

Front foglight

14 The foglight bulb is accessed from behind the light unit - if preferred, jack up the front of the car for better access.

S70 and V70 models

15 The bulbholder has two tabs to make it easier to turn - twist the bulbholder anti-clockwise to release it from the back of the light unit **(see illustration)**.

C70 models

16 Turn the rear cover anti-clockwise, and move it aside, taking care not to damage the wiring.

17 Squeeze together the legs of the wire retaining clip, and swing it to the side for access to the bulb.

8.11 Pulling out the sidelight bulbholder

8.12 The sidelight bulb pulls out of its holder

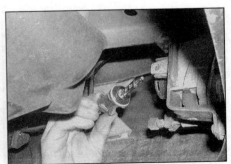

8.15 Use the tabs on the bulbholder to twist and remove it

12

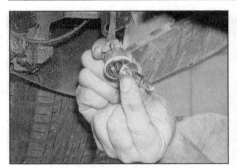

8.18 Pull out the foglight bulb

8.20a Depress the plastic retaining catch . . .

8.20b . . . and withdraw the light unit

All models

18 Remove the bulb from the bulbholder (see illustration).
19 Refitting is a reversal of removal.

Front direction indicator

20 Open the bonnet and press down the plastic catch next to the wiring plug which secures the light unit in position. Carefully withdraw the light unit from the front of the car (see illustrations).
21 Pull the bulbholder out of the light unit - there is no need to disconnect the wiring plug (see illustration).
22 Push in and twist the bulb anti-clockwise to remove it from the bulbholder (see illustration).
23 Refitting is a reversal of removal. Make sure that the plastic catch is fully engaged when refitting the light unit, so that the unit is secure.

Front direction indicator side repeater

24 Slide the light unit forwards to release the retaining clip, then lift it out, rear edge first (see illustration).
25 Twist the bulbholder through a quarter-turn to release it from the light unit, and withdraw the holder (see illustration). It is not recommended that the wiring plug be disconnected, as there is a risk of losing the wiring through the hole in the wing. Tape the wiring to the wing to prevent this, if necessary.
26 Pull the bulb from its holder, and press the new one into position (see illustration).
27 Refitting is a reversal of removal. When refitted, press the light unit to the rear to secure the retaining clip.

Rear light clusters (S70 models)

Note: *This procedure applies both to the*

bulbs in the rear corner light housing, and to those in the boot lid housing.
28 With the boot open, unclip and remove the trim cover from behind the light unit.
29 Release the retaining catch by pressing down the plastic tab, and withdraw the bulbholder (see illustrations).
30 Remove the relevant bayonet fitting bulb from the holder (see illustration).
31 Refitting is a reversal of removal.

Rear light clusters (V70 models)

Upper light cluster

32 From within the luggage compartment, release the light unit access cover with the aid of a screwdriver (see illustration).
33 Where fitted, withdraw the speaker for access to the bulbholder.
34 Press the retaining catch down and withdraw the bulbholder from the pillar (see

8.21 Release the bayonet fitting bulbholder . . .

8.22 . . . and the bayonet fitting bulb

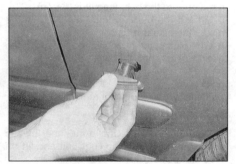

8.24 Removing the side repeater light

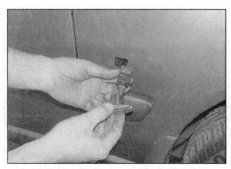

8.25 Twist and release the bulbholder from the light

8.26 Pull out the wedge-base bulb

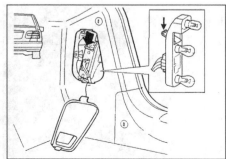

8.29a Rear corner light bulb renewal details - S70 models

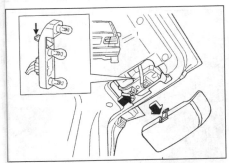

8.29b Rear boot lid light bulb renewal details - S70 models

8.29c Bulbholder removed from rear boot lid light

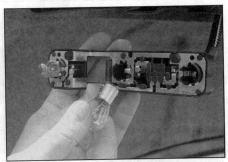

8.30 Twist and remove the bulb from the bulbholder

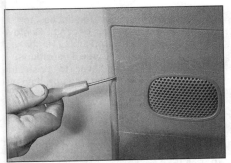

8.32 Releasing the upper light cluster access cover

illustration). Withdraw the relevant bayonet fitting bulb from the holder.

35 Refitting is a reversal of removal.

Lower light cluster

36 From within the luggage compartment, lift

out the outer rear floor covering on the side concerned (see illustration).

37 Remove the access cover in front of the light unit by turning the locking clip through 90°, moving the cover down and lifting out (see illustration).

38 Depress the two retaining catches and withdraw the bulbholder (see illustration). Withdraw the relevant bayonet fitting bulb from the holder.

39 Refitting is a reversal of removal.

Rear light cluster (C70 models)

40 From within the boot, unclip the trim cover from behind the light unit.

41 Unscrew the plastic wing nut, disconnect the wiring plug, and withdraw the bulbholder.

42 Remove the relevant bayonet fitting bulb from the holder.

43 Refitting is a reversal of removal.

High-level brake light

44 The high-level brake light does not contain conventional light bulbs, but rather, a row of LEDs (light-emitting diodes). As a result, if the high-level brake light stops working, it may ultimately be necessary to replace the light unit complete - see Section 10. Before deciding that this is necessary, however, check the fuse and all wiring, using the information in Section 2 and the wiring diagrams at the end of this Chapter.

Number plate light

45 Undo the two screws securing the relevant light unit or lens (see illustration).

46 Carefully prise out the light lens. The wedge-base bulb can be pulled from its holder - a pair of thin-nosed pliers may be necessary, due to the awkward access (see illustration).

47 Refitting is a reversal of removal.

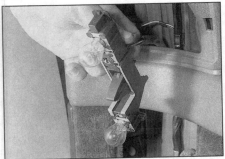

8.34 Press the retaining catch down and withdraw the bulbholder from the pillar

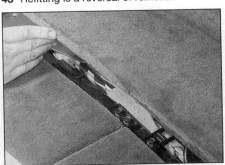

8.36 Lift out the outer rear floor covering for access to the lower light cluster

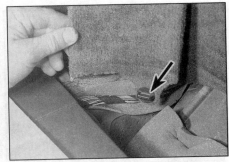

8.37 Turn the locking clip (arrowed) and lift off the cover

8.38 Withdraw the bulbholder from the pillar

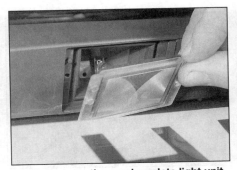

8.45 Remove the number plate light unit lens . . .

8.46 . . . for access to the push-fit bulb

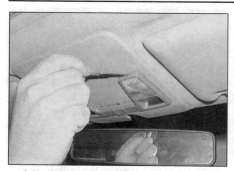

9.3a Using a small screwdriver, prise out . . .

9.3b . . . and remove the light lens

9.4 Removing the bayonet fitting bulb

9 Bulbs (interior lights) - renewal

General

1 Whenever a bulb is renewed, note the following points:

a) *Disconnect the battery negative lead before starting work (see Section 1).*

b) *Remember that if the light has just been in use, the bulb may be extremely hot.*

c) *Always check the bulb contacts and holder, ensuring that there is clean metal-to-metal contact between the bulb and its live(s) and earth. Clean off any corrosion or dirt before fitting a new bulb.*

d) *Wherever bayonet-type bulbs are fitted,*

ensure that the live contact(s) bear firmly against the bulb contact.

e) *Always ensure that the new bulb is of the correct rating and that it is completely clean before fitting it.*

2 Some switch illumination/pilot bulbs are integral with their switches, and cannot be renewed separately.

Interior/vanity mirror lights

3 Carefully prise the light unit or lens from its location using a screwdriver **(see illustrations)**.

4 Renew the bulb(s), which may be bayonet or end clip fitting **(see illustration)**.

5 Refitting is a reversal of removal.

Front reading lights

6 Prise out the front interior light lenses from

the roof console panel, for access to the console retaining screws beneath. Remove the two screws, then unclip and lower the roof console from its location **(see illustrations)**.

7 Use a small screwdriver to prise the bulbholder from the reading light unit, then pull out the wedge-base bulb **(see illustrations)**.

8 Refitting is a reversal of removal.

Glovebox light

9 Empty the contents of the glovebox, then undo the six Torx screws on the front face.

10 Pull the box rearwards to disengage the retaining clips, and withdraw the box from the facia **(see illustration)**.

11 Pull the black dimmer sleeve off the bulbholder, then remove the bayonet fitting bulb **(see illustrations)**.

12 Ensure that the dimmer sleeve light

9.6a Remove the roof console retaining screws . . .

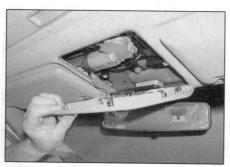

9.6b . . . then lower the console for access to the reading light bulbholder

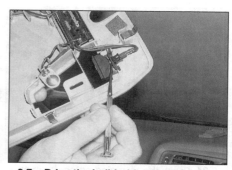

9.7a Prise the bulbholder from the light unit . . .

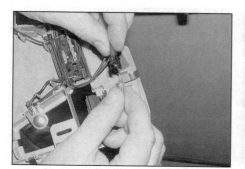

9.7b . . . and pull out the wedge-base bulb

9.10 Remove the screws, then pull the glovebox from the facia

9.11a Pull the dimmer sleeve from the bulbholder . . .

9.11b . . . then remove the bayonet fitting bulb

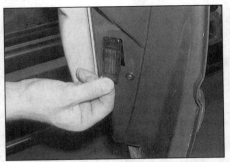

9.15 Release the light unit from the door edge

9.16a Twist off the lens from the bulbholder . . .

aperture faces the glovebox window when refitting.

13 Refitting is a reversal of removal. Do not over-tighten the glovebox screws.

Heater control panel illumination bulb

14 Refer to Chapter 3, Section 10 or 11 as applicable.

Door edge marker light bulb

15 Push the light unit upwards and release it at the bottom **(see illustration)**.
16 Withdraw the unit from the door, twist the lens from the bulbholder and pull out the wedge-base bulb **(see illustrations)**.
17 Refitting is a reversal of removal.

Automatic transmission selector panel illumination bulb

18 Apply the handbrake fully, then carefully prise free the trim panel below the handbrake lever. The panel must be moved sideways to disengage the main retaining clip. Unclip the panel at the top of the handbrake lever, then carefully work the gaiter over the lever and remove the trim panel.
19 Working through the aperture below the handbrake lever, release the selector panel from the console by first disengaging the clips at the rear. Once the rear edge is released, prise up the rest of the gaiter or selector panel.

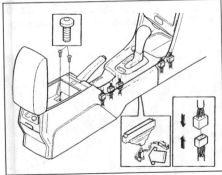

9.20 Selector panel illumination bulb renewal details

Unless difficulty is experienced, it should not be necessary to remove the centre console

20 Working through the selector lever and handbrake apertures, it should now be possible to pull the bulbholder from the base of the elongated selector panel illumination shroud **(see illustration)**. If access cannot be gained using this method, remove the centre console completely, as described in Chapter 11.
21 Trace the wiring from the bulbholder back to the connector plug, and disconnect it. The bulb and holder cannot be separated, and must be renewed as a unit.
22 Refitting is a reversal of removal.

Switch illumination bulbs

23 Not all switch illumination bulbs are renewable separately. Remove the switch as described in Section 4 for examination.
24 Usually, the bulbholder is removed by turning through 90° with a small screwdriver; with the bulbholder removed, the bulb can then be pulled out **(see illustrations)**.
25 On some switches, the bulb is simply pulled from the switch directly.

Instrument panel bulbs

26 Refer to Section 6.

Front ashtray illumination bulb

27 Remove the ashtray, then undo the screws securing the ashtray compartment and withdraw the compartment.
28 Pull out the ashtray light bulbholder, and remove the bulb and holder from the contacts.
29 Refitting is a reversal of removal.

9.16b . . . and remove the wedge-base bulb

Rear ashtray illumination bulb

30 Remove the ashtray, then pull the top of the ashtray panel upwards to release its bottom edge - if necessary, prise up the retaining tabs using a small screwdriver.
31 Pull out the bulbholder, and remove the bulb and holder from the contacts.
32 Refitting is a reversal of removal.

Cigarette lighter illumination bulb

Front cigar lighter

33 Remove the centre console as described in Chapter 11. Whilst it is possible to gain access to the cigar lighter body by prising out the oddments tray at the front of the console, removing the bulbholder requires that the console be removed.

9.24a Hazard warning light switch bulb renewal - turn the bulbholder using a small screwdriver . . .

9.24b . . . and remove the bulbholder from the switch - the bulb can be pulled out

9.34 Use a small screwdriver to release the cigar lighter retaining clips

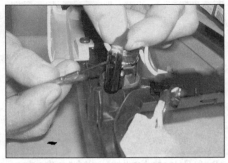

9.35a Prise out the bulbholder from the side of the cigar lighter . . .

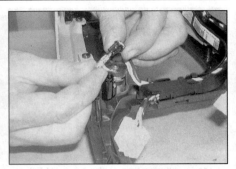

9.35b . . . and pull out the bulb

34 Using a small screwdriver, release the two retaining tabs which secure the cigar lighter to the underside of the console **(see illustration)**. The cigar lighter will remain attached by its wiring, but releasing it from its location makes bulb renewal easier.

35 Again using a small screwdriver, release the bulbholder from the cigar lighter body, and pull out the bulb **(see illustrations)**.

36 Refitting is a reversal of removal. Check the operation of the bulb before refitting the centre console.

Rear cigar lighter

37 Remove the ashtray, then pull the top of the ashtray panel upwards to release its bottom edge - if necessary, prise up the retaining tabs using a small screwdriver **(see illustrations)**.

38 Proceed as described in paragraphs 34 and 35 **(see illustration)**.

39 Refitting is a reversal of removal.

Footwell lights

40 Taking care not to damage the facia trim, prise down the top edge of the light unit, then disconnect its wiring plug and remove it **(see illustrations)**.

41 Carefully unclip the metal cover from the rear of the light unit, then pull out the wedge-base bulb from the holder **(see illustrations)**.

42 Refitting is a reversal of removal.

9.37a Remove the rear ashtray . . .

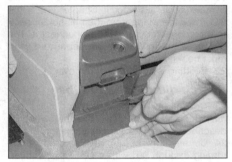

9.37b . . . then release the retaining catches and pull out the ashtray panel

9.38 Rear cigar lighter bulbholder removed for access to the bulb

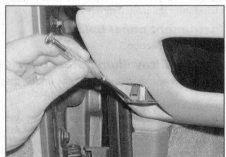

9.40a Prise down the footwell light . . .

9.40b . . . and disconnect its wiring plug

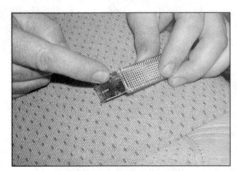

9.41a Unclip the metal cover . . .

9.41b . . . then withdraw it from the light unit for access to the bulbholder

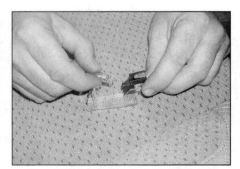

9.41c Pull out the wedge-base bulb

10.2a Disconnect the main headlight wiring connector at the base of the light unit

10.2b Where applicable, also disconnect the beam control motor wiring plug

10.4a Remove the two inner bolts (arrowed) . . .

10 Exterior light units - removal and refitting

Note: *Disconnect the battery negative lead before removing any light unit.*

Headlight

1 On models with headlight wash/wipe, pivot the headlight wiper arms out of the way while the headlight is being worked on.
2 Disconnect the wiring connector on the lower rear face of the light unit. Where a beam height control motor is fitted, disconnect the wiring connectors on the motor **(see illustrations)**.
3 Remove the front direction indicator by pressing down its plastic catch next to the wiring plug. Carefully withdraw the light unit from the front of the car, and disconnect the wiring plug from the bulbholder.

4 Undo the three retaining bolts and withdraw the headlight unit from the front of the car **(see illustrations)**.
5 Refitting is a reversal of removal. Have the headlight beam alignment checked on completion (see Section 11).

Headlight lens

6 If necessary, the headlight lens can be replaced separately, as described below.
7 Remove the headlight as described above.
8 On models with headlight wash/wipe, remove the screw from the base of the light unit which secures the wiper arm stop, and remove the stop from the light.
9 The lens is secured by a total of eight metal clips around its edge, which can be released using a flat-bladed screwdriver **(see illustration)**.
10 Lift off the glass, and recover the seal. The seal should always be renewed when a new glass is being fitted. Try not to touch the

headlight reflector while the glass is removed.
11 Reassembly is a reversal of removal, taking care that the new seal is located correctly, and that all the lens securing clips are firmly in position - if any were broken, or have lost their tension, fit new ones.
12 On completion, refit the headlight as described previously.

Front foglight

13 Apply the handbrake, chock the rear wheels, then jack up the front of the car.
14 The foglight unit is removed complete with its metal mounting bracket - the two can then be separated if required.
15 Disconnect the wiring plug from the rear of the unit **(see illustration)**. On C70 models, remove the bulb as described in Section 8.
16 Remove the Torx screw at the base of the bracket, then remove the two small bolts at the top, and remove the light unit and bracket from the car **(see illustrations)**.

10.4b . . . and the outer bolt . . .

10.4c . . . and withdraw the headlight from the car

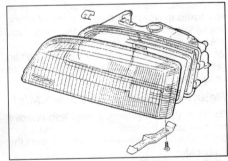

10.9 Headlight lens renewal details - there are eight metal clips in total (one shown)

10.15 Disconnect the wiring plug from the rear of the foglight

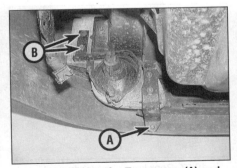

10.16a Remove the Torx screw (A) and two upper bolts (B) . . .

10.16b . . . and withdraw the foglight and bracket from its location

12

10.19a Depress the plastic retaining catch . . .

10.19b . . . and withdraw the light unit

10.20 Disconnect the wiring plug from the bulbholder, and remove the light

17 If required, remove the three screws securing the mounting bracket to the light unit, and separate the two.

18 Refitting is a reversal of removal.

Front direction indicator

19 Press down the plastic catch next to the wiring plug which secures the light unit in position. Carefully withdraw the light unit from the front of the car (see illustrations).

20 Disconnect the wiring plug from the rear of the bulbholder (see illustration).

21 Refitting is a reversal of removal. Make sure that the plastic catch is fully engaged when refitting the light unit, so that the unit is secure.

Front direction indicator side repeater

22 Slide the light unit forwards to release the retaining clip, then lift it out, rear edge first.

23 Disconnect the wiring plug from the bulbholder, and remove the light unit (see illustration). Note that there is a risk of losing the wiring through the hole in the wing; tape the wiring to the wing to prevent this.

24 Refitting is a reversal of removal. When refitted, press the light unit to the rear to secure the retaining clip.

Rear light clusters (S70 models)

25 With the boot open, unclip and remove the trim cover from behind the light unit.

26 Disconnect the wiring plug from the bulbholder.

27 Remove the four nuts securing the light unit to the rear wing or boot lid (see

illustration). If the boot lid-mounted light cluster is being removed, squeeze together the two retaining lugs.

28 Remove the light unit from the car. Check the condition of the seal to the bodywork, and renew it if necessary.

29 Refitting is a reversal of removal.

Rear light clusters (V70 models)

Upper light cluster

30 From within the luggage compartment, release the light unit access cover with the aid of a screwdriver.

31 Where fitted, withdraw the speaker for access to the bulbholder.

32 Press the retaining catch down and withdraw the bulbholder from the pillar. Disconnect the bulbholder wiring connector.

33 Using a long socket, undo the two nuts and remove the light cluster unit from the rear of the vehicle (see illustration).

34 Refitting is a reversal of removal.

Lower light cluster

35 Remove the upper rear light cluster as described previously (the two units overlap, and the upper must be removed first).

36 From within the luggage compartment, lift out the outer rear floor covering on the side concerned.

37 Remove the access cover in front of the light unit by turning the locking clip through 90°, moving the cover down and lifting out.

38 Depress the two retaining catches and withdraw the bulbholder. Disconnect the bulbholder wiring connector.

39 Fold back the luggage compartment rear floor panel, undo the screws and remove the sill guard.

40 Release the side trim panels as necessary for access to the two cluster unit retaining nuts.

41 Using a long socket, undo the nuts and remove the light cluster unit from the rear of the vehicle.

42 Refitting is a reversal of removal.

High-level brake light (S70 and C70 models)

43 On S70 models, fold the rear seat forwards, then remove the rear seat side cushions.

44 Unclip and remove the rear pillar trim panels, then release the two clips securing the rear edge of the headlining, and lower the headlining for access to the light unit.

45 Disconnect the wiring plug from the light unit, then push the light unit to one side to release the retaining hooks (see illustration). Remove the light unit from the car.

46 Note that the bulbs in the high-level brake light are actually LEDs (light-emitting diodes), and these cannot be replaced separately. If the brake light has stopped working, it may be necessary to replace the unit complete. Check the fuse, and all wiring and connections, before assuming the light unit is faulty.

10.23 Disconnect the wiring plug from the bulbholder

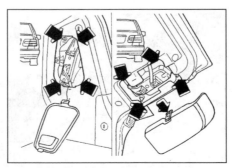

10.27 Rear light cluster renewal - retaining nuts arrowed

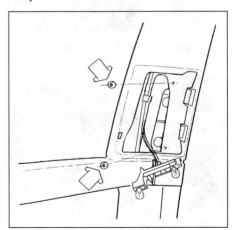

10.33 Upper rear light cluster retaining nuts (arrowed) - V70 models

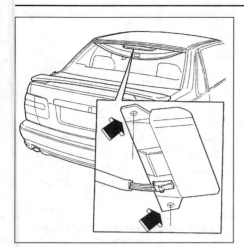

10.45 High-level brake light is retained by hooks which lock into holes (arrowed) in the mounting flange

47 Refitting is a reversal of removal. Check that the light unit is working before reassembling the trim.

High-level brake light (V70 models)

48 Remove the tailgate interior trim panels as described in Chapter 11, Section 13.
49 Disconnect the wiring plug from the light unit.
50 Undo and remove the two retaining screws, and remove the light unit from the car **(see illustration)**.
51 Note that the bulbs in the high-level brake light are actually LEDs (light-emitting diodes), and these cannot be replaced separately. If the brake light has stopped working, it may be necessary to replace the unit complete. Check the fuse, and all wiring and connections, before assuming the light unit is faulty.
52 Refitting is a reversal of removal. Check that the light unit is working before reassembling the trim.

Number plate light

53 Undo the two screws securing the relevant light unit.

54 Carefully prise out the light unit, disconnect the wiring connector and remove the unit. Note that on V70 models, the two number plate light units are different.
55 Refitting is a reversal of removal.

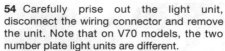

11 Headlight beam alignment - checking and adjusting

1 Beam alignment should be carried out by a Volvo dealer or other specialist heaving the necessary optical alignment equipment.
2 For reference, the headlights can be adjusted by means of the vertical and horizontal adjuster controls at the rear of the headlight unit.
3 Some models are equipped with an electrically-operated headlight beam adjustment system which is controlled through the switch on the facia. On these models, ensure that the switch is set to the off position before adjusting the headlight aim.

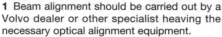

12 Headlight beam control motor - removal and refitting

Removal

1 Although not essential, this operation is much easier (especially refitting) if the headlight unit is removed as described in Section 10.
2 If not already done, disconnect the wiring connector at the beam control motor on the rear of the headlight unit.
3 Turn the motor 90° anti-clockwise to release the motor bayonet fitting attachment.
4 Pull the motor rearwards off the light unit until the motor shaft disengages from its socket location in the headlight reflector. Remove the motor **(see illustration)**.

Refitting

5 Turn the beam height control adjuster on the motor anti-clockwise as far as it will go to extend the motor shaft fully.

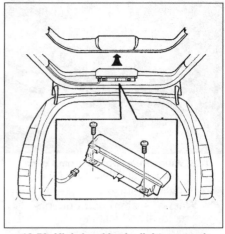

10.50 High-level brake light removal details - V70 models

6 Lightly lubricate the end of the motor shaft with medium grease.
7 Unclip and remove the inner cover from the rear of the headlight. Hold the headlight reflector, while engaging the motor ball into the reflector socket **(see illustration)**.
8 Turn the height control adjuster clockwise to shorten the shaft until the motor can be located in the light unit. Turn the motor clockwise to lock the bayonet attachment.
9 Reconnect the wiring connectors and check the operation of the motor.
10 Have the beam adjustment basic setting checked and if necessary adjusted, by a dealer or specialist.

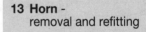

13 Horn - removal and refitting

Removal

1 Open the bonnet and disconnect the wires from the horn.
2 Unbolt the horn from its bracket and remove it **(see illustration)**.

Refitting

3 Refitting is a reversal of removal.

12.4 Removing the motor from the headlight

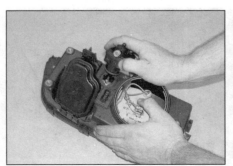

12.7 Hold the headlight reflector as the motor is engaged

13.2 Horn retaining bolt and wiring connector

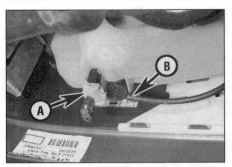

14.3 Windscreen washer pump wiring plug (A) and fluid hose (B)

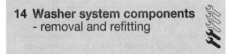

14 Washer system components
   - removal and refitting

Windscreen washer pump

Removal

1 Jack up the front right-hand corner of the car, and support on axle stands.
2 Place a container under the reservoir, and be prepared for spillage.
3 Using long-nosed pliers and a protective cloth, grip the washer pump and pull it out of the reservoir. Disconnect the wiring connector, detach the hose and remove the pump **(see illustration)**.

Refitting

4 Refitting is a reversal of removal.

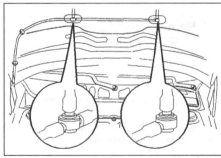

14.13 Front washer jet supply tubes and connection pieces, accessed with the bonnet open

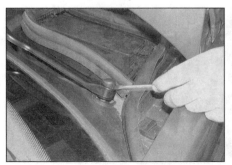

15.1a Prise off the cover . . .

14.6 Tailgate washer pump and wiring connector (arrowed)

Tailgate washer pump

Removal

5 From within the engine compartment, remove the washer fluid reservoir filler neck by pulling it up and out of the tank.
6 Using long-nosed pliers and a protective cloth, grip the washer pump and pull it up and out of the reservoir. Disconnect the wiring connector, detach the hose and remove the pump **(see illustration)**.

Refitting

7 Refitting is a reversal of removal.

Washer reservoir

Removal

8 From within the engine compartment, remove the washer fluid reservoir filler neck by pulling it up and out of the tank.
9 Disconnect the fluid level sensor. Also disconnect the wiring connector and fluid hose from the tailgate washer pump (where applicable).
10 From under the front right-hand wheel arch, disconnect the fluid hose and wiring connector at the washer pump.
11 Undo the reservoir retaining bolts, and withdraw the unit from under the car **(see illustration)**.

Refitting

12 Refitting is a reversal of removal.

Washer jets

Removal

13 If working on the rear washer jet, remove

15.1b . . . then unscrew and remove the wiper arm nut

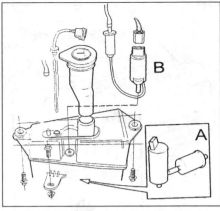

14.11 Washer reservoir and related components

A Windscreen washer pump
B Tailgate washer pump

the relevant trim panel for access, then disconnect the fluid hose. The front washer jets can be accessed by opening the bonnet **(see illustration)**.
14 Release the jet from its location using a deep socket which will push the side catches together and allow removal.

Refitting

15 Push the jet into its location until the side catches spring out to lock. Reconnect the fluid hose
16 Adjust the jet nozzles using a pin so that liquid is sprayed onto the centre of the glass.

Washer fluid level sensor

17 Refer to Section 7.

15 Wiper arms -
   removal and refitting

Removal

1 Lift up or prise off the cover (where applicable) then remove the nut at the base of the wiper arm **(see illustrations)**.
2 Pull the arm off the splines, using a twisting motion to most effectively release the arm **(see illustration)**.

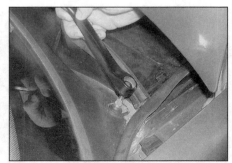

15.2 Pull the wiper arm off the splined spindle

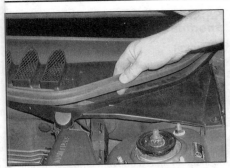

16.4 Lift off the rubber weatherseal

16.5a Release the spring clips . . .

16.5b . . . and detach the drain hoses from the cowl panel

3 If the wiper arms will not release, refit the nut loosely, then use a pair of slip-joint pliers (water pump pliers) under the end of the wiper arm and on the end of the spindle to free the splines.

Refitting

4 Switch the relevant wiper on, then switch it off again to ensure that the motor and linkage are parked. Position the windscreen wiper arms so that the driver's side arm is 35 mm from the top edge of the cowl panel, and the passenger's side arm is 45 mm from the edge of the panel. Position the tailgate wiper arm so that it is horizontal.

16.6a Remove four screws and take off the fusebox lid . . .

16.6b . . . then remove the cowl panel, unclipping it at the rear

16 Windscreen wiper motor and linkage - removal and refitting

Removal

1 Switch the wipers on, then off again to ensure that the motor and linkage are parked.
2 Disconnect the battery negative lead.
3 Remove the windscreen wiper arms as described in Section 15.
4 Lift off the rubber weatherseal from the rear edge of the engine compartment (**see illustration**), then undo the five Torx screws securing the windscreen wiper cowl panel to the scuttle at the front.
5 Using a suitable pair of pliers, release the spring clips securing the two drain hoses at the front of the cowl panel (**see illustrations**).

6 Remove the four screws securing the fusebox lid, then lift off the cowl panel, disengaging it from the rubber seal at the rear edge (**see illustrations**).
7 Undo the two bolts securing the mounting frame to the wiper well (**see illustration**).
8 Unhook the frame assembly from its location, noting how the locating peg fits into the central mounting. Disconnect the wiring connector and remove the unit from the car (**see illustrations**).
9 Mark the position of the motor crank arm relative to the frame, undo the nut and remove the crank arm from the motor.
10 Undo the three motor retaining bolts and remove the motor from the frame. The frame and linkage arms are an assembly, and cannot be individually renewed.

Refitting

11 Refit the motor to the frame, and secure with the three mounting bolts.
12 If a new motor is being fitted, temporarily reconnect the wiring connectors at the car, switch on the motor then switch it off again to ensure that it is parked.
13 Position the crank arm on the motor, with the marks made on removal aligned. Prevent the crank arm from turning by holding it with a spanner, then refit and tighten the nut.
14 Alternatively, if a new frame and linkage are being fitted, set the motor to the park position as described previously then, when connecting the crank arm to the motor, position it so that it is parallel with the linkage arm directly above.
15 The assembled components can now be refitted using a reversal of removal.

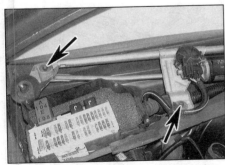

16.7 Wiper motor frame securing bolts (arrowed)

16.8a Unhook the wiper motor frame from the mounting (arrowed)

16.8b Disconnect the motor wiring plug, and remove the assembly

17.6 Removing the tailgate wiper motor assembly

17 Tailgate wiper motor - removal and refitting

Removal

1 Switch the wiper on then off again to ensure that the motor and linkage are parked.
2 Disconnect the battery negative lead.
3 Remove the tailgate wiper arm as described in Section 15.
4 Remove the tailgate interior trim panel as described in Chapter 11.
5 Undo the three nuts securing the mounting frame to the tailgate.
6 Release the frame assembly from its location, disconnect the wiring connector and remove the unit from the car (see illustration).
7 Mark the position of the motor crank arm relative to the frame, then undo the nut and remove the crank arm from the motor.
8 Undo the three motor retaining bolts and remove the motor from the frame. The frame and linkage arm are an assembly, and cannot be individually renewed.

Refitting

9 Refit the motor to the frame and secure with the three mounting bolts.
10 If a new motor is being fitted, temporarily reconnect the wiring connector at the car, switch on the motor then switch it off again to ensure that it is parked.

11 Position the crank arm on the motor, with the marks made on removal aligned. Prevent the crank arm from turning by holding it with a spanner, then refit and tighten the nut.
12 Alternatively, if a new frame and linkage are being fitted, set the motor to the park position as described previously then, when connecting the crank arm to the motor, position it so that it is parallel with the linkage arm directly above.
13 The assembled components can now be refitted using a reversal of removal.

18 Headlight wiper motor - removal and refitting

Left-hand motor

Removal

1 Disconnect the battery negative lead.
2 Lift up the cover, then remove the nut at the base of the wiper arm and pull the arm off the splines. Use a twisting motion to most effectively release the arm. Disconnect the washer tube from the wiper arm (see illustrations).
3 Remove the headlight and front direction indicator light units as described in Section 10.
4 Undo the two bolts securing the motor to the body panel.
5 Disconnect the wiper motor wiring connector, which is located either above the headlight unit or in front of the radiator according to model.
6 Remove the radiator left-hand mounting bolt completely, and loosen the right-hand bolt, so that the radiator can be moved slightly to the rear, to allow the wiper motor to be withdrawn. Remove the wiper motor from the engine compartment.

Refitting

7 Refitting is a reversal of removal. Take care not to trap the washer hose when installing the motor. Before refitting the wiper arm, switch the motor on and off so that it is in the park position.
8 Fit the headlight wiper arm with the blade resting on the stop.

Right-hand motor (models without air conditioning)

Removal

9 Disconnect the battery negative lead.
10 Remove the ECU box air duct behind the headlight. Remove the washer reservoir filler neck by pulling it upwards out of the washer reservoir.
11 Remove the headlight wiper arm as described in paragraph 2.
12 Disconnect the wiper motor wiring connector located above the headlight unit.
13 Undo the two bolts now exposed securing the motor to the body panel. Withdraw the motor from its location and remove it from the engine compartment (see illustration).

Refitting

14 Refitting is a reversal of removal. Take care not to trap the washer hose when installing the motor. Before refitting the wiper arm, switch the motor on and off so that it is in the park position.
15 Fit the headlight wiper arm by positioning it with the blade just below the stop. Secure the arm, then lift the blade over the stop.

Right-hand motor (models with air conditioning)

Removal

16 Disconnect the battery negative lead.
17 Remove the ECU box air duct behind the headlight. Remove the washer reservoir filler neck by pulling it upwards out of the washer reservoir.
18 Lift the cooling system expansion tank out of its location, and move it to one side without disconnecting any of the hoses.
19 Disconnect the wiring plug for the washer motor, which is located on the radiator support panel above the headlight.
20 Remove the headlight wiper arm as described in paragraph 2.
21 Remove the right-hand headlight unit as described in Section 10.
22 Clean off the top of the ECU box lid, to make sure no debris falls inside when it is removed. Release the catch on the side of the ECU module box lid. Lift off the lid and place it to one side.

18.2a Remove the wiper arm nut . . .

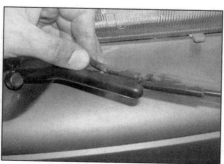

18.2b . . . and disconnect the washer tube

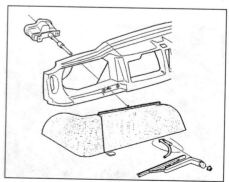

18.13 Right-hand headlight wiper motor and related components

23 Remove the bolt securing the upper section of the ECU box, and disconnect the rear air intake pipe from the box. Release the retaining catches at the front and side, and lift the upper section out **(see illustration)**.

24 Undo the module box lower section retaining bolt, then move the box rearward to release it from the body at the front. Lift up the module box cable duct to gain access to the wiper motor.

25 Disconnect the wiper motor wiring connector, which is located either above the headlight unit or in front of the radiator according to model.

26 Remove the three bolts securing the radiator support panel, and the two bolts securing the motor to the body panel **(see illustration)**.

27 Withdraw the radiator support panel and the wiper motor, turning the motor on its side to clear adjacent components, and remove it from the engine compartment.

Refitting

28 Refitting is a reversal of removal, noting the following points:

a) Take care not to trap the washer hose or any wiring when installing the motor.

b) Before refitting the wiper arm, switch the motor on and off so that it is in the park position.

c) Fit the right-hand headlight wiper arm by positioning it with the blade just below the stop. Secure the arm, then lift the blade over the stop.

19 Electrically-operated/heated front seat - information and component renewal

Information

1 An electrically-operated front seat with programmable memory is optionally available for both the driver and passenger. The seat incorporates four electric motors, three under the seat and one in the backrest. The three motors under the seat control the height of the front and rear edges of the seat cushion, and the fore-and-aft position of the complete seat. The fourth motor controls the backrest vertical position.

2 A control panel on the side of the seat contains the motor control switches and the memory buttons which are used to store and adjust the various settings.

3 The operation of the seat is controlled by an electronic control unit (ECU) which also incorporates a diagnostic function. In the event of a fault in the seat components or control circuitry, a fault code will be stored in the ECU memory for subsequent read-out using diagnostic equipment (typically, a fault code reader).

Component renewal

 Warning: There is a risk of injury if the SIPS bag is triggered inadvertently when working on the front

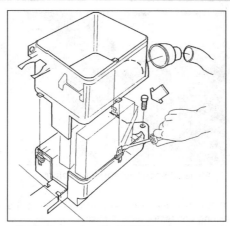

18.23 Removing the ECU box for access to the headlight wiper motor

seat. Ensure that the safety device described in the following paragraphs is installed, and never apply external force to the side of the seat. It is strongly recommended that any work involving the front seat is entrusted to a Volvo dealer. Refer to Section 24 for further information on the SRS system.

4 Removal and refitting any of the electric seat components except the control panel will entail re-calibration of the seat ECU by a Volvo dealer. Until this is done the new components will not operate correctly, and a fault code will be logged in the ECU memory. For any operation other than removing the control panel, it is therefore advisable to consult a Volvo dealer.

Control panel

5 Ensure that the ignition is switched off, then disconnect the battery negative lead. Wait at least 10 minutes before proceeding.

6 Disconnect the yellow wiring connector from the ECU under the front edge of the seat cushion.

7 Remove the seat side compartment by releasing the forward edge and pushing backwards.

8 Remove the red plastic safety device from its holder in the side compartment, and fit the safety device to the SIPS bag sensor unit on the side of the seat.

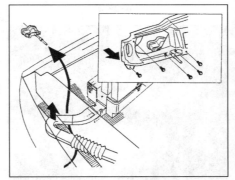

18.26 Right-hand headlight wiper motor removal details

9 Undo the three screws on the rear of the side compartment, and remove the control panel.

10 Refitting is a reversal of removal.

Heating elements

11 On models equipped with heated seats, a heating element is fitted to both the seat back and the seat cushion. Renewal of the heating elements entails completely removing all the seat upholstery and partially dismantling the internal frame.

12 Note that upholstery removal and refitting requires considerable skill and experience if it is to be carried out successfully, and is therefore best entrusted to a Volvo dealer. In practice it will be very difficult for anyone unskilled in this work, or without the necessary tools to carry out the job without ruining the upholstery.

13 An additional danger is that the side airbag (SIPS bag) could be damaged or triggered by any attempt to dismantle the seat - see the warning earlier in this Section.

Seat heater switches

14 Refer to Section 4.

20 Radio/cassette player - removal and refitting

Note: *Radio/cassette players of various designs may be fitted, according to model, territory and optional equipment. The removal and refitting procedures for one of the common types are as follows.*

Removal

1 Disconnect the battery negative lead. If the radio/cassette player is equipped with an anti-theft security code, refer to the information given in the *Reference* sections at the end of this manual before disconnecting the battery.

2 The removal handles are concealed on either side of the front face - press in the handles, and they will spring out for use.

3 Pull the handles slowly rearwards, and withdraw the radio from the facia sufficiently to gain access to the wiring at the rear **(see illustration)**.

20.3 Pull the radio/cassette unit from the facia using the built-in handles

4 Disconnect the wiring multi-plugs and the aerial lead, and remove the unit from the car **(see illustrations)**.

Refitting

5 Refitting is a reversal of removal. Press the removal handles in on completion, so that they are concealed.

21 Speakers -
removal and refitting

20.4a Disconnect the multi-plugs . . .

20.4b . . . and the aerial lead from the rear of the unit, and remove it

Facia speaker

1 Carefully prise up the speaker grilles on the side of the facia top cover **(see illustration)**.
2 Remove the speaker by pressing down the centre of the plastic expanding rivets and lifting the speaker up **(see illustration)**. Disconnect the wiring and remove the speaker.
3 Refitting is a reversal of removal, making sure the speaker is correctly located. Pull out the centre of the expanding rivets before fitting, then press the centre to lock.

Door speaker

4 Remove the door trim panel as described in Chapter 11.
5 Undo the speaker retaining screw at the base, then turn the plastic fasteners either side through 90°. Supporting the speaker, prise the plastic pegs either side out of the door **(see illustrations)**.

6 Remove the speaker and disconnect the wiring connector **(see illustration)**.
7 Refitting is a reversal of removal.

Rear speaker (S70 and C70 models)

8 Working in the boot, disconnect the wiring plugs from the base of each speaker, noting their locations.
9 If the speaker retaining screws are visible from below, unscrew and remove them. The speakers can then be lifted out of the shelf from inside the car.
10 If no screws could be seen from below, carefully prise off the speaker covers. The speakers will either be retained by screws, or by the expanding rivets described in paragraphs 2 and 3. Once released, lift the speakers out of the shelf.
11 Refitting is a reversal of removal.

Rear speaker (V70 models)

12 From within the luggage compartment, release the rear light unit access cover with the aid of a screwdriver.
13 Undo the four speaker retaining screws, remove the speaker and disconnect the wiring connectors.
14 Refitting is a reversal of removal.

22 Radio aerial -
general information

On S70 and C70 models, various aerial types may be fitted as standard or optional equipment, according to model and market. The aerial is typically fitted to the left-hand rear wing - access to the aerial assembly is

21.1 Prise up the speaker grille from the top of the facia

21.2 Press down the centres of the expanding rivets (arrowed) to release the speaker

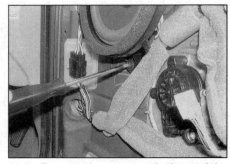

21.5a Remove the screw at the base of the speaker . . .

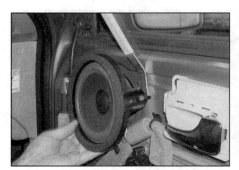

21.5b . . . then turn the plastic fasteners through 90° and using a flat-bladed tool . . .

21.5c . . . prise the pegs out of the door

21.6 Disconnect the wiring plug from the speaker

gained by removing the left-hand side trim panel in the boot. Removal should be fairly straightforward in all cases - unclip and disconnect the wiring to the aerial as necessary, then remove the retaining screws (electric aerial) or the nut at the aerial base inside the wing (manual aerial). No specific information was available at the time of writing concerning removal and refitting procedures.

On V70 models, the aerial is a wire filament incorporated into the rear window glass on the left-hand side. The aerial works in conjunction with a signal booster located behind the trim panel under the rear window. Repair of small breaks in the glass filament may be possible with special metallic repair paste but must ideally be dealt with by a specialist for satisfactory results.

In the event of aerial breakage or poor audio quality, seek the advice of a Volvo dealer or audio equipment specialist. Many aerial problems, like electrical faults, are caused by poor connections. Check the aerial wiring plugs both at the aerial itself and at the rear of the radio (remove the radio as described in Section 20 for access). Some aerials rely on making a good earth connection between the aerial mounting and the body of the car - if necessary, remove the aerial and clean its connection point on the body. If an earth fault is suspected, solder a length of wire to the aerial, and connect the other end to a known good earth point.

There is a chance that the aerial wiring may be broken or shorted out somewhere along its length - this could be checked by performing a continuity test. Using suitable lengths of wire securely connected to both ends of the aerial lead, check for continuity with an ohmmeter - continuity will be indicated by obtaining any reading other than infinity.

23 Anti-theft alarm and immobiliser system - general information

Note: *This information is applicable only to the systems fitted by Volvo as original equipment.*

All models are equipped with an anti-theft alarm, and most are also equipped with an ignition immobiliser.

Immobiliser

The electronic immobiliser is automatically activated when the ignition key is removed from the ignition switch. When activated, it cuts the ignition circuit, preventing the engine from being started.

The system is disarmed when the ignition key is inserted into the ignition switch, as follows. The head of the ignition key contains a transponder micro-chip, and the ignition lock contains a reader coil. When the key enters the lock, the reader coil recognises the signal from the micro-chip, and de-activates the immobiliser. It is essential that the key tag showing the key number is not lost (this will be

supplied with the car when new). Any duplicate keys will have to be obtained from a Volvo dealer, who will need the key number to supply a duplicate - any keys cut elsewhere will work the door locks, but will not contain the transponder chip necessary to de-activate the immobiliser and allow the engine to be started.

The immobiliser reader coil can be removed from the ignition switch, after removing the column lower shroud. However, it is unclear at the time of writing whether a new reader coil can be matched to a particular key or control unit.

Any problems or work involving the immobiliser system should be entrusted to a Volvo dealer, as dedicated electronic equipment is required to diagnose faults, or to 'match' the various components.

Alarm

An anti-theft alarm system is fitted as standard equipment. The alarm has switches on all the doors (including the tailgate/boot lid), the bonnet and ignition switch. If the tailgate/boot lid, bonnet or any of the doors are opened or the ignition switch is switched on whilst the alarm is set, the alarm horn will sound and the hazard warning lights will flash. The alarm also has an immobiliser function which makes the ignition inoperable whilst the alarm is triggered.

The alarm system may be upgraded with various options, to give greater security:

a) *The glass breakage sensor detects the sound of glass breaking, such as when a side or rear window is attacked by a thief trying to gain entry. If this is not fitted, and the doors are not opened, the standard alarm will not sound. Estate models may have resistive wires (similar to those for the heated rear window) set into the rear side glass - when the glass is broken, the current flow through the wires is interrupted, and the alarm will sound.*

b) *The movement sensor system detects movement inside the car - if access has been gained without the alarm sounding, this sensor should trigger the alarm. The system consists of an emitter and a sensor - the emitter sends out a high-frequency wave signal, which is detected by the sensor. If the wave pattern is distorted or interrupted, the alarm will be triggered.*

c) *The inclination sensor detects movement of the vehicle body, and in particular, any change in attitude resulting from it being jacked up. The sensor often takes the form of a mercury switch, or it may be a ball-bearing and saucer type. Once the alarm is set and the position of the switch has been noted, any attempt to rock the car, or to jack it up, will result in the alarm sounding.*

d) *The backup battery is perhaps the most useful of any of the alarm options. One of the most common methods of disabling an alarm is to disconnect the vehicle*

battery. If a backup battery is fitted, the alarm will still sound even after being tampered with in this way.

Signals from the alarm system switches and contacts which are integral with the door, bonnet and tailgate/boot lid locks are sent to a central control unit inside the car once the system is set. The control unit monitors the signals and activates the alarm if any of the signal loops are broken, or if an attempt is made to start the car (or to hot-wire the ignition).

The status of the system is displayed by means of a flashing LED located in the centre of the facia.

Should the alarm system become faulty, bear in mind the following points:

a) *As with other electrical equipment, many faults are caused by poor connections or bad earths.*

b) *Check the operation of all the door, bonnet and boot lid/tailgate switches, and the operation of all interior lights.*

c) *The alarm system may behave oddly if the vehicle battery is in poor condition, or if its terminals are loose.*

d) *If the system is operating correctly, but gives too many false alarms, a Volvo dealer may be able to reduce the sensitivity of some of the system sensors (where fitted).*

e) *Ultimately, the vehicle may have to be taken to a Volvo dealer or a suitably-equipped garage for examination. They will have access to a special diagnostic tester which will quickly trace any fault present in the system.*

24 Supplemental Restraint System (SRS) - general information and precautions

General information

A supplemental restraint system is fitted in various forms as standard or optional equipment depending on model and territory.

The main system component is a driver's airbag, which is designed to prevent serious chest and head injuries to the driver during an accident. A similar bag for the front seat passenger is also available on certain models. A crash sensor, which detects frontal impact, is located under the centre console, with a standby power unit mounted alongside. The crash sensor incorporates a deceleration sensor, and a microprocessor ECU, to monitor the severity of the impact and trigger the airbag where necessary. The airbag is inflated by a gas generator, which forces the bag out of the module cover in the centre of the steering wheel, or out of a cover on the passenger's side of the facia. A contact reel behind the steering wheel at the top of the steering column, ensures that a good electrical connection is maintained with the airbag at all times, as the steering wheel is turned in each direction.

12

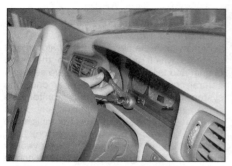

25.2 Removing an airbag securing screw from the rear of the steering wheel

25.4a Lift out the airbag unit . . .

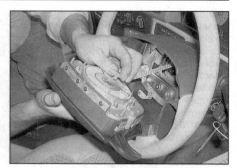

25.4b . . . and disconnect the wiring connector at the rear

In addition to the airbag units, the supplemental restraint system also incorporates pyrotechnical seat belt tensioners operated by gas cartridges in the belt inertia reel assembly. The pyrotechnical units are also triggered by the crash sensor, in conjunction with the air bag, to tighten the seat belts and provide additional collision protection.

All models also incorporate a side impact protection system (SIPS) as standard equipment. In its basic form, the SIPS system is essentially an integral part of the vehicle structure in which strengthening agents are used to distribute side impacts through the bodywork. This is done by reinforcing the lower areas of the doors and door pillars, and providing strengthening bars in the seats and centre console. In this way, side impacts are absorbed by the body structure as a whole, giving exceptional impact strength.

In addition to the body reinforcement of the SIPS system, all models are fitted with a SIPS bag for both front passengers. The SIPS bag is an airbag located in a cushion module in the side of the front seat. The unit is triggered in the event of a severe side impact. The SIPS bag is inflated by two gas generators, which cause the bag to break open the module cover, rip open the seat upholstery seam, and inflate to its full volume towards the door.

Precautions

⚠ *Warning: The safe handling of the SRS components requires the use of Volvo special equipment. Any attempt to dismantle the airbag module, SIPS bag, crash sensors, contact reel, seat*

belt tensioners or any associated wiring or components without this equipment, and the specialist knowledge needed to use it correctly, could result in severe personal injury and/or malfunction of the system. For this reason, the only procedures covered in this manual relating to the SRS components are those which are absolutely essential to enable access to be gained to other components or systems. It is imperative that any other work involving the SRS components is entrusted to a Volvo dealer.

Before carrying out any work on the SRS components, disconnect the battery and wait for at least 10 minutes before proceeding.

Handle the airbag unit with extreme care as a precaution against personal injury, and always hold it with the cover facing away from the body. If in doubt concerning any proposed work involving the airbag unit or its control circuitry, consult a Volvo dealer.

Note that the airbag(s) must not be subjected to temperatures in excess of 90°C (194°F). When the airbag is removed, ensure that it is stored the correct way up to prevent possible inflation.

Do not allow any solvents or cleaning agents to contact the airbag assemblies. They must be cleaned using only a damp cloth.

The airbag(s) and control unit are both sensitive to impact. If either is dropped or damaged they should be renewed.

Disconnect the airbag control unit wiring plug prior to using arc-welding equipment on the vehicle.

25 Supplemental Restraint System (SRS) - component renewal

Note: *Before proceeding, refer to the warnings in Section 25.*

Driver's airbag

Removal

1 Disconnect the battery negative lead, and wait 10 minutes before proceeding.
2 Using a suitable Torx type socket bit, undo the two airbag module retaining screws from the rear of the steering wheel. Turn the steering wheel 90° in each direction to gain access to the screws (see illustration).
3 Return the wheel to the straight-ahead position.
4 Lift the airbag module off the steering wheel, disconnect the wiring connector from the rear of the unit and remove it from the vehicle (see illustrations).

⚠ *Warning: Position the airbag unit in a safe place, with the mechanism facing downwards as a precaution against accidental operation. Do not attempt to open or repair the airbag unit, or apply any electrical current to it. Do not use any airbag which is visibly damaged or which has been tampered with.*

5 Lock the airbag contact reel using the plastic strip provided in the steering wheel. Remove the screw at the bottom left of the wheel, and making sure that the screw is not removed from the plastic strip, insert the screw into the hole in the top right of the contact reel (see illustrations). Once it has been locked, no attempt should be made to turn the steering wheel, or the contact reel will be damaged.

Refitting

6 Unlock the contact reel by removing the screw securing the plastic strip, and returning it to its original location.
7 Rest the airbag unit on the bottom edge of the steering wheel hub and reconnect the wiring connector. Swing the airbag unit up into position, checking carefully that the wiring is not pinched.

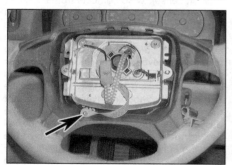

25.5a Remove the screw from its original location (arrowed) . . .

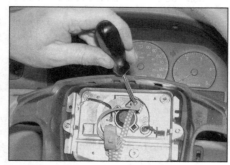

25.5b . . . and use it to lock the contact reel by screwing it in as shown

8 Refit the airbag unit retaining screws and tighten to the specified torque.

9 Make sure that no-one is inside the car. Switch on the ignition, then reconnect the battery negative lead. Switch the ignition off, then on again, and check that the SRS warning light comes on, then goes out within 15 seconds.

Driver's airbag contact reel

Removal

10 Remove the airbag unit as described above, and the steering wheel as described in Chapter 10.

11 Taking care not to rotate the contact unit, undo the three retaining screws and remove it from the steering wheel. Disconnect the wiring plug **(see illustration)**.

Refitting

12 If a new contact unit is being fitted, cut the cable-tie which is fitted to prevent the unit accidentally rotating.

13 A new reel should be supplied in the centralised position - if not, or there is a chance the unit is not centralised, proceed as follows. Turn the reel gently clockwise as far as it will go, then turn it back anti-clockwise approximately three turns. Continue turning until the lug on the reel is at the 1 o'clock position. Lock the reel in this position by screwing in the locking screw located in the plastic retaining strip.

14 Fit the unit to the steering wheel and securely tighten its retaining screws.

15 Refit the steering wheel as described in Chapter 10, and the airbag unit as described above.

Passenger's airbag

Removal

16 Disconnect the battery negative lead, and wait 10 minutes before proceeding.

17 Undo the six screws on the front face of the glovebox, then pull the box rearwards to release the retaining clips, and remove it from the facia.

18 Confirm that the battery is disconnected, then disconnect the wiring connector from the base of the airbag module.

19 Undo the three screws securing the airbag module bracket above the glovebox, then remove the six nuts securing the module to the inside of the facia panel.

Refitting

20 Refitting is a reversal of removal.

21 On completion, make sure that no-one is inside the car. Switch on the ignition, then reconnect the battery negative lead. Switch the ignition off, then on again, and check that the SRS warning light comes on, then goes out within 15 seconds.

Airbag control unit

Removal

22 The airbag control unit is fitted in the centre of the car, under the front of the centre console between the handbrake and gear/selector lever. The control unit incorporates the crash sensor.

23 Remove the centre console as described in Chapter 11.

24 It may be necessary to make a small cut in the carpet for access to the control unit.

25 Release the securing catch and disconnect the wiring plug from the side of the unit.

26 Undo the securing nuts and remove the control unit from the car.

Refitting

27 Refitting is a reversal of removal.

28 On completion, make sure that no-one is inside the car. Switch on the ignition, then reconnect the battery negative lead. Switch the ignition off, then on again, and check that the SRS warning light comes on, then goes out within 15 seconds.

Side airbags

29 The side air bag units are built into the front seats, and their removal requires that the seat fabric be removed. This is not considered to be a DIY operation, and should be referred to a Volvo dealer.

---

26 Central locking components - removal and refitting

Lock motors

1 The lock motor is most easily removed once the lock mechanism has been completely removed, as described in Chapter 11, Section 11.

2 Unscrew and remove the cover/motor securing screws, and lift off the cover.

3 Lift out the motor and wiring plug from the lock assembly. Unsolder the wiring from the plug, noting how it connects, then remove the motor completely.

4 Refitting is a reversal of removal. Check the operation of the motor before refitting the door trim panel.

Door lock microswitch

5 Remove the lock assembly as described in Chapter 11, Section 11.

6 Remove the cover securing screws, and take off the lock assembly cover.

7 Detach the switch wiring from the slot on the lock assembly, then prise the switch from its location.

8 Unsolder the switch wiring, noting how it connects, then remove the switch completely.

9 Refitting is a reversal of removal. Check the operation of the motor before refitting the door trim panel.

Boot lid/tailgate lock microswitch

10 Remove the boot lid or tailgate handle as described in Chapter 11.

11 Unclip the cover which fits over the switch, for access to the switch wiring.

12 The switch wiring has to be unsoldered to remove the switch - note the location of all wires for use when refitting.

13 Refitting is a reversal of removal. Check the operation of the motor before refitting the door trim panel.

Control unit(s)

Central locking control unit

14 Disconnect the battery negative lead, and position the lead away from the battery terminals.

15 The main central locking control unit is located inside the car. Depending on model, it will either be behind the glovebox, or behind the driver's side lower facia.

16 Remove the under-facia trim from the driver's and passenger's side of the facia, then reach up and locate the control unit. On models with the control unit on the passenger's side, it may be useful to remove the glovebox as described in Chapter 11, Section 29.

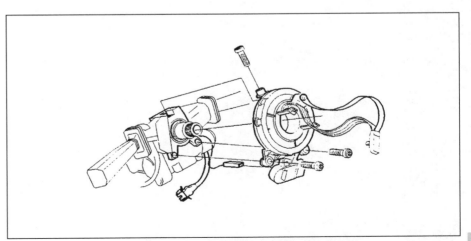

25.11 Driver's airbag contact reel removal details

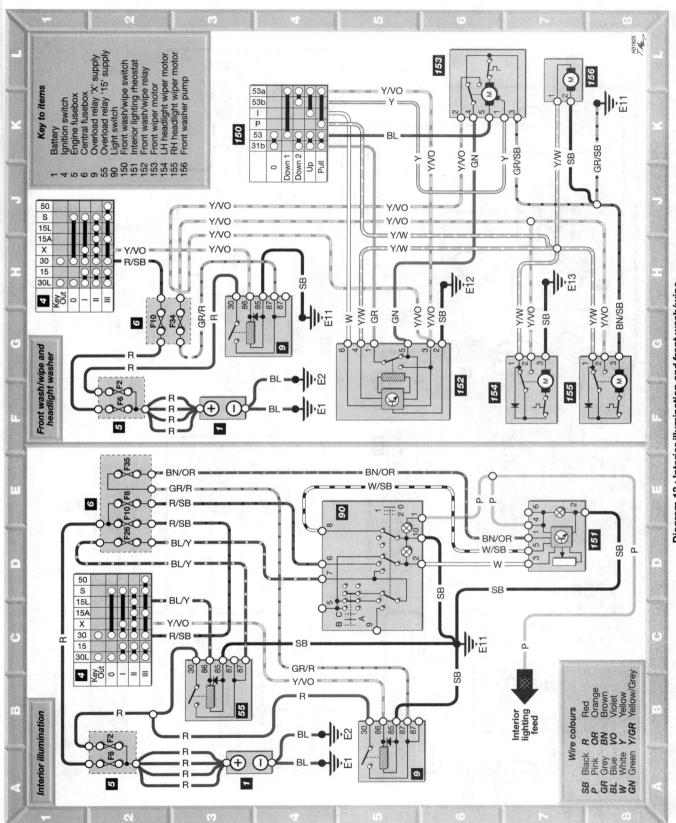

Diagram 13 : Interior illumination and front wash/wipe

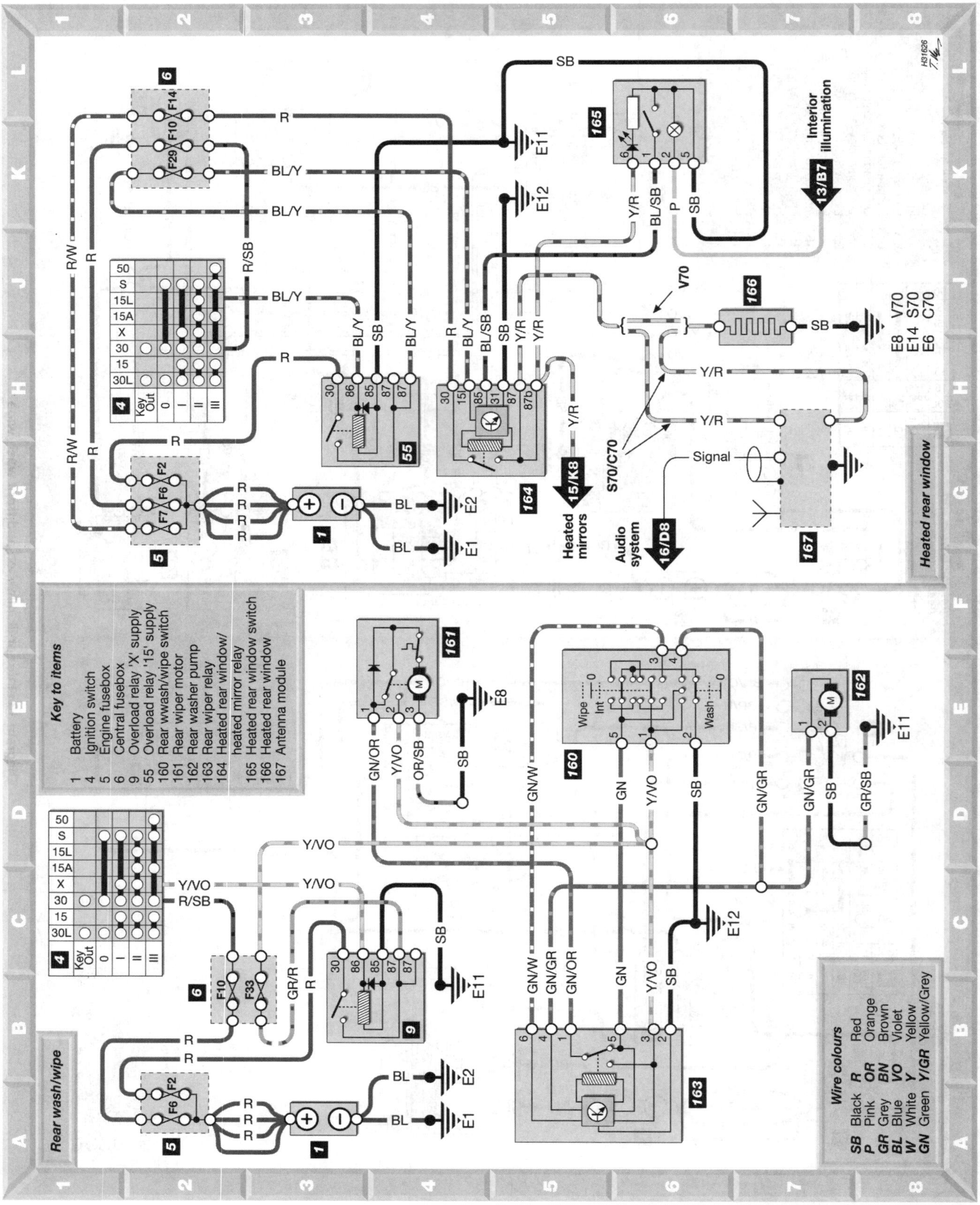

Key to items

1 Battery
4 Ignition switch
5 Engine fusebox
6 Central fusebox
9 Overload relay 'X' supply
55 Overload relay '15' supply
160 Rear wash/wipe switch
161 Rear wiper motor
162 Rear washer pump
163 Rear wiper relay
164 Heated rear window/
    heated mirror relay
165 Heated rear window switch
166 Heated rear window
167 Antenna module

Wire colours

SB	Black	R	Red
P	Pink	OR	Orange
GR	Grey	BN	Brown
BL	Blue	VO	Violet
W	White	Y	Yellow
GN	Green	Y/GR	Yellow/Grey

Diagram 14 : Rear wash/wipe and heated rear window

Rear wash/wipe

Heated rear window

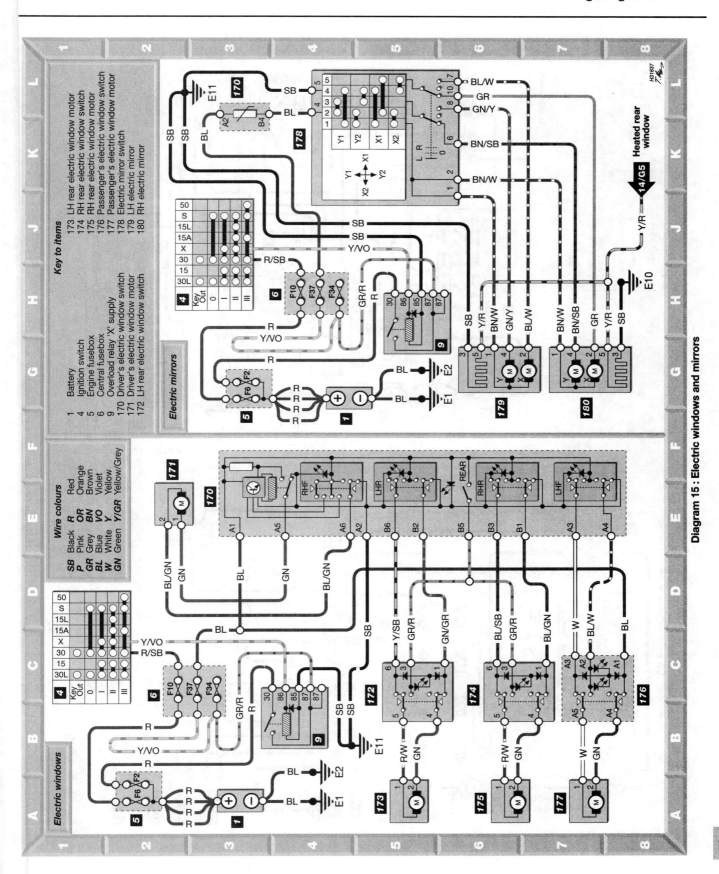

Diagram 15 : Electric windows and mirrors

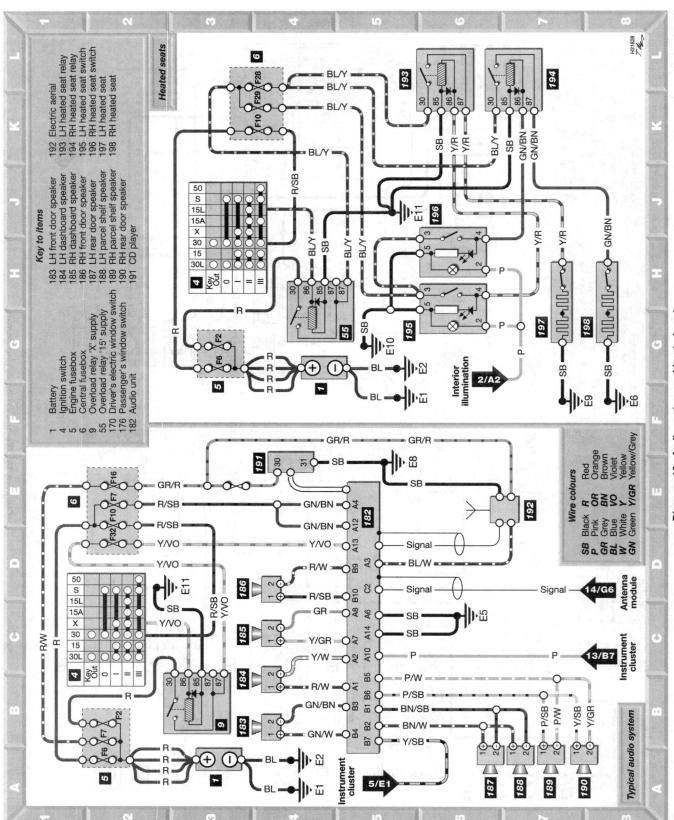

Heated seats

Key to items

1	Battery	183	LH front door speaker
4	Ignition switch	184	LH dashboard speaker
5	Engine fusebox	185	RH dashboard speaker
6	Central fusebox	186	RH front door speaker
9	Overload relay 'X' supply	187	LH rear door speaker
55	Overload relay '15' supply	188	LH parcel shelf speaker
170	Driver's electric window switch	189	RH parcel shelf speaker
176	Passenger's window switch	190	RH rear door speaker
182	Audio unit	191	CD player
		192	Electric aerial
		193	LH heated seat relay
		194	RH heated seat relay
		195	LH heated seat switch
		196	RH heated seat switch
		197	LH heated seat
		198	RH heated seat

Wire colours

SB	Black	**R**	Red
P	Pink	**OR**	Orange
GR	Grey	**BN**	Brown
BL	Blue	**VO**	Violet
W	White	**Y**	Yellow
GN	Green	**Y/GR**	Yellow/Grey

Interior illumination

Antenna module

Instrument cluster

Typical audio system

Diagram 16 : Audio system and heated seats

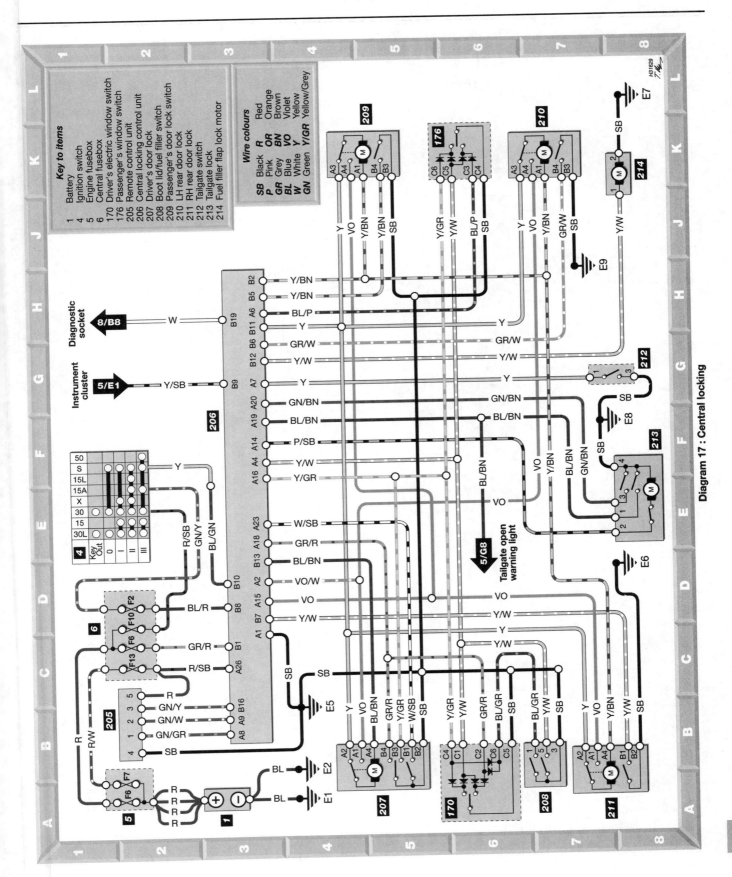

Key to items

1 Battery
4 Ignition switch
5 Engine fusebox
6 Central fusebox
170 Driver's electric window switch
176 Passenger's window switch
205 Remote control unit
206 Central locking control unit
207 Driver's door lock
208 Boot lid/fuel filler switch
209 Passenger's door lock switch
210 LH rear door lock
211 RH rear door lock
212 Tailgate switch
213 Tailgate lock
214 Fuel filler flap lock motor

Wire colours

SB Black   R Red
P Pink   OR Orange
GR Grey   BN Brown
BL Blue   VO Violet
W White   Y Yellow
GN Green   Y/GR Yellow/Grey

Diagram 17 : Central locking

Notes

Dimensions and weights

Note: *All figures are approximate, and may vary according to model. Refer to manufacturer's data for exact figures.*

Dimensions

Overall length	4720 mm
Overall width:	
S70 and V70 models	1760 mm
C70 models	1820 mm
Overall height:	
S70 models	1420 mm
V70 models	1440 mm
C70 models	1410 mm
Wheelbase	2660 mm

Weights

Kerb weight	Consult vehicle registration certificate (or a Volvo dealer)
Maximum gross vehicle weight	Consult type designation plate behind left-hand headlight in engine compartment
Maximum roof rack load	100 kg
Maximum trailer weight:	
Braked	1600 kg
Unbraked	500 kg

Conversion factors

Length (distance)

Inches (in)	x 25.4	= Millimetres (mm)	x 0.0394	= Inches (in)
Feet (ft)	x 0.305	= Metres (m)	x 3.281	= Feet (ft)
Miles	x 1.609	= Kilometres (km)	x 0.621	= Miles

Volume (capacity)

Cubic inches (cu in; in^3)	x 16.387	= Cubic centimetres (cc; cm^3)	x 0.061	= Cubic inches (cu in; in^3)
Imperial pints (Imp pt)	x 0.568	= Litres (l)	x 1.76	= Imperial pints (Imp pt)
Imperial quarts (Imp qt)	x 1.137	= Litres (l)	x 0.88	= Imperial quarts (Imp qt)
Imperial quarts (Imp qt)	x 1.201	= US quarts (US qt)	x 0.833	= Imperial quarts (Imp qt)
US quarts (US qt)	x 0.946	= Litres (l)	x 1.057	= US quarts (US qt)
Imperial gallons (Imp gal)	x 4.546	= Litres (l)	x 0.22	= Imperial gallons (Imp gal)
Imperial gallons (Imp gal)	x 1.201	= US gallons (US gal)	x 0.833	= Imperial gallons (Imp gal)
US gallons (US gal)	x 3.785	= Litres (l)	x 0.264	= US gallons (US gal)

Mass (weight)

Ounces (oz)	x 28.35	= Grams (g)	x 0.035	= Ounces (oz)
Pounds (lb)	x 0.454	= Kilograms (kg)	x 2.205	= Pounds (lb)

Force

Ounces-force (ozf; oz)	x 0.278	= Newtons (N)	x 3.6	= Ounces-force (ozf; oz)
Pounds-force (lbf; lb)	x 4.448	= Newtons (N)	x 0.225	= Pounds-force (lbf; lb)
Newtons (N)	x 0.1	= Kilograms-force (kgf; kg)	x 9.81	= Newtons (N)

Pressure

Pounds-force per square inch (psi; lbf/in^2; lb/in^2)	x 0.070	= Kilograms-force per square centimetre (kgf/cm^2; kg/cm^2)	x 14.223	= Pounds-force per square inch (psi; lbf/in^2; lb/in^2)
Pounds-force per square inch (psi; lbf/in^2; lb/in^2)	x 0.068	= Atmospheres (atm)	x 14.696	= Pounds-force per square inch (psi; lbf/in^2; lb/in^2)
Pounds-force per square inch (psi; lbf/in^2; lb/in^2)	x 0.069	= Bars	x 14.5	= Pounds-force per square inch (psi; lbf/in^2; lb/in^2)
Pounds-force per square inch (psi; lbf/in^2; lb/in^2)	x 6.895	= Kilopascals (kPa)	x 0.145	= Pounds-force per square inch (psi; lbf/in^2; lb/in^2)
Kilopascals (kPa)	x 0.01	= Kilograms-force per square centimetre (kgf/cm^2; kg/cm^2)	x 98.1	= Kilopascals (kPa)
Millibar (mbar)	x 100	= Pascals (Pa)	x 0.01	= Millibar (mbar)
Millibar (mbar)	x 0.0145	= Pounds-force per square inch (psi; lbf/in^2; lb/in^2)	x 68.947	= Millibar (mbar)
Millibar (mbar)	x 0.75	= Millimetres of mercury (mmHg)	x 1.333	= Millibar (mbar)
Millibar (mbar)	x 0.401	= Inches of water (inH$_2$O)	x 2.491	= Millibar (mbar)
Millimetres of mercury (mmHg)	x 0.535	= Inches of water (inH$_2$O)	x 1.868	= Millimetres of mercury (mmHg)
Inches of water (inH$_2$O)	x 0.036	= Pounds-force per square inch (psi; lbf/in^2; lb/in^2)	x 27.68	= Inches of water (inH$_2$O)

Torque (moment of force)

Pounds-force inches (lbf in; lb in)	x 1.152	= Kilograms-force centimetre (kgf cm; kg cm)	x 0.868	= Pounds-force inches (lbf in; lb in)
Pounds-force inches (lbf in; lb in)	x 0.113	= Newton metres (Nm)	x 8.85	= Pounds-force inches (lbf in; lb in)
Pounds-force inches (lbf in; lb in)	x 0.083	= Pounds-force feet (lbf ft; lb ft)	x 12	= Pounds-force inches (lbf in; lb in)
Pounds-force feet (lbf ft; lb ft)	x 0.138	= Kilograms-force metres (kgf m; kg m)	x 7.233	= Pounds-force feet (lbf ft; lb ft)
Pounds-force feet (lbf ft; lb ft)	x 1.356	= Newton metres (Nm)	x 0.738	= Pounds-force feet (lbf ft; lb ft)
Newton metres (Nm)	x 0.102	= Kilograms-force metres (kgf m; kg m)	x 9.804	= Newton metres (Nm)

Power

Horsepower (hp)	x 745.7	= Watts (W)	x 0.0013	= Horsepower (hp)

Velocity (speed)

Miles per hour (miles/hr; mph)	x 1.609	= Kilometres per hour (km/hr; kph)	x 0.621	= Miles per hour (miles/hr; mph)

Fuel consumption*

Miles per gallon, Imperial (mpg)	x 0.354	= Kilometres per litre (km/l)	x 2.825	= Miles per gallon, Imperial (mpg)
Miles per gallon, US (mpg)	x 0.425	= Kilometres per litre (km/l)	x 2.352	= Miles per gallon, US (mpg)

Temperature

Degrees Fahrenheit = (°C x 1.8) + 32   Degrees Celsius (Degrees Centigrade; °C) = (°F - 32) x 0.56

It is common practice to convert from miles per gallon (mpg) to litres/100 kilometres (l/100km), where mpg x l/100 km = 282

Spare parts are available from many sources, including maker's appointed garages, accessory shops, and motor factors. To be sure of obtaining the correct parts, it may sometimes be necessary to quote the vehicle identification number. If possible, it can also be useful to take the old parts along for positive identification. Items such as starter motors and alternators may be available under a service exchange scheme - any parts returned should always be clean.

Our advice regarding spare part sources is as follows:

Officially-appointed garages

This is the best source of parts which are peculiar to your car, and are not otherwise generally available (eg badges, interior trim, certain body panels, etc). It is also the only place at which you should buy parts if the vehicle is still under warranty.

Accessory shops

These are very good places to buy materials and components needed for the maintenance of your car (oil, air and fuel filters, spark plugs, light bulbs, drivebelts, oils and greases, brake pads, touch-up paint, etc). Parts like this sold by a reputable shop are of the same standard as those used by the car manufacturer.

Motor factors

Good factors will stock all the more important components which wear out comparatively quickly and can sometimes supply individual components needed for the overhaul of a larger assembly. They may also handle work such as cylinder block reboring, crankshaft regrinding and balancing, etc.

Tyre and exhaust specialists

These outlets may be independent or members of a local or national chain. They frequently offer competitive prices when compared with a main dealer or local garage, but it will pay to obtain several quotes before making a decision. Also ask what extras may be added to the quote - for instance, fitting a new valve and balancing the wheel are both often charged on top of the price of a new tyre.

Other sources

Beware of parts of materials obtained from market stalls, car boot sales or similar outlets. Such items are not invariably sub-standard, but there is little chance of compensation if they do prove unsatisfactory. In the case of safety-critical components such as brake pads there is the risk not only of financial loss but also of an accident causing injury or death.

Second-hand components or assemblies obtained from a car breaker can be a good buy in some circumstances, but this sort of purchase is best made by the experienced DIY mechanic.

Modifications are a continuing and unpublicised process in vehicle manufacture, quite apart from major model changes. Spare parts manuals and lists are compiled upon a numerical basis, the individual vehicle identification numbers being essential to correct identification of the component concerned.

When ordering spare parts, always give as much information as possible. Quote the type designation, chassis number, engine number

and, where applicable, the vehicle identification number as appropriate **(see illustration)**.

On models for the UK market only, the Vehicle Identification Number (VIN) is located on the top left-hand side of the facia, and can be viewed through the windscreen **(see illustration)**.

The vehicle identification number is also stamped in the engine compartment bulkhead, below the windscreen **(see illustration)**.

Vehicle loading details, and codes for

colour and upholstery, are located on a plate on the left-hand inner wing behind the headlight **(see illustration)**.

Engine type designation and serial numbers are stamped on the upper side of the cylinder block beside the coolant pump. These numbers may also appear on a sticker on the upper timing belt cover.

The transmission identification numbers are located on a plate attached to the transmission casing.

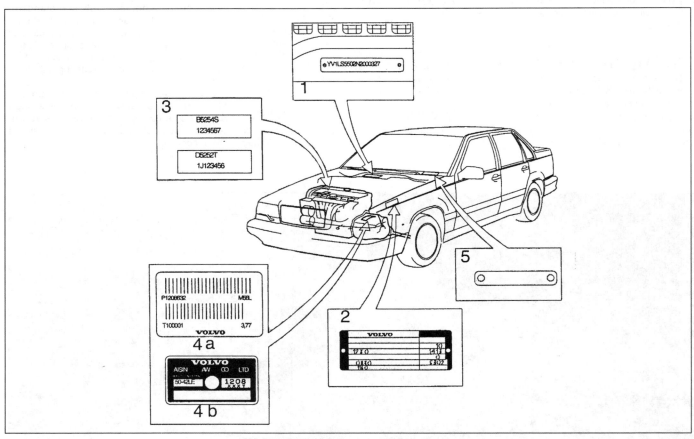

Vehicle identification number locations

1   Vehicle Identification Number (VIN)
2   Type designation, chassis number, loading details, colour and
*   upholstery codes*
3   Engine number

4a Manual gearbox type and serial number (on front)
4b Automatic transmission type and serial number (on top)
5   Vehicle Identification Number (VIN)

Visible VIN viewed through the windscreen

VIN is also stamped at the top of the engine compartment bulkhead

Information plate on left-hand inner wing

Whenever servicing, repair or overhaul work is carried out on the car or its components, observe the following procedures and instructions. This will assist in carrying out the operation efficiently and to a professional standard of workmanship.

Joint mating faces and gaskets

When separating components at their mating faces, never insert screwdrivers or similar implements into the joint between the faces in order to prise them apart. This can cause severe damage which results in oil leaks, coolant leaks, etc upon reassembly. Separation is usually achieved by tapping along the joint with a soft-faced hammer in order to break the seal. However, note that this method may not be suitable where dowels are used for component location.

Where a gasket is used between the mating faces of two components, a new one must be fitted on reassembly; fit it dry unless otherwise stated in the repair procedure. Make sure that the mating faces are clean and dry, with all traces of old gasket removed. When cleaning a joint face, use a tool which is unlikely to score or damage the face, and remove any burrs or nicks with an oilstone or fine file.

Make sure that tapped holes are cleaned with a pipe cleaner, and keep them free of jointing compound, if this is being used, unless specifically instructed otherwise.

Ensure that all orifices, channels or pipes are clear, and blow through them, preferably using compressed air.

Oil seals

Oil seals can be removed by levering them out with a wide flat-bladed screwdriver or similar implement. Alternatively, a number of self-tapping screws may be screwed into the seal, and these used as a purchase for pliers or some similar device in order to pull the seal free.

Whenever an oil seal is removed from its working location, either individually or as part of an assembly, it should be renewed.

The very fine sealing lip of the seal is easily damaged, and will not seal if the surface it contacts is not completely clean and free from scratches, nicks or grooves. If the original sealing surface of the component cannot be restored, and the manufacturer has not made provision for slight relocation of the seal relative to the sealing surface, the component should be renewed.

Protect the lips of the seal from any surface which may damage them in the course of fitting. Use tape or a conical sleeve where possible. Lubricate the seal lips with oil before fitting and, on dual-lipped seals, fill the space between the lips with grease.

Unless otherwise stated, oil seals must be fitted with their sealing lips toward the lubricant to be sealed.

Use a tubular drift or block of wood of the appropriate size to install the seal and, if the seal housing is shouldered, drive the seal down to the shoulder. If the seal housing is unshouldered, the seal should be fitted with its face flush with the housing top face (unless otherwise instructed).

Screw threads and fastenings

Seized nuts, bolts and screws are quite a common occurrence where corrosion has set in, and the use of penetrating oil or releasing fluid will often overcome this problem if the offending item is soaked for a while before attempting to release it. The use of an impact driver may also provide a means of releasing such stubborn fastening devices, when used in conjunction with the appropriate screwdriver bit or socket. If none of these methods works, it may be necessary to resort to the careful application of heat, or the use of a hacksaw or nut splitter device.

Studs are usually removed by locking two nuts together on the threaded part, and then using a spanner on the lower nut to unscrew the stud. Studs or bolts which have broken off below the surface of the component in which they are mounted can sometimes be removed using a stud extractor. Always ensure that a blind tapped hole is completely free from oil, grease, water or other fluid before installing the bolt or stud. Failure to do this could cause the housing to crack due to the hydraulic action of the bolt or stud as it is screwed in.

When tightening a castellated nut to accept a split pin, tighten the nut to the specified torque, where applicable, and then tighten further to the next split pin hole. Never slacken the nut to align the split pin hole, unless stated in the repair procedure.

When checking or retightening a nut or bolt to a specified torque setting, slacken the nut or bolt by a quarter of a turn, and then retighten to the specified setting. However, this should not be attempted where angular tightening has been used.

For some screw fastenings, notably cylinder head bolts or nuts, torque wrench settings are no longer specified for the latter stages of tightening, "angle-tightening" being called up instead. Typically, a fairly low torque wrench setting will be applied to the bolts/nuts in the correct sequence, followed by one or more stages of tightening through specified angles.

Locknuts, locktabs and washers

Any fastening which will rotate against a component or housing during tightening should always have a washer between it and the relevant component or housing.

Spring or split washers should always be renewed when they are used to lock a critical component such as a big-end bearing retaining bolt or nut. Locktabs which are folded over to retain a nut or bolt should always be renewed.

Self-locking nuts can be re-used in non-critical areas, providing resistance can be felt when the locking portion passes over the bolt or stud thread. However, it should be noted that self-locking stiffnuts tend to lose their effectiveness after long periods of use, and should then be renewed as a matter of course.

Split pins must always be replaced with new ones of the correct size for the hole.

When thread-locking compound is found on the threads of a fastener which is to be re-used, it should be cleaned off with a wire brush and solvent, and fresh compound applied on reassembly.

Special tools

Some repair procedures in this manual entail the use of special tools such as a press, two or three-legged pullers, spring compressors, etc. Wherever possible, suitable readily-available alternatives to the manufacturer's special tools are described, and are shown in use. In some instances, where no alternative is possible, it has been necessary to resort to the use of a manufacturer's tool, and this has been done for reasons of safety as well as the efficient completion of the repair operation. Unless you are highly-skilled and have a thorough understanding of the procedures described, never attempt to bypass the use of any special tool when the procedure described specifies its use. Not only is there a very great risk of personal injury, but expensive damage could be caused to the components involved.

Environmental considerations

When disposing of used engine oil, brake fluid, antifreeze, etc, give due consideration to any detrimental environmental effects. Do not, for instance, pour any of the above liquids down drains into the general sewage system, or onto the ground to soak away. Many local council refuse tips provide a facility for waste oil disposal, as do some garages. If none of these facilities are available, consult your local Environmental Health Department, or the National Rivers Authority, for further advice.

With the universal tightening-up of legislation regarding the emission of environmentally-harmful substances from motor vehicles, most vehicles have tamperproof devices fitted to the main adjustment points of the fuel system. These devices are primarily designed to prevent unqualified persons from adjusting the fuel/air mixture, with the chance of a consequent increase in toxic emissions. If such devices are found during servicing or overhaul, they should, wherever possible, be renewed or refitted in accordance with the manufacturer's requirements or current legislation.

Note: It is antisocial and illegal to dump oil down the drain. To find the location of your local oil recycling bank, call this number free.

The jack supplied with the vehicle tool kit should **only** be used for changing the roadwheels in an emergency - see *Wheel changing* at the front of this book. When carrying out any other kind of work, raise the vehicle using a heavy-duty hydraulic (or trolley) jack, and always supplement the jack with axle stands positioned under the vehicle jacking points. If the roadwheels do not have to be removed, consider using wheel ramps - if wished, these can be placed under the wheels once the vehicle has been raised using a hydraulic jack, and the vehicle lowered onto the ramps so that it is resting on its wheels.

Only ever jack the vehicle up on a solid, level surface. If there is even a slight slope, take great care that the vehicle cannot move as the wheels are lifted off the ground. Jacking up on an uneven or gravelled surface is not recommended, as the weight of the vehicle will not be evenly distributed, and the jack may slip as the vehicle is raised.

As far as possible, do not leave the vehicle unattended once it has been raised, particularly if children are playing nearby.

Before jacking up the front of the car, ensure that the handbrake is firmly applied. When jacking up the rear of the car, place wooden chocks in front of the front wheels, and engage first gear (or P).

When using a hydraulic jack or axle stands, the jack head or axle stand head may be placed under one of the relevant jacking points or load-bearing areas **(see illustration)**.

To raise the front of the vehicle, the jack can be positioned under the engine subframe. **Do not** jack the vehicle under the sump, or any of the steering or suspension components. With the front raised, position axle stands under the subframe on each side **(see illustration)**.

To raise the rear of the vehicle, position the jack head under the reinforced plate below the spare wheel well - use a flat piece of wood on top of the jack head to further spread the load. With the rear raised, position axle stands under the structural members just in front of the rear suspension attachments on each side **(see illustrations)**.

The jack supplied with the vehicle locates in a reinforced bracket, located in the middle of the sill on each side of the car. This means that, when the jack is raised, the front AND rear wheel on that side will be lifted off the ground, placing a high load on the jack. Ensure that the jack head is correctly engaged before attempting to raise the vehicle **(see illustration)**.

Do not jack the vehicle under any other part of the sill, sump, floor pan, or directly under any of the steering or suspension components.

Never work under, around, or near a raised vehicle, unless it is adequately supported on stands. Do not rely on a jack alone, as even a hydraulic jack could fail under load. The Volvo is a heavy car, and makeshift methods should not be used to lift and support it during servicing work.

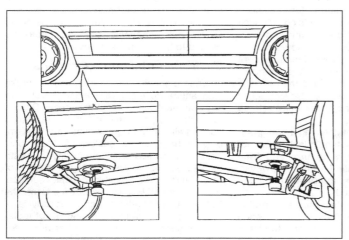

Jacking points for use with workshop or hydraulic (trolley) jack

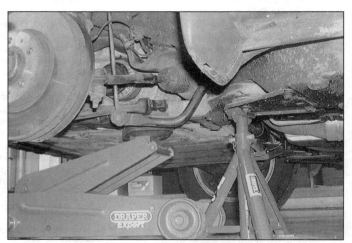

When jacking up the front of the car, jack and support under the engine subframe

Raise the rear of the car using the reinforced plate at the rear of the spare wheel well . . .

. . . and support in front of the rear suspension attachment points

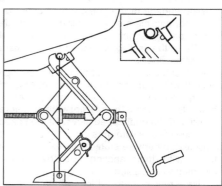

Ensure that the vehicle jack is securely located in the jacking point, as shown in the inset

The radio/cassette unit fitted as standard equipment by Volvo is equipped with a built-in security code, to deter thieves. If the power source to the unit is cut, the anti-theft system will activate. Even if the power source is immediately reconnected, the radio/cassette unit will not function until the correct security code has been entered. Therefore, if you do not know the correct security code for the radio/cassette unit, **do not** disconnect either of the battery terminals, or remove the radio/cassette unit from the vehicle.

To enter the correct security code, follow the instructions provided with the radio/cassette player or vehicle handbook. The code appears on the Radio Pass card, which is normally found with the vehicle handbook in the glovebox.

If an incorrect code is entered three times, the unit will become locked, and cannot be operated for 2 hours.

If this happens, or if the security code is lost or forgotten, seek the advice of your Volvo dealer.

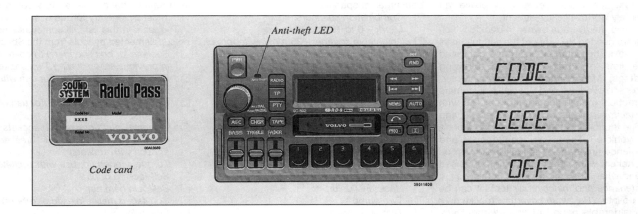

Anti-theft LED

Code card

Introduction

A selection of good tools is a fundamental requirement for anyone contemplating the maintenance and repair of a motor vehicle. For the owner who does not possess any, their purchase will prove a considerable expense, offsetting some of the savings made by doing-it-yourself. However, provided that the tools purchased meet the relevant national safety standards and are of good quality, they will last for many years and prove an extremely worthwhile investment.

To help the average owner to decide which tools are needed to carry out the various tasks detailed in this manual, we have compiled three lists of tools under the following headings: *Maintenance and minor repair, Repair and overhaul,* and *Special.* Newcomers to practical mechanics should start off with the *Maintenance and minor repair* tool kit, and confine themselves to the simpler jobs around the vehicle. Then, as confidence and experience grow, more difficult tasks can be undertaken, with extra tools being purchased as, and when, they are needed. In this way, a *Maintenance and minor repair* tool kit can be built up into a *Repair and overhaul* tool kit over a considerable period of time, without any major cash outlays. The experienced do-it-yourselfer will have a tool kit good enough for most repair and overhaul procedures, and will add tools from the *Special* category when it is felt that the expense is justified by the amount of use to which these tools will be put.

Maintenance and minor repair tool kit

The tools given in this list should be considered as a minimum requirement if routine maintenance, servicing and minor repair operations are to be undertaken. We recommend the purchase of combination spanners (ring one end, open-ended the other); although more expensive than open-ended ones, they do give the advantages of both types of spanner.

☐ *Combination spanners:*
  Metric - 8 to 19 mm inclusive
☐ *Adjustable spanner - 35 mm jaw (approx.)*
☐ *Spark plug spanner (with rubber insert) - petrol models*
☐ *Spark plug gap adjustment tool - petrol models*
☐ *Set of feeler gauges*
☐ *Brake bleed nipple spanner*
☐ *Screwdrivers:*
  Flat blade - 100 mm long x 6 mm dia
  Cross blade - 100 mm long x 6 mm dia
  Torx - various sizes (not all vehicles)
☐ *Combination pliers*
☐ *Hacksaw (junior)*
☐ *Tyre pump*
☐ *Tyre pressure gauge*
☐ *Oil can*
☐ *Oil filter removal tool*
☐ *Fine emery cloth*
☐ *Wire brush (small)*
☐ *Funnel (medium size)*
☐ *Sump drain plug key (not all vehicles)*

Repair and overhaul tool kit

These tools are virtually essential for anyone undertaking any major repairs to a motor vehicle, and are additional to those given in the *Maintenance and minor repair* list. Included in this list is a comprehensive set of sockets. Although these are expensive, they will be found invaluable as they are so versatile - particularly if various drives are included in the set. We recommend the half-inch square-drive type, as this can be used with most proprietary torque wrenches.

The tools in this list will sometimes need to be supplemented by tools from the *Special* list:

☐ *Sockets (or box spanners) to cover range in previous list (including Torx sockets)*
☐ *Reversible ratchet drive (for use with sockets)*
☐ *Extension piece, 250 mm (for use with sockets)*
☐ *Universal joint (for use with sockets)*
☐ *Flexible handle or sliding T "breaker bar" (for use with sockets)*
☐ *Torque wrench (for use with sockets)*
☐ *Self-locking grips*
☐ *Ball pein hammer*
☐ *Soft-faced mallet (plastic or rubber)*
☐ *Screwdrivers:*
  Flat blade - long & sturdy, short (chubby), and narrow (electrician's) types
  Cross blade – long & sturdy, and short (chubby) types
☐ *Pliers:*
  Long-nosed
  Side cutters (electrician's)
  Circlip (internal and external)
☐ *Cold chisel - 25 mm*
☐ *Scriber*
☐ *Scraper*
☐ *Centre-punch*
☐ *Pin punch*
☐ *Hacksaw*
☐ *Brake hose clamp*
☐ *Brake/clutch bleeding kit*
☐ *Selection of twist drills*
☐ *Steel rule/straight-edge*
☐ *Allen keys (inc. splined/Torx type)*
☐ *Selection of files*
☐ *Wire brush*
☐ *Axle stands*
☐ *Jack (strong trolley or hydraulic type)*
☐ *Light with extension lead*
☐ *Universal electrical multi-meter*

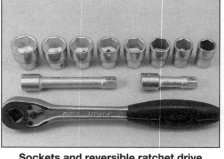

Sockets and reversible ratchet drive

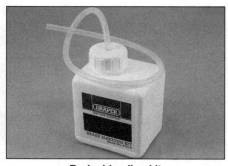

Brake bleeding kit

Torx key, socket and bit

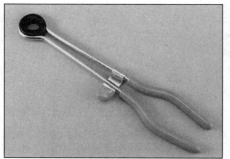

Hose clamp

Angular-tightening gauge

Special tools

The tools in this list are those which are not used regularly, are expensive to buy, or which need to be used in accordance with their manufacturers' instructions. Unless relatively difficult mechanical jobs are undertaken frequently, it will not be economic to buy many of these tools. Where this is the case, you could consider clubbing together with friends (or joining a motorists' club) to make a joint purchase, or borrowing the tools against a deposit from a local garage or tool hire specialist. It is worth noting that many of the larger DIY superstores now carry a large range of special tools for hire at modest rates.

The following list contains only those tools and instruments freely available to the public, and not those special tools produced by the vehicle manufacturer specifically for its dealer network. You will find occasional references to these manufacturers' special tools in the text of this manual. Generally, an alternative method of doing the job without the vehicle manufacturers' special tool is given. However, sometimes there is no alternative to using them. Where this is the case and the relevant tool cannot be bought or borrowed, you will have to entrust the work to a dealer.

☐ Angular-tightening gauge
☐ Valve spring compressor
☐ Valve grinding tool
☐ Piston ring compressor
☐ Piston ring removal/installation tool
☐ Cylinder bore hone
☐ Balljoint separator
☐ Coil spring compressors (where applicable)
☐ Two/three-legged hub and bearing puller
☐ Impact screwdriver
☐ Micrometer and/or vernier calipers
☐ Dial gauge
☐ Stroboscopic timing light
☐ Dwell angle meter/tachometer
☐ Fault code reader
☐ Cylinder compression gauge
☐ Hand-operated vacuum pump and gauge
☐ Clutch plate alignment set
☐ Brake shoe steady spring cup removal tool
☐ Bush and bearing removal/installation set
☐ Stud extractors
☐ Tap and die set
☐ Lifting tackle
☐ Trolley jack

Buying tools

Reputable motor accessory shops and superstores often offer excellent quality tools at discount prices, so it pays to shop around.

Remember, you don't have to buy the most expensive items on the shelf, but it is always advisable to steer clear of the very cheap tools. Beware of 'bargains' offered on market stalls or at car boot sales. There are plenty of good tools around at reasonable prices, but always aim to purchase items which meet the relevant national safety standards. If in doubt, ask the proprietor or manager of the shop for advice before making a purchase.

Care and maintenance of tools

Having purchased a reasonable tool kit, it is necessary to keep the tools in a clean and serviceable condition. After use, always wipe off any dirt, grease and metal particles using a clean, dry cloth, before putting the tools away. Never leave them lying around after they have been used. A simple tool rack on the garage or workshop wall for items such as screwdrivers and pliers is a good idea. Store all normal spanners and sockets in a metal box. Any measuring instruments, gauges, meters, etc, must be carefully stored where they cannot be damaged or become rusty.

Take a little care when tools are used. Hammer heads inevitably become marked, and screwdrivers lose the keen edge on their blades from time to time. A little timely attention with emery cloth or a file will soon restore items like this to a good finish.

Working facilities

Not to be forgotten when discussing tools is the workshop itself. If anything more than routine maintenance is to be carried out, a suitable working area becomes essential.

It is appreciated that many an owner-mechanic is forced by circumstances to remove an engine or similar item without the benefit of a garage or workshop. Having done this, any repairs should always be done under the cover of a roof.

Wherever possible, any dismantling should be done on a clean, flat workbench or table at a suitable working height.

Any workbench needs a vice; one with a jaw opening of 100 mm is suitable for most jobs. As mentioned previously, some clean dry storage space is also required for tools, as well as for any lubricants, cleaning fluids, touch-up paints etc, which become necessary.

Another item which may be required, and which has a much more general usage, is an electric drill with a chuck capacity of at least 8 mm. This, together with a good range of twist drills, is virtually essential for fitting accessories.

Last, but not least, always keep a supply of old newspapers and clean, lint-free rags available, and try to keep any working area as clean as possible.

Micrometers

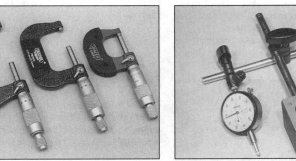

Dial test indicator ("dial gauge")

Strap wrench

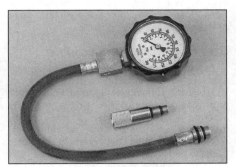

Compression tester

Fault code reader

This is a guide to getting your vehicle through the MOT test. Obviously it will not be possible to examine the vehicle to the same standard as the professional MOT tester. However, working through the following checks will enable you to identify any problem areas before submitting the vehicle for the test.

Where a testable component is in borderline condition, the tester has discretion in deciding whether to pass or fail it. The basis of such discretion is whether the tester would be happy for a close relative or friend to use the vehicle with the component in that condition. If the vehicle presented is clean and evidently well cared for, the tester may be more inclined to pass a borderline component than if the vehicle is scruffy and apparently neglected.

It has only been possible to summarise the test requirements here, based on the regulations in force at the time of printing. Test standards are becoming increasingly stringent, although there are some exemptions for older vehicles. For full details obtain a copy of the Haynes publication Pass the MOT! (available from stockists of Haynes manuals).

An assistant will be needed to help carry out some of these checks.

The checks have been sub-divided into four categories, as follows:

1 Checks carried out **FROM THE DRIVER'S SEAT**

2 Checks carried out **WITH THE VEHICLE ON THE GROUND**

3 Checks carried out **WITH THE VEHICLE RAISED AND THE WHEELS FREE TO TURN**

4 Checks carried out on **YOUR VEHICLE'S EXHAUST EMISSION SYSTEM**

1 Checks carried out **FROM THE DRIVER'S SEAT**

Handbrake

☐ Test the operation of the handbrake. Excessive travel (too many clicks) indicates incorrect brake or cable adjustment.

☐ Check that the handbrake cannot be released by tapping the lever sideways. Check the security of the lever mountings.

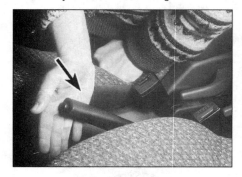

Footbrake

☐ Depress the brake pedal and check that it does not creep down to the floor, indicating a master cylinder fault. Release the pedal, wait a few seconds, then depress it again. If the pedal travels nearly to the floor before firm resistance is felt, brake adjustment or repair is necessary. If the pedal feels spongy, there is air in the hydraulic system which must be removed by bleeding.

☐ Check that the brake pedal is secure and in good condition. Check also for signs of fluid leaks on the pedal, floor or carpets, which would indicate failed seals in the brake master cylinder.

☐ Check the servo unit (when applicable) by operating the brake pedal several times, then keeping the pedal depressed and starting the engine. As the engine starts, the pedal will move down slightly. If not, the vacuum hose or the servo itself may be faulty.

Steering wheel and column

☐ Examine the steering wheel for fractures or looseness of the hub, spokes or rim.

☐ Move the steering wheel from side to side and then up and down. Check that the steering wheel is not loose on the column, indicating wear or a loose retaining nut. Continue moving the steering wheel as before, but also turn it slightly from left to right.

☐ Check that the steering wheel is not loose on the column, and that there is no abnormal

movement of the steering wheel, indicating wear in the column support bearings or couplings.

Windscreen and mirrors

☐ The windscreen must be free of cracks or other significant damage within the driver's field of view. (Small stone chips are acceptable.) Rear view mirrors must be secure, intact, and capable of being adjusted.

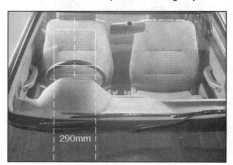

290mm

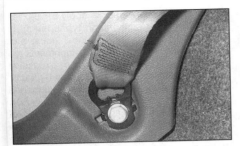

Seat belts and seats

Note: *The following checks are applicable to all seat belts, front and rear.*

☐ Examine the webbing of all the belts (including rear belts if fitted) for cuts, serious fraying or deterioration. Fasten and unfasten each belt to check the buckles. If applicable, check the retracting mechanism. Check the security of all seat belt mountings accessible from inside the vehicle.
☐ The front seats themselves must be securely attached and the backrests must lock in the upright position.

Doors

☐ Both front doors must be able to be opened and closed from outside and inside, and must latch securely when closed.

2 Checks carried out WITH THE VEHICLE ON THE GROUND

Vehicle identification

☐ Number plates must be in good condition, secure and legible, with letters and numbers correctly spaced – spacing at (A) should be at least twice that at (B).

☐ The VIN plate and/or homologation plate must be legible.

Electrical equipment

☐ Switch on the ignition and check the operation of the horn.
☐ Check the windscreen washers and wipers, examining the wiper blades; renew damaged or perished blades. Also check the operation of the stop-lights.

☐ Check the operation of the sidelights and number plate lights. The lenses and reflectors must be secure, clean and undamaged.
☐ Check the operation and alignment of the headlights. The headlight reflectors must not be tarnished and the lenses must be undamaged.
☐ Switch on the ignition and check the operation of the direction indicators (including the instrument panel tell-tale) and the hazard warning lights. Operation of the sidelights and stop-lights must not affect the indicators - if it does, the cause is usually a bad earth at the rear light cluster.
☐ Check the operation of the rear foglight(s), including the warning light on the instrument panel or in the switch.

Footbrake

☐ Examine the master cylinder, brake pipes and servo unit for leaks, loose mountings, corrosion or other damage.

☐ The fluid reservoir must be secure and the fluid level must be between the upper (**A**) and lower (**B**) markings.

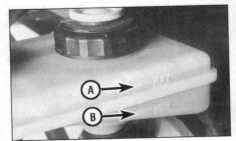

☐ Inspect both front brake flexible hoses for cracks or deterioration of the rubber. Turn the steering from lock to lock, and ensure that the hoses do not contact the wheel, tyre, or any part of the steering or suspension mechanism. With the brake pedal firmly depressed, check the hoses for bulges or leaks under pressure.

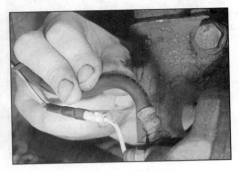

Steering and suspension

☐ Have your assistant turn the steering wheel from side to side slightly, up to the point where the steering gear just begins to transmit this movement to the roadwheels. Check for excessive free play between the steering wheel and the steering gear, indicating wear or insecurity of the steering column joints, the column-to-steering gear coupling, or the steering gear itself.
☐ Have your assistant turn the steering wheel more vigorously in each direction, so that the roadwheels just begin to turn. As this is done, examine all the steering joints, linkages, fittings and attachments. Renew any component that shows signs of wear or damage. On vehicles with power steering, check the security and condition of the steering pump, drivebelt and hoses.
☐ Check that the vehicle is standing level, and at approximately the correct ride height.

Shock absorbers

☐ Depress each corner of the vehicle in turn, then release it. The vehicle should rise and then settle in its normal position. If the vehicle continues to rise and fall, the shock absorber is defective. A shock absorber which has seized will also cause the vehicle to fail.

Exhaust system

☐ Start the engine. With your assistant holding a rag over the tailpipe, check the entire system for leaks. Repair or renew leaking sections.

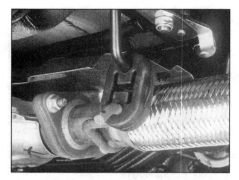

3 Checks carried out
WITH THE VEHICLE RAISED AND THE WHEELS FREE TO TURN

Jack up the front and rear of the vehicle, and securely support it on axle stands. Position the stands clear of the suspension assemblies. Ensure that the wheels are clear of the ground and that the steering can be turned from lock to lock.

Steering mechanism

☐ Have your assistant turn the steering from lock to lock. Check that the steering turns smoothly, and that no part of the steering mechanism, including a wheel or tyre, fouls any brake hose or pipe or any part of the body structure.
☐ Examine the steering rack rubber gaiters for damage or insecurity of the retaining clips. If power steering is fitted, check for signs of damage or leakage of the fluid hoses, pipes or connections. Also check for excessive stiffness or binding of the steering, a missing split pin or locking device, or severe corrosion of the body structure within 30 cm of any steering component attachment point.

Front and rear suspension and wheel bearings

☐ Starting at the front right-hand side, grasp the roadwheel at the 3 o'clock and 9 o'clock positions and shake it vigorously. Check for free play or insecurity at the wheel bearings, suspension balljoints, or suspension mountings, pivots and attachments.
☐ Now grasp the wheel at the 12 o'clock and 6 o'clock positions and repeat the previous inspection. Spin the wheel, and check for roughness or tightness of the front wheel bearing.

☐ If excess free play is suspected at a component pivot point, this can be confirmed by using a large screwdriver or similar tool and levering between the mounting and the component attachment. This will confirm whether the wear is in the pivot bush, its retaining bolt, or in the mounting itself (the bolt holes can often become elongated).

☐ Carry out all the above checks at the other front wheel, and then at both rear wheels.

Springs and shock absorbers

☐ Examine the suspension struts (when applicable) for serious fluid leakage, corrosion, or damage to the casing. Also check the security of the mounting points.
☐ If coil springs are fitted, check that the spring ends locate in their seats, and that the spring is not corroded, cracked or broken.
☐ If leaf springs are fitted, check that all leaves are intact, that the axle is securely attached to each spring, and that there is no deterioration of the spring eye mountings, bushes, and shackles.

☐ The same general checks apply to vehicles fitted with other suspension types, such as torsion bars, hydraulic displacer units, etc. Ensure that all mountings and attachments are secure, that there are no signs of excessive wear, corrosion or damage, and (on hydraulic types) that there are no fluid leaks or damaged pipes.
☐ Inspect the shock absorbers for signs of serious fluid leakage. Check for wear of the mounting bushes or attachments, or damage to the body of the unit.

Driveshafts (fwd vehicles only)

☐ Rotate each front wheel in turn and inspect the constant velocity joint gaiters for splits or damage. Also check that each driveshaft is straight and undamaged.

Braking system

☐ If possible without dismantling, check brake pad wear and disc condition. Ensure that the friction lining material has not worn excessively, (A) and that the discs are not fractured, pitted, scored or badly worn (B).

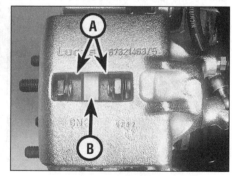

☐ Examine all the rigid brake pipes underneath the vehicle, and the flexible hose(s) at the rear. Look for corrosion, chafing or insecurity of the pipes, and for signs of bulging under pressure, chafing, splits or deterioration of the flexible hoses.
☐ Look for signs of fluid leaks at the brake calipers or on the brake backplates. Repair or renew leaking components.
☐ Slowly spin each wheel, while your assistant depresses and releases the footbrake. Ensure that each brake is operating and does not bind when the pedal is released.

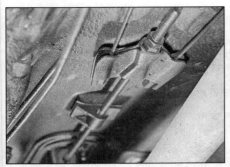

□ Examine the handbrake mechanism, checking for frayed or broken cables, excessive corrosion, or wear or insecurity of the linkage. Check that the mechanism works on each relevant wheel, and releases fully, without binding.

□ It is not possible to test brake efficiency without special equipment, but a road test can be carried out later to check that the vehicle pulls up in a straight line.

Fuel and exhaust systems

□ Inspect the fuel tank (including the filler cap), fuel pipes, hoses and unions. All components must be secure and free from leaks.

□ Examine the exhaust system over its entire length, checking for any damaged, broken or missing mountings, security of the retaining clamps and rust or corrosion.

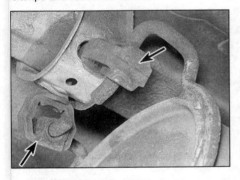

Wheels and tyres

□ Examine the sidewalls and tread area of each tyre in turn. Check for cuts, tears, lumps, bulges, separation of the tread, and exposure of the ply or cord due to wear or damage. Check that the tyre bead is correctly seated on the wheel rim, that the valve is sound and

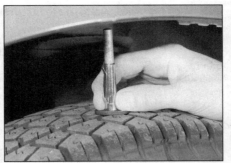

properly seated, and that the wheel is not distorted or damaged.

□ Check that the tyres are of the correct size for the vehicle, that they are of the same size and type on each axle, and that the pressures are correct.

□ Check the tyre tread depth. The legal minimum at the time of writing is 1.6 mm over at least three-quarters of the tread width. Abnormal tread wear may indicate incorrect front wheel alignment.

Body corrosion

□ Check the condition of the entire vehicle structure for signs of corrosion in load-bearing areas. (These include chassis box sections, side sills, cross-members, pillars, and all suspension, steering, braking system and seat belt mountings and anchorages.) Any corrosion which has seriously reduced the thickness of a load-bearing area is likely to cause the vehicle to fail. In this case professional repairs are likely to be needed.

□ Damage or corrosion which causes sharp or otherwise dangerous edges to be exposed will also cause the vehicle to fail.

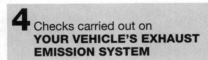

4 Checks carried out on **YOUR VEHICLE'S EXHAUST EMISSION SYSTEM**

Petrol models

□ Have the engine at normal operating temperature, and make sure that it is in good tune (ignition system in good order, air filter element clean, etc).

□ Before any measurements are carried out, raise the engine speed to around 2500 rpm, and hold it at this speed for 20 seconds.

Allow the engine speed to return to idle, and watch for smoke emissions from the exhaust tailpipe. If the idle speed is obviously much too high, or if dense blue or clearly-visible black smoke comes from the tailpipe for more than 5 seconds, the vehicle will fail. As a rule of thumb, blue smoke signifies oil being burnt (engine wear) while black smoke signifies unburnt fuel (dirty air cleaner element, or other carburettor or fuel system fault).

□ An exhaust gas analyser capable of measuring carbon monoxide (CO) and hydrocarbons (HC) is now needed. If such an instrument cannot be hired or borrowed, a local garage may agree to perform the check for a small fee.

CO emissions (mixture)

□ At the time of writing, the maximum CO level at idle is 3.5% for vehicles first used after August 1986 and 4.5% for older vehicles. From January 1996 a much tighter limit (around 0.5%) applies to catalyst-equipped vehicles first used from August 1992. If the CO level cannot be reduced far enough to pass the test (and the fuel and ignition systems are otherwise in good condition) then the carburettor is badly worn, or there is some problem in the fuel injection system or catalytic converter (as applicable).

HC emissions

□ With the CO emissions within limits, HC emissions must be no more than 1200 ppm (parts per million). If the vehicle fails this test at idle, it can be re-tested at around 2000 rpm; if the HC level is then 1200 ppm or less, this counts as a pass.

□ Excessive HC emissions can be caused by oil being burnt, but they are more likely to be due to unburnt fuel.

Diesel models

□ The only emission test applicable to Diesel engines is the measuring of exhaust smoke density. The test involves accelerating the engine several times to its maximum unloaded speed.

Note: *It is of the utmost importance that the engine timing belt is in good condition before the test is carried out.*

□ Excessive smoke can be caused by a dirty air cleaner element. Otherwise, professional advice may be needed to find the cause.

Engine

- ☐ Engine fails to rotate when attempting to start
- ☐ Engine rotates but will not start
- ☐ Engine difficult to start when cold
- ☐ Engine difficult to start when hot
- ☐ Starter motor noisy or excessively-rough in engagement
- ☐ Engine starts but stops immediately
- ☐ Engine idles erratically
- ☐ Engine misfires at idle speed
- ☐ Engine misfires throughout the driving speed range
- ☐ Engine hesitates on acceleration
- ☐ Engine stalls
- ☐ Engine lacks power
- ☐ Engine backfires
- ☐ Oil pressure warning light illuminated with engine running
- ☐ Engine runs-on after switching off
- ☐ Engine noises
- ☐ Engine oil consumption excessive

Cooling system

- ☐ Overheating
- ☐ Overcooling
- ☐ External coolant leakage
- ☐ Internal coolant leakage
- ☐ Corrosion

Fuel and exhaust systems

- ☐ Excessive fuel consumption
- ☐ Fuel leakage and/or fuel odour
- ☐ Excessive noise or fumes from exhaust system

Clutch

- ☐ Pedal travels to floor - no pressure or very little resistance
- ☐ Clutch fails to disengage (unable to select gears)
- ☐ Clutch slips (engine speed increases with no increase in vehicle speed)
- ☐ Judder as clutch is engaged
- ☐ Noise when depressing or releasing clutch pedal

Manual transmission

- ☐ Noisy in neutral with engine running
- ☐ Noisy in one particular gear
- ☐ Difficulty engaging gears
- ☐ Jumps out of gear
- ☐ Vibration
- ☐ Lubricant leaks

Automatic transmission

- ☐ Fluid leakage
- ☐ Transmission fluid brown, or has burned smell
- ☐ General gear selection problems
- ☐ Transmission will not downshift (kickdown) with accelerator pedal fully depressed
- ☐ Engine will not start in any gear, or starts in gears other than Park or Neutral
- ☐ Transmission slips, is noisy, or has no drive in forward or reverse gears

Driveshafts

- ☐ Clicking or knocking noise on turns (at slow speed on full lock)
- ☐ Vibration when decelerating or accelerating

Braking system

- ☐ Vehicle pulls to one side under braking
- ☐ Noise (grinding or high-pitched squeal) when brakes applied
- ☐ Excessive brake pedal travel
- ☐ Brake pedal feels spongy when depressed
- ☐ Excessive brake pedal effort required to stop vehicle
- ☐ Judder felt through brake pedal or steering wheel when braking
- ☐ Brakes binding

Suspension and steering systems

- ☐ Vehicle pulls to one side
- ☐ Wheel wobble and vibration
- ☐ Excessive pitching and/or rolling around corners, or during braking
- ☐ Wandering or general instability
- ☐ Excessively-stiff steering
- ☐ Excessive play in steering
- ☐ Lack of power assistance
- ☐ Tyre wear excessive

Electrical system

- ☐ Battery will not hold a charge for more than a few days
- ☐ Ignition/no-charge warning light remains illuminated with engine running
- ☐ Ignition/no-charge warning light fails to come on
- ☐ Lights inoperative
- ☐ Instrument readings inaccurate or erratic
- ☐ Horn inoperative, or unsatisfactory in operation
- ☐ Windscreen/tailgate wipers inoperative or unsatisfactory in operation
- ☐ Windscreen/tailgate washers inoperative, or unsatisfactory in operation
- ☐ Electric windows inoperative, or unsatisfactory in operation
- ☐ Central locking system inoperative, or unsatisfactory in operation

Introduction

The vehicle owner who does his or her own maintenance according to the recommended service schedules should not have to use this section of the manual very often. Modern component reliability is such that, provided those items subject to wear or deterioration are inspected or renewed at the specified intervals, sudden failure is comparatively rare. Faults do not usually just happen as a result of sudden failure, but develop over a period of time. Major mechanical failures in particular are usually preceded by characteristic symptoms over hundreds or even thousands of miles. Those components which do occasionally fail without warning are often small and easily carried in the vehicle.

With any fault-finding, the first step is to decide where to begin investigations. Sometimes this is obvious, but on other occasions, a little detective work will be necessary. The owner who makes half a dozen haphazard adjustments or replacements may be successful in curing a fault (or its symptoms), but will be none the wiser if the fault recurs, and ultimately may have spent more time and money than was necessary. A calm and logical approach will be found to be more satisfactory in the long run. Always take into account any warning signs or abnormalities that may have been noticed in the period preceding the fault - power loss, high or low gauge readings, unusual smells, etc - and remember that failure of components such as fuses or spark plugs may only be pointers to some underlying fault.

These pages provide an easy reference guide to the more common problems which may occur during the operation of the vehicle. These problems and their possible causes are grouped under headings denoting various components or systems, such as Engine, Cooling system, etc. The Chapter and/or Section which deals with the problem is also shown in brackets. Whatever the fault, certain basic principles apply. These are as follows:

Verify the fault. This is simply a matter of being sure that you know what the symptoms are before starting work. This is particularly important if you are investigating a fault for someone else, who may not have described it very accurately.

Don't overlook the obvious. For example, if the vehicle won't start, is there petrol in the tank? (Don't take anyone else's word on this particular point, and don't trust the fuel gauge either!) If an electrical fault is indicated, look for loose or broken wires before digging out the test gear.

Cure the disease, not the symptom. Substituting a flat battery with a fully-charged one will get you off the hard shoulder, but if the underlying cause is not attended to, the new battery will go the same way. Similarly, changing oil-fouled spark plugs for a new set will get you moving again, but remember that the reason for the fouling (if it wasn't simply an incorrect grade of plug) will have to be established and corrected.

Don't take anything for granted. Particularly, don't forget that a new component may itself be defective (especially if it's been rattling around in the boot for months), and don't leave components out of a fault diagnosis sequence just because they are new or recently fitted. When you do finally diagnose a difficult fault, you'll probably realise that all the evidence was there from the start.

Consider what work, if any, has recently been carried out. Many faults arise through careless or hurried work. For instance, if any work has been performed under the bonnet, could some of the wiring have been dislodged or incorrectly routed, or a hose trapped? Have all the fasteners been properly tightened? Were new gaskets used? There is often a certain amount of detective work to be done in this case, as an apparently-unrelated task can have far-reaching consequences.

Engine

Engine fails to rotate when attempting to start
☐ Battery terminal connections loose or corroded (*Weekly checks*).
☐ Battery discharged or faulty (Chapter 5A).
☐ Broken, loose or disconnected wiring in the starting circuit (Chapter 5A).
☐ Defective starter solenoid or switch (Chapter 5A).
☐ Defective starter motor (Chapter 5A).
☐ Starter pinion or flywheel ring gear teeth loose or broken (Chapter 2A or 5A).
☐ Engine earth leads broken or disconnected (Chapter 5A).
☐ Automatic transmission not in Park/Neutral position, or selector cable adjustment incorrect (Chapter 1).

Engine rotates but will not start
☐ Fuel tank empty.
☐ Battery discharged (engine rotates slowly) (Chapter 5A).
☐ Battery terminal connections loose or corroded (*Weekly checks*).
☐ Ignition components damp or damaged (Chapter 1 or 5B).
☐ Broken, loose or disconnected wiring in the ignition circuit (Chapter 1 or 5B).
☐ Immobiliser fault (Chapter 12).
☐ Worn, faulty or incorrectly-gapped spark plugs (Chapter 1).
☐ Low cylinder compressions (Chapter 2A) .
☐ Major mechanical failure (eg timing belt) (Chapter 2A).

Engine difficult to start when cold
☐ Battery discharged (Chapter 5A).
☐ Battery terminal connections loose or corroded (*Weekly checks*).
☐ Worn, faulty or incorrectly-gapped spark plugs (Chapter 1).
☐ Other ignition system fault (Chapter 1 or 5B).
☐ Engine management system fault (Chapter 1, 4A or 5B).
☐ Low cylinder compressions (Chapter 2A).

Engine difficult to start when hot
☐ Air cleaner element dirty or clogged (Chapter 1).
☐ Engine management system fault (Chapter 1, 4A or 5B).
☐ Low cylinder compressions (Chapter 2A).

Starter motor noisy or excessively-rough in engagement
☐ Starter pinion or flywheel ring gear teeth loose or broken (Chapter 2A or 5A).
☐ Starter motor mounting bolts loose or missing (Chapter 5A).
☐ Starter motor internal components worn or damaged (Chapter 5A).

Engine starts but stops immediately
☐ Loose or faulty electrical connections in the ignition circuit (Chapter 1 or 5B).
☐ Engine management system fault (Chapter 1, 4A or 5B).
☐ Vacuum leak at the inlet manifold or associated hoses (Chapter 1, 4A or 4B).

Engine idles erratically
☐ Engine management system fault (Chapter 1, 4A or 5B).
☐ Fuel injectors partially blocked (Chapter 4A).
☐ Air cleaner element dirty or clogged (Chapter 1).
☐ Vacuum leak at the inlet manifold or associated hoses (Chapter 1, 4A or 4B).
☐ Worn, faulty or incorrectly-gapped spark plugs (Chapter 1).
☐ Uneven or low cylinder compressions (Chapter 2A).
☐ Camshaft lobes worn (Chapter 2A).

Engine misfires at idle speed
☐ Worn, faulty or incorrectly-gapped spark plugs (Chapter 1).
☐ Faulty spark plug HT leads (Chapter 1).
☐ Engine management system fault (Chapter 1, 4A or 5B).
☐ Fuel injectors partially blocked (Chapter 4A).
☐ Vacuum leak at the inlet manifold or associated hoses (Chapter 1, 4A or 4B).
☐ Uneven or low cylinder compressions (Chapter 2A).
☐ Disconnected, leaking or perished crankcase ventilation hoses (Chapter 1 or 4B).

Engine misfires throughout the driving speed range
☐ Fuel filter choked (Chapter 1).
☐ Fuel pump faulty (Chapter 4A).
☐ Fuel tank vent blocked or fuel pipes restricted (Chapter 4A or 4B).
☐ Vacuum leak at the inlet manifold or associated hoses (Chapter 1, 4A or 4B).
☐ Worn, faulty or incorrectly-gapped spark plugs (Chapter 1).
☐ Faulty spark plug HT leads (Chapter 1).
☐ Engine management system fault (Chapter 1, 4A or 5B).
☐ Fuel injectors partially blocked (Chapter 4A).
☐ Uneven or low cylinder compressions (Chapter 2A).

Engine hesitates on acceleration
☐ Worn, faulty or incorrectly-gapped spark plugs (Chapter 1).
☐ Engine management system fault (Chapter 1, 4A or 5B).
☐ Fuel injectors partially blocked (Chapter 4A).
☐ Vacuum leak at the inlet manifold or associated hoses (Chapter 1, 4A or 4B).

Engine (continued)

Engine stalls

- ☐ Engine management system fault (Chapter 1, 4A or 5B).
- ☐ Fuel injectors partially blocked (Chapter 4A).
- ☐ Vacuum leak at the inlet manifold or associated hoses (Chapter 1, 4A or 4B).
- ☐ Fuel filter choked (Chapter 1).
- ☐ Fuel pump faulty (Chapter 4A).
- ☐ Fuel tank vent blocked or fuel pipes restricted (Chapter 4A or 4B).

Engine lacks power

- ☐ Engine management system fault (Chapter 1, 4A or 5B).
- ☐ Fuel injectors partially blocked (Chapter 4A).
- ☐ Timing belt incorrectly fitted (Chapter 2A)
- ☐ Fuel filter choked (Chapter 1).
- ☐ Fuel pump faulty (Chapter 4A).
- ☐ Uneven or low cylinder compressions (Chapter 2A).
- ☐ Worn, faulty or incorrectly-gapped spark plugs (Chapter 1).
- ☐ Vacuum leak at the inlet manifold or associated hoses (Chapter 1, 4A or 4B).
- ☐ Brakes binding (Chapter 1 or 9).
- ☐ Clutch slipping (Chapter 6).
- ☐ Automatic transmission fluid level incorrect (Chapter 1).

Engine backfires

- ☐ Engine management system fault (Chapter 1, 4A or 5B).
- ☐ Timing belt incorrectly fitted (Chapter 2A).
- ☐ Vacuum leak at the inlet manifold or associated hoses (Chapter 1, 4A or 4B).
- ☐ Emission control system fault (Chapter 4B).

Oil pressure warning light illuminated with engine running

- ☐ Low oil level or incorrect oil grade (Chapter 1).
- ☐ Faulty oil pressure sensor (Chapter 12).
- ☐ Worn engine bearings and/or oil pump (Chapter 2A or 2B).
- ☐ High engine operating temperature (Chapter 3).
- ☐ Oil pressure relief valve defective (Chapter 2A).
- ☐ Oil pick-up pipe strainer clogged (Chapter 2B).

Engine runs-on after switching off

- ☐ Engine management system fault (Chapter 1, 4A or 5B).
- ☐ Excessive carbon build-up in engine (Chapter 2A or 2B).
- ☐ High engine operating temperature (Chapter 3).

Engine noises

Pre-ignition (pinking) or knocking during acceleration or under load

- ☐ Incorrect grade of fuel (Chapter 4A).
- ☐ Vacuum leak at the inlet manifold or associated hoses (Chapter 1, 4A or 4B).
- ☐ Excessive carbon build-up in engine (Chapter 2A or 2B).

Whistling or wheezing noises

- ☐ Leaking inlet manifold gasket (Chapter 4A).
- ☐ Leaking exhaust manifold gasket or front pipe-to-manifold joint (Chapter 4B).
- ☐ Leaking vacuum hose (Chapter 1, 4A, 5B or 9).
- ☐ Blowing cylinder head gasket (Chapter 2A).

Tapping or rattling noises

- ☐ Worn valve gear or camshafts (Chapter 2A or 2B).
- ☐ Worn or faulty hydraulic tappets (Chapter 2A or 2B).
- ☐ Worn timing belt, tensioner, or idler pulleys (Chapter 2A).
- ☐ Ancillary component fault (coolant pump, alternator, etc) (Chapter 3 or 5A).

Knocking or thumping noises

- ☐ Worn big-end bearings (regular heavy knocking, perhaps less under load) (Chapter 2B).
- ☐ Worn main bearings (rumbling and knocking, perhaps worsening under load) (Chapter 2B).
- ☐ Piston slap (most noticeable when cold - engine worn) (Chapter 2B).
- ☐ Ancillary component fault (coolant pump, alternator, etc) (Chapter 3 or 5A).

Engine oil consumption excessive

- ☐ Wrong grade of oil, or oil level too high (*Weekly checks*).
- ☐ Oil filter or sump drain plug loose (Chapter 1).
- ☐ Oil seal leaking (Chapter 2A or 2B).
- ☐ Camshaft cover/engine top cover seal leaking (Chapter 2A or 2B).
- ☐ Sump gasket leaking (Chapter 2B).
- ☐ Cylinder head gasket leaking (Chapter 2B).
- ☐ Engine burning oil - piston ring or cylinder bore wear (Chapter 2B).

Cooling system

Overheating

- ☐ Insufficient coolant in system (*Weekly checks*).
- ☐ Thermostat faulty (Chapter 3).
- ☐ Radiator core blocked or grille restricted (Chapter 3).
- ☐ Radiator electric cooling fan(s) or coolant temperature sensor faulty (Chapter 3).
- ☐ Engine management system fault (Chapter 1, 4A or 5B).
- ☐ Pressure cap faulty (Chapter 3).
- ☐ Auxiliary drivebelt worn or slipping (Chapter 1).
- ☐ Air-lock in cooling system (Chapter 1, Section 29).

Overcooling

- ☐ Thermostat faulty (Chapter 3).
- ☐ Inaccurate coolant temperature sensor (Chapter 3).

External coolant leakage

- ☐ Deteriorated or damaged hoses or hose clips (Chapter 1).
- ☐ Radiator core or heater matrix leaking (Chapter 3).
- ☐ Pressure cap faulty (Chapter 3).
- ☐ Coolant pump seal leaking (Chapter 3).
- ☐ Boiling due to overheating (Chapter 3).

Internal coolant leakage

- ☐ Leaking cylinder head gasket (Chapter 2A).
- ☐ Cracked cylinder head or cylinder bore (Chapter 2B).

Corrosion

- ☐ Infrequent draining and flushing (Chapter 1).
- ☐ Incorrect antifreeze mixture, or inappropriate antifreeze type (Chapter 1 or 3).

Fuel and exhaust systems

Excessive fuel consumption

☐ Unsympathetic driving style, or adverse conditions.
☐ Air cleaner filter element dirty or clogged (Chapter 1).
☐ Engine management system fault (Chapter 1, 4A or 5B).
☐ Fuel injectors partially blocked (Chapter 4A).
☐ Tyres under-inflated (*Weekly checks*).

Fuel leakage and/or fuel odour

☐ Damaged or corroded fuel tank, pipes or connections (Chapter 1).

Excessive noise or fumes from exhaust system

☐ Leaking exhaust system or manifold joints (Chapter 1 or 4B).
☐ Leaking, corroded or damaged silencers or pipe (Chapter 1 or 4B).
☐ Broken mountings, causing body or suspension contact (Chapter 1 or 4B).

Clutch

Pedal travels to floor - no pressure or very little resistance

☐ Air in clutch hydraulic system (Chapter 6).
☐ Faulty clutch slave cylinder (Chapter 6).
☐ Faulty clutch master cylinder (Chapter 6).
☐ Broken diaphragm spring in clutch pressure plate (Chapter 6).

Clutch fails to disengage (unable to select gears)

☐ Air in clutch hydraulic system (Chapter 6).
☐ Faulty clutch slave cylinder (Chapter 6).
☐ Faulty clutch master cylinder (Chapter 6).
☐ Clutch disc sticking on transmission mainshaft splines (Chapter 6).
☐ Clutch disc sticking to flywheel or pressure plate (Chapter 6).
☐ Faulty pressure plate assembly (Chapter 6).
☐ Clutch release mechanism worn or incorrectly assembled (Chapter 6).

Clutch slips (engine speed increases with no increase in vehicle speed)

☐ Clutch disc linings excessively worn (Chapter 6).
☐ Clutch disc linings contaminated with oil or grease (Chapter 6).
☐ Faulty pressure plate or weak diaphragm spring (Chapter 6).

Judder as clutch is engaged

☐ Clutch disc linings contaminated with oil or grease (Chapter 6).
☐ Clutch disc linings excessively worn (Chapter 6).
☐ Faulty or distorted pressure plate or diaphragm spring (Chapter 6).
☐ Worn or loose engine/transmission mountings (Chapter 2A).
☐ Clutch disc hub or transmission input shaft splines worn (Chapter 6).

Noise when depressing or releasing clutch pedal

☐ Worn clutch release bearing (Chapter 6).
☐ Worn or dry clutch pedal bushes (Chapter 6).
☐ Faulty pressure plate assembly (Chapter 6).
☐ Pressure plate diaphragm spring broken (Chapter 6).
☐ Broken clutch disc cushioning springs (Chapter 6).

Manual transmission

Noisy in neutral with engine running

☐ Mainshaft bearings worn (noise apparent with clutch pedal released, but not when depressed) (Chapter 7A).*
☐ Clutch release bearing worn (noise apparent with clutch pedal depressed, possibly less when released) (Chapter 6).

Noisy in one particular gear

☐ Worn, damaged or chipped gear teeth (Chapter 7A).*
☐ Worn bearings (Chapter 7A).*

Difficulty engaging gears

☐ Clutch fault (Chapter 6).
☐ Selector cables out of adjustment (Chapter 7A).
☐ Worn synchroniser assemblies (Chapter 7A).*

Jumps out of gear

☐ Selector cables out of adjustment (Chapter 7A).
☐ Worn synchroniser assemblies (Chapter 7A).*
☐ Worn selector forks (Chapter 7A).*

Vibration

☐ Lack of oil (Chapter 1).
☐ Worn bearings (Chapter 7A).*

Lubricant leaks

☐ Leaking differential side gear oil seal (Chapter 7A).
☐ Leaking housing joint (Chapter 7A).*
☐ Leaking input shaft oil seal (Chapter 7A).

* Although the corrective action necessary to remedy the symptoms described is beyond the scope of the home mechanic, the above information should be helpful in isolating the cause of the condition, so that the owner can communicate clearly with a professional mechanic.

Automatic transmission

Note: *Due to the complexity of the automatic transmission, it is difficult for the home mechanic to properly diagnose and service this unit. For problems other than the following, the vehicle should be taken to a dealer service department or automatic transmission specialist.*

Fluid leakage

☐ Automatic transmission fluid is usually dark in colour. Fluid leaks should not be confused with engine oil, which can easily be blown onto the transmission by airflow.

☐ To determine the source of a leak, first remove all built-up dirt and grime from the transmission housing and surrounding areas, using a degreasing agent, or by steam-cleaning. Drive the vehicle at low speed, so airflow will not blow the leak far from its source. Raise and support the vehicle, and determine where the leak is coming from. The following are common areas of leakage:
   a) *Transmission oil sump (Chapter 1 or 7B).*
   b) *Dipstick tube (Chapter 1 or 7B).*
   c) *Transmission-to-fluid cooler pipes/unions (Chapter 1 or 7B).*
   d) *Transmission oil seals (Chapter 7B).*

Transmission fluid brown, or has burned smell

☐ Transmission fluid level low, or fluid in need of renewal (Chapter 1).

General gear selection problems

☐ Checking and adjusting the selector cable is covered in Chapter 1 and 7B. The following are common problems which may be caused by a poorly-adjusted cable:
   a) *Engine starting in gears other than Park or Neutral.*
   b) *Indicator on gear selector lever pointing to a gear other than the one actually being used.*

c) *Vehicle moves when in Park or Neutral.*
d) *Poor gear shift quality or erratic gear changes.*
   Refer to Chapter 7B for the selector cable adjustment procedure.
☐ If the selector lever will not move out of Park, the Shiftlock system may not be operating correctly. Turn the ignition key to position I, and press the Shiftlock override button on the front right of the selector housing while moving the lever to another position.

Transmission will not downshift (kickdown) with accelerator pedal fully depressed

☐ Low transmission fluid level (Chapter 1).
☐ Incorrect selector cable adjustment (Chapter 1 or 7B).
☐ Automatic transmission ECU or sensor fault (Chapter 7B).

Engine will not start in any gear, or starts in gears other than Park or Neutral

☐ Incorrect selector cable adjustment (Chapter 7B).
☐ Automatic transmission ECU or sensor fault (Chapter 7B).

Transmission slips, is noisy, or has no drive in forward or reverse gears

☐ There are many probable causes for the above problems, but the home mechanic should be concerned with only one possibility - fluid level. Before taking the vehicle to a dealer or transmission specialist, check the fluid level and condition of the fluid as described in Chapter 1. Correct the fluid level as necessary, or change the fluid if needed. If the problem persists, professional help will be necessary.

Driveshafts

Clicking or knocking noise on turns (at slow speed on full lock)

☐ Lack of constant velocity joint lubricant, possibly due to damaged gaiter (Chapter 8).
☐ Worn outer constant velocity joint (Chapter 8).

Vibration when decelerating or accelerating

☐ Worn inner constant velocity joint (Chapter 8).
☐ Bent or distorted driveshaft (Chapter 8).

Braking system

Note: *Before assuming that a brake problem exists, make sure that the tyres are in good condition and correctly inflated, that the front wheel alignment is correct, and that the vehicle is not loaded with weight in an unequal manner. Apart from checking the condition of all pipe and hose connections, any faults occurring on the Anti-lock Braking System (ABS) should be referred to a Volvo dealer for repair.*

Vehicle pulls to one side under braking

☐ Worn, defective, damaged or contaminated front or rear brake pads on one side (Chapter 9).
☐ Seized or partially-seized front or rear brake caliper piston (Chapter 9).
☐ A mixture of brake pad lining materials fitted between sides (Chapter 9).
☐ Brake caliper mounting bolts loose (Chapter 9).
☐ Worn or damaged steering or suspension components (Chapter 10).

Noise (grinding or high-pitched squeal) when brakes applied

☐ Brake pad friction lining material worn down to metal backing (Chapter 9).
☐ Excessive corrosion of brake disc (may be apparent after the vehicle has been standing for some time) (Chapter 9).

Excessive brake pedal travel

☐ Faulty master cylinder (Chapter 9).
☐ Air in hydraulic system (Chapter 9).

Brake pedal feels spongy when depressed

☐ Air in hydraulic system (Chapter 9).
☐ Deteriorated flexible rubber brake hoses (Chapter 9).
☐ Master cylinder mounting nuts loose (Chapter 9).
☐ Faulty master cylinder (Chapter 9).

Braking system (continued)

Excessive brake pedal effort required to stop vehicle

☐ Faulty vacuum servo unit (Chapter 9).
☐ Disconnected, damaged or insecure brake servo vacuum hose (Chapter 9).
☐ Primary or secondary hydraulic circuit failure (Chapter 9).
☐ Seized brake caliper piston(s) (Chapter 9).
☐ Brake pads incorrectly fitted (Chapter 9).
☐ Incorrect grade of brake pads fitted (Chapter 9).
☐ Brake pad linings contaminated (Chapter 9).

Judder felt through brake pedal or steering wheel when braking

☐ Excessive run-out or distortion of front or rear discs (Chapter 9).
☐ Brake pad linings worn (Chapter 9).
☐ Brake caliper mounting bolts loose (Chapter 9).
☐ Wear in suspension or steering components or mountings (Chapter 10).

Brakes binding

☐ Seized brake caliper piston(s) (Chapter 9).
☐ Faulty handbrake mechanism (Chapter 9).
☐ Faulty master cylinder (Chapter 9).

Suspension and steering systems

Note: *Before diagnosing suspension or steering faults, be sure that the trouble is not due to incorrect tyre pressures, mixtures of tyre types, or binding brakes.*

Vehicle pulls to one side

☐ Defective tyre (*Weekly checks*).
☐ Excessive wear in suspension or steering components (Chapter 10).
☐ Incorrect front or rear wheel alignment (Chapter 10).
☐ Accident damage to steering or suspension components (Chapter 10).

Wheel wobble and vibration

☐ Front roadwheels out of balance (vibration felt mainly through the steering wheel) (*Weekly checks*).
☐ Rear roadwheels out of balance (vibration felt throughout the vehicle) (*Weekly checks*).
☐ Roadwheels damaged or distorted (*Weekly checks*).
☐ Faulty or damaged tyre (*Weekly checks*).
☐ Worn steering or suspension joints, bushes or components (Chapter 10).
☐ Roadwheel bolts loose (Chapter 1).

Excessive pitching and/or rolling around corners, or during braking

☐ Defective shock absorbers (Chapter 10).
☐ Broken or weak coil spring and/or suspension component (Chapter 10).
☐ Worn or damaged anti-roll bar or mountings (Chapter 10).

Wandering or general instability

☐ Incorrect wheel alignment (Chapter 10).
☐ Worn steering or suspension joints, bushes or components (Chapter 10).
☐ Roadwheels out of balance (*Weekly checks*).
☐ Faulty or damaged tyre (*Weekly checks*).
☐ Roadwheel bolts loose (Chapter 1).
☐ Defective shock absorbers (Chapter 10).

Excessively-stiff steering

☐ Broken or slipping steering pump (auxiliary) drivebelt (Chapter 1).
☐ Steering pump faulty (Chapter 10).
☐ Seized track rod end balljoint or suspension balljoint (Chapter 10).
☐ Incorrect front wheel alignment (Chapter 10).
☐ Steering rack or column bent or damaged (Chapter 10).

Excessive play in steering

☐ Worn steering column universal joint(s) (Chapter 10).
☐ Worn steering track rod end balljoints (Chapter 10).
☐ Worn steering gear (Chapter 10).
☐ Worn steering or suspension joints, bushes or components (Chapter 10).

Lack of power assistance

☐ Broken or slipping steering pump (auxiliary) drivebelt (Chapter 1).
☐ Incorrect fluid level (*Weekly checks*).
☐ Restriction in fluid hoses (Chapter 10).
☐ Faulty steering pump (Chapter 10).
☐ Faulty steering gear (Chapter 10).

Tyre wear excessive

Tyres worn on inside or outside edges

☐ Tyres under-inflated (*Weekly checks*).
☐ Incorrect camber or castor angles (wear on one edge only) (Chapter 10).
☐ Worn steering or suspension joints, bushes or components (Chapter 10).
☐ Excessively-hard cornering.
☐ Accident damage.

Tyre treads exhibit feathered edges

☐ Incorrect toe setting (Chapter 10).

Tyres worn in centre of tread

☐ Tyres over-inflated (*Weekly checks*).

Tyres worn on inside and outside edges

☐ Tyres under-inflated (*Weekly checks*).

Tyres worn unevenly

☐ Tyres out of balance (*Weekly checks*).
☐ Excessive wheel or tyre run-out (*Weekly checks*).
☐ Worn shock absorbers (Chapter 10).
☐ Faulty tyre (*Weekly checks*).

Electrical system

Note: *For problems associated with the starting system, refer to the faults listed under **Engine** earlier in this Section.*

Battery will not hold a charge for more than a few days

☐ Battery defective internally (Chapter 5A).
☐ Battery electrolyte level low (Chapter 1).
☐ Battery terminal connections loose or corroded (*Weekly checks*).
☐ Auxiliary drivebelt worn or slipping (Chapter 1).
☐ Alternator not charging at correct output (Chapter 5A).
☐ Alternator or voltage regulator faulty (Chapter 5A).
☐ Short-circuit causing continual battery drain (Chapter 5A or 12).

Ignition/no-charge warning light remains illuminated with engine running

☐ Auxiliary drivebelt worn or slipping (Chapter 1).
☐ Alternator brushes worn, sticking, or dirty (Chapter 5A).
☐ Alternator brush springs weak or broken (Chapter 5A).
☐ Internal fault in alternator or voltage regulator (Chapter 5A).
☐ Broken, disconnected, or loose wiring in charging circuit (Chapter 5A).

Ignition/no-charge warning light fails to come on

☐ Warning light bulb blown (Chapter 12).
☐ Broken, disconnected, or loose wiring in warning light circuit (Chapter 12).
☐ Alternator faulty (Chapter 5A).

Lights inoperative

☐ Bulb blown (Chapter 12).
☐ Corrosion of bulb or bulbholder contacts (Chapter 12).
☐ Blown fuse (Chapter 12).
☐ Faulty relay (Chapter 12).
☐ Broken, loose, or disconnected wiring (Chapter 12).
☐ Faulty switch (Chapter 12).

Instrument readings inaccurate or erratic

Instrument readings increase with engine speed

☐ Faulty instrument panel control components or circuitry (Chapter 12).

Tachometer gives no reading, or gives inaccurate reading

☐ Faulty instrument panel control components or circuitry (Chapter 12).
☐ Faulty RPM sensor (Chapter 5B).
☐ Engine management system fault (Chapter 4A or 5B).
☐ Wiring open-circuit (Chapter 12).
☐ Faulty gauge (Chapter 12).

Fuel or temperature gauges give no reading

☐ Faulty instrument panel control components or circuitry (Chapter 12).
☐ Engine management system fault (Chapter 4A or 5B).
☐ Faulty gauge sender unit (Chapter 3 or 4A).
☐ Wiring open-circuit (Chapter 12).
☐ Faulty gauge (Chapter 12).

Fuel or temperature gauges give continuous maximum reading

☐ Faulty instrument panel control components or circuitry (Chapter 12).
☐ Faulty gauge sender unit (Chapter 3 or 4A).
☐ Wiring short-circuit (Chapter 12).
☐ Faulty gauge (Chapter 12).

Horn inoperative, or unsatisfactory in operation

Horn fails to operate

☐ Blown fuse (Chapter 12).
☐ Steering wheel wiring connections loose, broken or disconnected (Chapter 10).
☐ Faulty horn (Chapter 12).

Horn emits intermittent or unsatisfactory sound

☐ Steering wheel cable connections loose, broken or disconnected (Chapter 10).
☐ Horn mountings loose (Chapter 12).
☐ Faulty horn (Chapter 12).

Horn operates all the time

☐ Horn push either earthed or stuck down (Chapter 10).
☐ Steering wheel cable connections earthed (Chapter 10).

Windscreen/tailgate wipers inoperative or unsatisfactory in operation

Wipers fail to operate, or operate very slowly

☐ Wiper blades stuck to screen, or linkage seized or binding (Chapter 12).
☐ Blown fuse (Chapter 12).
☐ Wiring or connections loose, broken or disconnected (Chapter 12).
☐ Faulty relay (Chapter 12).
☐ Faulty wiper motor (Chapter 12).

Wiper blades sweep over too large or too small an area of the glass

☐ Wiper arms incorrectly positioned on spindles (Chapter 12).
☐ Excessive wear of wiper linkage (Chapter 12).
☐ Wiper motor or linkage mountings loose or insecure (Chapter 12).

Wiper blades fail to clean the glass effectively

☐ Wiper blade rubbers worn or perished (*Weekly checks*).
☐ Wiper arm tension springs broken, or arm pivots seized (Chapter 12).
☐ Insufficient windscreen washer additive to adequately remove road film (*Weekly checks*).

Windscreen/tailgate washers inoperative, or unsatisfactory in operation

One or more washer jets inoperative

☐ Blocked washer jet (Chapter 12).
☐ Disconnected, kinked or restricted fluid hose (Chapter 12).
☐ Insufficient fluid in washer reservoir (*Weekly checks*).

Washer pump fails to operate

☐ Broken or disconnected wiring or connections (Chapter 12).
☐ Blown fuse (Chapter 12).
☐ Faulty washer switch (Chapter 12).
☐ Faulty washer pump (Chapter 12).

Washer pump runs for some time before fluid is emitted from jets

☐ Faulty one-way valve in fluid supply hose (Chapter 12).

Electrical system (continued)

Electric windows inoperative, or unsatisfactory in operation

Window glass will only move in one direction

☐ Faulty switch (Chapter 12).

Window glass slow to move

☐ Incorrectly-adjusted door glass guide channels (Chapter 11).
☐ Regulator seized or damaged, or in need of lubrication (Chapter 11).
☐ Door internal components or trim fouling regulator (Chapter 11).
☐ Faulty motor (Chapter 12).

Window glass fails to move

☐ Incorrectly-adjusted door glass guide channels (Chapter 11).
☐ Blown fuse (Chapter 12).
☐ Faulty relay (Chapter 12).
☐ Broken or disconnected wiring or connections (Chapter 12).
☐ Faulty motor (Chapter 12).

Central locking system inoperative, or unsatisfactory in operation

Complete system failure

☐ Blown fuse (Chapter 12).
☐ Faulty relay (Chapter 12).
☐ Broken or disconnected wiring or connections (Chapter 12).

Latch locks but will not unlock, or unlocks but will not lock

☐ Faulty door lock microswitch (Chapter 11).
☐ Broken or disconnected latch operating rods or levers (Chapter 11).
☐ Faulty relay (Chapter 12).

One lock motor fails to operate

☐ Broken or disconnected wiring or connections (Chapter 12).
☐ Faulty lock motor (Chapter 11).
☐ Broken, binding or disconnected latch operating rods or levers (Chapter 11).
☐ Fault in door latch (Chapter 11).

A

ABS (Anti-lock brake system) A system, usually electronically controlled, that senses incipient wheel lockup during braking and relieves hydraulic pressure at wheels that are about to skid.

Air bag An inflatable bag hidden in the steering wheel (driver's side) or the dash or glovebox (passenger side). In a head-on collision, the bags inflate, preventing the driver and front passenger from being thrown forward into the steering wheel or windscreen.

Air cleaner A metal or plastic housing, containing a filter element, which removes dust and dirt from the air being drawn into the engine.

Air filter element The actual filter in an air cleaner system, usually manufactured from pleated paper and requiring renewal at regular intervals.

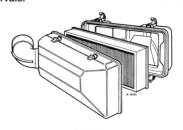

Air filter

Allen key A hexagonal wrench which fits into a recessed hexagonal hole.

Alligator clip A long-nosed spring-loaded metal clip with meshing teeth. Used to make temporary electrical connections.

Alternator A component in the electrical system which converts mechanical energy from a drivebelt into electrical energy to charge the battery and to operate the starting system, ignition system and electrical accessories.

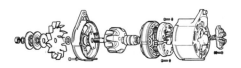

Alternator (exploded view)

Ampere (amp) A unit of measurement for the flow of electric current. One amp is the amount of current produced by one volt acting through a resistance of one ohm.

Anaerobic sealer A substance used to prevent bolts and screws from loosening. Anaerobic means that it does not require oxygen for activation. The Loctite brand is widely used.

Antifreeze A substance (usually ethylene glycol) mixed with water, and added to a vehicle's cooling system, to prevent freezing of the coolant in winter. Antifreeze also contains chemicals to inhibit corrosion and the formation of rust and other deposits that

would tend to clog the radiator and coolant passages and reduce cooling efficiency.

Anti-seize compound A coating that reduces the risk of seizing on fasteners that are subjected to high temperatures, such as exhaust manifold bolts and nuts.

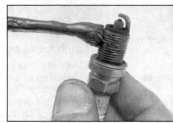

Anti-seize compound

Asbestos A natural fibrous mineral with great heat resistance, commonly used in the composition of brake friction materials. Asbestos is a health hazard and the dust created by brake systems should never be inhaled or ingested.

Axle A shaft on which a wheel revolves, or which revolves with a wheel. Also, a solid beam that connects the two wheels at one end of the vehicle. An axle which also transmits power to the wheels is known as a live axle.

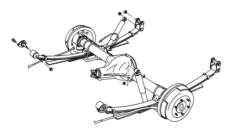

Axle assembly

Axleshaft A single rotating shaft, on either side of the differential, which delivers power from the final drive assembly to the drive wheels. Also called a driveshaft or a halfshaft.

B

Ball bearing An anti-friction bearing consisting of a hardened inner and outer race with hardened steel balls between two races.

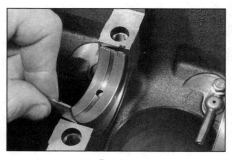

Bearing

Bearing The curved surface on a shaft or in a bore, or the part assembled into either, that permits relative motion between them with minimum wear and friction.

Big-end bearing The bearing in the end of the connecting rod that's attached to the crankshaft.

Bleed nipple A valve on a brake wheel cylinder, caliper or other hydraulic component that is opened to purge the hydraulic system of air. Also called a bleed screw.

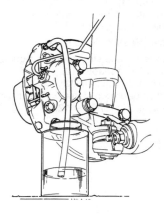

Brake bleeding

Brake bleeding Procedure for removing air from lines of a hydraulic brake system.

Brake disc The component of a disc brake that rotates with the wheels.

Brake drum The component of a drum brake that rotates with the wheels.

Brake linings The friction material which contacts the brake disc or drum to retard the vehicle's speed. The linings are bonded or riveted to the brake pads or shoes.

Brake pads The replaceable friction pads that pinch the brake disc when the brakes are applied. Brake pads consist of a friction material bonded or riveted to a rigid backing plate.

Brake shoe The crescent-shaped carrier to which the brake linings are mounted and which forces the lining against the rotating drum during braking.

Braking systems For more information on braking systems, consult the *Haynes Automotive Brake Manual*.

Breaker bar A long socket wrench handle providing greater leverage.

Bulkhead The insulated partition between the engine and the passenger compartment.

C

Caliper The non-rotating part of a disc-brake assembly that straddles the disc and carries the brake pads. The caliper also contains the hydraulic components that cause the pads to pinch the disc when the brakes are applied. A caliper is also a measuring tool that can be set to measure inside or outside dimensions of an object.

Camshaft A rotating shaft on which a series of cam lobes operate the valve mechanisms. The camshaft may be driven by gears, by sprockets and chain or by sprockets and a belt.

Canister A container in an evaporative emission control system; contains activated charcoal granules to trap vapours from the fuel system.

Canister

Carburettor A device which mixes fuel with air in the proper proportions to provide a desired power output from a spark ignition internal combustion engine.

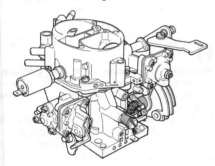

Carburettor

Castellated Resembling the parapets along the top of a castle wall. For example, a castellated balljoint stud nut.

Castellated nut

Castor In wheel alignment, the backward or forward tilt of the steering axis. Castor is positive when the steering axis is inclined rearward at the top.

Catalytic converter A silencer-like device in the exhaust system which converts certain pollutants in the exhaust gases into less harmful substances.

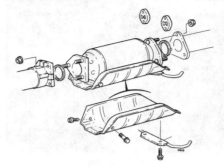

Catalytic converter

Circlip A ring-shaped clip used to prevent endwise movement of cylindrical parts and shafts. An internal circlip is installed in a groove in a housing; an external circlip fits into a groove on the outside of a cylindrical piece such as a shaft.

Clearance The amount of space between two parts. For example, between a piston and a cylinder, between a bearing and a journal, etc.

Coil spring A spiral of elastic steel found in various sizes throughout a vehicle, for example as a springing medium in the suspension and in the valve train.

Compression Reduction in volume, and increase in pressure and temperature, of a gas, caused by squeezing it into a smaller space.

Compression ratio The relationship between cylinder volume when the piston is at top dead centre and cylinder volume when the piston is at bottom dead centre.

Constant velocity (CV) joint A type of universal joint that cancels out vibrations caused by driving power being transmitted through an angle.

Core plug A disc or cup-shaped metal device inserted in a hole in a casting through which core was removed when the casting was formed. Also known as a freeze plug or expansion plug.

Crankcase The lower part of the engine block in which the crankshaft rotates.

Crankshaft The main rotating member, or shaft, running the length of the crankcase, with offset "throws" to which the connecting rods are attached.

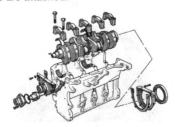

Crankshaft assembly

Crocodile clip See Alligator clip

D

Diagnostic code Code numbers obtained by accessing the diagnostic mode of an engine management computer. This code can be used to determine the area in the system where a malfunction may be located.

Disc brake A brake design incorporating a rotating disc onto which brake pads are squeezed. The resulting friction converts the energy of a moving vehicle into heat.

Double-overhead cam (DOHC) An engine that uses two overhead camshafts, usually one for the intake valves and one for the exhaust valves.

Drivebelt(s) The belt(s) used to drive accessories such as the alternator, water pump, power steering pump, air conditioning compressor, etc. off the crankshaft pulley.

Accessory drivebelts

Driveshaft Any shaft used to transmit motion. Commonly used when referring to the axleshafts on a front wheel drive vehicle.

Driveshaft

Drum brake A type of brake using a drum-shaped metal cylinder attached to the inner surface of the wheel. When the brake pedal is pressed, curved brake shoes with friction linings press against the inside of the drum to slow or stop the vehicle.

Drum brake assembly

E

EGR valve A valve used to introduce exhaust gases into the intake air stream.

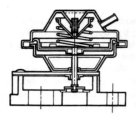

EGR valve

Electronic control unit (ECU) A computer which controls (for instance) ignition and fuel injection systems, or an anti-lock braking system. For more information refer to the *Haynes Automotive Electrical and Electronic Systems Manual*.

Electronic Fuel Injection (EFI) A computer controlled fuel system that distributes fuel through an injector located in each intake port of the engine.

Emergency brake A braking system, independent of the main hydraulic system, that can be used to slow or stop the vehicle if the primary brakes fail, or to hold the vehicle stationary even though the brake pedal isn't depressed. It usually consists of a hand lever that actuates either front or rear brakes mechanically through a series of cables and linkages. Also known as a handbrake or parking brake.

Endfloat The amount of lengthwise movement between two parts. As applied to a crankshaft, the distance that the crankshaft can move forward and back in the cylinder block.

Engine management system (EMS) A computer controlled system which manages the fuel injection and the ignition systems in an integrated fashion.

Exhaust manifold A part with several passages through which exhaust gases leave the engine combustion chambers and enter the exhaust pipe.

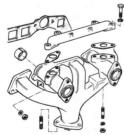

Exhaust manifold

F

Fan clutch A viscous (fluid) drive coupling device which permits variable engine fan speeds in relation to engine speeds.

Feeler blade A thin strip or blade of hardened steel, ground to an exact thickness, used to check or measure clearances between parts.

Feeler blade

Firing order The order in which the engine cylinders fire, or deliver their power strokes, beginning with the number one cylinder.

Flywheel A heavy spinning wheel in which energy is absorbed and stored by means of momentum. On cars, the flywheel is attached to the crankshaft to smooth out firing impulses.

Free play The amount of travel before any action takes place. The "looseness" in a linkage, or an assembly of parts, between the initial application of force and actual movement. For example, the distance the brake pedal moves before the pistons in the master cylinder are actuated.

Fuse An electrical device which protects a circuit against accidental overload. The typical fuse contains a soft piece of metal which is calibrated to melt at a predetermined current flow (expressed as amps) and break the circuit.

Fusible link A circuit protection device consisting of a conductor surrounded by heat-resistant insulation. The conductor is smaller than the wire it protects, so it acts as the weakest link in the circuit. Unlike a blown fuse, a failed fusible link must frequently be cut from the wire for replacement.

G

Gap The distance the spark must travel in jumping from the centre electrode to the side

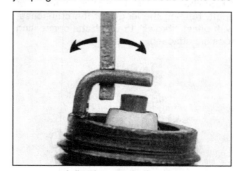

Adjusting spark plug gap

electrode in a spark plug. Also refers to the spacing between the points in a contact breaker assembly in a conventional points-type ignition, or to the distance between the reluctor or rotor and the pickup coil in an electronic ignition.

Gasket Any thin, soft material - usually cork, cardboard, asbestos or soft metal - installed between two metal surfaces to ensure a good seal. For instance, the cylinder head gasket seals the joint between the block and the cylinder head.

Gasket

Gauge An instrument panel display used to monitor engine conditions. A gauge with a movable pointer on a dial or a fixed scale is an analogue gauge. A gauge with a numerical readout is called a digital gauge.

H

Halfshaft A rotating shaft that transmits power from the final drive unit to a drive wheel, usually when referring to a live rear axle.

Harmonic balancer A device designed to reduce torsion or twisting vibration in the crankshaft. May be incorporated in the crankshaft pulley. Also known as a vibration damper.

Hone An abrasive tool for correcting small irregularities or differences in diameter in an engine cylinder, brake cylinder, etc.

Hydraulic tappet A tappet that utilises hydraulic pressure from the engine's lubrication system to maintain zero clearance (constant contact with both camshaft and valve stem). Automatically adjusts to variation in valve stem length. Hydraulic tappets also reduce valve noise.

I

Ignition timing The moment at which the spark plug fires, usually expressed in the number of crankshaft degrees before the piston reaches the top of its stroke.

Inlet manifold A tube or housing with passages through which flows the air-fuel mixture (carburettor vehicles and vehicles with throttle body injection) or air only (port fuel-injected vehicles) to the port openings in the cylinder head.

J

Jump start Starting the engine of a vehicle with a discharged or weak battery by attaching jump leads from the weak battery to a charged or helper battery.

L

Load Sensing Proportioning Valve (LSPV) A brake hydraulic system control valve that works like a proportioning valve, but also takes into consideration the amount of weight carried by the rear axle.

Locknut A nut used to lock an adjustment nut, or other threaded component, in place. For example, a locknut is employed to keep the adjusting nut on the rocker arm in position.

Lockwasher A form of washer designed to prevent an attaching nut from working loose.

M

MacPherson strut A type of front suspension system devised by Earle MacPherson at Ford of England. In its original form, a simple lateral link with the anti-roll bar creates the lower control arm. A long strut - an integral coil spring and shock absorber - is mounted between the body and the steering knuckle. Many modern so-called MacPherson strut systems use a conventional lower A-arm and don't rely on the anti-roll bar for location.

Multimeter An electrical test instrument with the capability to measure voltage, current and resistance.

N

NOx Oxides of Nitrogen. A common toxic pollutant emitted by petrol and diesel engines at higher temperatures.

O

Ohm The unit of electrical resistance. One volt applied to a resistance of one ohm will produce a current of one amp.

Ohmmeter An instrument for measuring electrical resistance.

O-ring A type of sealing ring made of a special rubber-like material; in use, the O-ring is compressed into a groove to provide the sealing action.

O-ring

Overhead cam (ohc) engine An engine with the camshaft(s) located on top of the cylinder head(s).

Overhead valve (ohv) engine An engine with the valves located in the cylinder head, but with the camshaft located in the engine block.

Oxygen sensor A device installed in the engine exhaust manifold, which senses the oxygen content in the exhaust and converts this information into an electric current. Also called a Lambda sensor.

P

Phillips screw A type of screw head having a cross instead of a slot for a corresponding type of screwdriver.

Plastigage A thin strip of plastic thread, available in different sizes, used for measuring clearances. For example, a strip of Plastigage is laid across a bearing journal. The parts are assembled and dismantled; the width of the crushed strip indicates the clearance between journal and bearing.

Plastigage

Propeller shaft The long hollow tube with universal joints at both ends that carries power from the transmission to the differential on front-engined rear wheel drive vehicles.

Proportioning valve A hydraulic control valve which limits the amount of pressure to the rear brakes during panic stops to prevent wheel lock-up.

R

Rack-and-pinion steering A steering system with a pinion gear on the end of the steering shaft that mates with a rack (think of a geared wheel opened up and laid flat). When the steering wheel is turned, the pinion turns, moving the rack to the left or right. This movement is transmitted through the track rods to the steering arms at the wheels.

Radiator A liquid-to-air heat transfer device designed to reduce the temperature of the coolant in an internal combustion engine cooling system.

Refrigerant Any substance used as a heat transfer agent in an air-conditioning system. R-12 has been the principle refrigerant for many years; recently, however, manufacturers have begun using R-134a, a non-CFC substance that is considered less harmful to the ozone in the upper atmosphere.

Rocker arm A lever arm that rocks on a shaft or pivots on a stud. In an overhead valve engine, the rocker arm converts the upward movement of the pushrod into a downward movement to open a valve.

Rotor In a distributor, the rotating device inside the cap that connects the centre electrode and the outer terminals as it turns, distributing the high voltage from the coil secondary winding to the proper spark plug. Also, that part of an alternator which rotates inside the stator. Also, the rotating assembly of a turbocharger, including the compressor wheel, shaft and turbine wheel.

Runout The amount of wobble (in-and-out movement) of a gear or wheel as it's rotated. The amount a shaft rotates "out-of-true." The out-of-round condition of a rotating part.

S

Sealant A liquid or paste used to prevent leakage at a joint. Sometimes used in conjunction with a gasket.

Sealed beam lamp An older headlight design which integrates the reflector, lens and filaments into a hermetically-sealed one-piece unit. When a filament burns out or the lens cracks, the entire unit is simply replaced.

Serpentine drivebelt A single, long, wide accessory drivebelt that's used on some newer vehicles to drive all the accessories, instead of a series of smaller, shorter belts. Serpentine drivebelts are usually tensioned by an automatic tensioner.

Serpentine drivebelt

Shim Thin spacer, commonly used to adjust the clearance or relative positions between two parts. For example, shims inserted into or under bucket tappets control valve clearances. Clearance is adjusted by changing the thickness of the shim.

Slide hammer A special puller that screws into or hooks onto a component such as a shaft or bearing; a heavy sliding handle on the shaft bottoms against the end of the shaft to knock the component free.

Sprocket A tooth or projection on the periphery of a wheel, shaped to engage with a chain or drivebelt. Commonly used to refer to the sprocket wheel itself.

Starter inhibitor switch On vehicles with an automatic transmission, a switch that prevents starting if the vehicle is not in Neutral or Park.

Strut See MacPherson strut.

T

Tappet A cylindrical component which transmits motion from the cam to the valve stem, either directly or via a pushrod and rocker arm. Also called a cam follower.

Thermostat A heat-controlled valve that regulates the flow of coolant between the cylinder block and the radiator, so maintaining optimum engine operating temperature. A thermostat is also used in some air cleaners in which the temperature is regulated.

Thrust bearing The bearing in the clutch assembly that is moved in to the release levers by clutch pedal action to disengage the clutch. Also referred to as a release bearing.

Timing belt A toothed belt which drives the camshaft. Serious engine damage may result if it breaks in service.

Timing chain A chain which drives the camshaft.

Toe-in The amount the front wheels are closer together at the front than at the rear. On rear wheel drive vehicles, a slight amount of toe-in is usually specified to keep the front wheels running parallel on the road by offsetting other forces that tend to spread the wheels apart.

Toe-out The amount the front wheels are closer together at the rear than at the front. On front wheel drive vehicles, a slight amount of toe-out is usually specified.

Tools For full information on choosing and using tools, refer to the *Haynes Automotive Tools Manual*.

Tracer A stripe of a second colour applied to a wire insulator to distinguish that wire from another one with the same colour insulator.

Tune-up A process of accurate and careful adjustments and parts replacement to obtain the best possible engine performance.

Turbocharger A centrifugal device, driven by exhaust gases, that pressurises the intake air. Normally used to increase the power output from a given engine displacement, but can also be used primarily to reduce exhaust emissions (as on VW's "Umwelt" Diesel engine).

U

Universal joint or U-joint A double-pivoted connection for transmitting power from a driving to a driven shaft through an angle. A U-joint consists of two Y-shaped yokes and a cross-shaped member called the spider.

V

Valve A device through which the flow of liquid, gas, vacuum, or loose material in bulk may be started, stopped, or regulated by a movable part that opens, shuts, or partially obstructs one or more ports or passageways. A valve is also the movable part of such a device.

Valve clearance The clearance between the valve tip (the end of the valve stem) and the rocker arm or tappet. The valve clearance is measured when the valve is closed.

Vernier caliper A precision measuring instrument that measures inside and outside dimensions. Not quite as accurate as a micrometer, but more convenient.

Viscosity The thickness of a liquid or its resistance to flow.

Volt A unit for expressing electrical "pressure" in a circuit. One volt that will produce a current of one ampere through a resistance of one ohm.

W

Welding Various processes used to join metal items by heating the areas to be joined to a molten state and fusing them together. For more information refer to the *Haynes Automotive Welding Manual*.

Wiring diagram A drawing portraying the components and wires in a vehicle's electrical system, using standardised symbols. For more information refer to the *Haynes Automotive Electrical and Electronic Systems Manual*.

Note: *References throughout this index are in the form "Chapter number" • "Page number"*

Haynes Manuals – The Complete List

Title	Book No.
ALFA ROMEO	
Alfa Romeo Alfasud/Sprint (74 - 88)	0292
Alfa Romeo Alfetta (73 - 87)	0531
AUDI	
Audi 80 (72 - Feb 79)	0207
Audi 80, 90 (79 - Oct 86) & Coupe (81 - Nov 88)	0605
Audi 80, 90 (Oct 86 - 90) & Coupe (Nov 88 - 90)	1491
Audi 100 (Oct 82 - 90) & 200 (Feb 84 - Oct 89)	0907
Audi 100 & A6 Petrol & Diesel (May 91 - May 97)	3504
AUSTIN	
Austin/MG/Rover Maestro 1.3 & 1.6 (83 - 95)	0922
Austin/MG Metro (80 - May 90)	0718
Austin/Rover Montego 1.3 & 1.6 (84 - 94)	1066
Austin/MG/Rover Montego 2.0 (84 - 95)	1067
Mini (59 - 69)	0527
Mini (69 - Oct 96)	0646
Austin/Rover 2.0 litre Diesel Engine (86 - 93)	1857
BEDFORD	
Bedford CF (69 - 87)	0163
Bedford/Vauxhall Rascal & Suzuki Supercarry (86 - Oct 94)	3015
BMW	
BMW 316, 320 & 320i (4-cyl) (75 - Feb 83)	0276
BMW 320, 320i, 323i & 325i (6-cyl) (Oct 77 - Sept 87)	0815
BMW 3-Series (Apr 91 - 96)	3210
BMW 3- & 5-Series (sohc) (81 - 91)	1948
BMW 520i & 525e (Oct 81 - June 88)	1560
BMW 525, 528 & 528i (73 - Sept 81)	0632
CITROEN	
Citroën 2CV, Ami & Dyane (67 - 90)	0196
Citroën AX Petrol & Diesel (87 - 97)	3014
Citroën BX (83 - 94)	0908
Citroën C15 Van Petrol & Diesel (89 - Oct 98)	3509
Citroën CX (75 - 88)	0528
Citroën Saxo Petrol & Diesel (96 - 98)	3506
Citroën Visa (79 - 88)	0620
Citroën Xantia Petrol & Diesel (93 - 98)	3082
Citroën XM Petrol & Diesel (89 - 98)	3451
Citroën ZX Diesel (91 - 93)	1922
Citroën ZX Petrol (91 - 94)	1881
Citroën 1.7 & 1.9 litre Diesel Engine (84 - 96)	1379
COLT	
Colt/Mitsubishi 1200, 1250 & 1400 (79 - May 84)	0600
FIAT	
Fiat 126 (73 - 87)	0305
Fiat 127 (71 - 83)	0193
Fiat 500 (57 - 73)	0090
Fiat Cinquecento (93 - 98)	3501
Fiat Panda (81 - 95)	0793
Fiat Punto Petrol & Diesel (94 - 99)	3251
Fiat Regata (84 - 88)	1167
Fiat Tipo (88 - 91)	1625
Fiat Uno (83 - 95)	0923
Fiat X1/9 (74 - 89)	0273

Title	Book No.
FORD	
Ford Capri II (& III) 1.6 & 2.0 (74 - 87)	0283
Ford Capri II (& III) 2.8 & 3.0 (74 - 87)	1309
Ford Cortina Mk IV (& V) 1.6 & 2.0 (76 - 83)	0343
Ford Escort (75 - Aug 80)	0280
Ford Escort (Sept 80 - Sept 90)	0686
Ford Escort & Orion (Sept 90 - 97)	1737
Ford Escort Mk II Mexico, RS 1600 & RS 2000 (75 - 80)	0735
Ford Fiesta (76 - Aug 83)	0334
Ford Fiesta (Aug 83 - Feb 89)	1030
Ford Fiesta (Feb 89 - Oct 95)	1595
Ford Fiesta Petrol & Diesel (Oct 95 - 97)	3397
Ford Granada (Sept 77 - Feb 85)	0481
Ford Granada & Scorpio (Mar 85 - 94)	1245
Ford Ka (96 - 99)	3570
Ford Mondeo Petrol (93 - 99)	1923
Ford Mondeo Diesel (93 - 96)	3465
Ford Orion (83 - Sept 90)	1009
Ford Sierra 4 cyl. (82 - 93)	0903
Ford Sierra V6 (82 - 91)	0904
Ford Transit Petrol (Mk 2) (78 - Jan 86)	0719
Ford Transit Petrol (Mk 3) (Feb 86 - 89)	1468
Ford Transit Diesel (Feb 86 - 99)	3019
Ford 1.6 & 1.8 litre Diesel Engine (84 - 96)	1172
Ford 2.1, 2.3 & 2.5 litre Diesel Engine (77 - 90)	1606
FREIGHT ROVER	
Freight Rover Sherpa (74 - 87)	0463
HILLMAN	
Hillman Avenger (70 - 82)	0037
HONDA	
Honda Accord (76 - Feb 84)	0351
Honda Accord (Feb 84 - Oct 85)	1177
Honda Civic (Feb 84 - Oct 87)	1226
Honda Civic (Nov 91 - 96)	3199
HYUNDAI	
Hyundai Pony (85 - 94)	3398
JAGUAR	
Jaguar E Type (61 - 72)	0140
Jaguar MkI & II, 240 & 340 (55 - 69)	0098
Jaguar XJ6, XJ & Sovereign; Daimler Sovereign (68 - Oct 86)	0242
Jaguar XJ6 & Sovereign (Oct 86 - Sept 94)	3261
Jaguar XJ12, XJS & Sovereign; Daimler Double Six (72 - 88)	0478
JEEP	
Jeep Cherokee Petrol (93 - 96)	1943
LADA	
Lada 1200, 1300, 1500 & 1600 (74 - 91)	0413
Lada Samara (87 - 91)	1610
LAND ROVER	
Land Rover 90, 110 & Defender Diesel (83 - 95)	3017
Land Rover Discovery Diesel (89 - 95)	3016
Land Rover Series IIA & III Diesel (58 - 85)	0529
Land Rover Series II, IIA & III Petrol (58 - 85)	0314
MAZDA	
Mazda 323 (Mar 81 - Oct 89)	1608
Mazda 323 (Oct 89 - 98)	3455

Title	Book No.
Mazda 626 (May 83 - Sept 87)	0929
Mazda B-1600, B-1800 & B-2000 Pick-up (72 - 88)	0267
MERCEDES-BENZ	
Mercedes-Benz 190, 190E & 190D Petrol & Diesel (83 - 93)	3450
Mercedes-Benz 200, 240, 300 Diesel (Oct 76 - 85)	1114
Mercedes-Benz 250 & 280 (68 - 72)	0346
Mercedes-Benz 250 & 280 (123 Series) (Oct 76 - 84)	0677
Mercedes-Benz 124 Series (85 - Aug 93)	3253
MG	
MGB (62 - 80)	0111
MG Midget & AH Sprite (58 - 80)	0265
MITSUBISHI	
Mitsubishi Shogun & L200 Pick-Ups (83 - 94)	1944
MORRIS	
Morris Ital 1.3 (80 - 84)	0705
Morris Minor 1000 (56 - 71)	0024
NISSAN	
Nissan Bluebird (May 84 - Mar 86)	1223
Nissan Bluebird (Mar 86 - 90)	1473
Nissan Cherry (Sept 82 - 86)	1031
Nissan Micra (83 - Jan 93)	0931
Nissan Micra (93 - 99)	3254
Nissan Primera (90 - Oct 96)	1851
Nissan Stanza (82 - 86)	0824
Nissan Sunny (May 82 - Oct 86)	0895
Nissan Sunny (Oct 86 - Mar 91)	1378
Nissan Sunny (Apr 91 - 95)	3219
OPEL	
Opel Ascona & Manta (B Series) (Sept 75 - 88)	0316
Opel Ascona (81 - 88) (Not available in UK see Vauxhall Cavalier 0812)	3215
Opel Astra (Oct 91 - Feb 98) (Not available in UK see Vauxhall Astra 1832)	3156
Opel Calibra (90 - 98) see Vauxhall/Opel Calibra Book No. 3502	
Opel Corsa (83 - Mar 93) (Not available in UK see Vauxhall Nova 0909)	3160
Opel Corsa (Mar 93 - 97) (Not available in UK see Vauxhall Corsa 1985)	3159
Opel Frontera Petrol & Diesel (91 - 98) see Vauxhall/Opel Frontera Book No. 3454	
Opel Kadett (Nov 79 - Oct 84)	0634
Opel Kadett (Oct 84 - Oct 91) (Not available in UK see Vauxhall Astra & Belmont 1136)	3196
Opel Omega & Senator (86 - 94) (Not available in UK see Vauxhall Carlton & Senator 1469)	3157
Opel Omega (94 - 99) (See Vauxhall/Opel Omega Book No. 3510)	
Opel Rekord (Feb 78 - Oct 86)	0543
Opel Vectra (Oct 88 - Oct 95) (Not available in UK see Vauxhall Cavalier 1570)	3158
Opel Vectra Petrol & Diesel (95 - 98) (Not available in UK see Vauxhall Vectra 3396)	3523

Title	Book No.
PEUGEOT	
Peugeot 106 Petrol & Diesel (91 - 98)	1882
Peugeot 205 (83 - 95)	0932
Peugeot 305 (78 - 89)	0538
Peugeot 306 Petrol & Diesel (93 - 99)	3073
Peugeot 309 (86 - 93)	1266
Peugeot 405 Petrol (88 - 96)	1559
Peugeot 405 Diesel (88 - 96)	3198
Peugeot 406 Petrol & Diesel (96 - 97)	3394
Peugeot 505 (79 - 89)	0762
Peugeot 1.7/1.8 & 1.9 litre Diesel Engine (82 - 96)	0950
Peugeot 2.0, 2.1, 2.3 & 2.5 litre Diesel Engines (74 - 90)	1607
PORSCHE	
Porsche 911 (65 - 85)	0264
Porsche 924 & 924 Turbo (76 - 85)	0397
PROTON	
Proton (89 - 97)	3255
RANGE ROVER	
Range Rover V8 (70 - Oct 92)	0606
RELIANT	
Reliant Robin & Kitten (73 - 83)	0436
RENAULT	
Renault 5 (Feb 85 - 96)	1219
Renault 9 & 11 (82 - 89)	0822
Renault 18 (79 - 86)	0598
Renault 19 Petrol (89 - 94)	1646
Renault 19 Diesel (89 - 95)	1946
Renault 21 (86 - 94)	1397
Renault 25 (84 - 92)	1228
Renault Clio Petrol (91 - May 98)	1853
Renault Clio Diesel (91 - June 96)	3031
Renault Espace Petrol & Diesel (85 - 96)	3197
Renault Laguna Petrol & Diesel (94 - 96)	3252
Renault Mégane & Scénic Petrol & Diesel (96 - 98)	3395
ROVER	
Rover 213 & 216 (84 - 89)	1116
Rover 214 & 414 (89 - 96)	1689
Rover 216 & 416 (89 - 96)	1830
Rover 211, 214, 216, 218 & 220 Petrol & Diesel (Dec 95 - 98)	3399
Rover 414, 416 & 420 Petrol & Diesel (May 95 - 98)	3453
Rover 618, 620 & 623 (93 - 97)	3257
Rover 820, 825 & 827 (86 - 95)	1380
Rover 3500 (76 - 87)	0365
Rover Metro, 111 & 114 (May 90 - 96)	1711
SAAB	
Saab 90, 99 & 900 (79 - Oct 93)	0765
Saab 900 (Oct 93 - 98)	3512
Saab 9000 (4-cyl) (85 - 95)	1686
SEAT	
Seat Ibiza & Cordoba Petrol & Diesel (Oct 93 - 99)	3571
Seat Ibiza & Malaga (85 - 92)	1609

Title	Book No.
SKODA	
Skoda Estelle (77 - 89)	0604
Skoda Favorit (89 - 96)	1801
Skoda Felicia Petrol & Diesel (95 - 99)	3505
SUBARU	
Subaru 1600 & 1800 (Nov 79 - 90)	0995
SUZUKI	
Suzuki SJ Series, Samurai & Vitara (4-cyl) (82 - 97)	1942
Suzuki Supercarry (86 - Oct 94)	3015
TALBOT	
Talbot Alpine, Solara, Minx & Rapier (75 - 86)	0337
Talbot Horizon (78 - 86)	0473
Talbot Samba (82 - 86)	0823
TOYOTA	
Toyota Carina E (May 92 - 97)	3256
Toyota Corolla (Sept 83 - Sept 87)	1024
Toyota Corolla (80 - 85)	0683
Toyota Corolla (Sept 87 - Aug 92)	1683
Toyota Corolla (Aug 92 - 97)	3259
Toyota Hi-Ace & Hi-Lux (69 - Oct 83)	0304
TRIUMPH	
Triumph Acclaim (81 - 84)	0792
Triumph GT6 & Vitesse (62 - 74)	0112
Triumph Spitfire (62 - 81)	0113
Triumph Stag (70 - 78)	0441
Triumph TR7 (75 - 82)	0322
VAUXHALL	
Vauxhall Astra (80 - Oct 84)	0635
Vauxhall Astra & Belmont (Oct 84 - Oct 91)	1136
Vauxhall Astra (Oct 91 - Feb 98)	1832
Vauxhall/Opel Calibra (90 - 98)	3502
Vauxhall Carlton (Oct 78 - Oct 86)	0480
Vauxhall Carlton & Senator (Nov 86 - 94)	1469
Vauxhall Cavalier 1600, 1900 & 2000 (75 - July 81)	0315
Vauxhall Cavalier (81 - Oct 88)	0812
Vauxhall Cavalier (Oct 88 - 95)	1570
Vauxhall Chevette (75 - 84)	0285
Vauxhall Corsa (Mar 93 - 97)	1985
Vauxhall/Opel Frontera Petrol & Diesel (91 - Sept 98)	3454
Vauxhall Nova (83 - 93)	0909
Vauxhall/Opel Omega (94 - 99)	3510
Vauxhall Vectra Petrol & Diesel (95 - 98)	3396
Vauxhall/Opel 1.5, 1.6 & 1.7 litre Diesel Engine (82 - 96)	1222
VOLKSWAGEN	
VW Beetle 1200 (54 - 77)	0036
VW Beetle 1300 & 1500 (65 - 75)	0039
VW Beetle 1302 & 1302S (70 - 72)	0110
VW Beetle 1303, 1303S & GT (72 - 75)	0159
VW Golf & Jetta Mk 1 1.1 & 1.3 (74 - 84)	0716
VW Golf, Jetta & Scirocco Mk 1 1.5, 1.6 & 1.8 (74 - 84)	0726
VW Golf & Jetta Mk 1 Diesel (78 - 84)	0451
VW Golf & Jetta Mk 2 (Mar 84 - Feb 92)	1081

Title	Book No.
VW Golf & Vento Petrol & Diesel (Feb 92 - 96)	3097
VW LT vans & light trucks (76 - 87)	0637
VW Passat & Santana (Sept 81 - May 88)	0814
VW Passat Petrol & Diesel (May 88 - 96)	3498
VW Polo & Derby (76 - Jan 82)	0335
VW Polo (82 - Oct 90)	0813
VW Polo (Nov 90 - Aug 94)	3245
VW Polo Hatchback Petrol & Diesel (94 - 98)	3500
VW Scirocco (82 - 90)	1224
VW Transporter 1600 (68 - 79)	0082
VW Transporter 1700, 1800 & 2000 (72 - 79)	0226
VW Transporter (air-cooled) (79 - 82)	0638
VW Transporter (water-cooled) (82 - 90)	3452
VOLVO	
Volvo 142, 144 & 145 (66 - 74)	0129
Volvo 240 Series (74 - 93)	0270
Volvo 262, 264 & 260/265 (75 - 85)	0400
Volvo 340, 343, 345 & 360 (76 - 91)	0715
Volvo 440, 460 & 480 (87 - 97)	1691
Volvo 740 & 760 (82 - 91)	1258
Volvo 850 (92 - 96)	3260
Volvo 940 (90 - 96)	3249
Volvo S40 & V40 (96 - 99)	3569
Volvo S70, C70 & V70 (96 - 99)	3573
YUGO/ZASTAVA	
Yugo/Zastava (81 - 90)	1453
AUTOMOTIVE TECHBOOKS	
Automotive Brake Manual	3050
Automotive Carburettor Manual	3288
Automotive Diagnostic Fault Codes Manual	3472
Automotive Diesel Engine Service Guide	3286
Automotive Disc Brake Manual	3542
Automotive Electrical and Electronic Systems Manual	3049
Automotive Engine Management and Fuel Injection Systems Manual	3344
Automotive Gearbox Overhaul Manual	3473
Automotive Service Summaries Manual	3475
Automotive Timing Belt Manual - Ford	3474
Automotive Timing Belts Manual - Austin/Rover	3549
Automotive Timing Belts Manual - Peugeot/Citroën	3568
Automotive Timing Belt Manual - Vauxhall/Opel	3577
Automotive Welding Manual	3053
In-Car Entertainment Manual (3rd Edition)	3363
OTHER TITLES	
Automotive Fuel Injection Systems	9755
Car Bodywork Repair Manual (2nd Edition)	9864
Caravan Manual (2nd Edition)	9894
Motorcaravan Manual, The	L7322
Small Engine Repair Manual	1755
SU Carburettors	0299
Weber Carburettors (to 79)	0393

CL08.09/99

All the products featured on this page are available through most motor accessory shops, cycle shops and book stores. Our policy of continuous updating and development means that titles are being constantly added to the range. For up-to-date information on our complete list of titles, please telephone: (UK) **+44 1963 440635** • (USA) **+1 805 498 6703** • (France) **+33 1 47 78 50 50** • (Sweden) **+46 18 124016** • (Australia) **+61 3 9763 8100**

Preserving Our Motoring Heritage

<
*The Model J Duesenberg
Derham Tourster.
Only eight of these
magnificent cars were
ever built – this is the
only example to be found
outside the United States
of America*

Almost every car you've ever loved, loathed or desired is gathered under one roof at the Haynes Motor Museum. Over 300 immaculately presented cars and motorbikes represent every aspect of our motoring heritage, from elegant reminders of bygone days, such as the superb Model J Duesenberg to curiosities like the bug-eyed BMW Isetta. There are also many old friends and flames. Perhaps you remember the 1959 Ford Popular that you did your courting in? The magnificent 'Red Collection' is a spectacle of classic sports cars including AC, Alfa Romeo, Austin Healey, Ferrari, Lamborghini, Maserati, MG, Riley, Porsche and Triumph.

A Perfect Day Out

Each and every vehicle at the Haynes Motor Museum has played its part in the history and culture of Motoring. Today, they make a wonderful spectacle and a great day out for all the family. Bring the kids, bring Mum and Dad, but above all bring your camera to capture those golden memories for ever. You will also find an impressive array of motoring memorabilia, a comfortable 70 seat video cinema and one of the most extensive transport book shops in Britain. The Pit Stop Cafe serves everything from a cup of tea to wholesome, home-made meals or, if you prefer, you can enjoy the large picnic area nestled in the beautiful rural surroundings of Somerset.

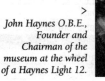

>
*John Haynes O.B.E.,
Founder and
Chairman of the
museum at the wheel
of a Haynes Light 12.*

<
*Graham Hill's Lola
Cosworth Formula 1
car next to a 1934
Riley Sports.*

The Museum is situated on the A359 Yeovil to Frome road at Sparkford, just off the A303 in Somerset. It is about 40 miles south of Bristol, and 25 minutes drive from the M5 intersection at Taunton.
Open 9.30am - 5.30pm (10.00am - 4.00pm Winter) 7 days a week, *except Christmas Day, Boxing Day and New Years Day*
Special rates available for schools, coach parties and outings Charitable Trust No. 292048